# THE PSYCHOLOGY OF
# ATTITUDES
# & ATTITUDE
# CHANGE

SAGE was founded in 1965 by Sara Miller McCune to support the dissemination of usable knowledge by publishing innovative and high-quality research and teaching content. Today, we publish more than 750 journals, including those of more than 300 learned societies, more than 800 new books per year, and a growing range of library products including archives, data, case studies, reports, conference highlights, and video. SAGE remains majority-owned by our founder, and on her passing will become owned by a charitable trust that secures our continued independence.

Los Angeles | London | Washington DC | New Delhi | Singapore

# THE PSYCHOLOGY OF
# ATTITUDES & ATTITUDE CHANGE

2ND EDITION

## GREGORY R. MAIO & GEOFFREY HADDOCK

Los Angeles | London | New Delhi
Singapore | Washington DC

**SAGE**

Los Angeles | London | New Delhi
Singapore | Washington DC

SAGE Publications Ltd
1 Oliver's Yard
55 City Road
London EC1Y 1SP

SAGE Publications Inc.
2455 Teller Road
Thousand Oaks, California 91320

SAGE Publications India Pvt Ltd
B 1/I 1 Mohan Cooperative Industrial Area
Mathura Road
New Delhi 110 044

SAGE Publications Asia-Pacific Pte Ltd
3 Church Street
#10-04 Samsung Hub
Singapore 049483

Editor: Michael Carmichael
Assistant editor: Keri Dickens
Production editor: Imogen Roome
Copyeditor: Solveig Gardner Servian
Proofreader: Leigh C. Timmins
Indexer: Adam Pozner
Marketing manager: Alison Borg
Cover design: Wendy Scott
Typeset by: C&M Digitals (P) Ltd, Chennai, India
Printed and bound by
CPI Group (UK) Ltd, Croydon, CR0 4YY

1007366112

First published 2009

Reprinted in 2010 and twice in 2012
Figure 3.2: Images downloaded from wikimedia commons under the Free Art Licence (Carrot by Meul, 14 Jan 2013, http://commons.wikimedia.org/wiki/File:Carotte.svg#), Creative Commons Attribution-Share Alike 3.0 Unreported license, (Peanut by Linuxerist and W:User:ClockworkSoul, 20 Mar 2006, http://commons.wikimedia.org/wiki/File:Smallpeanut.png#), Creative Commons CC0 1.0 Universal Public Domain Dedication (Sheep by Anonymous, 8 Apr 2014, http://commons.wikimedia.org/wiki/File:Sheep_clipart.svg#), and the Open Clip Art Library's Public Domain release (Cheese pizza by Linuxerist, 26 Apr 2006, http://commons.wikimedia.org/wiki/File:Cheese_pizza.svg#; Motorbike by TheresaKnott, 7 Apr 2007, http://commons.wikimedia.org/wiki/File:Motorbike.svg#; Jean Victor Balin Bread by Jean Victor Balin and Eugenio Hansen OFS, 23 Oct 2010, http://commons.wikimedia.org/wiki/File:Jean_victor_balin_bread.svg#).

**Library of Congress Control Number: 2014939125**

**British Library Cataloguing in Publication data**

A catalogue record for this book is available from the British Library

ISBN 978-1-4462-7225-1
ISBN 978-1-4462-7226-8 (pbk)

MIX
Paper from responsible sources
FSC
www.fsc.org    FSC® C013604

At SAGE we take sustainability seriously. Most of our products are printed in the UK using FSC papers and boards. When we print overseas we ensure sustainable papers are used as measured by the Egmont grading system. We undertake an annual audit to monitor our sustainability.

# CONTENTS

# LIST OF FIGURES AND TABLES

## FIGURES

## TABLES

# PREFACE

Back in 2006, SAGE gauged our interest in writing a textbook on the psychology of attitudes. We were pleased (and honored) to be asked to become involved in such a project. From our perspective, it was a new and exciting challenge that would be unlike anything we had done before. It also gave us the opportunity to consolidate some of our thinking about the field and become even more acquainted with some areas of attitudes research. The end result of our labors was the first edition of *The Psychology of Attitudes and Attitude Change*. It is gratifying to know that the first edition was well received by academics, students, and practitioners, and we are very happy to have been invited to develop a second edition.

You won't be surprised to learn that this second edition contains a number of novel developments. Of course, we have updated the coverage in order to incorporate research that has been conducted since we wrote the first edition. In addition, we received valuable feedback from academics, students, and practitioners who adopted and read the first edition. This feedback was beneficial in suggesting new ideas that we hope will further benefit the volume. For teachers, we have added materials such as presentation notes and sample assessment questions. For students, we have added a glossary as well as a set of questions that you can use to test your own understanding of individual chapters. Some of these developments are available via the new website **study.sagepub.com/maiohaddock** that accompanies the book, others are contained within the book itself. We hope that these will be beneficial in maximizing your learning experience.

## OVERVIEW

It is difficult to listen to a talk show without getting agitated. Talk shows love to get our attention with debates on a whole catalogue of issues, with common topics being war, global warming, discrimination, sexuality, terrorism, morality, and religion. Debates on these issues can leave us dumbstruck. We might be left aghast that others vehemently support a war that we oppose or that they are opposed to an energy saving initiative that we like. We might be particularly perturbed when our friends or relatives chime in with unexpected views, and we may desperately wish to change their minds. In these situations, we are all united by a desire to understand and shape other people's *attitudes*.

This desire has long been held by human beings. Some of the attitude conflicts that puzzle people now (e.g., health care, immigration) are different from those that perturbed people in prior generations (e.g., slavery), but the basic quest to understand attitudes is the same. Fortunately, there has been an exciting advance in this quest. At the beginning of the previous century, social psychologists began to realize that scientific methods can be used to better understand attitudes and how they change. This recognition eventually grew into a conviction that attitudes are indispensable for understanding social psychological processes (e.g., Allport, 1935; Eagly & Chaiken, 1993; Eiser, 1994).

Research on attitudes is now flourishing. In the past century, the field has moved from questions like "Can attitudes be measured?" to questions like "Which measures are most useful?" Research is now using complex and intriguing perspectives to tackle fascinating theoretical and practical problems in the study of attitudes.

As research has progressed, it has become clear that it is time to rethink the nature of this important construct and how it is taught. This textbook offers a novel approach to this issue, focusing on what attitudes are and on what they do for us. The text attempts to cover the essential items of information that have been garnered from past research, while integrating recent advances in a simple way. The book will focus on basic theory and research in the area, while highlighting applications and real life examples.

The text is aimed at upper-year undergraduates and postgraduates who are enrolled in courses on attitudes and attitude change. Because of this aim at higher levels of study, it is important that the text stimulates critical thinking about the models and evidence that are presented. Consequently, the book frequently presents questions that challenge students to think more deeply about the issues. Our hope is that students who read this text will come away with a better understanding of what we know *and* do not know about attitudes.

At the same time, we have done our best to create a text with relevance to the treatment of attitudes in institutions of higher education around the world. Although the bulk of the pivotal research on attitudes has emerged from the United States, key findings have also emerged from studies in numerous countries, including Australia, Belgium, Canada, China, France, Germany, Great Britain, Italy, Japan, the Netherlands, New Zealand, Portugal, and Spain. We have attempted to cover key research from most if not all of these nations, which helps to integrate diverse perspectives on the psychology of attitudes.

This book includes four sections. The first section looks at what attitudes are and why they are important. The second section examines the ability of attitudes to predict behavior. From there, we consider how attitudes are formed and changed. Finally, we present a variety of major issues for understanding internal (e.g., neurological) and external influences on attitude (e.g., culture), along with unresolved questions.

# Section 1: Why do attitudes matter?

This section outlines some of the issues that galvanized researchers to begin studying attitudes. In doing so, it introduces core conceptualizations of attitudes. To illustrate these views, it will be necessary to describe how attitudes are measured. This component of Section 1 will focus on the most common and interesting attitude measurement techniques, while showing how these measures are useful and important.

Within this section of the book, we introduce the metaphor of the "three witches" of attitudes: content, structure, and function. Put simply, attitudinal *content* can include cognitive, affective, and behavioral information about an object; attitude *structure* refers to how this information is organized along dimensions within attitudes; and attitude *function* encompasses diverse psychological needs served by attitudes (e.g., self-esteem, utility enhancement). We label these as three "witches" because they operate more effectively together than in isolation, in the same way that three witches in folklore make a better brew together than separately. This section foreshadows how content, structure, and function are relevant to each subsequent section of the volume. In later chapters, their relevance is identified by using "three witches" side-bars to come back to this theme.

# Section 2: What do attitudes do?

This section addresses how attitudes are influential in helping us navigate our social environment. First, we will consider how our attitudes influence our interpretation of information. Second, we will consider how our attitudes guide our behavior. The question of precisely *how* attitudes predict actions has been the focus of several models of attitude–behavior relations. Thus, the second portion of this section will describe and review important models and evaluate the evidence testing them.

# Section 3: What shapes attitudes?

This section is the largest portion of the book because a large number of important models have been developed to explain attitude formation and change. Most of these models focus on cognitive processes, although other models have specifically examined affective influences or behavioral processes. Consequently, this section of the text focuses on cognitive, affective, and behavioral processes in separate chapters. Nonetheless, these processes strongly overlap, and we attempt to highlight some common principles in a fourth chapter.

# Section 4: What more is there to learn?

This section will describe how research on attitudes is being enriched by a variety of methodological and theoretical developments. One chapter describes advances in understanding diverse "internal" aspects of attitudes, including neurological activity, motor actions, and lifespan development. The next chapter describes advances in understanding diverse "external" aspects of attitudes, including influences of time, relationships, groups, and culture. The final chapter highlights themes from across the book by bringing us back to attitude content, structure, and function. This chapter also closes with some challenging questions about the nature and importance of attitudes.

# HOW TO USE THIS BOOK

Every chapter in the book shares the same underlying structure. We start every chapter by listing some *Questions to ponder*. These questions are intended to stimulate thinking about some of the major themes relevant to the chapter's content. Next, the *Preview* acts as a brief guide of what is covered in the chapter – a road map of what will be discussed. From there, we move to the "meat" of the chapter. Here, we provide a look at important research and theories that are relevant to the theme of the chapter. At various points in each chapter, we review *Key points* and describe how our three witches of attitude play a role in understanding and guiding research questions. Chapter 1 has *More to know* information. Also, throughout the book we provide some *Research highlights* – and our "three witches" of attitudes (described above) appear in side-bars to indicate where there are interesting questions pertaining to attitude content, structure, and function.

At the end of each chapter, we offer some other tools to help the reader. The sections titled *What we have learned* review the most important points within the chapter. Following from that, the sections titled *What do you think?* present a series of big-picture questions that are relevant to the chapter's theme. We hope that these are questions that you can begin to answer having read the chapter. Then we present a set of *Key terms*, allowing the reader to have a firm understanding of core concepts. Finally, each chapter ends with a section titled *Further reading*. Here we present some references to papers, both basic and applied, that we find especially interesting.

# THANKS (AGAIN)

We want to end this Preface by thanking a series of people for their help in bringing this revision to fruition. Let's start with some people from SAGE. As ever, we thank Michael Carmichael for his support (and his updates on the wavering fortunes of the Toronto Blue Jays, Maple Leafs, and Raptors). Keri Dickens was always helpful in making things get done on time. From a professional perspective, we are extremely grateful for the efforts of our mentors, Jim Olson and Mark Zanna, who nurtured our interest in the study of attitudes. We are very fortunate to have fantastic social psychology colleagues in the School of Psychology at Cardiff University – Tony Manstead, Job van der Schalk, and Ulrich von Hecker. We also want to thank Richard Petty and Mark Conner for their work in reading an early draft of the first edition and providing very helpful feedback.

Last, and certainly not least, our families deserve special mention. Our wives and children have been patient and supportive throughout the entire process. Because of their support, this project has been a lot of fun. Thanks Audra, Kestrel, and Gabriella. Thanks Maggie, Charlotte, and Ceara.

# REFERENCES

Allport, G. W. (1935) Attitudes. In C. Murchison (ed.), *Handbook of Social Psychology* (pp. 798–844). Worcester, MA: Clark University Press.

Eagly, A. H. and Chaiken, S. (1993) *The Psychology of Attitudes*. Orlando, FL: Harcourt Brace Jovanovich.

Eiser, J. R. (1994) *Attitudes, Chaos, and the Connectionist Mind*. Oxford: Blackwell.

# SECTION 1

## INTRODUCTION: WHY DO ATTITUDES MATTER?

In our daily lives, we often use the term *attitude* to mean different things. Have you ever met someone with a "bad attitude?" We might say that a person has a "bad attitude" because he has a negative outlook on life. From a social psychological perspective, the term attitude has a somewhat different meaning. In this section of the book, we want to tell you what social psychologists mean when they use the term attitude.

In Chapter 1, we will begin by introducing past and present conceptualizations of attitudes. This discussion will highlight the basic characteristic of an attitude – an association in memory between an attitude object and an evaluation of it. Basically, an attitude refers to how much we like (and/or dislike) something. After showing how social psychologists define the concept of attitude, we will describe some of the issues that motivated researchers to begin investigating attitudes and how the empirical study of attitudes has evolved over time. We will see that scientists who study attitudes seek to discover how people's opinions are shaped and how their attitudes influence their behavior. Chapter 1 also deals with how we measure attitudes. Through the years, attitudes have been assessed using a variety of techniques. In the last half of the opening chapter, we will introduce you to some of the more prominent ways of measuring people's opinions.

The primary aim of Chapter 2 is to introduce the metaphor of the *three witches* of attitudes: content, structure, and function. We label these as three "witches" because we strongly believe that they operate more effectively together than in isolation, in the same way that three witches combine in folklore to make a potent brew. Attitude *content* refers to cognitive, affective, and behavioral information that people associate with attitude objects. Attitude *structure* refers to whether attitudes are best conceptualized as unidimensional (e.g., like/dislike as a single continuum) or bidimensional (e.g., like and dislike as separate continuums). Attitude *function* refers to the psychological needs that are served by attitudes. Chapter 2 will introduce some basic insights regarding each of the witches and foreshadow how attitude content, structure, and function are relevant to each section of the book.

# SECTION 1

## INTRODUCTION: WHY DO ATTITUDES MATTER?

# 1

---

# WHAT ARE ATTITUDES AND HOW ARE THEY MEASURED?

---

## QUESTIONS TO PONDER

1. What do we mean by the term "attitude"?
2. Why are attitudes interesting and important?
3. Why did social psychologists first start studying attitudes?
4. How do we measure attitudes?

### PREVIEW

Within this chapter we consider what attitudes are and how they are measured. We see how common definitions emphasize that attitudes are summary evaluations (e.g., like/dislike) of objects. We provide a brief history of research on the attitude construct, explaining why social psychologists first started studying attitudes, how research interests have changed over the past century, and why attitudes are interesting and important. We also discuss how attitudes are measured. We will see that a person's attitudes can be assessed in many different ways.

## WHAT IS AN ATTITUDE?

Do you remember the last great party you attended? What did you talk about? Who did you talk about? Chances are you talked about things and people that you like or dislike. You might have expressed the view that you disliked your country's President or Prime Minister, had mixed feelings about the latest Meryl Streep film, or that you really liked your social psychology class. In every case, you were talking about your attitudes – your likes and dislikes. Attitudes are important. They influence how we view the world, what we think, and what we do. Because attitudes are vital in understanding human thought and behavior, social psychologists have devoted a lot of attention to understanding how we form attitudes, how our attitudes influence our daily life, and how our attitudes change over time. In this book, we want to tell you about what social psychologists call an attitude.

In thinking about these questions, perhaps the best place to start is by defining the term *attitude*. Like most constructs in psychology, the attitude concept has been defined in many ways. In their influential text *The Psychology of Attitudes*, Alice Eagly and Shelly Chaiken (1993, p. 1) define attitude as "a psychological tendency that is expressed by evaluating a particular entity with some degree of favor or disfavor." Russell Fazio (1995, p. 247) defines attitude as "an association in memory between a given object and a given summary evaluation of the object." Richard Petty and John Cacioppo (1981, p. 7) define attitude as "a general and enduring positive or negative feeling about some person, object, or issue." Finally, Mark Zanna and John Rempel (1988, p. 319) define attitude as "the categorization of a stimulus object along an evaluative dimension."

Notice that all of these definitions emphasize evaluative judgments about an object. Indeed, most attitude theorists would argue that evaluation is *the* predominant aspect of the attitude concept. In other words, reporting an attitude involves making a decision of liking versus disliking, or favoring versus disfavoring a particular issue, object, or person. As such, attitudes summarize different types of information about an issue, object, or person. That is, all of our relevant thoughts, feelings, and past experiences get rolled up into a single evaluative summary. As we will see in Chapter 2, thoughts, feelings, and past behaviors are important sources of information for attitudes. Thus, we define *attitude* as an overall evaluation of an object that is based on cognitive, affective, and behavioral information.

An attitude, when conceptualized as an evaluative judgment, can vary in two important ways (see Eagly & Chaiken, 1993, 1998). First, attitudes differ in *valence*, or positive versus negative direction of evaluation. For instance, both authors of this text hold some positive attitudes (we like the music of The Police), negative attitudes (we dislike liver), and neutral attitudes (we feel pretty average toward tomato juice). Second, attitudes differ in *strength*, which is a term encompassing their stability, ability to withstand attack, capacity to influence how we process information, and ability to guide behavior (see Petty & Krosnick, 1995). For example, while one of us really hates liver, the other feels less strongly. Throughout the book (and especially in Chapter 4), we will see that differences in valence and strength play an important role in understanding *how* attitudes guide our processing of information and our behavior.

Until now, we have used a number of objects when providing examples of our own attitudes. This leads to the question "What is an *attitude object*?" Basically, attitude objects can be anything that is evaluated along a dimension of favorability. As others have noted (see Eagly & Chaiken, 1993), some attitude objects are abstract (e.g., liberalism) and others are concrete (e.g., a red Corvette car). One's own self (e.g., self-esteem) and other individuals (e.g., a particular politician) can also serve as attitude objects, as can social policy issues (e.g., death penalty) and social groups (e.g., people from Canada). Throughout the book, we will use a number of examples when describing research that social psychologists have carried out on the attitude concept.

## KEY POINTS

- An attitude is an evaluative judgment about a stimulus object.
- Attitudes differ in valence and strength.
- Attitude objects can be anything that is liked or disliked.

# A SHORT HISTORY OF ATTITUDES RESEARCH

The study of attitudes has an extensive history within social psychology, with both emerging at the turn of the 20th century. Indeed, Gordon Allport (1935, p. 198), a renowned researcher who helped inspire attitudes research, noted that "the concept of attitude is probably the most distinctive and indispensable concept in contemporary American social psychology." This view was also shared by experts outside of social psychology, such as sociologists and behavioral psychologists (see McGuire, 1986). In this section of the chapter, we consider why social psychologists first started to study attitudes, and why this fascination has continued. Our aim is to highlight the central role that the study of attitudes has played, and continues to play, within social psychology. To achieve this aim, we will time-travel backwards, but, for the sake of brevity, we present a short history – one that is more like an episode of Dr. Who than a feature-length documentary. Readers who are interested in learning more are invited to read the work of William McGuire (e.g., McGuire, 1985, 1986), who wrote extensively on the history of attitude research.

## A starting point

As noted above, empirical research relevant to the psychology of attitudes can be traced to the early 20th century. In the 1920s, a number of individuals became interested in measuring subjective mental properties like attitudes. At that time, such was the importance of work on attitude measurement that social psychology was often defined as the study of attitudes (McGuire, 1985). Two significant researchers from that era were Louis Thurstone and Rensis Likert. Thurstone and Likert developed various ways for measuring attitudes, most notably the Equal Appearing Interval method (Thurstone, 1928; Thurstone & Chave, 1929) and the Likert scale (see Likert, 1932). Thurstone's and Likert's research was highly influential because it demonstrated that attitudes can be quantifiably measured – paving the way for the development of the discipline. In fact, the ability of scientists to measure attitudes was seen as an enormous breakthrough, as evidenced by the title of one Thurstone's first journal articles on this topic: "Attitudes can be measured." Even today, Likert scales remain an important tool for researchers interested in assessing attitudes and opinions. We will learn about Thurstone's and Likert's contributions later in this chapter.

In addition to developing strategies designed to measure attitudes, early research also considered the degree to which individuals' attitudes influence their behavior. In a famous paper, Richard LaPiere (1934) reported his experience traveling across the United States of America with a young Chinese couple. At the time of the travels, there was widespread anti-Asian prejudice in the United States. As a result of this prejudice, LaPiere was concerned whether he and his traveling companions would be refused service in hotels and restaurants. Much to his surprise, only once (in over 250 establishments) were they not served. A few months after the completion of the journey, LaPiere sent a letter to each of the visited establishments and asked whether they would serve Chinese visitors. Of the establishments that replied, only one indicated that it would serve them. This finding was taken as evidence that a person's attitudes do not necessarily impact their behavior. While there were a number of problems with LaPiere's work (e.g., the measures of attitude and behavior are not suitable by modern standards; see Chapter 3), the study was seminal in its consideration of *whether* attitudes predict behavior. The study of when and how attitudes guide behavior (and how behavior influences attitudes) remains at the forefront of attitude research. Indeed, we devote an entire section of this book to this issue.

## The real world

Perhaps not surprisingly, the focus of research in social psychology is often influenced by real world events. The atrocities of World War II led social psychologists like Kurt Lewin, who escaped Nazi Germany in the 1930s, and many of social psychology's progenitors, such as Solomon Asch, Leon Festinger, and Muzafer Sherif, to study processes such as conformity, power, and group dynamics. Their research had direct relevance to the study of attitudes and the types of questions that people began to address. Basically, the study of attitudes picked up momentum in an attempt to tackle greater societal concerns.

For instance, Theodore Adorno and colleagues (Adorno, Frenkel-Brunswick, Levinson, & Sanford, 1950) were curious about the processes that lead individuals to develop authoritarian attitudes. In particular, they studied the social psychological bases of anti-Semitic attitudes. Their development of the F-scale (the F stood for Fascism) and their research on authoritarianism played an important role in understanding the development of prejudice against minority ethnic groups. Several decades later, research by Bob Altemeyer (1996) further developed this line of investigation, provoking a resurgence of interest in the concept of authoritarianism.

World War II affected social psychological research in other ways. Although attempts to understand the dynamics of persuasion can be traced back to Greek philosophy, the success of Nazi propaganda campaigns made Allied powers realize the importance of understanding how to mobilize and change public opinion. During the war, one of the founders of attitude research, Carl Hovland, took a leave of absence from Yale to become Chief Psychologist and Director of Experimental Studies for the United States War Department. His research during this time attempted to discover methods for making the United States' war propaganda more effective at sustaining public morale.

After the war, interest in persuasion remained strong due to the emergence of the Cold War and developments in telecommunications (such as the wide availability of television). Consequently, upon returning to Yale, Hovland, Irving Janis, and others within the "Yale School" continued to study how individuals respond to persuasive messages. These researchers instigated scientific research on attitude change examining *when* and *how* attitudes are most likely to change (see, e.g., Hovland, Janis, & Kelley, 1953). As noted by McGuire (1986), the Yale School's approach was *convergent* in that it started with a particular phenomenon (i.e., attitude change) that needed explanation. The researchers would assess a wide array of variables in order to determine which ones are important in explaining the phenomenon. Most important, these researchers addressed how factors such as characteristics of the message source, message recipient, and the persuasive message itself determine the likelihood of attitude change. Their findings were highly influential in helping social psychologists understand how and when persuasion is most likely to occur. Further, their work had an enormous impact on subsequent models of attitude change (see Chapter 5).

While Hovland and colleagues were developing their research on persuasion, Leon Festinger and colleagues addressed other issues relevant to attitude change. As noted by McGuire (1986), Festinger's approach was *divergent*: it started with a particular theory and applied it to a wide range of attitudinal phenomena. One theory that Festinger applied was Cognitive Dissonance Theory (Festinger, 1957). *Cognitive dissonance* refers to a state of imbalance among beliefs, including the beliefs that support a person's attitudes. The theory suggests that holding inconsistent beliefs produces a negative feeling that we are motivated to reduce. As applied to attitudes, cognitive dissonance theory suggests that a person with two inconsistent attitudes would be motivated to change one of these attitudes to regain a state of consonance (see Chapter 6).

A final key development during this era was a consideration of the reasons *why* people hold attitudes – the study of *attitude functions* – encompassing the psychological needs served by attitudes. Two groups of researchers developed taxonomies of attitude functions. M. Brewster Smith and colleagues (Smith, Bruner, & White, 1956) and Daniel Katz and colleagues (e.g., Katz, 1960; Katz & Stotland, 1959) both postulated that attitudes can serve a number of functions or needs for an individual. The most important of these functions is the object appraisal function – the capacity of attitudes to serve as energy saving devices that make judgments easier and faster to perform. Attitudes can also help us express our values, identify with people we like, and protect ourselves from negative feedback. As we show later in the book, knowing the primary function of an attitude is important, because attempts at attitude change are more likely to be successful when a persuasive appeal matches the function of the attitude.

## The growth of a social cognition perspective

In the mid-1960s, there was a change in the *zeitgeist* of social psychology (and psychology as a whole). While much of the previous research was largely grounded in behaviorism, this new perspective – referred to as *social cognition* – was grounded in understanding *how* individuals elaborate upon and process socially relevant information. The social cognition perspective includes convergent and divergent approaches alongside "systems" approaches, which attempt to map linkages among many causal factors, mediating variables, and outcomes (McGuire, 1986). This perspective remains the dominant framework within contemporary social psychology. From the perspective of attitude research, this framework led attitude researchers to consider new questions about *how* attitudes affect information processing and behavior. For instance, in thinking about how attitudes influence behavior, Icek Ajzen and Martin Fishbein developed the Theory of Reasoned Action (Ajzen & Fishbein, 1977, 1980; see Chapter 4). As its name suggests, the Theory of Reasoned Action was developed to predict deliberative and thoughtful (i.e., reasoned) behavior from attitudes. This theory (and subsequent variations) paved the way for hundreds of studies that shared a common goal – understanding effects of attitudes on behavior.

This theory was a factor in a resurgence of research examining the relation between attitudes and behavior during the 1970s. In 1969, Alan Wicker had reviewed studies examining the relation between attitudes and behavior and reached the sobering conclusion that attitudes are a relatively poor predictor of behavior. His findings led a number of social psychologists to question the value of the attitude concept (see Eagly, 1992; Elms, 1975). It was argued that, if attitudes do not predict actions, then the construct is of limited use. Fishbein and Ajzen's theory and related research (Ajzen & Fishbein, 1977, 1980) showed that these concerns were overstated and that there needed to be greater attention to the study of *when* and *how* attitudes predict behavior. In the last 30 years, research findings have led to the conclusion that attitudes *do* predict behavior, but in some conditions better than others. In Chapter 3, we discuss when attitudes are most likely to predict behavior. In Chapter 4, we discuss models that have been developed to understand how attitudes predict behavior.

# A new wave of attitude research

Attitude researchers have frequently noted that attitudes are based on cognitive, affective, and behavioral information (see Chapter 2). In the 1980s, research on this *content* of attitudes began to flourish (and it continues to flourish today). For example, this research has addressed questions such as how people organize their thoughts, feelings, and past experiences about a particular attitude object. Throughout the book, we devote considerable attention to the study of how the cognitive, affective, and behavioral content of attitudes interact and how they shape the development and expression of attitudes.

The 1980s also saw the introduction of two important models of persuasion: the Elaboration Likelihood Model (ELM; Petty & Cacioppo, 1981, 1986) and the Heuristic-Systematic Model (HSM; Chaiken, 1980; Chaiken, Liberman, & Eagly, 1989). The ELM and HSM are both dual-process models in that they specify two different routes to persuasion. The ELM refers to a central route and a peripheral route: the central route requires an individual to pay close attention to the contents of a persuasive appeal, whereas the peripheral route requires less thought. According to the HSM, one route involves systematic processing, while the other involves heuristic processing: systematic processing requires individuals to carefully scrutinize the contents of a persuasive appeal, whereas heuristic processing requires less effort. While sharing many similarities, the

ELM and HSM differ in a number of ways (see Chapter 5). Together, these models have provided and continue to provide important insights into the processes underlying attitude change (see Maio & Haddock, 2007).

## Ongoing developments

In the past two decades, research on the attitude concept has continued to flourish. One of the primary themes has been the study of *attitude strength*. As noted earlier in this chapter, some of our attitudes are held with great strength, while others are less strong. Strong attitudes have been found to differ from weak attitudes in a number of ways. Strong attitudes are more (a) persistent over time, (b) resistant to change, (c) likely to influence information processing, and (d) likely to predict behavior (Krosnick & Petty, 1995). Research on attitude strength has also played a major role in answering questions surrounding the degree to which attitudes are stable versus temporary (see Wilson, Lindsey, & Schooler, 2000).

The new millennium has been extremely exciting for attitude researchers. While there have been a number of key developments, two areas of study in particular may make long-lasting impressions. First, advances in computer technology (e.g., millisecond timing accuracy for key-stroke responses) and concerns about dishonest responding to questionnaires led researchers to develop new ways to measure attitudes. Without question, the most influential of these new techniques employs implicit measurement. Put simply, *implicit measures assess attitudes without requiring individual's awareness of their attitude or how it is being measured*. Interestingly, research has revealed that in many domains, responses on implicit measures of attitude are often not consistent with people's self-reported ratings of their own attitudes (see Petty, Fazio, & Briñol, 2009). Similarly, implicit measures of attitude often predict different outcomes from self-report measures (see Perugini, Richetin, & Zogmaister, 2010).

Advances in technology have benefited attitude research in other ways. One exciting development has been the application of brain imaging techniques to study attitudinal phenomena. For instance, structural and functional Magnetic Resonance Imaging (MRI and fMRI), Electroencephalography (EEG), and Magnetoencephalography (MEG) are being used to identify where attitude judgments are made in the brain (e.g., Cunningham, Johnson, Gatenby, Gore, & Banaji, 2003; Cunningham, Raye, & Johnson, 2004). Similarly, experiments have begun using event-related potential (ERP) methodology to develop understanding of the time-course in which attitude judgments are made (see Cacioppo, Crites, & Gardner, 1996; Cunningham, Espinet, DeYoung, & Zelazo, 2005). The use of these (and complementary) technologies is providing fascinating insights about attitudinal processes (see Chapter 9).

## Beyond social psychology

Social psychologists are not the only scientists who study attitudes. For example, research on attitude change has obvious implications for understanding areas such as consumer behavior, political science, and health. Marketers are keenly aware of the strategies that are most effective to elicit persuasion, and politicians continually try to convince us of the need to vote for them and support their policies. Further, research assessing how attitudes predict behavior has important applied implications. Health psychologists have adopted models such as the Theory of Reasoned Action (and its revised version, the Theory of Planned Behavior) in an attempt to get individuals to engage in a healthier lifestyle (e.g., exercising, eating a better diet).

## KEY POINTS

- The scientific study of attitudes has maintained a core role in the development of social psychology.
- Attitude research plays an important role in understanding how opinions are formed, changed, and measured.

### MORE TO KNOW 1.1

### WHAT ARE THE MOST IMPORTANT AND INFLUENTIAL PAPERS ON THE PSYCHOLOGY OF ATTITUDES?

We think it's important for all students, even those taking their first course in social psychology, to go beyond textbooks and read journal articles. By reading articles you get an insight into the types of research questions being asked and how social psychologists seek to answer these questions. If you're a novice at reading journal articles, don't be turned off by the jargon sometimes used or be afraid that the statistics used are beyond what you've learned. To help, we recommend an excellent paper by Christian Jordan and Mark Zanna (1999) on how to read a research article. These scientists offer advice on how to gather the main points being made in a research paper.

After you've made the decision to read journal articles, the next decision is more difficult – what to read! If you were to access every article that has been written on the psychology of attitudes, you'd find yourself snowed under a huge pile of paper. To help provide a single reference point for key readings in the field, we recently produced a five-volume set that brings together many of the most important papers ever published on the psychology of attitudes. Presented by thematic areas, these volumes serve as a useful compendium for everyone interested in attitudes (Haddock & Maio, 2012).

## HOW ARE ATTITUDES MEASURED?

So far, we have learned what attitudes are and how attitudes research has developed over time. Of course, to understand attitudes we need to have a sense of how attitudes are measured. In the remainder of the chapter, we deal will the question of how to measure attitudes.

Attitudes, like most psychological constructs, are not directly observable. You cannot "see" an attitude like you see a person's height or the speed of a car. Attitudes are in people's heads and can only be inferred from their responses (Fazio & Olson, 2003; Himmelfarb, 1993). As a result, social psychologists have needed to develop various methodologies in order to effectively assess individuals' attitudes.

We want to introduce some of the most commonly used techniques that have been developed over the past 75 years. To introduce different measures of attitude, we have elected to distinguish them on the basis of whether they are *explicit* (i.e., direct) or *implicit* (i.e., indirect). The distinction between explicit and implicit processes has a long history within psychology. Psychologists usually think of explicit processes as those that require conscious attention, while implicit processes are those that do not require conscious attention. As applied to attitude measurement, these terms can be used to distinguish between measures in which the respondent is aware *or* unaware of how an attitude is being assessed. Put simply, explicit attitude measures directly ask respondents to indicate their attitude, whereas implicit attitude measures assess attitudes without respondents' awareness or control over of how their attitude is being measured.

## Direct (explicit) measures of attitudes

The vast majority of attitude measures can be conceptualized as direct (explicit) indicators of attitude. Historically, explicit measures of attitudes have been extremely popular among social psychologists (Greenwald & Banaji, 1995; Krosnick, Judd, & Wittenbrink, 2005). Usually, these measures are self-report questionnaires in which participants respond to direct questions about their opinions (e.g., "What is your opinion about abortion?"). As we learned in our trip back in time, initial research into attitude measurement is generally associated with the work of Thurstone (1928). In a seminal paper, Thurstone demonstrated how methods of psychophysical scaling could be adapted to measuring attitudes.

Thurstone's most significant contribution to the measurement of attitudes was his development of the *equal appearing intervals* method (Thurstone & Chave, 1929). The equal appearing intervals (EAI) approach involves multiple stages (Himmelfarb, 1993). First, the researcher constructs a set of belief statements that are relevant to the attitude being measured. Assume for a minute that a researcher was interested in creating an EAI measure of attitudes toward capital punishment. The researcher would begin by creating a pool of statements that are relevant to the issue (e.g., "Capital punishment would decrease the homicide rate" and "The death penalty should never be used").

Second, after these belief statements had been created, judges are asked to order these statements along a scale containing many intervals (e.g., 11). This ordering separates the statements into different subsets that imply similar levels of favorability or unfavorability toward the topic (e.g., capital punishment). For example, if judge A placed an item in the seventh interval, that item would have a score of 7 for that judge. The value for a particular item is the median of the placements made for that item across all judges. Thus, after the second stage, each item has been allocated a (median) score on the interval scale.

In the third stage, the belief statements are given to the individuals whose attitudes are to be examined. Respondents are asked to indicate the items with which they agree. A respondent's score is the mean (or median) of the scale value of the items to which they agreed. For example, if a respondent agreed with four items that had scale values of 5, 6, 6, and 7, this individual would have a score of 6.

Because he believed that Thurstone's methodology was too time consuming, Likert (1932) developed a technique of summated ratings. In this approach, belief statements are written to indicate either a favorable or unfavorable attitude. An example of a Likert scale to assess attitudes toward capital punishment is shown in Figure 1.1. For each item, respondents indicate their degree of agreement or disagreement. As you read the items presented in Figure 1.1, you will notice that items can be written such that a strong positive attitude toward the death penalty will produce either a "strongly agree" response (e.g., to item 2) or a "strongly disagree" response (e.g., to item 3). Researchers create items that are worded in opposite directions in order to help avoid tendencies to agree or disagree with *every* item.

How are Likert scales scored? In a questionnaire like that in Figure 1.1, each response alternative is allocated a score (in this case from 1 to 5). Traditionally, a low score is taken to indicate a negative attitude and a high score is taken to indicate a positive attitude. Thus, for item 2, an individual who strongly disagrees with the statement will be given a score of 1, while a person who strongly agrees will be given a score of 5. For item 3 (a reverse keyed item), an individual who strongly disagrees with the statement is expressing a positive attitude (and is given a score of 5 for that item), whereas an individual who strongly agrees with that item is expressing a negative attitude (and is allocated a score of 1). A person's response on each item can be averaged to form a single score. For example, a respondent who answered 5, 4, 1, 5, and 1 to the items listed in Figure 1.1 would have total score of 4.8 (after items 3 and 5 have been reverse coded).

An important characteristic of Likert scales is that different items are used which have unknown scale values, unlike EAI scales. Moreover, it is important to check that the items actually can be seen as reflecting the same construct (i.e., a respondent's attitude). It could be the case that some items tap different attitudes from others. For instance, in Figure 1.1, the first item is about making euthanasia legal, while the second item is about holding a referendum. Although both items are keyed positively (i.e., a high score suggesting a positive attitude), it could be the case that participants' responses to the second item have more to do with their attitude toward referendums or their attitude toward the likely outcome of a referendum on euthanasia, rather than their attitude toward euthanasia per se. If this is the case, then people's responses on item 2 should exhibit weak correlations with the other items. However, if we are right in suggesting that these items can form a reliable scale, then correlations among responses to each item should be high. If they are sufficiently high, scores on the individual items are averaged to form a single attitude score.

Another important consideration is that the numbers produced by the summation across items aren't "real" in the sense that you cannot use them to compare attitudes toward different attitude objects. Because of the way in which items are worded, a 4.8 score toward "euthanasia" does not necessarily reflect a more positive attitude than, say, a 3.1 score for "cycling to work." To compare between attitude topics, it is necessary to use a methodology that measures attitudes toward a variety of attitude objects along a common scale with matching items.

---

The following statements are part of a survey on public attitudes. There are no right or wrong answers, only opinions. For each statement, indicate the number that best represents your personal opinion by using the following scale:

If you strongly disagree with the statement, indicate 1
If you disagree with the statement, indicate 2
If you neither disagree nor agree with the statement, indicate 3
If you agree with the statement, indicate 4
If you strongly agree with the statement, indicate 5

1   I think euthanasia should be made legal.                                      _____

2   I would support a referendum for the institution of euthanasia.     _____

3   Euthanasia should never be used.                                          _____

4   Euthanasia is appropriate when someone wants to die.            _____

5   I am against the use of euthanasia in all circumstances.         _____

---

**Figure 1.1**   *An example of a Likert scale to assess attitudes toward euthanasia*

Among the efforts to develop such a technique, the most influential method is the *semantic differential* approach (Osgood, Suci, & Tannenbaum, 1957). An example of a semantic differential scale is shown in Figure 1.2. In this technique, participants are given a set of bipolar adjective scales, each of which is separated a number of categories. Participants are asked to evaluate the attitude object by indicating the response that best represents their opinion. To measure overall attitudes, the bipolar adjectives use general evaluative terms such as favorable/ unfavorable, good/bad, and like/dislike. Similar to the need for Likert scale items to show high intercorrelations, responses to the bipolar adjectives should also be highly correlated if we are to assume that they all assess the same construct (i.e., a respondent's attitude). If the correlations are sufficiently high, responses to the bipolar adjectives can be averaged to form a single attitude score.

If the bipolar scales assess attitudes in the same way across objects, then it is possible to compare scores across different objects. However, there can be instances where the same adjectives could mean different things for different attitude objects. For instance, the dimension "cold/warm" is likely to mean different things if you were reporting your attitude toward "Canada" versus "my best friend." In fact, attitude objects like "Canada" and "my best friend" differ in so many ways (e.g., concreteness, personal relevance) that it is questionable whether there is any value in comparing them. Thus, the usefulness of bipolar semantic differential scales for comparing across objects must always be considered in light of potential differences between the attitude objects being compared.

Please respond to each scale by placing an 'x' on the line that best represents your opinion.

EUTHANASIA

BAD: _____ : _____ : _____ : _____ : _____ : _____ : _____ : GOOD
NEGATIVE: _____ : _____ : _____ : _____ : _____ : _____ : _____ : POSITIVE
DISLIKE : _____ : _____ : _____ : _____ : _____ : _____ : _____ : LIKE

**Figure 1.2**   *A semantic differential measure of attitudes*

# Issues in the direct measurement of attitudes

Direct measures of attitude have dominated research on the psychology of attitudes. Indeed, their usefulness will be demonstrated throughout this book. However, despite their usefulness and wide appeal, they possess a number of limitations. For example, individuals might occasionally be unaware of their underlying attitude toward an object (Fazio, Jackson, Dunton, & Williams, 1995; Greenwald & Banaji, 1995; Nisbett & Wilson, 1977). There are also effects of how the items in direct measures are presented. Even very subtle differences in item presentation (e.g., item order) can influence responses to direct measures of attitude (see Schwarz, 1999; Schwarz, Strack, & Mai, 1991), and items can elicit different responses depending on whether the questionnaire invites people to rate their attitudes relative to other people's attitudes or not (see Olson, Goffin, & Haynes, 2007). It is also noteworthy that people make finer distinctions in their levels of positivity than in their levels of negativity, using more options in scales denoting positive evaluations (Smallman, Becker, & Roese, 2014).

Probably the most important criticism about direct measures of attitude is that of impression management. Impression management involves giving responses that present the respondents in a favorable way, even if the responses are inaccurate (Paulhus & John, 1998). To the extent that the researcher is interested in studying attitudes toward sensitive issues or issues relevant to norms of political or social appropriateness, individuals' responses might not necessarily reflect their own opinion, but instead may reflect a desire to present themselves in a positive manner. For example, in some cultures, it may be considered socially inappropriate to express a prejudicial attitude toward ethnic minority groups. In such contexts, the use of explicit, direct measures may not provide an accurate portrayal of respondents' attitudes, as individuals may not want to appear prejudiced.

# Indirect (implicit) measures of attitudes

To circumvent problems associated with direct measures of attitude, social psychologists have developed a number of indirect or implicit response strategies. It is beyond the scope of this chapter to review all of these approaches (see Fazio & Olson, 2003, for a review). We therefore focus on the most influential and important techniques: evaluative priming (EP; see Fazio et al., 1995) and the Implicit Association Test (IAT; Greenwald, McGhee, & Schwartz, 1998).

## Evaluative priming (EP)

As highlighted earlier in this chapter, Russell Fazio (1995, p. 247) defines an attitude as "an association in memory between a given object and a given summary evaluation of the object." According to Fazio and colleagues, these associations vary in strength, and the strength of the association reflects the *accessibility* of an attitude from memory and the likelihood that the evaluation is spontaneously activated when we encounter the attitude object. Let us describe this perspective more concretely. One of the authors of this book *really* hates the bread spread Marmite, and is he continually amazed that this product is sold throughout the world. Even thinking about Marmite sets off an immediate and strong negative reaction within him. Fazio's model would postulate that the author has a strong association in memory between the attitude object "Marmite" and the evaluation "bad." While this same author also dislikes pickles, they don't elicit the same level of repulsion. Fazio's approach would postulate that the author's evaluation of Marmite is activated more spontaneously than his negative attitude toward pickles. That is, if he was asked whether Marmite is bad, he could make this response faster compared to if he was asked whether pickles are bad.

How can this speed difference in association be quantified? In a typical study, a participant is seated in front of a computer. The name of the attitude object is then presented on the computer screen (e.g., the word "Marmite"). Upon presentation of the attitude object, participants indicate their evaluation of the object by pressing a key labeled "good" or a key labeled "bad." The speed with which a key is pressed is taken as a measure of the strength of the association between the attitude object and its evaluation (see Fazio, 1990). In our example, the speed in which the author pressed the "bad" key in response to "Marmite" should be faster than the speed in which he pressed the "bad" key in response to "pickles."

This type of procedure can be taken a step further. Like before, imagine that you're sitting in front of a computer. This time, the task is different. Once again, you are shown the name of an attitude object on the screen – this serves as the stimulus prime. Shortly after the stimulus prime is presented, it is replaced by an evaluative adjective (e.g., "disgusting"). Your task is to accurately classify the *meaning* of the adjective as rapidly as possible, by pressing one key to indicate that the adjective (not the stimulus prime) signifies a "good" thing and another key to indicate that the adjective signifies a "bad" thing. Of interest to the researcher is the latency or speed with which you make the judgment.

---

### MORE TO KNOW 1.2

### WHAT ARE THE IMPORTANT JOURNALS THAT PUBLISH RESEARCH ON THE PSYCHOLOGY OF ATTITUDES?

Social psychologists publish their research in academic journals. Here are some of the most important social psychology journals that serve as outlets for attitude research: *Basic and Applied Social Psychology*; *British Journal of Social Psychology*; *European Journal of Social*

*(Continued)*

(Continued)

*Psychology; Journal of Applied Social Psychology; Journal of Experimental Social Psychology; Journal of Personality and Social Psychology; Personality and Social Psychology Bulletin; Personality and Social Psychology Review; Social Cognition; Social Influence; Social Psychological;* and *Personality Science.*

In addition, attitude research is often published in academic journals outside social psychology. Here is a sample of other journals where attitude research is often published: *Canadian Journal of Behavioural Science; Developmental Psychology; Environment and Behavior; European Review of Social Psychology; Group Processes & Intergroup Relations; Health Psychology; Journal of Consumer Policy; Journal of Consumer Research; Journal of Consumer Psychology; Journal of Environmental Psychology; Journal of Management Studies; Journal of Social and Personal Relationships; Journal of Personality; Journal of Politics; Journal of Social Issues; Nature Climate Change; Personality and Individual Differences; Political Psychology; Psychological Science; Psychology, Public Policy, and Law; Psychonomic Bulletin and Review; Public Opinion Quarterly; Social Development; Social Justice Research;* and *Social Psychology.*

Why is the researcher interested in the speed of these judgments? Our cognitive processes make it easier for us to interpret the meaning of an object that shares the same meaning as an item we have just seen than to process completely unrelated items. So, we should be faster at classifying a positive adjective (e.g., "good") after seeing a stimulus prime that we like than after seeing a stimulus prime we dislike. Similarly, we should be faster at classifying a negative adjective (e.g., "bad") after seeing a stimulus prime that we dislike than after seeing a stimulus prime we like. In our case, the presentation of Marmite as a stimulus prime should inhibit (i.e., slow down) responses to a subsequent positive adjective and facilitate (i.e., speed up) responses to a subsequent negative adjective. Further, these facilitation and inhibition effects should be larger when presented with Marmite as the stimulus prime, rather than pickles as the stimulus prime. Thus, the presentation of the stimulus prime affects how quickly we decide whether an evaluative word is positive or negative.

Fazio and colleagues have adapted this evaluative priming paradigm to assess attitudes, most notably for domains in which explicit measures might be subject to social desirability concerns (such as prejudicial attitudes). For example, in a study by Fazio et al. (1995), participants were instructed that their task was to indicate the meaning of positive and negative adjectives. However, prior to the presentation of the target adjective, participants were briefly shown a photo of a person who was either Black or White. Fazio et al. (1995) found that, among White participants, the presentation of a Black face produced faster responding to negative adjectives and slower responses to positive adjectives (relative to what was found in response to the presentation of a White face). Thus, in this study, a negative attitude toward African Americans was represented by differences in the time required to categorize positive and negative adjectives after the presentation of a Black face compared to a White face.

## The Implicit Association Test

The second indirect procedure we want to describe is the Implicit Association Test (IAT; Greenwald et al., 1998). Like the evaluative priming measure, it is based on the assumption that attitude objects can spontaneously activate evaluations which influence subsequent responses and the speed with which these responses are made. In a typical IAT study, participants are seated at a computer and asked to classify adjectives *and* attitude objects. (Recall that the evaluative priming method asks people only to classify the adjectives and does not ask people to classify the attitude object.) Participants are instructed to make their responses as quickly as possible; the computer records the time it takes them to respond. By recording the speed of responses, this task is similar to the evaluative priming method.

As originally designed, an IAT study involves various blocks. In our example, we will describe an IAT with five separate blocks of trials to examine attitudes toward men versus women. In block 1 of a gender IAT, participants are shown a variety of male and female names (see Figure 1.3). They are instructed to make one response (e.g., press the "s" key on a keyboard) when they see a male name and a different response (e.g., press the "k" key) when they see a female name. They are asked to perform this task (and all others in the test) as quickly as possible, with multiple trials in a block. In block 2, participants are presented with a variety of positive and negative adjectives. Again, they are asked to make one response (press the "s" key) when a positive adjective appears on the screen and a different response (press the "k" key") when a negative adjective appears on the screen. In block 3, participants are instructed that they will see names or adjectives, and that they are to press the "s" key when they see a male name or positive adjective, and press the "k" key when they see a female name or negative adjective. Block 4 is similar to block 2, but this time the responses are reversed: a participant now presses the "s" key when a negative word appears and the "k" key when a positive word appears. Block 5 is similar to block 3, but this time participants are to press the "s" key when a male name or negative adjective appears and the "k" key when a female name or positive adjective appears.

Blocks 3 and 5 are crucial – they measure the strength of association between an attitude object (in this example, gender categories) and evaluations. How does the IAT use these blocks to compute an attitude score? Imagine an individual who is more positive about men compared to women. For this individual, the task in block 3 should be quite simple. If the individual evaluates men more favorably than women, trials in which men are associated with positive adjectives and women are associated with negative adjectives should lead to fast responses, because the links between these categories and evaluations are congruent. Let's imagine that our participant's mean response time to trials in this block is 800 milliseconds. In contrast, responses in block 5 should take longer for this participant. Given the participant's favorability to men over women, trials that associate women with positivity and men with negativity should take more time to elicit a response. Let's imagine that our participant's mean response time for this block is 1100 milliseconds. If so, our participant's mean response time for block 3 is shorter than that for block 5 by 300 milliseconds. As originally conceived, this difference is referred to as the IAT effect (see Greenwald et al., 1998 for additional details about computing IAT effects; see also Greenwald, Nosek, & Banaji, 2003 for alternative scoring algorithms for the IAT).

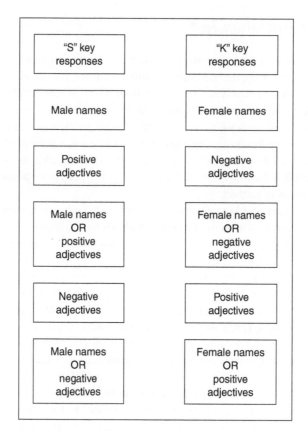

**Figure 1.3**   *A sample procedure sequence for a five-block IAT*

Since its development, the IAT has evoked a substantial amount of interest. In the decade after its publication, the original journal article introducing the measure was cited by over 900 articles – an amazing citation rate. Furthermore, since its development, the IAT has been refined in numerous ways. For example, the IAT's developers have generated new scoring formulae for the measure (see Greenwald et al., 2003), a recent adaptation simplifies the structure of trials (Rothermund, Teige-Mocigemba, Gast, & Wentura, 2009), and there is a formula that helps to disentangle non-attitudinal components of IAT scores (e.g., task switching demands) from the attitudinal components (Meissner & Rothermund, 2013).

The IAT has also been developed for different participant populations, including even a variant for a non-human primate, the rhesus macaque (Mahajan et al., 2011). One useful development was provided by Andrew Baron and Mahzarin Banaji (2006), who modified the IAT for use with young children. This child-friendly IAT was developed by making several alterations to the basic IAT. First, children are allowed more time to respond. Second, the positive and negative attributes are words that are frequently used in a child's vocabulary (e.g., nice, yucky), and are spoken aloud through headphones or speakers (rather than written words on a computer screen). Third, bright buttons are used to record responses, rather than keys on a keyboard. Baron and Banaji (2006) successfully used a child-friendly race-IAT in a sample of six and 10 year olds. They found that six year olds demonstrated strong explicit and implicit pro-white/anti-black attitudes, while 10 year olds were positive toward African Americans on the explicit measure and remained negative on the implicit measure. Thus, the IAT can yield important findings even among very young people.

Initially, a wave of excitement led to unwarranted assumptions about the power of the measure. One of these was the notion that respondents could not bias their scores on the measure. Yet people can exert some control over the influence of their attitudinal biases on responses in the IAT after training (e.g., Calanchini, Gonsalkorale, Sherman, & Klauer, 2013). Another assumption was that the IAT represented a tool that could uncover an individual's "unconscious" attitudes. This idea is difficult to test and we, like most others, do not believe this to be accurate (see also Fazio & Olson, 2003). Rather, the IAT represents an implicit *measure* of attitude; the attitude may or may not be entirely unconscious to the individual.

Similarly, researchers wondered whether the IAT might represent a "gold standard" of attitude measurement. That said, scores on the IAT are more malleable than initially assumed. For example, Dasgupta and Greenwald (2001) assessed whether showing participants pictures of liked and disliked Black and White individuals would influence racial attitudes on the IAT. One group of participants was shown pictures of admired Black individuals (e.g., the actor Will Smith) and disliked White individuals (e.g., serial murderer Charles Manson), whereas a second group was shown pictures of admired White individuals (e.g., the actor Tom Hanks) and disliked Black individuals (e.g., boxer Mike Tyson). Compared to participants in a control group (shown pictures of flowers and insects), participants in the "pro-Black" (i.e., Will Smith) condition subsequently showed less prejudicial attitudes than participants in the "pro-White" (i.e., Mike Tyson) or control conditions. Further, these effects were found when the race IAT was administered immediately after or 24 hours after the presentation of the famous faces (see also Blair, Ma, & Lenton, 2001). Thus, the IAT manifests variability similar to that seen in self-report measures, which are also affected by context (as noted earlier in this chapter).

Notwithstanding these issues, there is a lot of cogent evidence to support the usefulness of the IAT (Greenwald, Poehlman, Uhlmann, & Banaji, 2009). Greenwald, Banaji, and colleagues have also developed very interesting and educational websites about the IAT (see, e.g., https://implicit. harvard.edu/implicit and www.briannosek.com/iat/ – accessed May 20, 2014). As we will see below and in the rest of the book, numerous studies have found that its use helps to complement self-report measures of attitudes and that further adaptations of the IAT may be very useful.

## Other types of indirect measures of attitude

Just as it is a sign of respect for the original work when people try to remake a film or song, scientists' esteem for the evaluative priming measure and the IAT is shown in how they have tried to develop the approaches further, but in different ways. For instance, a recent complement to the EP approach is the Affect Misattribution Paradigm (AMP), developed by Keith Payne and his collaborators (Payne, Burkley, & Stokes, 2008; Payne, Cheng, Govorun, & Stewart, 2005). Like the EP method, this measure is implemented on a computer. Participants are shown images of an attitude object over a number of trials, and, immediately after each presentation, participants are briefly shown an ambiguous stimulus, such as a Chinese writing character (if the participants are not Chinese speaking). Participants are asked to quickly rate the pleasantness of the ambiguous stimulus, while *ignoring* the stimulus before (which is described as being a mere cue for the next stimulus). Because people tend to misattribute their current feelings to salient stimuli, the researchers predicted that the characters would be rated more positively following objects that are pleasant (e.g., a baby) than after objects that are unpleasant (e.g., a shark). Results supported this prediction, and many studies revealed that ratings of the pleasantness in the AMP could be used to detect political and racial attitudes. Furthermore, the attitude scores from the AMP correlated significantly with relevant self-report attitudes, intentions, and observed behaviors.

Independent evidence has supported Payne and colleagues' assumptions that affect misattribution is the mechanism shaping participants' scores on the measure (Gawronski & Ye, 2014). In addition, a recent meta-analysis of 167 studies has found that the AMP, the original evaluative priming method, and other approaches that rely on effects of primes to detect attitudes are reliable predictors of behavior, even after controlling for responses to explicit measures of attitude (Cameron, Brown-Iannuzzi, & Payne, 2012). Thus, priming procedures, and the AMP in particular, are promising procedures for implicitly assessing attitudes.

There have also been many new variations on the IAT. Michael Olson and Russell Fazio suggested that a "personalized" IAT could be a more effective measure of attitude (Olson & Fazio, 2004a). According to Olson and Fazio, performance on the IAT can be affected by *extrapersonal* associations, or knowledge about what others think or feel about the attitude object. For example, as noted by Han, Olson, and Fazio (2006), the responses of a participant completing an IAT in which the categories are apples and chocolates might be influenced by whether the participant is dating someone who loves apples or chocolates. The other person's feelings can be a part of the knowledge tapped by an IAT, even though those feelings do not necessarily affect the individual's own attitude. (The author's wife loves Marmite.) Olson and Fazio argue that influence of extrapersonal associations can be removed by making the tasks in the IAT more personal. They suggest that this can be achieved by having people classify objects and adjectives using the personal dimensions "I like/I don't like," rather than using the general dimensions of "favorable/unfavorable" (see also Han, Czellar, Olson, & Fazio, 2010).

Another procedural refinement tackles the relative nature of the IAT. For example, in a gender IAT, the category "women" is presented along with the category "men." As a result, the IAT score reflects a favorability to women over men (or vice-versa). The score depends on attitudes toward women *and* on attitudes toward men. This means that we cannot tell from a positive score whether a person actually likes women or just dislikes them less than he or she dislikes men. This problem can be important in many contexts. For example, in studies of prejudice, positive IAT scores in favor of an ingroup (e.g., Whites liking Whites) may occur even if spontaneous associations to the ingroup (e.g., Whites) and outgroup (e.g., Blacks) are *both* significantly favorable. Furthermore, in some contexts, it is not always clear which group should be the contrast category. In countries with diverse social groups, would prejudice toward Blacks be best assessed in comparison with Whites or in comparison with Asians? Similarly, what should be the contrast category in an IAT evaluating (say) Starbucks coffee? To avoid problems that are inherent in comparing across different categories, researchers have developed single category IATs (Blanton, Jaccard, Gonzales, Christie, 2006; Bluemke & Friese, 2008; Karpinski & Steinman, 2006). Single category IATs use subtly different response tasks and blocks to focus on one category (e.g., Blacks, Starbucks) without a comparison to another category.

Another adaptation of the IAT assesses attitudes without a computer. You might have noticed that the implicit measures we have discussed use computers to obtain response latencies. This can be cumbersome in many research settings where computers are not easily available, so paper-and-pencil IAT tasks have been developed (see Lowery, Hardin, & Sinclair, 2001). In this technique, stimuli (e.g., male and female names, positive and negative adjectives) are presented as series of items running down the center of a page. At the top of the page there are two categories, with one on each side of the column of items. Participants are asked to indicate beside each item whether it belongs in the category that is left or right of it. For example, the column of items may contain male and female names, interspersed among positive and negative adjectives. In one block, participants may be asked to sort the names and adjectives into both a male/positive column and a female/negative column. In another block, participants may be asked to sort the names and adjectives into a male/negative column and a female/positive column.

Sounds easy, doesn't it? But there is an important twist: participants are asked to categorize the items as quickly and accurately as possible in a specific amount of time. The time pressure causes them to make mistakes. As in the computerized version of the task, a participant who favors men to women should find it easier to complete the task in which male/positive and female/negative are categorized together. This difference in ease should cause the participant to make fewer mistakes in the male/positive and female/negative block than in the male/negative and female/positive block. To reflect this difference, an IAT score is derived by computing the difference between the number of correct categorizations across the two blocks.

## MORE TO KNOW 1.3

### IMPORTANT TEXTS ON THE PSYCHOLOGY OF ATTITUDES

A number of important books (besides this one!) have been written about the attitude construct. Here are five of our favorites:

Albarracín, D., Johnson, B. T., and Zanna, M. P. (eds) (2005) *The Handbook of Attitudes*. Mahwah, NJ: Erlbaum.
Bohner, G. and Wänke, M. (2002) *Attitudes and Attitude Change*. New York: Psychology Press.
Cialdini, R. (2008) *Influence: Science and Practice* (5th edn). Boston, MA: Allyn & Bacon.
Eagly, A. and Chaiken, S. (1993) *The Psychology of Attitudes*. Fort Worth, TX: Harcourt Brace Jovanovich.
Petty, R. E. and Cacioppo, J. T. (1981) *Attitudes and Persuasion: Classic and Contemporary Approaches*. Dubuque, IA: Brown.

Other types of indirect measures of attitude have been developed. For example, during the 1960s and 1970s, researchers experimented with a number of psychophysiological measures. These measures include the galvanic skin response (GSR), pupillary dilation, and facial electromyographic activity (facial EMG). The use of GSR was based on the assumption that activity in the sweat glands would increase skin conductance and, therefore, higher scores would reflect greater stress or aversion. However, research found that GSR responses can be elicited by both negative *and* positive responses, meaning that the GSR is not sensitive to attitude valence (Himmelfarb, 1993). In contrast, pupillary dilation was based on the assumption that the pupils of the eye should expand to take in more light when people see things they like. Yet subsequent research found that pupillary dilation (like GSR) is less sensitive to valence and more sensitive to the attention an individual devotes to an attitude object (see Petty & Cacioppo, 1983). Thus, despite some initial promise, the popularity of these measures has waned.

EMG addressed the issue of valence sensitivity and initially offered greater potential. This technique assesses the contractions of core facial muscles. Research using this procedure has revealed that such measures can distinguish positive from negative responses. For example, Cacioppo and Petty (1979a) tested whether an EMG measure would be able to distinguish participants' positive and negative responses to a persuasive appeal. These scientists found that participants' EMG patterns revealed facial expressions of happiness when the participants heard an appeal that supported their attitude. In contrast, when participants heard an appeal that ran counter to their attitude, their facial muscles displayed the pattern of sadness. While provocative, practical limitations and technological advances have made EMG assessments uncommon among contemporary attitude researchers.

In recent times, other types of physiological measures have shown promise. First, *event-related potentials* (ERPs) measure electrical activity in the brain. Research using this technique has helped develop our understanding of the time course in which individuals make attitudinal judgments; that is, when individuals show brain activity while making evaluative responses about an attitude object. For example, experiments by Cacioppo, Crites, and Gardner (1996) and Cunningham et al. (2005) have found that event-related potentials often occur between 450–600 milliseconds after the presentation of an attitude object.

A second physiological measure that is eliciting interest is *functional magnetic resonance imaging* (fMRI). fMRI attempts to uncover the brain locations associated with attitudinal responding by assessing changes in blood flow and blood oxygenation within the brain. Changes in blood flow within a region of the brain can be used to infer the degree to which that brain region is "active." As applied to the study of attitudes, a number of researchers have used fMRI to help understand where attitudinal responses are occurring in the brain (see, e.g., Cunningham et al., 2003, 2004, 2008, 2009). We'll learn more about this exciting technique in the final section of the book.

## Issues relevant to the measurement of attitudes

A sound measure of any psychological construct must be both reliable and valid. In its broadest sense, *reliability* refers to "the degree to which test scores are free from errors in measurement" (American Psychological Association, 1985, p. 19). When assessing a psychological construct, we want the measure to be a true indication of the individual's status on the construct being assessed. In the context of attitude measurement, reliability has two important meanings. First, internal consistency refers to whether the individual items are assessing the same psychological construct. As noted earlier, items that assess the same construct should be positively correlated. Second, test-retest reliability refers to consistency in scores across time. A sound attitude measure should produce similar scores across repeated testing (in the absence of any true attitude change).

## RESEARCH HIGHLIGHT 1.1

### IS IT A GUN OR A WALLET?

Back in 1999, a 22 year old Ghanaian man named Amadou Diallo was stopped by New York City police officers, who thought that Diallo matched the description of a rape suspect. When ordered not to move, Diallo reacted not by raising his hands in the air, but by reaching into his pocket. Police, perhaps assuming that Diallo was reaching for a weapon, fired 41 shots, hitting Diallo 19 times. It turned out that Diallo had reached into his pocket to present his wallet. The four officers involved in the shooting were later acquitted, on the basis that in the split-second they had to make a decision, they did not have the conscious intent to commit any crime (Payne, 2006). (Readers might also be interested in knowing that the tragic story of Amadou Diallo inspired the song "American Skin (41 Shots)" by Bruce Springsteen.)

Not long after this tragic event, social psychologists began to consider how police make split-second decisions in which they have to decide whether someone might be reaching for a gun. In one fascinating set of studies, Keith Payne and colleagues (see Payne, 2001, 2006; Payne, Lambert, & Jacoby, 2002; Payne, Shimizu, & Jacoby, 2005) adapted some of Russell Fazio's methodological paradigms to develop a task in which participants have to decide whether an object presented on a computer screen is a gun or a hand tool.

In Payne and colleagues' *weapon bias* paradigm, participants are first presented with an image of a Black or White face, which is followed by a picture of an object. Participants are told to ignore the face and to name the object, which after presentation is replaced by a "mask." Payne and colleagues have found that, when people were allowed to perform the object discrimination task at their own pace, they were very good at distinguishing between guns and hand tools. However, when they were forced to make a fast decision (within 500 ms), participants detected guns faster when the picture of the gun was preceded by a Black face compared to a White face. Moreover, Payne and colleagues have found that White participants were more likely to mistakenly see a gun more often when the face preceding the weapon was Black compared to when it was White (Payne, 2001, 2006).

Other research teams, using somewhat different experimental paradigms, have found similar results. For example, Joshua Correll and colleagues (see e.g., Correll, Park, Judd, & Wittenbrink, 2002; Correll et al., 2007) developed a video-game task in which participants were shown images (on a computer screen) of Black and White individuals holding objects such as guns or cell phones. Participants were instructed to "shoot" anyone holding a gun by pressing one key, and to "not shoot" any unarmed person by pressing another key. Similar to Payne (2001, 2006), studies using this paradigm have also shown that people are biased to mistakenly seeing weapons possessed by Black men (see, e.g., Correll et al., 2002).

A number of studies have investigated the reliability of explicit and implicit measures of attitude. Explicit measures have been shown to exhibit high reliability. For example, semantic differential scales using the evaluative dimensions of good/bad, positive/negative, and favorable/unfavorable exhibit high internal consistency (Huskinson & Haddock, 2004). Generally speaking, explicit measures that contain more items tend to be more reliable, as long as the items are somewhat similar. That said, research has found that even single-item semantic differential measures possess high test-retest reliability (Haddock, Zanna, & Esses, 1993).

Given their recent introduction, less research has been conducted assessing the reliability of implicit measures of attitude. However, Cunningham, Preacher, and Banaji (2001) found that implicit measures possessed reasonably high internal consistency and test-retest correlations. In the context of measuring prejudice, Cunningham et al. (2001) compared the reliability of the evaluative priming technique, the IAT, and an explicit measure of racial prejudice. Attitudes were assessed on four occasions, each time separated by two weeks. The study revealed that the implicit measures of prejudice were consistent over time. That is, participants who demonstrated an anti-Black bias at one point in time usually expressed an anti-Black bias at other points in time.

The *validity* of a scale refers to the extent that it assesses the construct it is designed to measure. Developing a valid measure of a psychological construct is not as simple and straightforward as one might expect. For example, testing the validity of a new measure of attitudes toward capital punishment would require demonstrating that the new measure is (a) related to other measures of capital punishment (i.e., convergent validity), (b) unrelated to measures of other constructs irrelevant to capital punishment (i.e., discriminant validity), and (c) predictive of future behavior (i.e., predictive validity).

A number of studies have investigated the validity of explicit and implicit measures of attitude. Explicit measures of attitude are often valid. For example, Haddock et al. (1993) demonstrated that a semantic differential measure of prejudicial attitudes was highly predictive of a subsequent measure of discriminatory behavior (see Eagly & Chaiken, 1993, for more examples). In later chapters (most notably Chapters 3 and 4), we will see additional evidence that semantic differential and Likert scales can yield scores that are highly predictive of judgments and behavior.

Several reviews of studies including implicit measures have found evidence to support their convergent and predictive validity (e.g., Cameron et al., 2012; Fazio & Olson, 2003; Greenwald et al., 2009; Maio, Haddock, Watt, Hewstone, & Rees, 2009; Perugini et al., 2010). Specific examples include Cunningham et al.'s (2001) finding that responses to the evaluative priming and IAT measures are significantly interrelated after statistically controlling for measurement unreliability. (Measurement error or unreliability weakens correlations between measures.) Also, in one compelling study using fMRI technology, Phelps et al. (2000) found that an IAT measure of racial prejudice was highly predictive of amygdala activation when presented with pictures of Black individuals (the amygdala is an area of the brain associated with fearful evaluations). This type of research highlights how implicit measures of attitude may be able to provide a window into deeper workings of the brain.

At the same time, however, we caution readers that the reliability and validity of any measure must always be viewed in the context of the measure. A measure that is reliable and valid in one context might not be reliable and valid in another context. With regard to the measurement of attitudes, the nature of the attitude object is perhaps the most significant variable to consider. For instance, the IAT has been viewed as a window into better prediction of ethnic and racial discrimination, but a recent meta-analysis disputes this claim (Oswald, Mitchell, Blanton, Jaccard, & Tetlock, 2013). Furthermore, other research suggests that the IAT exhibits weak validity in assessing attitudes toward the self (Buhrmester, Blanton, & Swann, 2011). On the other hand, there are many examples of the unique predictive validity of implicit measures, such as evidence of their validity in assessing preference for physical attractiveness in romantic partners, beyond the variance explained by explicit measures of this preference (Eastwick, Eagly, Finkel, & Johnson, 2011). Perhaps implicit measures are more strongly handicapped when they are applied to attitude targets and evaluative dimensions that are multifaceted and complex (e.g., social outgroups, the self) rather than targets or dimensions that are simple (e.g., attractiveness). The same may be true for explicit measures, and many other variables (e.g., distractions, salient norms) may affect the performance of both types of measure.

Finally, if responses to explicit measures are strongly correlated with responses to implicit measures, then both measures should exhibit similar properties. This high correspondence can arise in diverse circumstances. For instance, responses to both types of measure can be similar when people are willing to express their true attitudes and can easily access them (Fazio & Olson, 2003), are asked to rely on their "gut feelings" in response to explicit measures (Loersch, McCaslin, & Petty, 2011), or are given prior tasks that narrow their conceptual focus (Huntsinger, 2013). In such cases, both types of measures should provide similar perspectives on the attitudes people hold.

Nevertheless, it is important not to dismiss the instances in which the measures reveal quite different attitudes. Chapter 9 will highlight instances where it is interesting to calculate discrepancies between implicit and explicit measures of attitude within individuals. These discrepancies can also predict phenomena that are psychologically interesting (e.g., defensiveness, social group discrimination).

## KEY POINTS

- Different types of attitude measures can be distinguished on the basis of whether they are explicit or implicit.
- Implicit measures have gained popularity because they assess attitudes without the necessity of asking the participant for a verbal report.
- Part of the appeal of implicit measures is due to the belief that responses on these measures are less likely to be affected by social desirability concerns.
- In many areas of study, scores on implicit attitude measures tend to be only moderately correlated with explicit measures of the same construct (something we'll learn about more throughout the book).
- Implicit measures of attitude often predict variability in behavior that cannot be explained by explicit measures of attitude alone. Thus, they have become an important part of our tools for assessing attitudes.

# WHAT WE HAVE LEARNED

- Attitudes are overall evaluations of attitude objects.
- Attitudes can differ in valence and intensity.
- Attitudes influence our actions.
- Attitudes have a core role in the study of social psychology.
- Attitudes can be measured in a number of ways.
- Responses on direct and indirect measures of attitude are not necessarily related.

# WHAT DO YOU THINK?

- Attitudes are overall evaluations of objects that influence how we behave. When you think about your own attitudes, do you believe they are stored in memory, or are they constructed on the spot, depending upon what you're thinking at the time? Is this distinction important?
- What makes an attitude strong? Can you think of ways in which people come to possess strong attitudes? Perhaps particular types of experiences are important, or there are special ways in which strong attitudes are stored in memory?
- Responses on implicit and explicit measures of attitude are not always correlated with each other. Why might this be? What are the implications of the relative independence? Can you think of circumstances that should affect the degree to which implicit and explicit measures should be correlated?

# KEY TERMS

*AMP* – affect misattribution paradigm, an implicit measure assessing attitudes through effects of primes on evaluations of stimuli.

*Attitude* – an overall evaluation of an object that is based on cognitive, affective, and behavioral information.

*Attitude accessibility* – the ease of retrieval of the attitude from memory.

*Attitude content* – the types of information that influence attitudes.

*Attitude functions* – the reasons why people hold attitudes, including the psychological needs served by attitudes.

*Attitude objects* – anything that is evaluated along a dimension of favorability.

*Attitude strength* – their stability, ability to withstand attack, capacity to influence how we process information, and ability to guide behavior.

*Attitude valence* – the positive versus negative direction of evaluation.

*Cognitive dissonance* – a state of imbalance among beliefs, including the beliefs that support a person's attitudes.

*EAI scales* – equal appearing interval scales, a technique that classifies self-report items according to degree of valence, prior to asking respondents to indicate their agreement or disagreement with each item.

*EP* – evaluative priming, a technique for implicitly measuring attitudes by examining the speed with which we classify evaluative stimuli after seeing evaluatively congruent or incongruent primes.

*ERPs* – event-related potentials, measure electrical activity in the cerebral cortex.

*Explicit measures* – techniques that measure attitudes by directly asking respondents.

*Extrapersonal associations* – knowledge about what others think or feel about the attitude object.

*facial EMG* – facial electromyography, assesses electrical activity in facial muscles that control smiling, frowning, and other emotional expressions.

*fMRI* – functional magnetic resonance imaging, measures oxygen utilization in areas of the brain.

*GSR* – galvanic skin response, assessing activity in the sweat glands along surfaces of the hand.

*IAT* – Implicit Association Test, an implicit measure assessing attitudes by examining effects of pairing attitude object targets with positive or negative targets in a task that categorizes the identity or valence (e.g., good or bad) of the targets.

*Implicit measures* – techniques for assessing attitudes without individuals' awareness of their attitude or how it is being measured.

*Likert scales* – self-report measures of attitude that ask respondents to rate their extent of agreement versus disagreement with items.

*Measurement reliability* – the degree to which test scores are free from errors in measurement.

*Measurement validity* – the extent to which test scores assess the construct they are designed to measure.

*Personalized IAT* – Personalized Implicit Association Test, an implicit measure assessing attitudes by examining effects of pairing attitude object targets with positive or negative targets in a task that categorizes the identity of the targets and their *personal* attitude valence (e.g., I like or I dislike).

*Semantic differential scales* – a self-report measure of attitude that uses responses to bipolar scales anchored by oppositely valenced adjectives at the ends (e.g., very good to very bad).

*Social cognition* – how individuals elaborate upon and process socially relevant information.

# FURTHER READING

Here are references to some key papers and books we have mentioned throughout this chapter. These readings would help you to learn about basic ideas in the study of attitudes and approaches to their measurement. In future chapters, we will also highlight readings that are applied in emphasis.

Fazio, R. H., Jackson, J. R., Dunton, B. C. and Williams, C. J. (1995) Variability in automatic activation as an unobtrusive measure of racial attitudes: A bona fide pipeline? *Journal of Personality and Social Psychology, 69*, 1013–1027.

Fazio, R. H. and Olson, M. A. (2003) Implicit measures in social cognition research: Their meaning and use. *Annual Review of Psychology, 54*, 297–327.

Greenwald, A. G., McGhee, D. and Schwartz, J. (1998) Measuring individual differences in implicit cognition: The Implicit Association Test. *Journal of Personality and Social Psychology, 74*, 1464–1480.

Krosnick, J. A, Judd, C. M. and Wittenbrink, B. (2005) Attitude measurement. In D. Albarracín, B. T. Johnson and M. P. Zanna (eds), *Handbook of Attitudes and Attitude Change*. Mahwah, NJ: Erlbaum.

McGuire, W. J. (1986) The vicissitudes of attitudes and similar representational constructs in twentieth century psychology. *European Journal of Social Psychology, 16*, 89–130.

Petty, R. E., Fazio, R. H. and Briñol, P. (eds) (2009) *Attitudes: Insights from the New Implicit Measures*. New York: Psychology Press.

Wittenbrink, B. and Schwarz, N. (eds) (2007) *Implicit Measures of Attitudes: Procedures and Controversies*. New York: Guilford Press.

# 2

---

# THE THREE WITCHES OF ATTITUDES

---

## QUESTIONS TO PONDER

1. How do we decide whether we like or dislike something?
2. Do different people derive their attitudes in different ways?
3. What does it mean to have a neutral attitude? Are there different types of neutral attitudes?
4. What are the implications of liking and disliking something at the same time?
5. Why do we hold attitudes?

---

### PREVIEW

Within this chapter we introduce three important aspects of attitude: content, structure, and function. These aspects of attitude pertain to the types of information we incorporate within attitudes (content), the way in which this information is organized and integrated (structure), and the psychological needs that this integrative process help to satisfy (function). These three aspects are different in many ways, but are closely intertwined. None of these three aspects of attitude can be understood without consideration of the others. In this way, these aspects are like the three witches in William Shakespeare's *Macbeth* and popular folklore; together they make a potent brew called "attitude." A better understanding of attitudes comes from considering the links among attitude content, structure, and function.

---

## ATTITUDE CONTENT

So far, we have seen that attitudes can be thought of as a global evaluation (e.g., like/dislike) of an object. This perspective has generated a number of conceptual models of the attitude concept.

The most influential model of attitude has been the *multicomponent model* (see Eagly & Chaiken, 1993; Zanna & Rempel, 1988). According to this perspective (see Figure 2.1), attitudes are summary evaluations of an object that have *cognitive*, *affective*, and *behavioral* components. We like to think of these components as a taxi CAB that will get you where you want to go. A number of researchers have considered how the CAB components contribute to the formation and expression of attitudes.

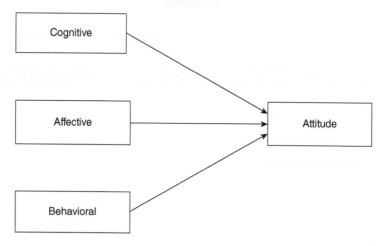

**Figure 2.1**   *The Multicomponent Model of Attitude*

## Getting into the CAB (cognition, affect, and behavior)

What do we mean when we say that attitudes have cognitive, affective, and behavioral components? The *cognitive* component of attitudes refers to the beliefs, thoughts, and attributes we associate with an object. In many cases, a person's attitude might be based primarily upon the positive and negative attributes the individual associates with an object. For example, when one author recently bought a new car, he devoted considerable attention to different vehicles' safety records, gas mileage, and repair costs. In this example, attitudes toward the different cars were formed through a consideration of the positive and negative characteristics of each car. As other examples, we may form attitudes toward a particular politician based on our beliefs about the politician's policy aims, intelligence, and values, and we may form attitudes toward a new cleaning product based on beliefs about its effectiveness, environmental friendliness, and cost.

The *affective* component of attitudes refers to feelings or emotions linked to an attitude object. Affective responses influence attitudes in a number of ways. A primary way in which feelings shape attitudes is through feelings that are aroused in response to an attitude object. For instance, many people indicate that spiders make them feel scared. This negative affective response is likely to cause a negative attitude toward spiders. In contrast, many people indicate that ice cream tastes great, and this positive affective response is likely to cause a positive attitude toward ice cream.

The *behavioral* component of attitudes refers to past behaviors or experiences regarding an attitude object. For instance, in a response to a survey asking our opinion on "global food security," we might infer that we have a positive attitude if we remember having donated to alleviate famine in a drought-stricken country. Alternatively, we might infer that we have a negative attitude toward global food security if we remember having signed a petition against factory farming of animals. This kind of mental process was best articulated by Daryl Bem. According to Bem's (1972) Self-Perception Theory, individuals do not always have access to their opinions about different objects (see also Nisbett & Wilson, 1977), especially if their feelings on the issue are vague or uncertain. Sometimes people infer their attitudes by thinking about how they have behaved with respect to the attitude object in the past.

## Are the CAB components really different?

Having read the previous section, you might be thinking "Hey, aren't these components pretty much the same thing?" You will be pleased to hear that attitude researchers have asked the same question and have devoted a lot of energy to answering it. To cut a long story short, the components are different.

Perhaps the best evidence showing that the CAB components are not the same comes from research conducted by Steven Breckler (1984). In one experiment, Breckler had participants report their cognitive, affective, and behavioral responses about snakes. Whilst in the presence of a real snake, participants indicated whether (i) snakes are kind or cruel (cognition), (ii) snakes make them feel anxious or happy (affect), and (iii) they like to handle snakes (behavior). Breckler (1984) used the content of participants' responses to compute a score for each of the components. He found that these cognitive, affective, and behavioral scores were only moderately correlated with each other. Thus, these components were empirically distinct.

While Breckler (1984) provided strong evidence that the cognitive, affective, and behavioral components of attitude are not the same, this does not mean that they are completely independent of each other. For example, one of the authors is a big fan of the music of Bruce Springsteen. If you asked him for his thoughts about Bruce Springsteen's music, he would answer that the music has well-constructed lyrics that express the importance Springsteen places on equality and social justice. If you asked the author about the feelings he associates with the music, he would say that the music makes him feel happy. If you asked him about his past experiences with Bruce Springsteen's music, he would wax lyrically about the many times he has attended a Springsteen concert. Unsurprisingly, the positive cognitions, affects, and behaviors all contribute to the author's positive attitude toward Bruce Springsteen.

That said, it isn't always the case that the CAB components have the same evaluative implications. Instead of asking this author about his perceptions of Bruce Springsteen, ask him about blood donation. He would tell you that blood donation is a noble endeavor that helps others; implying that he has positive cognitions. However, if you asked him about his feelings about blood donation, he would admit that it makes him feel afraid. He would also recall the negative experience of having once been jabbed repeatedly by a sadistic nurse who was unable to locate a vein in his arm. Thus, his cognitive, affective, and behavioral responses about blood donation differ in valence. (If you're wondering, it turns out this author does not donate blood, though he thinks it is an important thing to do.) Taken together, while the cognitive, affective, and behavioral components are (usually) consistent in their evaluative implications, they are not simply different ways of saying the same thing.

## Semantic differential measures of the CAB components

Another way of demonstrating the relative independence of the CAB components is to address how they can be measured. While attitude researchers have used a number of techniques to measure these components, this section describes some measures that are psychometrically sound and most popular among researchers.

The first type of measure we want to discuss is the semantic differential approach to measuring attitudinal components. We have already learned that researchers often use semantic differential scales such as positive/negative and good/bad to measure overall attitudes. This framework can also be used to measure the cognitive and affective components of attitude. Most often, researchers using semantic differential scales to assess cognition and affect have either used content-specific semantic differential scales or they have used generic scales applicable to both cognition and affect. In other words, some researchers use specific semantic differential scales to assess cognition and other semantic differential scales to assess affect. In contrast, other researchers have used the *same* semantic differential scales to assess both cognitive and affective responses toward a particular attitude object, while changing the instructions to highlight either cognition or affect.

Regarding the content-specific approach, Crites, Fabrigar, and Petty (1994) developed semantic differential measures of the cognitive and affective components of attitude. Their measure of the cognitive component features dimensions such as useful/useless, wise/foolish, beneficial/harmful, valuable/worthless, perfect/imperfect, and wholesome/unhealthy, while the affect component features dimensions such as lovely/hateful, delighted/sad, happy/annoyed, calm/tense, excited/bored, relaxed/angry, acceptance/disgusted, and joy/sorrow. These measures have the advantage of being reliable and valid, and can be used across different attitude objects (see Crites et al., 1994). Similarly, for both components, the word pairs are more specific than the broad, evaluative semantic dimensions (good/bad, like/dislike) used to measure overall attitudes.

In contrast to the content-specific approach, Breckler and Wiggins (1989) used the *same* semantic differential scales to assess *both* cognition and affect for a particular object, but framed the scales differently. For instance, in assessing cognitive and affective reactions toward blood donation, Breckler and Wiggins (1989) measured cognitions by having participants respond to the stem "Blood donation is" on the dimensions bad/good, wise/foolish, useless/useful, and important/unimportant. Affective responses toward this object were assessed by having participants respond to the stem "Blood donation makes me feel" on the same semantic differential scales.

Both approaches to measuring attitudinal components are useful. First, they are simple to administer and complete. Second, by presenting the same items for different attitude objects, they can be used to compare the favorability of responses across attitude objects. That said, there are also some problems with this type of measure. Most importantly, the attentive reader will have noticed that the semantic differential measures mentioned only the cognitive and affective components. The diffuse nature of behavior has made it difficult for researchers to imagine valid semantic differential scales for this component.

## Open-ended measures of the CAB components

A second type of measure uses open-ended questions to measure all three attitudinal components. In this technique, people are asked to write down the thoughts, feelings, and behavioral experiences they associate with an attitude object. An example of this type of measure is provided in Figure 2.2. Looking at these measures, you can see that the cognition measure asks participants to list the characteristics, attributes, and values they associate with the attitude object. The affect measure asks participants to list the feelings and emotions they associate with the attitude object. The behavior measure asks participants to list relevant past experiences they have had with the attitude object.

So if participants list their own cognitive, affective, and behavioral responses, how are scores derived for each component? Let's explain how this is done by using the affect measure as an example. For this exercise, let's assume that we are doing a survey of attitudes toward the topic "Drilling for oil in the Arctic." A participant with a negative attitude toward drilling might indicate that this activity elicits two affective responses: "anger" and "disgust." Having listed these feelings, the participant then rates how positive or negative each emotion is in relation to the attitude object. Our participant might indicate that anger gets a rating of −1, while disgust gets a score of −2. From these responses, we can compute a score that is the average of these valence ratings (in this case, −1.5).

Limitations of this approach include the fact that participants may find it hard to articulate the thoughts, feelings, and past experiences they associate with a particular attitude object, meaning that they might not provide any responses for one or more components. Similarly, these measures require more time and effort from participants. If researchers are interested in measuring cognitions, affective responses, and past behaviors for many attitude objects, it might not be feasible to use the open-ended approach.

Notwithstanding these limitations, the open-ended technique for measuring attitudinal components has been used in many studies (Bell, Esses, & Maio, 1996; Haddock, Zanna, & Esses, 1994a, 1994b; see Esses & Maio, 2002, and Haddock & Zanna, 1998, for reviews), and there are a number of advantages of this approach. First, this technique enabled researchers to devise a measure of the behavioral component, allowing for a more comprehensive test of the multi-component model of attitude (see, e.g., Haddock et al., 1994b). Second, respondents are asked to indicate the cognitive, affective, and behavioral responses that are the most personally salient and relevant, permitting them to be unrestrained from the dimensions provided by "close-ended" response formats. This feature enables people to provide responses that matter to them, even though they may have no significance to others. For instance, a person describing their behaviors regarding apples might say "feed them to my horse" – a behavior that would be unlikely to appear on any researcher-designed, closed-ended questionnaire.

## COGNITION (PART 1)

We are interested in the characteristics that people use in describing members of various social groups. Your task is to provide a description of typical members of the group. Your description should consist of a list of characteristics or, if necessary, short phrases which **you** would use to describe typical members of the group (e.g., 'they are cheap', 'they are intelligent'). Provide as many characteristics or short phrases as you think are necessary to convey your impression of the group and to describe them adequately. **Please be honest.** Your responses will be kept strictly confidential.

CANADIAN MEN ARE:

_____
_____
_____
_____
_____
_____
_____
_____
_____

## COGNITION (PART 2)

Please go back to each of the characteristics that you have provided. Decide for each characteristic whether it is favorable, unfavorable, or neutral, as you have used it to describe the group. Indicate the degree of favorability of each characteristic as follows:

1.   If the characteristic is positive, write a plus (+) beside it. If it is very positive, write two pluses (++) beside it.
2.   If the characteristic is neutral, write a zero (0) beside it.
3.   If the characteristic is negative, write a minus (–) beside it. If it is very negative, write two minuses (—) beside it.

Give your immediate first impression. Don't spend too much time on any one characteristic.

## AFFECT (PART 1)

We are interested in examining how members of particular groups make you feel, that is the emotions you experience when you see, meet or even think about typical members of a group. Your task is to provide a list of the feelings **you** experience (e.g., proud, angry, disgusted, happy) when you think about typical members of that group. Provide as many feelings or emotions as you believe are necessary to accurately convey your impression of the group and to describe them adequately. **Please be honest.** Your responses will be kept strictly confidential.

CANADIAN MEN MAKE ME FEEL:

_____
_____
_____

_____
_____
_____
_____

### AFFECT (PART 2)

Please go back to each of the feelings or emotions that you have provided. Decide for each feeling or emotion whether it is favorable, unfavorable, or neutral, as you have experienced it in reference to the group. Indicate the degree of favorability of each feeling or emotion as follows:

1. If the emotion is positive, write a plus (+) beside it. If it is very positive, write two pluses (++) beside it.
2. If the emotion is neutral, write a zero (0) beside it.
3. If the emotion is negative, write a minus (–) beside it. If it is very negative, write two minuses (––) beside it.

Give your immediate first impression. Don't spend too much time on any one emotion.

### BEHAVIOR (PART 1)

We are interested in the past experiences you have had with members of different social groups. Your task is to provide a list of recent experiences which **you** have had with typical group members. Provide as many experiences as you believe are necessary. **Please be honest.** Your responses will be kept strictly confidential.

MY BEHAVIORS RELEVANT TO CANADIAN MEN ARE:

_____
_____
_____
_____
_____
_____
_____

### BEHAVIOR (PART 2)

Please go back to the behaviors that you have provided. Decide for each **behavior** whether it is positive, negative, or neutral, as you have experienced it. Indicate your rating of each behavior as follows:

1. If the behavior is positive, write a plus (+) beside it. If it is very positive, write two pluses (+ +) beside it.
2. If the behavior is neutral, write a zero (0) beside it.
3. If the behavior is negative, write a minus (–) beside it. If it is very negative, write two minuses (– –) beside it.

Please give your first impression. Don't spend too much time on any one behavior.

**Figure 2.2** _Open-ended measures of attitudinal components_

# Do the CAB components predict attitudes?

So far, we have shown that cognitive, affective, and behavioral information are different components of attitude. But how well do they actually predict a person's attitude? Numerous studies have addressed this important question. The primary idea behind this line of research is to examine the degree to which the favorability of people's cognitions, feelings, and behaviors are correlated with their overall attitude. In addition, the research tests whether each component explains the overall attitude in complementary and unique ways; in other words, does each component explain some part of the overall attitude that is not explained by the other components?

Before we introduce this research, we have to add an important caveat. For the most part, this research has concentrated on how cognitive and affective information predict attitudes, in the absence of behavioral information. Why? As we just discussed, semantic differential measures of the components have been limited to assessments of the cognitive and affective components. Given the popularity of these measures, most studies have focused on these two components. However, as described below, the studies have also examined the role of these two components in a broad variety of attitudes.

One of the first studies examining the relative importance of cognition and affect was reported by Robert Abelson, Donald Kinder, Mark Peters, and Susan Fiske (1982), who explored the role of thoughts and feelings in predicting attitudes toward American presidential candidates. In this study, survey respondents ascribed personality traits to the Democratic and Republican primary candidates in 1980 and reported their feelings about each candidate. The participants were also asked to indicate their attitude toward each candidate. Abelson and colleagues found that the favorability of affective responses to the presidential candidates correlated with individuals' overall evaluations above and beyond the correlations with the favorability of beliefs about the candidates. Nonetheless, the beliefs were also uniquely predictive of attitudes. Subsequent research by Eagly, Mladinic, and Otto (1994), Haddock and Zanna (1997), and Lavine, Thomsen, Zanna, and Borgida (1998) has produced similar findings. Thus, both cognitive and affective information contribute to the prediction of political attitudes.

Steven Breckler and colleagues (e.g., Breckler, 1984; Breckler & Berman, 1991; Breckler & Wiggins, 1989, 1991) expanded the examination of the cognitive and affective components beyond the political domain. Using a number of different assessment strategies (e.g., equal appearing interval scales, semantic differential scales, and thought-listing procedures) and attitude objects (e.g., legalized abortion, blood donation, and college comprehensive exams), they discovered that both cognitive and affective information predicted attitudes. Breckler and colleagues found that the relative importance of each class of information was, to some extent, a function of the stimulus object under examination. For instance, affect was found to best predict attitudes toward blood donation, whereas cognitive information was found to best predict attitudes toward abortion and comprehensive exams.

In the domain of intergroup attitudes, Vicki Esses, Geoff Haddock, and Mark Zanna (1993) conducted a series of studies assessing the relative importance of cognitive and affective information in prejudicial attitudes. This research employed open-ended measures of cognition and affect. Participants listed the beliefs and feelings they associated with various ethnic groups and rated the positivity and negativity of each belief or feeling. Correlations between participants' overall attitudes and the average ratings for the beliefs and for the feelings indicated that the cognitive and affective responses were both important for predicting prejudice. Further, the relative contribution of the cognitive and affective responses depended on the target group under study. For instance, Esses et al. (1993) found that attitudes toward strongly disliked groups were best predicted by cognitive information, in the form of symbolic beliefs (i.e., beliefs that typical group members violate or promote the attainment of cherished values), whereas attitudes toward liked groups were best predicted by affective information (e.g., feelings or emotions elicited by members of the target group).

Eagly et al. (1994) suggested that the open-ended approach is better suited to examining the roles of cognitive and affective information than closed-ended rating scales. Using open-ended elicitation measures similar to those used by Esses et al. (1993), Eagly et al. asked American undergraduates to rate the positivity and negativity of their feelings and beliefs regarding their attitudes to different groups (e.g., women, the United States Republican Party supporters) and issues (e.g., abortion on demand, financial aid for the poor). Eagly and colleagues discovered that participants who rated their beliefs or feelings more positively expressed more favorable attitudes than participants who rated their beliefs or feelings more negatively. Consistent with Breckler's earlier findings, Eagly et al. also found that the unique contribution of each class of information was to some degree a function of the attitude object under examination. Affect contributed significantly to the prediction of some attitudes (e.g., attitudes to Republicans), but beliefs were the most important predictor in most instances.

A smaller number of studies have used measures of all three CAB components. One such study was conducted by Haddock and colleagues (1994b). In this study, the researchers were interested in assessing the content of Canadian university students' attitudes toward Native Canadians. Using open-ended measures of cognition, affect, and behavior, and a measure of overall attitudes, the researchers found that the quality of participants' past experiences with Native Canadians predicted attitudes independent of the favorability of participants' thoughts and feelings about the group.

Across the studies described above, there is abundant evidence that evaluative implications of cognitive, affective, and/or behavioral information are positively correlated. In particular, these studies show that maintaining positive beliefs about an attitude object is associated with positive affective responses about that object, whereas negative beliefs about an object are typically associated with unfavorable feelings. This evidence is consistent with the idea that the components share a synergistic relation (Eagly & Chaiken, 1993) – they work in concert to support a particular attitude. For this reason, it was important that the researchers conducted additional analyses that revealed reliable associations between each component and attitude even after the other type of information was held constant in a statistical analysis (multiple regression). This shows how the components work together but are distinct.

Another line of inquiry has found that *people* differ in the degree to which their attitudes are derived from different sources of information. In a series of studies, Huskinson and Haddock (2004) asked participants to report their attitudes, beliefs, and feelings toward a large number of attitude objects. These researchers found that people differ reliably in the extent to which they use the favorability of their beliefs and feelings to derive their overall attitudes. Some people based their attitudes predominantly on their affective responses, whereas others based their attitudes predominantly on their cognitive responses. Because of the synergistic relation between these components, these scientists also found that many people had attitudes that were based equally on cognition and affect. Importantly, these differences were found to have important implications for a number of outcomes, such as persuasion (see Research Highlight 2.1; Haddock & Huskinson, 2004).

It turns out that there are personality variables that predict the extent to which people form attitudes derived from affective or cognitive information (Huskinson & Haddock, 2004). For instance, use of affective information is greater among people who are higher on a trait labeled *need for affect*, which is the tendency to seek out and enjoy emotional experiences (Maio & Esses, 2001). In addition, there are personality differences in the extent to which people view their own attitudes as generally stemming from affective or cognitive information (See, Petty, & Fabrigar, 2008). Later in the text (Chapter 8), we will see that such individual differences have implications for how people react to emotional and cognitive content in persuasive messages that target their attitudes.

## KEY POINTS

- Attitudes have cognitive, affective, and behavioral components.
- The cognitive component refers to beliefs, thoughts, and attributes associated with an attitude object; the affective component refers to feelings or emotions associated with an attitude object; the behavioral component refers to past behaviors with respect to an attitude object.
- These components have a "synergistic" relation. When an individual possesses positive beliefs about an attitude object, they typically have positive affective and behavioral associations with the object.
- Despite their synergism, the cognitive, affective, and behavioral components are quantitatively and qualitatively distinct. Further, people differ in the degree to which their attitudes are based on affective or cognitive components.

### RESEARCH HIGHLIGHT 2.1

#### ATTITUDE CONTENT

When we were kids in the 1970s, a series of famous television advertisements featured former professional athletes exalting their preference for a particular brand of beer. While some of the athletes noted that the beer was *less filling* than other beers, others replied that it *tasted great*. The first component of the message highlighted a positive attribute about the beverage (i.e., its low caloric intake), whereas the second component highlighted a positive affective response associated with the beverage (i.e., its taste). Which part of the message would you find more persuasive? Perhaps it depends on whether your attitudes tend to be based more upon the content of your beliefs or more upon the content of your feelings.

In one set of studies, Huskinson and Haddock (2004) considered the degree to which people differ in the extent to which their attitudes are derived from their cognitions or affects. Using a strategy in which respondents completed measures of attitudes, beliefs, and feelings for a range of attitude objects, within-person correlations showed that indeed some people (let's call them *thinkers*) based their attitudes much more upon the favorability of their beliefs than on the favorability of their feelings, while other people (let's call them *feelers*) based their attitudes much more upon the favorability of their feelings than on the favorability of their beliefs. Huskinson and Haddock then explored whether these individual differences in attitude content would be related to how people responded to a persuasive appeal that was either cognitively-based or affectively-based.

In the study, thinkers and feelers were randomly assigned to receive one persuasive appeal about a new beverage. Some participants read an advertisement highlighting the positive qualities about the drink (e.g., that it contained pure fruit extracts). This appeal is cognition-based, as it emphasizes the positive attributes of the object. Other participants, instead of reading about the drink's properties, were given the opportunity to taste the beverage. This appeal is affect-based, because of the feelings resulting from tasting the pleasant drink. Later, participants were asked to indicate how much they liked the beverage. The results revealed that the two appeals had different effects on thinkers and feelers. Specifically, among participants who were presented with the cognition-based appeal, thinkers tended to form more positive attitudes to the drink than feelers. In contrast, among participants who were presented with the affect-based appeal, feelers formed more positive attitudes to the drink than thinkers. Thus, this study shows how personality differences in attitude content influence how we react to different types of information.

# ATTITUDE STRUCTURE

The cognitive, affective, and behavioral components of attitudes can contain a wealth of information, but how do we organize this information according to attitude valence (i.e., positivity versus negativity)? It is typically assumed that the existence of positive beliefs, feelings, and behaviors inhibits the occurrence of negative beliefs, feelings, and behaviors. For example, an individual with positive beliefs, feelings, and behaviors about the New York Yankees baseball team may be unlikely to have negative beliefs, feelings, and behaviors about this team. In other words, according to this *one-dimensional* perspective, the positive and negative elements are at opposite ends of a single dimension, and people tend to experience either end of the dimension or a location in between.

This one-dimensional view is opposed by a perspective suggesting that cognitive, affective, and behavioral information is organized along two separate dimensions: one dimension reflects whether the attitude has few or many positive elements, and the other dimension reflects whether the attitude has few or many negative elements (Cacioppo, Gardner, & Berntson, 1997). If this *two-dimensional* view is correct, then people can possess any combination of positivity or negativity in their attitudes. Some of these combinations fit the one-dimensional view: attitudes may consist of few positive and many negative elements, few negative and many positive elements, or few positive and few negative elements (i.e., a neutral position). Another combination is inconsistent with the one-dimensional view: attitudes might occasionally contain many positive *and* many negative elements, leading to *attitudinal ambivalence*. The two-dimensional perspective explicitly allows for this ambivalence to occur, whereas the one-dimensional perspective does not.

The one-dimensional and two-dimensional perspectives are presented in Figure 2.3. The top panel depicts the one-dimensional view of attitudes. In this panel, Person X would be slightly negative. The single axis does not permit one to mark Person X as being both negative and positive. The bottom panel of Figure 2.3 depicts the two-dimensional view of attitudes, with one axis (from middle to top) representing variability in negative evaluations and the other axis (from middle to right) depicting variability in positive evaluations. From this perspective, a person can possess high amounts of negativity and positivity toward an object. For example, Person Y in the figure could be considered highly ambivalent.

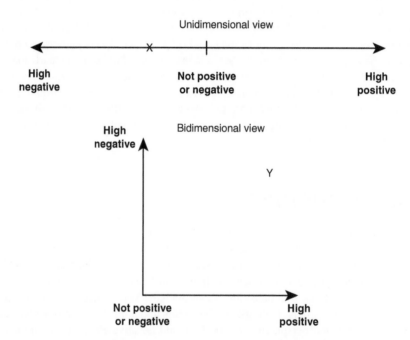

**Figure 2.3**    *Unidimensional and bidimensional views of attitude structure*

Which perspective is superior? At first glance, the two-dimensional perspective seems as though it should be superior because it allows for the same patterns of positivity and negativity as the one-dimensional view, while also allowing for ambivalence. For instance, it is difficult to interpret the meaning of the neutral point in one-dimensional scales for assessing attitudes (Kaplan, 1972). Imagine that people were asked to report their attitude toward eating rhubarb (a tart vegetable) on a nine-point scale that ranged from "1 – extremely unfavorable" to "9 – extremely favorable" as the end points, with "5 – neither unfavorable nor favorable" in the middle. If someone indicated that his or her attitude was 5, it is half-way between the most extreme positive response option and the most extreme negative response option. People could choose this option because it is a compromise between many positive and negative elements of their attitude (e.g., they have many positive and negative thoughts, feelings, and behaviors regarding eating rhubarb) *or* because they have no positive or negative elements whatsoever (e.g., they have never eaten rhubarb).

The failure to distinguish between these two reasons for the neutral selection is important, because measures that directly assess attitudinal ambivalence predict a variety of outcomes. The best known outcome is *response polarization* (Bell & Esses, 2002; MacDonald & Zanna, 1998). People who are highly ambivalent toward an object are more strongly influenced by features of their environment that make salient the object's positive or negative attributes. This causes them to behave more favorably toward the object when the positive elements are salient than when the negative elements are salient. In contrast, non-ambivalent people are less strongly influenced by the salience of the positive or negative attributes.

Research has also revealed that ambivalent and non-ambivalent attitudes influence how people process issue-relevant information and the degree to which attitudes predict behavior. With regard to the former issue, ambivalent attitudes tend to cause greater scrutiny of information that can help to resolve the ambivalence (Clark, Wegener, & Fabrigar, 2008; Maio, Bell, & Esses, 1996). With regard to the latter issue, research suggests that ambivalent attitudes are less likely to predict behavior than non-ambivalent attitudes (Conner & Armitage, 2009). A recent model suggests that these effects may occur because of ways in which ambivalence affects decision-making processes (van Harreveld, van der Pligt, & De Liver, 2009).

## RESEARCH HIGHLIGHT 2.2

### ATTITUDE STRUCTURE

One reason for the emergence of attitudinal ambivalence as an important property of attitudes is its potential to explain why people sometimes react in polarized ways to controversial groups or issues. This notion was nicely illustrated by Tara MacDonald and Mark Zanna (1998), who examined the consequences of students' ambivalence toward feminists. In an initial set of data, these investigators found that some students tended to both admire feminists *and* dislike them. This pattern can be labeled as cognitive-affective ambivalence, because it represents conflict between how the individuals think (e.g., admiring feminists for their perceived

*(Continued)*

*(Continued)*

courage) and feel (e.g., disliking feminists because of their perceived stridency). MacDonald and Zanna's study examined an important potential consequence of this ambivalence: polarized evaluations of a feminist's suitability for employment. The researchers expected that ambivalent people would be more strongly influenced by an innocuous prior event, which was whether a prior candidate who was admirable-but-dislikeable succeeded or failed in an interview.

To test this hypothesis, participants first completed a measure assessing their ambivalence toward feminists. This questionnaire assessed the extent to which participants admired feminists and disliked them. Ambivalent and nonambivalent participants were then informed in a subsequent experimental session that they were taking part in a study of how people make hiring decisions. They listened to a 10-minute audio recording of a job interview, which featured an admirable but dislikeable man who was to be successful (positive prime condition) or unsuccessful (negative prime condition) with his application. Participants then completed questions about the candidate's admirable qualities (positive prime condition) or dislikeable qualities (negative prime condition). Finally, participants read and evaluated the applications of several women, including one who had completed a thesis and another who had jobs that suggested a feminist political perspective. As part of this final task, participants rated the likelihood that they would hire each woman for a job. The main dependent measure was the rated likelihood of hiring the feminist applicant.

The results of the study showed that participants who exhibited a high degree of ambivalence toward feminists reported stronger intentions to hire the feminist candidate after seeing the admirable-but-dislikeable male candidate succeed than after seeing him fail. In contrast, participants who exhibited a low degree of ambivalence toward feminists were not affected by the success or failure of the admirable-but-dislikeable male candidate. Thus, only the ambivalent participants' intentions were affected by the prime.

MacDonald and Zanna (1998) concluded that cognitive-affective ambivalence has important consequences. When people possess this ambivalence, making them mindful of either the cognitive (e.g., admiration) or affective (e.g., dislike) elements of their attitudes causes their behavior to reflect the salient elements. As a result, ambivalent people might appear to strongly favor a person who is a target of their ambivalence (e.g., a feminist) in some situations (e.g., after a positive event), but strongly disfavor the individual in other situations (e.g., after a negative event). Thus, behavior that may seem quizzical and contradictory on the surface may be explicable by considering the extent to which there is ambivalence in the underlying attitude.

# Types of ambivalence

Researchers interested in attitude ambivalence have described different types of ambivalence (see Conner & Armitage, 2009; van Harreveld et al., 2009). As noted in Research Highlight 2.2, there may be ambivalence between attitude components and not just within them. For example, people might possess many positive beliefs and negative feelings about an object. Ambivalence can also exist between cognitions and behaviors and between emotions and behaviors. Such instances of *intercomponent* ambivalence are conceptually different from *intracomponent* ambivalence, arising when people have positive *and* negative beliefs, positive *and* negative feelings, or positive *and* negative behaviors.

At the same time, there are two major types of ambivalence that can reside within or between components. *Potential ambivalence* is a state of conflict that exists when people simultaneously possess positive and negative evaluations of an attitudinal object. This conflict can be measured by asking people to indicate the positive and negative elements of their attitude, perhaps by asking them to list the beliefs, emotions, and behaviors that occur to them (as outlined earlier in the chapter). Inspection of these elements might reveal many positive and negative beliefs (cognitive ambivalence), positive and negative feelings (affective ambivalence), positive and negative behavioral experiences (behavioral ambivalence), or ambivalence between components (e.g., cognitive-affective ambivalence). Researchers can then calculate the amount of conflict between people's positive and negative evaluations of an attitude object, using one of several different formulae that have been developed (e.g., Priester & Petty, 1996; Thompson, Zanna, & Griffin, 1995).

An important reason for labeling this type of ambivalence as "potential" ambivalence is that the ambivalence may or may not be consciously perceived by the individual (see McGregor, Newby-Clark, & Zanna, 1999). In contrast, *felt ambivalence* is the actual feeling of tension that people experience when they consciously think about the attitude object. This type of ambivalence is assessed by asking people to rate the extent to which their feelings are conflicted, mixed, and indecisive (e.g., "How mixed is your opinion about chocolate cake?"; see Wegener, Downing, Krosnick, & Petty, 1995).

Numerous studies have examined the antecedents and consequences of potential and felt ambivalence (e.g., Holbrook & Krosnick, 2005; Priester & Petty, 2001; see Conner & Armitage, 2009, for an excellent review). To date, research has revealed that measures of potential and felt ambivalence don't correlate highly, suggesting that they are distinct concepts (Priester & Petty, 1996; Riketta, 2004). At the same time, researchers have suggested that discrepancies between implicit measures and explicit measures of attitude can also provide another type of indicator of ambivalence (Briñol, Petty, & Wheeler, 2006). These discrepancies are discussed in Chapter 9.

## KEY POINTS

- There are important questions about how positive and negative evaluations may be organized within and between the components of attitude.
- The one-dimensional view postulates that the positive and negative elements are stored as opposite ends of a single dimension, whereas the two-dimensional view postulates that positive and negative elements are stored along two separate dimensions.
- Feelings of ambivalence may only partly reflect the potential ambivalence in thoughts, feelings, and behaviors relevant to our attitude.

# ATTITUDE FUNCTIONS

Individuals hold attitudes for a variety of reasons. For example, the authors' affinity for the Toronto Maple Leafs hockey team might have developed from their relatives and friends supporting the team. In contrast, each author's attitude toward abortion might be based on the value they place on an individual's freedom of choice or the sanctity of life. As introduced in Chapter 1, attitude researchers have devoted considerable attention to understanding the needs or functions that are fulfilled by attitudes.

The most prominent models of attitude functions were developed over 50 years ago (Katz, 1960; Smith et al., 1956). Smith et al. (1956) suggested that attitudes serve three primary functions: object-appraisal, social-adjustment, and externalization. *Object-appraisal* refers to the ability of attitudes to summarize the positive and negative attributes of objects in our social world. For example, attitudes can help people to approach things that are beneficial for them and avoid things that are harmful to them (Maio, Esses, Arnold, & Olson, 2004). *Social-adjustment* is fulfilled by attitudes that help us to identify with people whom we like and to dissociate from people whom we dislike. For example, individuals may buy a certain soft drink because their favorite singer endorses this drink. *Externalization* is fulfilled by attitudes that defend the self against internal conflict. For example, bad golfers might develop an intense dislike for the game because their poor performance threatens their self-esteem.

In his own program of research, Daniel Katz (1960) proposed four attitude functions, some of which relate to those proposed by Smith et al. (1956): knowledge, utility, ego-defense, and value-expression. The *knowledge* function represents the ability of attitudes to organize information about attitude objects, while the *utilitarian* function exists in attitudes that maximize rewards and minimize punishments obtained from attitude objects. These functions are similar to Smith et al.'s (1956) object-appraisal function. Katz's *ego-defensive* function exists in attitudes that serve to protect an individual's self-esteem, and is similar to Smith et al.'s (1956) externalization function. Finally, Katz proposed that attitudes may serve a *value-expressive* function, such that an attitude may express an individual's self-concept and central values. For example, a person might cycle to work rather than take her car because she values the environment.

Interest in the study of attitude functions has fluctuated wildly. In the decade following the taxonomies developed by Smith et al. (1956) and Katz (1960), there was considerable interest in understanding the reasons people held particular attitudes and the implications of holding attitudes that fulfilled different functions. Interest in the functional perspective then waned for a period of time, as researchers found it difficult to conduct experimental studies testing various aspects of functional theories.

A new generation of research then provided new insights into the functional perspective. For example, Gregory Herek (e.g., Herek, 1986, 2000) suggested a distinction between evaluative functions, which pertain to the ability of attitudes to summarize information about the attitude object itself, and expressive functions, which are fulfilled upon the expression of an attitude. Herek (1987) also developed a measure assessing the degree to which an attitude fulfills different functions. His Attitudes Functions Inventory (AFI) is a self-report measure asking participants to rate the extent to which their attitude reflects various concerns. This approach provides a simple method for determining the primary function of an individual's attitude toward a particular object (see also Prentice, 1987).

At around the same time as the development of Herek's AFI measure, Sharon Shavitt (e.g., Shavitt, 1990; Shavitt & Nelson, 2000) considered whether different attitude objects are likely to fulfill a particular function. For example, Shavitt (1990) tested whether consumer products such as coffee, air conditioners, watches, and sunglasses serve as single or multiple functions. Shavitt found that coffee and air conditioners tended to serve a utilitarian function (as indicated by researchers' coding of participants' thoughts about these items) and that people's attitudes toward particular brands of these products were most likely to be changed by utilitarian arguments (e.g., the quality of a product). In contrast, Shavitt found that objects such as watches and sunglasses could fulfill different functions. One person might wear a particular brand of sunglasses because of the quality of the brand (e.g., they are effective in blocking UV rays), whereas another person might wear that same brand because of the social prestige associated with the brand name. This research has been instrumental in linking theories of attitude function to consumer behavior.

## RESEARCH HIGHLIGHT 2.3

### ATTITUDE FUNCTIONS

Back in our university student days, one of us had two very good friends who had extremely different personalities. One of the friends was very adept at changing his personality to fit the social environment in which he found himself. If the situation suggested that he needed to behave one way, he could act that way; if the situation suggested that he needed to behave the opposite way, he could do that as well. In contrast, the other friend did not show this behavioral variability. He tended not to mold his personality depending upon the situation; instead he always showed others his "true self."

Mark Snyder (1974, 1986) developed the personality construct of *self-monitoring* in order to describe how people differ in the degree to which they change their behavior to suit their situation. Snyder described high self-monitors as the type of people who are adept at changing their behavior across situations, while low self-monitors tend to present themselves in the same way across situations. Snyder and his colleagues (e.g., Snyder & DeBono, 1985) linked these individual differences in self-monitoring to the functions that are likely to be fulfilled by the attitudes of high and low self-monitors. In particular, these scientists argued that high self-monitors, given their propensity to change their personality when interacting with different people, might be likely to hold attitudes that fulfill a social-adjustive function. In contrast, they argued that low self-monitors, given their propensity to always "be themselves," might be more likely to hold attitudes that fulfill a value-expressive function.

*(Continued)*

*(Continued)*

In a creative set of studies, Mark Snyder and Ken DeBono (1985) tested whether these individual differences in attitude function would influence how people responded to different types of persuasive appeals. In one experiment, Snyder and DeBono (1985, Study 3) randomly assigned high and low self-monitors to receive one of two appeals about a new brand of shampoo. One of the appeals focused on the *image* associated with the shampoo (e.g., that the product was above average in "how good it makes your hair look"). The other appeal focused on the *quality* of the shampoo (e.g., that the product was above average in "how clean it gets your hair").

Snyder and DeBono (1985, Study 3) tested whether people who tend to hold social-adjustive attitudes (i.e., high self-monitors) would be more persuaded by the image appeal than the quality appeal, whereas people who tend to hold value-expressive attitudes (i.e., low self-monitors) would be more persuaded by the quality appeal than the image appeal. These predictions were strongly supported by the results, which found that an individual's willingness to try the shampoo depended upon whether the appeal "matched" their self-monitoring status. This study and others (see DeBono, 1987; Prentice, 1987) demonstrate the importance of knowing the needs fulfilled by a person's attitude.

In recent years, research on attitude functions has focused on particular functions served by attitudes. For instance, there is evidence indicating that the object-appraisal function is highly important, because attitudes can simplify interaction with the environment. The importance of this function was highlighted by Russell Fazio and colleagues, who found that highly accessible attitudes (which people recall quickly) increase the ease with which people make attitude-relevant judgments and decrease physiological arousal during these judgments (see Fazio, 1995, 2000). These findings support the conclusion that the object-appraisal function is more strongly served by attitudes that are spontaneously activated from memory than by attitudes that are not spontaneously activated.

Despite the recent advances in research on attitude function, key problems still limit progress in understanding the psychological needs that attitudes fulfill (Maio & Olson, 2000b, 2000c). One problem is limitations in the current measures of attitude function. For instance, Herek's AFI relies on people's ability to know the functions of their own attitudes, but evidence indicates that people are sometimes poor at knowing the basis for their attitudes (Nisbett & Wilson, 1977). This problem is particularly evident for so-called ego-defensive attitudes, which help to defend the self-concept precisely because the person is *unaware* that the attitude is defending the self. (As soon as you know that the attitude is merely helping you to feel better about yourself, it may no longer help to make you feel better about yourself.) A second problem is ambiguity in the distinctions between different attitude functions. For instance, a person's attitude toward partying the night before an exam might reflect the extent to which he or she values "achievement" and, therefore, be value-expressive. At the same time, the person's value of achievement itself reflects a utilitarian concern. So is the attitude value-expressive or utilitarian? A different type of taxonomy may be needed to address such issues (Maio & Olson, 2000a).

## KEY POINTS

- Attitudes can fulfill a variety of psychological needs.
- Among the attitude functions, the object appraisal function is especially important as it enables attitudes to serve as energy saving devices that make judgments easier and faster to perform.
- Research on attitude functions requires further improvement in the methods used to assess them.

# LINKING ATTITUDE CONTENT, STRUCTURE, AND FUNCTION

There are inexorable links among attitude content, attitude structure, and attitude function. Consider attitude structure and function. In some of our research, we have argued that the same attitude functions may operate at both the unidimensional and bidimensional structural levels, but to varying degrees (e.g., Maio & Haddock, 2004; Maio et al., 2004). For instance, the object-appraisal function should be served more strongly by unidimensional attitudes than by bidimensional attitudes, because the bidimensional attitudes evoke more decision conflict. In addition, it is possible that social norms make it occasionally desirable to have high ambivalence in an attitude, such as when an issue is controversial (Pillaud, Cavazza, & Butera, 2013). In this situation, people who appear ambivalent may give the impression of being fair and knowledgeable. These individuals may also be inoffensive to others because they "agree" with everyone to some extent.

The links between attitude content and attitude function are also important. Consider attitudes toward a car that are based on a need to protect the environment versus a need to impress others. These attitudes are value-expressive or social-adjustive in function, but they may also imply different beliefs. For instance, a person motivated to protect the environment forms beliefs about the car's fuel efficiency, carbon emissions, and durability with this value in mind. The person motivated to impress others forms beliefs about the car's appearance, popularity, and brand reputation. These individuals form qualitatively different beliefs about the car. In other words, attitude function has implications for attitude content (and vice versa).

Notice that the connections between function and structure also have implications for attitude content, because we may be drawn to content that supports the structure and function that suits a particular attitude. For example, people who seek non-ambivalent attitudes for object-appraisal reasons may be drawn to cognitive, affective, and behavioral information that is mutually reinforcing toward the same attitude, and they may avoid information when it threatens to undermine the attitude (e.g., by avoiding cognitive information if it seems counter-attitudinal). In contrast, people who seek ambivalence for social-adjustive reasons may be more likely to form a mix of relevant cognitions, emotions, and behaviors.

Of importance, the connections we have highlighted do *not* mean that attitude content, structure, and function are all essentially the same thing. For example, it might be tempting to conclude that different attitude functions are simply different types of attitude content, because the different functions in our car example relied on different beliefs. This conclusion would be mistaken because different motives can also rely on similar beliefs. In our example, people may decide that purchasing a car that protects the environment is the best way to impress others. In that event, all of the environmental beliefs about the car would be subsumed within a social-expressive attitude in the same way as they are subsumed in an attitude that is simply oriented to expressing the value. The beliefs would be the same, but the end motives differ. Thus, as with other connections among attitude content, structure, and function, the links are flexible (see Maio & Haddock, 2004).

## How strong are attitudes?

An important question that is relevant to the content, structure, and function of attitudes is the extent to which attitudes are strong. As mentioned at the beginning of the book, people feel more strongly about some topics than about others. Strong attitudes differ from weak attitudes in a number of other ways. Jon Krosnick and Richard Petty (1995) argue that there are four key manifestations of strong attitudes. First, strong attitudes are *more persistent*. That is, they are more temporally stable over the passage of time (Visser & Krosnick, 1998). Second, strong attitudes are *more resistant to change*. When faced with a persuasive appeal, strong attitudes are less likely to change than weak attitudes (Petty, Haugtvedt, & Smith, 1995). Third, strong attitudes are *more likely to influence information processing*. Research has revealed that people devote greater attention to information that is relevant to strong versus weak attitudes (Houston & Fazio, 1989). Finally, strong attitudes are *more likely to guide behavior*. Put simply, we are more likely to act upon strong versus weak attitudes (Holland, Verplanken, & van Knippenberg, 2002).

For many years, the topic of *attitude strength* has interested attitude researchers, and the strength of an attitude has been conceptualized and measured in many different ways. For example, individuals can be asked how *certain* they are of their attitude, as well as how *important* their attitude is to them personally (see Haddock, Rothman, Reber, & Schwarz, 1999; Wegener et al., 1995). These types of ratings are related, but different (Visser, Bizer, & Krosnick, 2006). This difference is relevant to our description of attitude content because certainty may draw on the amount of cognitive content supporting an attitude, while importance might draw on the amount of emotional content supporting an attitude. Similarly, strong attitudes can be retrieved from memory more quickly than others; such easily retrievable attitudes are referred to as being highly *accessible* (Fazio, 1995). Recall the evidence that accessible attitudes serve a stronger utilitarian/object-appraisal function (Fazio, 2000). In addition, high accessibility may also reflect a uni-polar attitude structure (Mellema & Bassili, 1995; Pomerantz, Chaiken, & Tordesillas, 1995).

The roles of attitude content, structure, and function in attitude strength is relevant for understanding a debate that has occurred among some attitude researchers. Through the years, a number of scholars have deliberated about the degree to which attitudes are best considered as evaluative representations of an attitude object that are *stored* in memory versus *temporary* evaluations. In its strong form, the first position implies that attitudes are stable across time and context – a popular analogy being that we have a file drawer of attitudes in our brain (see Eagly & Chaiken 2007; Fazio, 2007; Petty, Briñol, & DeMarree, 2007). In contrast, the strong form of the latter position implies that attitudes are simply constructed on the spot (see Schwarz, 2007). Proponents of both perspectives can generate research supporting their position.

At the same time, however, the answer may depend on attitude strength. Strong attitudes should be more stable and enduring, but weak attitudes should be more malleable and likely to be constructed on the spot. People may not need to construct attitudes if they are based on synergistic cognitive, affective, and behavioral information, while serving congruent psychological needs, and stored in a unidimensional, nonconflicting fashion. In contrast, when attitudes include a hodge-podge of conflicting information and motives, stored on different dimensions, then people may be forced to construct attitudes on the spot, depending on which information and motives are important to them at the time.

## KEY POINTS

- Attitude content, attitude structure, and attitude function are inexorably linked.
- Attitudes vary in the degree to which they are persistent over time, resistant to change, influential in guiding information processing, and influential in predicting behavior.

## WHAT WE HAVE LEARNED

- It is useful to consider attitude content, structure, and function as three inseparable but distinct aspects of attitudes.
- Attitudes have cognitive, affect, and behavioral (CAB) components.
- Positive and negative elements of attitude can be stored as opposite ends of a single dimension or along two separate dimensions.
- Attitudes serve a variety of psychological needs. The object appraisal function is especially important; it suggests that attitudes serve as energy saving devices that make judgments easier and faster to perform.
- Attitude content, attitude structure, and attitude function may influence attitude strength. Strong attitudes are more influential than weak attitudes.

## WHAT DO YOU THINK?

- We have seen that attitudes are based on cognitive, affective, and behavioral information. Further, we have described research demonstrating that people differ in the degree to which their attitudes are based on cognitive and affective information. Do you think people are aware of whether they might have a preference for cognitive or affective information?

- The two-dimensional structure perspective suggests that positive and negative elements of attitudes are stored along two separate dimensions (one for positive elements, a second for negative elements). Do you think that this structure is more or less efficient than a one-dimensional system? Is it possible that both systems can co-exist, with each being used in different circumstances?
- Attitudes can serve a number of different functions. Do people know the primary functions of their attitudes? If they do, what does this suggest for how attitude functions can be measured?

# KEY TERMS

*Affective component of attitudes* – feelings or emotions linked to an attitude object.

*Attitude accessibility* – the ease with which an attitude can be retrieved from memory.

*Attitudinal ambivalence* – the existence of many positive *and* many negative elements in an attitude.

*Attitude certainty* – individuals' degree of certainty and confidence in their attitude.

*Attitude importance* – individuals' judgments about the significance of their attitude to them personally.

*Behavioral component of attitudes* – past behaviors or experiences regarding an attitude object.

*Cognitive component of attitudes* – the beliefs, thoughts, and attributes we associate with an object.

*Content-specific measures of attitude components* – a methodology using semantic differential scales that refer to cognition, affect, or behavior.

*Ego-defensive function* – the ability of attitudes to protect an individual's self-esteem.

*Externalization function* – the ability of attitudes to defend the self against internal conflict.

*Knowledge function* – the ability of attitudes to organize information about attitude objects.

*Multicomponent model* – attitudes are evaluations of an object that summarize cognitive, affective, and behavioral information.

*Need for affect* – the tendency to seek out and enjoy emotional experiences.

*Object-appraisal function* – the ability of attitudes to summarize the positive and negative attributes of objects in our social world.

*Open-ended measures of attitude components* – a technique that asks participants to freely list beliefs, feelings, or behaviors linked to their attitude.

*Self-monitoring orientation* – individual differences in how people vary their behavior to suit the situation.

*Social-adjustment function* – the ability of attitudes to help us identify with people whom we like and to dissociate from people whom we dislike.

*Utilitarian function* – the ability of attitudes to maximize rewards and minimize punishments obtained from attitude objects.

*Value-expressive function* – the ability of an attitude to express an individual's self-concept and central values.

# FURTHER READING

## BASIC

Breckler, S. J. (1984) Empirical validation of affect, behavior and cognition as distinct components of attitude. *Journal of Personality and Social Psychology*, *47*, 1191–1205.

Fazio, R. H. (2000) Accessible attitudes as tools for object appraisal: Their costs and benefits. In G. R. Maio and J. M. Olson (eds), *Why We Evaluate: Functions of Attitudes* (pp. 1–36). Mahwah, NJ: Erlbaum.

Lavine, H., Thomsen, C. J., Zanna, M. P. and Borgida, E. (1998) On the primacy of affect in the determination of attitudes and behavior: The moderating role of affective-cognitive ambivalence. *Journal of Experimental Social Psychology*, *34*, 398–421.

## APPLIED

Crites, S. L., Fabrigar, L. R. and Petty, R. E. (1994) Measuring the affective and cognitive properties of attitudes: Conceptual and methodological issues. *Personality and Social Psychology Bulletin*, *20*, 619–634.

Kempf, D. S. (1999) Attitude formation from product trial: Distinct roles of cognition and affect for hedonic and functional products. *Psychology and Marketing*, *16*, 35–50.

Lipkus, I. M., Green, J. D., Feaganes, J. R. and Sedikides, C. (2001) The relationship between attitudinal ambivalence and desire to quit smoking among college smokers. *Journal of Applied Social Psychology*, *31*, 113–133.

Verplanken, B. and Orbell, S. (2003) Reflection on past behavior: A self-report index of habit strength. *Journal of Applied Social Psychology*, *33*, 1313–1330.

# SECTION 2

## INTRODUCTION: WHAT DO ATTITUDES DO?

Those of us who grew up in the 1970s and 1980s know that these were strange years. For example, Steve Austin possessed bionic, superhuman limbs in the television show *The Six Million Dollar Man*, but he still had to use a payphone to call his boss, Oscar Goldman. Then, in 1982, *Time* magazine's "Person of the Year" award went *not* to a person, but to a thing called the personal computer. Eventually, the personal computer's features and potential became clear, but at first it was just odd. Nowadays, we are going through the same process of discovery for other new people and ideas, ranging from nanotechnology to climate change. Over time, people will form attitudes toward these new entities in the same way as we did for Steve Austin and the personal computer.

Social psychologists hope that these diverse attitudes *do* something, otherwise a large number of us would not devote our lives to studying them. Despite some early controversy (and because of lessons learnt from it), research has found that attitudes *are* important. When the right methods are used, research has revealed that attitudes do a lot of things and that they are useful in a number of ways. In this section of the book, we will discover how attitudes are influential in helping us navigate our social environment.

Chapter 3 begins this discovery by considering whether attitudes predispose people to respond differently toward an attitude object. We will see that our attitudes influence how we process information. That is, attitudes serve as lenses through which we perceive and interpret information in our social world. Chapter 3 also addresses the degree to which our attitudes guide our actions and behaviors. To the extent that attitudes are a useful construct in social psychology, they should predict behavior, at least to some degree. We will see that there are specific conditions in which our attitudes do a good job in predicting and influencing what we do.

Building on the evidence presented in Chapter 3, Chapter 4 deals with *how* attitudes predict behavior. Here, we will focus on models that researchers have developed for understanding the mechanisms through which attitudes shape behavior. This chapter will describe and review important models, while evaluating evidence testing them. We will see that these models highlight different things and often compliment each other quite well.

# 3

# THE INFLUENCE OF ATTITUDES ON INFORMATION PROCESSING AND BEHAVIOR

## QUESTIONS TO PONDER

1. Do our attitudes influence what we see in our social environment?
2. Do our attitudes influence how we interpret information?
3. Do our attitudes influence what information we encode and what information we remember?
4. Do our attitudes predict our behavior?
5. When do our attitudes predict our behavior?

## PREVIEW

Attitudes are useful in many ways. Without them, we would be dazed by the information bombarding us, and unable to decide how to think and act. In this chapter, we address how attitudes are influential in helping us navigate our social environment. First, we will see that our attitudes influence how we process information. Second, we consider the degree to which our attitudes guide our actions and behaviors. Third, we will see that the role of attitudes depends on their strength. Strong and weak attitudes might have different effects on behavior as a result of differences in their content, structure, and function.

# ATTITUDES AND INFORMATION PROCESSING

A few years ago, one of the authors and a good friend were watching a baseball game together. While the author was cheering for one team, his friend was cheering for the other. Throughout the game, both the author and his friend complained about the quality of the umpires. The author thought that the team he was supporting was the victim of numerous bad calls. In contrast, his friend thought that his own team was getting unfair treatment from the umpires. It was hard to believe they were actually watching the same game! How can two people see the same thing yet draw completely different conclusions? In this part of the chapter, we consider how attitudes influence people's processing of information.

In addressing this issue, we first need to describe what we mean by the term *information processing*. Psychologists use the term to refer to how our mind deals with information we encounter in our social world. Within the chapter, we will describe how attitudes influence three stages of information processing. First, we discuss whether our attitudes influence the information to which we *attend*. Given the large amount of information we face in our social world, we pay attention to just a subset of that information. Do our attitudes affect what we actually notice? Second, we address whether our attitudes influence how we *encode and interpret* information. While two people might attend to the same information, their likes and dislikes can shape how they interpret that information (like our baseball example). Finally, we discuss whether attitudes also affect our ability to *remember* specific pieces of information. Do attitudes influence the information we remember?

## The influence of attitudes on attention

The idea that attitudes influence the information we see and hear is one of the oldest assumptions in the study of attitudes (see Allport, 1935; Asch, 1952). Indeed, Gordon Allport (1935, p. 806) wrote that our attitudes "determine for each individual what he will see and hear, what he will think and what we will do …; they are our methods for finding our way about in an ambiguous universe." Similarly, Leon Festinger's (1957) initial writings on cognitive dissonance can be traced back to how individuals seek out different types of information when making decisions. Recall from Chapter 1 that cognitive dissonance refers to an aversive feeling between attitude-relevant beliefs. Festinger argued that we use an open-minded information search strategy before we make a decision, in order to be well-informed, but after a decision is reached, the need to avoid cognitive dissonance (between our beliefs about our behavior and our attitude) leads us to search for information in a selective way. For example, when one of us recently bought a new car, he searched diligently for detailed information about the two models that he most liked. After he had reached a decision (and paid for the car), he tended to notice and search for information that confirmed his choice and to avoid information that made him feel like he had made the wrong decision.

Early experiments supported this proposal with evidence using a variety of experimental paradigms (see Frey, 1986, for a review). Nonetheless, some researchers were unconvinced by this research and the arguments behind the notion of *selective attention*. In particular, Jonathan

Freedman and David Sears (1965) argued that some of the early research on selective attention merely showed that people are more likely to encounter information that supports their attitudes; there was no evidence to suggest that individuals explicitly *sought out* attitude-congruent information (see Judd & Kulik, 1980). In response to this criticism, subsequent research used different procedures to test whether attitudes influence attention to different types of information.

A great example is Silvia Knobloch-Westerwick and Jingbo Meng's (2009) study of people's choice of political messages. To test whether individuals are selective in their exposure to information on political issues, Knobloch-Westerwick and Meng conducted two test sessions. In the first session, participants completed a survey of their attitudes to 17 political issues and measures of the strength of these attitudes (e.g., accessibility, importance, certainty). Six weeks later, participants completed a computer study that had no apparent connection to the first session. In this study, they were asked to browse an online magazine and read whichever articles they wished over a five-minute period. The initial screen presented eight headlines with taglines on four different issues that were among the 17 that were presented in the first session. The article headlines expressed opposing views on each of the four topics. The computer program recorded participants' selection of the online articles and how long they read the articles.

As shown in Figure 3.1, a significant and consistent difference emerged in both the selection of articles and the time spent reading them. In the five minutes allotted for reading, participants read more articles that were consistent with the attitudes they had expressed in the earlier survey than were inconsistent with their attitudes. They also spent more time reading the attitude-consistent articles. An interesting aspect of these findings is that it was not the case that people completely ignored the attitude-inconsistent articles. Despite the significant preference for articles that supported their attitudes, participants did spend an appreciable amount of time considering the opposing information.

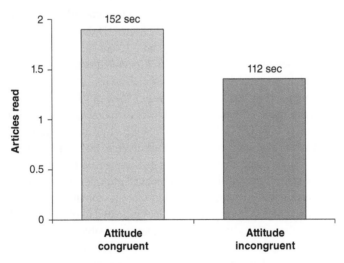

**Figure 3.1** *Number of articles read, and time spent looking at articles, as a function of article congruency (Knobloch-Westerwick & Meng, 2009)*

A recent meta-analysis of studies looking at selective exposure suggests that the amount of selective exposure to information supporting attitudes depends on a number of factors (Hart et al., 2009). For instance, selective exposure effects are much larger when the topics are value-relevant or there is high prior commitment to a particular attitude position, and new dissonant information must not seem highly useful, high in quality, or non-refutable (see also Frey, 1986; Jonas, Schulz-Hardt, Frey, & Thelen, 2001).

Another potential moderator is attitude strength. As we indicated earlier, strong attitudes can better serve as guides for thought and action. As a result, they may guide our attention more strongly. Fitting this view, participants in Knobloch-Westerwick and Meng's (2009) study were less likely to select counter-attitudinal articles when their attitudes were held with high certainty. Curiously, however, their participants were more likely to select counter-attitudinal articles when they had highly accessible and important attitudes.

It is not entirely clear why attitude accessibility and importance had this effect. One consideration is that the effects of specific attitude properties may differ from the effects of attitude strength on aggregate. Indeed, a different pattern emerged in two studies that combined many measures of attitude importance and attitude certainty with self-relevance and other self-report items assessing aspects of attitude strength. With this combined index, Laura Brannon, Michael Tagler, and Alice Eagly (2007) found that, when we have strong attitudes (e.g., they are important or we are certain about them), we are particularly drawn to information that supports our attitudes. This suggests that aggregate attitude strength may help predict selective exposure better than any one facet of attitude strength.

On the other hand, it may be the case that attitude importance and accessibility are two attitude properties that predict heightened attention to attitude-relevant stimuli in general, independently of whether the stimuli support or refute the attitude. For instance, individuals are more likely to seek out general information for topics that they personally considered important compared to individuals with less important attitudes about these issues (Holbrook, Berent, Krosnick, Visser, & Boninger, 2005; see also Blankenship & Wegener, 2008). Similarly, an elegant experiment by David Roskos-Ewoldsen and Russell Fazio (1992) showed that our visual attention is drawn toward objects for which we have highly accessible attitudes. In one experiment, participants sat in front of a computer screen that briefly (for about 1500 milliseconds) displayed six objects that were arranged in the shape of a circle. The objects included items such as a bicycle, a squirrel, a flower, and a purse. Figure 3.2 illustrates the style of presentation using a few items that the authors like or dislike (e.g., carrots, sheep). Participants' task was to notice as many of the displayed objects as possible and to write down the names of these objects. Previously, the researchers had assessed the accessibility of participants' attitudes toward each of the six objects in the array. The results of the experiment revealed that participants were more likely to notice objects for which they had highly accessible attitudes compared to objects for which they had less accessible attitudes. For the authors, it is likely that their accessible attitude to cheese pizza would make the pizza image most noticeable in Figure 3.2. Further, Roskos-Ewoldsen and Fazio (1992) showed that this type of visual attention effect occurs even when the experimental task does not require that participants pay attention to the objects in the array. In other words, participants do not have to be actively searching for these objects for them to be noticed.

Finally, results from a recent experiment indicate that it also matters whether we are attempting to predict selective exposure from self-report attitudes or from implicitly measured attitudes (Galdi, Gawronski, Arcuri, & Friese, 2012). Residents of Northern Italy were approached at home and asked to complete explicit and implicit measures of attitude regarding Turkey's possible inclusion in the European Union (EU). A week later, participants were asked to choose an article from each of six pairs of articles opposing or supporting Turkey's possible inclusion in the EU. Analyses of these choices revealed that self-reported attitudes predicted selective exposure when participants felt decided on the issue, whereas the implicit measures predicted selective exposure when participants reported being undecided on the issue. This evidence is a provocative indication that lower levels of attitude strength may lead us to use spontaneous associations with an issue as guides to information processing, more than our directly reported attitudes.

The effects of these specific attitude properties on selective exposure might also depend on other factors. Daphne Wiersema, Frenk van Harreveld, and Joop van der Plight (2012) found

**Figure 3.2**  *An illustration of the way in which Roskos-Ewoldsen and Fazio (1992) presented attitude objects*

that participants were likely to show selective exposure for value-relevant issues, but only if they were low in self-esteem. This result highlights the relevance of attitude function, in this case showing that simultaneous value-expressive and ego-defensive motivations may elicit selective exposure. Basically, if an issue is important to our values *and* our self-concept needs bolstering, we may seek out information to support our views about the issue as a means of supporting our self-esteem.

At the same time, there is evidence that the effects of two strength-related properties, ambivalence and certainty, depend on the extent to which the new information is likely to be familiar or unfamiliar to the individual (Sawicki et al., 2011, 2013). When the information is likely to be familiar (e.g., because they possess a lot of relevant knowledge), lower levels of ambivalence or uncertainty predict a preference for pro-attitudinal information. In contrast, when information is likely to be novel, higher levels of ambivalence or uncertainty predict the preference for pro attitudinal information. The effect when information is familiar is similar to the effect of attitude strength obtained by Brannon et al. (2007), but the opposite effect when information is novel suggests that the effects of attitude strength can be varied. The effects when information is novel also fit other evidence that, when people feel highly ambivalent toward an issue, they examine relevant persuasive messages *more* carefully than do people who have the same position but are relatively non-ambivalent (Briñol et al., 2006; Jonas, Diehl, & Bromer, 1997; Maio et al., 1996). This careful scrutiny makes people more able to detect *new* information that can support their attitude and help decrease their ambivalence, in a mechanism similar to dissonance reduction (Clark, Wegener, & Fabrigar, 2008).

Taken together, the role of attitude strength in selective exposure has become an interesting problem. At an aggregate level, stronger attitudes appear to elicit more selective exposure to attitude-congruent information. In contrast, when specific aspects of attitude strength are examined (e.g., importance, ambivalence), their effect on selective exposure depends on other variables, such as self-esteem and familiarity of the attitude-relevant knowledge. Further research is needed to help determine whether similar complexities may apply even when aggregate measures of attitude strength are used. A recent theoretical perspective on selective exposure effects stresses the role of uncertainty in deciding whether to expend greater cognitive effort in processing attitude inconsistent information (Fischer, 2011), but it remains to be seen whether certainty operates in a special way that is different from other attitude strength variables.

## KEY POINTS

- Our attitudes influence the type of information we are likely to process and seek out.
- Our attitudes influence the type of information that we actually perceive.
- The size of the effects of attitude on processing, exposure, and perception depend on attitude strength, including effects of its importance, value-relevance, ambivalence, certainty, and accessibility.
- The role of attitude strength depends on how it is measured and on relevant individual differences (e.g., self-esteem, topic familiarity).

# THE INFLUENCE OF ATTITUDES ON HOW INFORMATION IS INTERPRETED

So far, we have seen that our attitudes influence what we pay attention to in our social world. Attitudes also influence how we interpret information. In one of the best-known studies of this phenomenon, Hastorf and Cantril (1954) had students from Princeton University and Dartmouth College watch a film clip of a football game between these two universities. Presumably, students had an attachment (and therefore a positive attitude) toward their own university. The students' task was to record every penalty made by both teams. Hastorf and Cantril found that Princeton students reported more fouls by the Dartmouth team than by the Princeton team, while Dartmouth students reported more fouls by Princeton than by Dartmouth. This type of research implies that a person's attitudes can influence how they interpret information, and of course, the author's experience watching baseball corroborates this finding.

## Effects on political judgments

This effect has been found with issues of greater importance than perceptions of sporting events. In one study, Vallone, Ross, and Lepper (1985) examined how individuals with different attitudes about Middle Eastern politics perceived television coverage of events related to the conflict. Students with pro-Israel, pro-Palestine, or neutral attitudes evaluated the *same* news stories reporting on the Middle East conflict. Vallone and colleagues found that participants with pro-Israel attitudes and students with pro-Palestine attitudes both viewed the same news stories as biased against their view. That is, students with pro-Israel views found the stories to be biased in favor of Palestinians, while students with pro-Palestine views found the same stories to be biased in favor of Israelis. (Participants with neutral attitudes viewed the stories as being neutral.) This study provides further evidence that people's opinions can serve as filters that influence how they interpret information.

Since this research, studies using different measures and methods have poignantly illustrated the role of attitudes in biased judgments. In one recent example, Eric Knowles, Brian Lowery, and Rebecca Schaumberg (2010) found that an implicit measure of prejudice against Blacks predicted Americans' opposition to a health care reform plan, but only when the plan was attributed to Barack Obama and not to Bill Clinton. Also, a study tracking American students' attitudes toward the two primary candidates in the 2008 American presidential election (Barack Obama and John McCain) found that the students' *preferences* for who would win shaped their future *expectations* regarding who would win over time (Krizan, Miller, & Johar, 2010). All told, the extant evidence suggests that attitudes predict how we evaluate relevant evidence and ideas, while also predicting our beliefs about what *will* happen.

When are our attitudes most likely to produce such effects? One important variable is the *extremity* of the individual's attitude; that is, the attitude's deviation from neutrality. People with more extreme political attitudes are more likely to think that others have more extreme views on both sides of the topic than are people who are more moderate in their partisanship (Van Boven,

Judd, & Sherman, 2012). Another important variable is the accessibility of the individual's attitude. Recall from Chapter 2 that highly accessible (i.e., easy to recall) attitudes are more likely to serve an object-appraisal function. Houston and Fazio (1989) demonstrated the importance of attitude accessibility in how people interpret attitude-relevant information. These researchers asked students to evaluate the methodology of two supposed studies on the costs and benefits of capital punishment. One of these studies concluded that capital punishment was an effective deterrent, while the other study reached the opposite conclusion. Houston and Fazio found that participants' attitudes influenced their perceptions of the scientific rigor of the two studies. In particular, participants who had a favorable attitude toward capital punishment rated the pro-death penalty study as superior to the study arguing against the death penalty. In contrast, participants who had an unfavorable attitude toward capital punishment rated the study against the death penalty as superior to the study arguing for the death penalty (see also Lord, Ross, & Lepper, 1979). This effect, however, depended upon the accessibility of the participants' attitudes. As you might expect, the selective interpretation effect occurred only among those individuals with accessible (strong) attitudes toward the death penalty. As described in Chapter 2, accessible attitudes should be more likely to help appraise objects, and Houston and Fazio showed how these attitudes can bias these appraisals.

## Effects on face perceptions

The ability of attitudes to shape our interpretation of stimuli goes well beyond influences on how we judge news articles or research studies. They even influence how we judge faces. For instance, more positive attitudes to a racial group, as assessed in an IAT, predict faster speeds at judging the orientation of faces from members of the group (Ma, Yang, & Han, 2011). This suggests that we interpret the group membership of a face more easily when we like the group to which it belongs. At the same time, however, there is evidence that people who are prejudiced against an outgroup are more likely to interpret faces as belonging to that group when the faces display negative stereotype-relevant traits, but they are less likely to interpret faces as belonging to the group when the faces display positive stereotype-relevant traits (Dotsch, Wigboldus, & van Knippenberg, 2011). Thus, there is a complex interplay between attitudes, facial features, and categorization of faces.

In fact, a recent study has found that attitudes may affect the way we mentally picture faces (Young, Ratner, & Fazio, 2014). Using a technique called *reverse correlation data reduction*, the researchers examined the actual image of a political candidate's face (Mitt Romney) in people's minds. They did this by asking participants to look at pairs of digitally scrambled images of his face over many trials. In each pair, participants were asked to select the most accurate image. Next, the researchers combined the participant's chosen "accurate" images and superimposed them over the original face. These averaged faces presumably reflect how participants actually "saw" the candidate. When additional, new participants rated these averaged faces on trustworthiness and positivity, results indicated that the faces actually looked more trustworthy in appearance and better looking when they were derived from the scrambled images selected by those who liked the candidate than by those who disliked the candidate.

**RESEARCH HIGHLIGHT 3.1**

### INTERPRETATION OF AMBIGUOUS STIMULI

Our attitudes can play a role in how we interpret visually ambiguous stimuli. Look at the image in Figure 3.3. What do you see, a letter or a number? Is it possible that our attitudes influence whether you report seeing the letter B or the number 13? A clever set of experiments by Emily Balcetis and David Dunning (2006) tested whether our likes and desires influence how we interpret visually ambiguous stimuli. In their research, participants took part in what they thought was a study on taste-testing. They were informed that they would taste one of two beverages – one that was desirable (fresh orange juice) or one that was undesirable (a foul-smelling vegetable drink). Participants were allowed to smell both of the beverages – a manipulation that was expected to make salient a positive attitude toward one drink (the fresh orange juice) and a negative attitude toward the other drink (the foul vegetable drink). Participants then sat in front of a computer and were told that a computer program would randomly assign one of the beverages for their consumption. Half of the participants were told that a number would indicate that they would drink the orange juice, while the other participants were told that a letter would result in their assignment to the orange juice. The ambiguous letter/number shown in Figure 3.3 was then presented very briefly (for 400 milliseconds). The experimenters were interested in testing whether this ambiguous object would be interpreted differently as function of whether the positive attitude object (the orange juice) was associated with either a letter or a number.

    The results of the study revealed that participants' preference to drink the desirable beverage affected their interpretation of the ambiguous figure. When the orange juice was associated with a letter, 72% of participants reported seeing the letter B instead of the number 13. However, when the orange juice was associated with a number, 61% of participants reported seeing the number 13 instead of the letter B. Thus, associating a positive attitude object with a particular interpretation of ambiguous information elicited that particular interpretation.

## KEY POINTS

- Instead of seeing things objectively, our attitudes affect how we encode and interpret what we see and hear.
- Attitudes are more likely to bias encoding and interpretation when the attitudes are easy to retrieve from memory.

## THE INFLUENCE OF ATTITUDES ON MEMORY

So far we have learned that our attitudes influence what we attend to and how we interpret information. The next question is about *selective memory*: Do our attitudes influence the type of information we're most likely to remember?

**Figure 3.3**   *Is it a B or a 13? It depends on what you want to see (Balcetis & Dunning, 2006)*

This question is relevant to the baseball example that opened our chapter. Recall that one of the authors and his friend completely disagreed about how the umpire was calling the game, fitting Hastorf and Cantril's (1954) observations about fans' *interpretations* of events in a Princeton–Dartmouth football game. It turns out that fans of teams don't only interpret events differently. Fans of the New York Yankees and Boston Red Sox also *remember* recent World Series championships featuring these two baseball teams more vividly and accurately when their team won the game (Yankees in 2003, Red Sox in 2004) than when their team lost the game (Breslin & Safer, 2011).

## How robust is selective memory?

A tendency to rehearse information that we like was a significant factor in the study of Yankees and Red Sox fans (Breslin & Safer, 2011), but several decades of research on the selective memory question suggests that the strength of this effect and the mechanisms involved is fairly complex. The role of attitudes in memory has been examined in different ways. For example, Judd and Kulik (1980) tested the hypothesis that, when individuals have unipolar attitudes, extreme congruent and incongruent statements would be more likely to be noticed and remembered compared to less extreme congruent and incongruent statements. In their experiment, participants were presented with a series of statements on attitude issues for which they had an opinion. These statements varied in their extremity, such that some were very extreme and others were less extreme. Participants rated the statements on a number of dimensions and the next day returned to the lab, where they were asked to remember as many of the statements as possible. As expected, the results revealed that extreme statements were more likely to be noticed and recalled than less extreme statements. In other words, both attitude-congruent and attitude-incongruent statements exhibited a memory advantage over relatively neutral statements.

Other researchers have presented people with attitude-congruent and attitude-incongruent information and later tested their ability to remember both types of information. Because our attitudes influence the information we select and how this information is interpreted, it makes sense to think that we may be more likely to remember information that is congruent with our attitudes. However, if this so-called *congeniality effect* occurs, it is small. In a meta-analytic review of prior experiments, Eagly, Chen, Chaiken, and Shaw-Barnes (1999) found only a small memory advantage for attitude-congruent information.

## A potential role for attitude function?

Recall from earlier in this chapter that attitude function has a role to play in understanding selective exposure, because value-expressive attitudes are more likely to elicit selective exposure effects. Attitude function may also play a role in understanding the size of the congeniality effect in memory. In their meta-analysis, Eagly et al. (1999) found that the congeniality effect was larger when the attitude issue was value-relevant. From this finding, we can infer that the effect of attitudes on memory may be greatest among attitudes that fulfill a value-expressive function. This makes sense at many levels. If you have been presented with information about a topic that is important to your values, it seems logical for you to become highly motivated to remember information that is consistent with your attitudes and, hence, your values. Consistent with this idea, Eagly et al. (1999) argued that a value-relevant topic elicits a desire to defend the self-concept, which leads individuals to show enhanced recall and recognition of information that is consistent with their attitudes (see also Blankenship & Wegener, 2008).

> **Function Witch:** *Could the magnitude of the congeniality effect also be high for attitudes that strongly fulfill a social-adjustment function, because this function requires defense of an attitude that is socially adaptive?*

Of interest, this potential role of defensiveness fits another parallel between evidence regarding selective exposure and evidence regarding attitude congeniality in memory. Specifically, like selective exposure effects, attitude congeniality effects for value-expressive issues are stronger among individuals with lower self-esteem (Wiersema, van der Pligt, & van Harreveld, 2010). This finding fits the view that the conjunction of value-relevance and self-esteem defense is important for both selective exposure and attitude congeniality effects.

## Other types of effects of attitudes on memory

Our attitudes affect memory in other ways. For example, research has tested whether individuals' attitudes affect their memory for relevant behavior. In one demonstration of this effect, Ross, McFarland, and Fletcher (1981) initially manipulated Canadian students' attitudes toward tooth-brushing. All students were given dental hygiene information from a reputable and credible source (the Ontario Dental Association). Some students were informed that brushing your teeth every day was a necessary component of good dental hygiene. In contrast, other students were told that brushing your teeth every day was bad for dental hygiene, because frequent brushing removed tooth enamel. This manipulation was designed to elicit a positive or negative attitude toward tooth-brushing. After receiving this information, everyone was asked to report how often they had brushed their teeth in the past two weeks. The results revealed that students who had previously read about the costs of tooth-brushing reported having brushed their teeth less often than those who had previously read about the benefits of tooth-brushing. In interpreting their results, Ross and colleagues argued that people like to believe that their behavior is consistent with their attitudes. When attitudes are influenced, people have the misperception that they have always had the same attitude and reconstruct their past memories to fit this "perceived" attitude.

## Why do these effects occur?

So far we have seen that our attitudes influence different stages of information processing. The next question to address is *why* these effects occur. Historically, social psychologists have highlighted motivational or cognitive explanations for these effects.

From a motivational perspective, people may attend to attitude-congruent information and process it more deeply because this helps people to defend and feel good about their attitudes. This reasoning stems from Festinger's (1957) work on cognitive dissonance: we find it emotionally aversive to harbor inconsistent beliefs and feelings. Similarly, people should feel motivated to avoid information that contradicts their attitudes. Similar to Freud's concept of repression, individuals might avoid information that raises self-doubt by running counter to their attitudes and beliefs.

The same line of reasoning also applies to the other stages of information processing. When individuals encode attitude-relevant information, it is unlikely that this information will be stored without checking its consistency with the individual's attitudes. Because individuals are motivated to see the world in a way that is favorable to them (see Kunda, 1990), it makes sense for people to encode and store information in way that supports their attitudes. If we were to instead interpret information in ways that challenge our own views, we'd have trouble believing in ourselves and comprehending our place in the world. Further, as we have seen, memory processes are affected by our attitudes. Once again, from a motivational perspective it makes sense for us to be better able to retrieve information that supports our opinions of the world; otherwise, we'd start to believe that we are completely out of touch with the facts, and this belief would be disturbing. Indeed, it has been argued that such biases are a crucial part of normal mental health (Taylor & Brown, 1988).

This motivational argument again highlights the importance of attitude functions. The evidence for effects of value-relevance on attitude-congruent memory may reveal only part of the impact of the value-expressive function. We may also be more likely to seek out information that justifies our important attitudes and values. That strong attitudes show more pronounced attitude-information processing effects is also consistent with motivational explanations. Individuals should be especially motivated to defend and obtain information about attitudes that they hold with heightened conviction.

 ***Function Witch:*** *But what about the knowledge function of attitudes? Perhaps we risk running around with inaccurate views of the world if all we do is see things as we would like to see them. There must be some balance among these needs.*

## KEY POINTS

- Research has tested how attitudes influence different stages of information processing: attention, encoding, and memory.

- Studies have shown that attitudes influence the information we notice and process, how this information is then interpreted, and the extent to which we remember different types of information.

- There are motivational and cognitive explanations for the effects of attitudes on attention, interpretation, and memory.

# THE INFLUENCE OF ATTITUDES ON BEHAVIOR

Common sense dictates that attitudes should predict behavior. For example, it makes sense to expect that people who possess a positive attitude toward the environment would reduce their waste and recycle. Similarly, it seems sensible to predict that someone who supports saving endangered animals would make an annual donation to the World Wildlife Fund. However, is the link between attitudes and behavior really this simple? As we will see, the link between attitudes and behavior is not as straightforward as one might believe. In the rest of this chapter, we address the question of *when* attitudes predict behavior.

## A starting point

In Chapter 1 we told you about Richard LaPiere, who in the early 1930s traveled across the United States with a young Chinese couple. Despite widespread anti-Asian prejudice, only once were LaPiere and his traveling companions refused service in hotels and restaurants. A few months after the journey, LaPiere (1934, p. 233) sent a letter to each of the visited establishments and asked whether they would serve "members of the Chinese race as guests." Of the establishments that replied, only one indicated that it would serve such a customer, with over 90% stating that they definitely would not. At first glance, the results of this study seem to suggest that people's attitudes can be dramatically inconsistent with their actions.

Of course, when you consider the study in more detail, it's easy to spot some methodological flaws. Most notably, LaPiere was unable to ensure that the person who answered the letter was the same person who served LaPiere and his friends. It is also uncertain whether the presence of the American academic increased the likelihood that the couple was offered service. Although we can consider the LaPiere (1934) study as suggesting that people's behavior might not necessarily follow from their attitudes, problems with the study mean that its conclusions must be taken with caution.

Let us now move forward in time to approximately 30 years after LaPiere's study. By the late 1960s, a number of studies had examined the relation between attitudes and behavior. In 1969, Alan Wicker reviewed these studies and reached a rather sobering conclusion: attitudes were a relatively poor predictor of behavior. Across almost 40 studies that were conducted before 1969,

Wicker found that the average correlation between attitudes and behavior was a very meager 0.15. Put another way, attitudes accounted for only around 2% of the variation in behavior! Wicker (1969, p. 75) concluded that there is "little evidence to support the postulated existence of stable, underlying attitudes within the individual which influence both his verbal expression and his actions." Wicker's gloomy findings led some social psychologists to question the value of the attitude concept. It was argued that if attitudes do not guide actions, then what use are they?

Puzzled by this finding, researchers began to devote greater attention to the study of *when* attitudes are likely to predict behavior. In the last 40 years, research findings have led to a more optimistic conclusion: attitudes do predict behavior, but in some conditions more than others. In a large meta-analytic review of the literature, Steven Kraus (1995) compared the results of over 100 studies on the attitude–behavior relation. He found that the average correlation between opinions and actions was 0.38, a value much higher than that obtained by Wicker (1969). Why is there such a difference between the conclusions drawn by these reviews?

Well, the difference between the size of Wicker's and Kraus's attitude–behavior correlations can be explained in a number of ways. First, contemporary researchers might be using better measures of attitudes and/or behaviors. As noted earlier, one failing of LaPiere's (1934) study is that he could not be certain that the measures of attitude and behavior even came from the same individual. Attitude researchers in the 1970s and beyond improved their measures of attitude and behavior.

Second, contemporary researchers might be using better experimental paradigms for testing their predictions. One criticism of early research on the attitude–behavior relation is that their experimental paradigms lacked the rigor to draw appropriate conclusions based on the research findings. For instance, scientists often examined attitudes that were quite different from the behaviors they were trying to predict. If the key measures don't assess the same construct, it's unsurprising that one did not do an effective job of predicting the other.

Third, contemporary researchers might be doing a better job of uncovering situations *when* attitudes are highly predictive of behavior. There are undoubtedly instances when attitudes are especially likely (or not very likely) to predict actions. This possibility had not been sufficiently considered by early research, and the field badly needed theories pointing to potential factors. This theoretical deficit was addressed in the years between Wicker's review and Kraus's, and several meta-analyses of data since Wicker's review support Kraus's conclusions while pointing to relevant factors for when attitudes predict behavior (e.g., Cooke & Sheeran, 2004; Glasman & Albarracín, 2006).

In the remainder of this chapter, we consider diverse variables that influence the magnitude of the attitude–behavior relation. These variables pertain to measurement, research design, and theory.

# When do attitudes predict behavior? It depends upon the correspondence between attitudinal and behavioral measures

Many of the early studies designed to assess the attitude–behavior relation were plagued by methodological problems. In a number of these cases, there was a low degree of *correspondence* between the measures of attitude and behavior. By that, we mean that the attitude and behavior measures dealt with different things. For example, LaPiere's (1934) attitude measure asked respondents to indicate whether they would serve "members of the Chinese race." This statement is broad compared to the behavior measure, which involved service being offered to a highly educated, well-dressed Chinese couple accompanied by an American college professor. Had LaPiere asked "Would you serve a highly educated, well-dressed Chinese couple accompanied by an American college professor?", the relation between attitudes and behavior undoubtedly would have been higher.

Icek Ajzen and Martin Fishbein (1977) formally articulated the idea that there needs to be high correspondence between measures of attitude and behavior. They stated that measures of attitude and behavior should correspond in four key ways: action, target, context, and time. The *action* element refers to the behavior being performed. If we are interested in how attitudes toward recycling influence behavior, the action would refer to the recycling behavior of interest, which might be something like recycling empty beer bottles. The *target* element refers to the target of the behavior, which might be something like a particular brand of coffee or a particular political candidate. For example, if a researcher is interested in the relation between attitudes and behavior for a particular political candidate, it would be wrong for the attitude measure to pose general questions about attitudes toward politicians in general, while the measure of behavior concentrates on whether an individual voted for a particular political candidate. The *context* element refers to the environment in which the behavior is performed; for example, whether the behavior is performed alone or in the presence of others. If there is a different context in which the attitude and behavior are measured, it is less likely that the measures will yield the "true" extent of their relation. Finally, the *time* element refers to the time frame in which the behavior is performed. Is the measure of behavior being assessed immediately after the measure of attitude or is there a large delay?

Ajzen and Fishbein (1977) argued that attitudes are better predictors of behavior when the measures of attitude and behavior correspond on the elements described above. There is ample evidence in support of this idea. In one well-known test of this reasoning, Davidson and Jaccard (1979) were interested in predicting women's use of birth control pills. The women in their study were asked a number of questions about their attitudes toward this topic, ranging from questions that were very general (their attitude toward birth control) to somewhat specific (their attitude toward birth control pills) to very specific (their attitude toward using birth control pills during the next two years). Two years after participants responded to these attitude questions, they were contacted by the researchers and asked to indicate if they had used birth control pills in the previous two years.

Davidson and Jaccard (1979) predicted that the attitude–behavior relation would be higher as the measures of attitudes and behavior became more correspondent. The results of this study supported the authors' hypothesis. To start, the general attitude measure (participants' attitude toward birth control) did not predict behavior, with a non-significant correlation ($r$) of 0.08. This result is not surprising, because this measure of attitude was too broad in relation to the specific behavior measure. The attitude question that was somewhat specific (participants' attitude toward birth control pills) was relatively useful in predicting behavior ($r = 0.32$). Finally, the most specific question (their attitude toward using birth control pills in the next two years) was most effective in predicting behavior ($r = 0.57$). This study highlights that a proper test of the attitude–behavior relation requires that researchers ensure that their measures of attitude and behavior correspond with each other.

Another type of correspondence is relevant to understanding the relation between attitudes and behavior. In Chapter 1, we noted the distinction between explicit and implicit measures of attitude. We learned that explicit and implicit measures of attitude are not necessarily correlated with each other (Fazio & Olson, 2003; Payne et al., 2008). Measures of behavior can be distinguished along a similar dimension. Specifically, behavior can be distinguished as a function of whether it is *deliberative*, that is, relatively thoughtful, or *spontaneous*, and relatively automatic (see Fazio & Olson, 2003; Gawronski & Bodenhausen, 2006; Strack & Deutsch, 2004). Sometimes, our actions are based on deliberative thought, such as when we actively consider the pros and cons of performing a behavior (e.g., deciding to purchase a car). At other times, our behavior is more spontaneous or beyond conscious control. This category might include impulsive behaviors, such as quickly buying a couple of chocolate bars at the grocery store checkout line.

A number of researchers have considered whether the attitude–behavior relation differs depending upon whether the measures of attitude and behavior correspond on the degree to which they are deliberative or spontaneous. It has been suggested that explicit measures of attitude should be more likely to predict a deliberative (rather than spontaneous) behavior, whereas implicit measures of attitude should be more likely to predict a spontaneous (rather than deliberative) behavior.

One set of illustrative experiments was conducted by John Dovidio and colleagues, who have examined how explicit and implicit measures of prejudice predict deliberative and spontaneous discriminatory behaviors. One of these experiments asked participants to complete explicit and implicit measures of their attitudes toward African Americans (Dovidio, Kawakami, Johnson, Johnson, & Howard, 1997). The explicit measure was a questionnaire consisting of items such as "Discrimination against Blacks is no longer a problem in the United States," whereas the implicit measure consisted of a response latency task. After completing these measures, participants were met by a second experimenter who asked participants to complete an ostensibly unrelated study. In this other study, participants were asked a series of questions by a Black female and a White female. The interviews were highly structured such that both interviewers' questions were posed in a well-rehearsed manner.

After completing the interview, participants evaluated both interviewers. Their response to these questions served as the deliberative measure of behavior. The spontaneous measure of behavior was derived from participants' non-verbal behavior during the interaction, which had been videotaped. Two non-verbal measures were considered – participants' eye contact with the experimenters and the frequency with which participants blinked. Less eye contact and more frequent blinking are indicators of less favorable behavior. Further, these behaviors are seen as spontaneous because they are difficult to consciously monitor and control.

Dovidio et al. (1997) expected that the explicit measure of prejudice would best predict participants' deliberative evaluations of their interactions with the Black and White experimenters, while the implicit measure of prejudice would best predict participants' spontaneous behaviors toward the Black and White experimenters. The results were consistent with predictions. Only the explicit measure of prejudice was correlated with participants' conscious assessment of their interaction, while only the implicit measure of prejudice was correlated with participants' non-verbal behavior.

Many studies have since tested the extent to which explicit and implicit measures of attitude predict different types of behavior. Another example of evidence supporting this view is in Research Highlight 3.2. However, the evidence for a greater role of explicit measures in predicting relatively deliberate behavior should not be taken as evidence to dismiss the role of implicit measures for such behavior. Even if implicit measures tend to predict deliberative judgments and behavior more weakly, they may still predict the behavior *uniquely*. For instance, the aforementioned study of attitudes toward United States President Obama and his health care reform plan showed that people who exhibited more prejudice against Blacks on an implicit measure of attitude expressed more reluctance to vote for him and his policy, even *after* controlling for their scores on explicit measures of attitude (Knowles et al., 2010). Furthermore, one recent review of relevant evidence has not supported the idea that implicit and explicit measures differentially predict deliberative behaviors (Greenwald et al., 2009), although this review offers different studies as ideal tests than are found in other reviews (e.g., Richetin, Conner, & Perugini, 2011).

Notwithstanding this debate, Fritz Strack and Roland Deutsch have proposed a theoretical model of the attitude–behavior relation that fits the idea that explicit and implicit measures tap into different processes. Their Reflective-Impulsive Model (RIM) proposes that behavior is controlled by two interacting systems: a *reflective* system that guides and elicits behavior via a reasoned consideration of available information, and an *impulsive* system that guides and elicits behavior through automatic associative links. The reflective system can be seen as involving processes that resemble how people respond to explicit measures of attitude, whereas the impulsive system involves processes that bear greater resemblance to implicit measures of attitude. Strack and Deutsch (2004) suggest that the reflective system should have a greater influence on deliberative behavior, while the impulsive system should have a greater influence on spontaneous behavior (see also Gawronski & Bodenhausen, 2006).

## RESEARCH HIGHLIGHT 3.2

### PREJUDICE AGAINST PEOPLE WITH AIDS

In an interesting demonstration of the correspondence between explicit and implicit measures of attitude and deliberative and spontaneous measures of behavior, Neumann, Hülsenbeck, and Seibt (2004) tested whether explicit and implicit measures of attitude differentially predicted reflective and automatic behavior toward individuals with AIDS. In this study, participants completed both explicit and implicit measures of attitudes toward people with AIDS. The explicit measure of attitude consisted of a questionnaire featuring items such as "What is your general attitude toward people with AIDS?", whereas the implicit measure of attitude consisted of an IAT (Greenwald et al., 1998). As for the behavioral measures, the reflective

*(Continued)*

(Continued)

measure of behavior asked participants to answer questions such as "There is no problem sharing an apartment with a person with AIDS," while the automatic measure of behavior assessed approach/avoidance tendencies in response to seeing a picture of a person with AIDS. This measure assesses how fast people move a computer mouse toward themselves (an approach movement) or away from themselves (an avoidance movement) in response to different types of images. This behavior is deemed to be automatic because it does not require conscious effort in order to complete the task. In this context, automatic negative behavior is revealed by faster avoidance behavior than approach behavior.

Neumann et al. (2004) found that the reflective behavior was predicted by the explicit but not the implicit measure of attitude, while the impulsive avoidance tendency was predicted by the implicit but not the explicit measure of attitude. In other words, the explicit measure was the best predictor of deliberative behavior, while the implicit measure of attitude was the best predictor of spontaneous behavior.

# When do attitudes predict behavior? It depends on the domain of behavior

In addition to considering the level of correspondence among measures, research has demonstrated that the attitude–behavior relation differs depending upon the topic under investigation. In his review, Kraus (1995) found that topics varied greatly in the degree to which opinions predicted actions. At one extreme, the relation between political attitudes and voting behavior tends to be very high. For example, in a study conducted during the 1984 American presidential election, Russell Fazio and Carol Williams (1986) first measured participants' attitudes toward the incumbent United States President Ronald Reagan, as well as attitudes toward his opponent, Walter Mondale. Approximately five months later (and very soon after the election), Fazio and Williams measured whether their participants voted for Reagan or Mondale. Despite the relatively long time lag between the measures of attitude and behavior, the correlation between voters' initial attitude and their subsequent voting behavior was an impressive 0.78 for Reagan and 0.63 for Mondale. The size of these correlations is quite impressive, especially given the six-month gap between the measurement of attitudes and behavior.

On the other hand, Kraus (1995) noted that there is a relatively low correlation between individuals' attitudes toward blood donation and the act of donating blood. For example, Charng, Piliavin, and Callero (1988) found a correlation of just 0.24 between attitudes toward blood donation and intentions to donate blood. At first glance, it is perhaps not surprising that blood donation is a domain where one might expect a low attitude–behavior relation. It may be that the low relation arises because the behavior of donating blood is much more difficult to enact than the simple expression of attitude through a behavior like voting. Thus, some of the difference between topics in attitude–behavior correlations may be due to differences in the difficulty inherent in executing the relevant behavior.

## When do attitudes predict behavior? It depends on the function of the attitude

Attitudes fulfill different needs, and attitudes serving different functions may be more or less likely to predict behavior. This idea fits Kraus's (1995) evidence that attitude–behavior relations vary across topics. For instance, the stronger relations observed for voting than for blood donation may have to do with a stronger value-expressive function for voting than for blood donation, because political attitudes are more value-expressive than utilitarian, and blood donation is a behavior with much stronger immediate implications for people (e.g., discomfort, time, fear of blood). Indeed, people report feeling more comfortable acting on attitudes that are seen as being expressive of core moral values and convictions, particularly when they have no material stake in the issue (Effron & Miller, 2012). Furthermore, this speculation about the power of value-expressive attitudes matches what we might expect given the stronger effects of value-expressive attitudes on memory (Eagly et al., 1999), as mentioned earlier in this chapter. If value-expressive attitudes are more likely to bias memory, then it seems plausible that they are also more likely to affect behavior.

Nonetheless, another attitude function may be particularly important for determining correspondence between attitudes and behavior. In Chapter 4, we will examine evidence indicating that the object-appraisal function is vital. Attitudes that fulfill this function strongly may be particularly strong predictors of behavior (Fazio, 2000).

## When do attitudes predict behavior? It depends on the strength of the attitude

As noted earlier, one of us absolutely loves the music of Bruce Springsteen; the other feels less strongly. Attitude researchers would say that one author has a very strong positive attitude toward the music of Bruce Springsteen, while the other has a weak positive attitude. Which author has seen Bruce Springsteen perform live 10 times, and once drove all night in order to do so? Not surprisingly, it is the one with the strong attitude.

A number of studies have demonstrated that strong attitudes are more likely than weak attitudes to predict behavior. In one study, Ross Norman (1975) had students complete measures of their attitudes toward volunteering as a participant in psychology research. The questionnaires included general evaluative items ("What is your overall favorability toward acting as a participant in psychology research?") and items assessing the cognitive component of attitude ("Does psychological research help others?"). Three weeks after these evaluations and cognitions were measured, participants were all offered the opportunity to volunteer for a psychology experiment. Norman was particularly interested in participants' *evaluative-cognitive consistency*; that is, the extent to which their attitudes and beliefs were highly congruent. He found that those participants who exhibited higher evaluative-cognitive consistency behaved in a way that better matched their attitudes. If they had a positive attitude about participating, they participated. If they had a negative attitude about participating, they did not participate. This pattern was reflected by a strong positive attitude–behavior correlation ($r = 0.63$). In contrast, individuals low in evaluative-cognitive consistency (i.e., those individuals whose attitudes and beliefs were independent) behaved in a way that was not related to their attitude ($r = -0.28$).

 **Content Witch:** *Could other affective and behavioral content work the same way? Perhaps attitude–behavior correspondence is higher when there is evaluative-affective and evaluative-behavioral consistency too (Chaiken, Pomerantz, & Giner-Sorolla, 1995).*

A number of researchers have considered how attitude strength moderates the attitude–behavior relation. In a comprehensive review, Richard Cooke and Paschal Sheeran (2004) examined seven indicators of attitude strength: accessibility, temporal stability, direct experience, involvement, certainty, ambivalence, and affective-cognitive consistency. Cooke and Sheeran found that all of the measures except involvement moderated the attitude–behavior relation, with stronger attitudes being more likely to predict behavior. This evidence provides a clear conclusion: strong attitudes are more likely to predict behavior than weak attitudes. That's why Bruce Springsteen is probably delighted that one of the authors is a strong fan. (Any day now he will call and invite the author on stage at a concert.)

## When do attitudes predict behavior? It depends on the person

In addition to examining how situations influence behavior, social psychologists are interested in understanding how personality differences help to account for our actions. With respect to the attitude–behavior relation, researchers have examined how various personality constructs moderate the degree to which opinions influence actions.

A key personality construct frequently tested as a moderator of the attitude–behavior relation is *self-monitoring* (Snyder, 1974, 1986). As noted in Chapter 2, self-monitoring refers to differences in how people vary their behavior across social situations. Low self-monitors are individuals who do not constantly monitor the fit between themselves and their situations: they tend not to change the way they behave depending upon the situation in which they find themselves. In contrast, high self-monitors more frequently assess the fit between their behavior and their situation: they tend to present themselves in a different light depending upon the social situation.

Studies have investigated whether the relation between attitudes and behavior is more pronounced for low self-monitors than high self-monitors. In one study, Snyder and Kendzierski (1982) investigated the relation between attitudes and behavior towards affirmative action policies. Snyder and Kendzierski (1982) gave students who favored or opposed affirmative action the opportunity to participate in a social situation that supported the behavioral expression of a positive attitude toward this issue. The results revealed that, among low self-monitors, decisions on whether to participate were predicted by their attitude toward affirmative action. In contrast, the behavioral decision of high self-monitors was unrelated to their attitude.

Another relevant individual difference variable is the *need for cognition*. Need for cognition refers to stable differences in the desire to engage in and enjoy effortful cognitive activity (Cacioppo & Petty, 1982). Individuals high in need for cognition are more likely to show attitude–behavior correspondence compared to individuals low in need for cognition. An interesting study of the 1984 American presidential election illustrates this difference. Specifically, Cacioppo, Petty, Kao, and Rodriguez (1986) found that pre-election voting preferences (as measured two months before the election) were more predictive of behavior among individuals high in need for cognition than among individuals low in need for cognition. In theory, this difference emerges because people higher in need for cognition are more likely to have thought carefully about their attitudes, causing them to be stronger.

The individual difference variables that we have highlighted are much smaller than the total number of potentially relevant constructs. It must be remembered that most of the participants involved in social psychology experiments on attitudes (and experiments from most other areas of psychology) are university students. Researchers do employ non-student samples to examine attitude–behavior consistency, but have done so less often. For example, a researcher might use a representative national sample to assess how society feels about a particular issue and behaviors relevant to the issue. Does the type of sample influence the attitude–behavior relation? Research has found that university students show *lower* attitude–behavior relations than non-students. For example, in his meta-analysis, Kraus (1995) observed that the average correlation between attitudes and behavior was 0.34 in studies that used student samples; the correlation was 0.48 in studies with non-student samples.

Why are students less likely to act in ways consistent with their attitudes? Again, attitude strength may be the key factor. This is a likely explanation of the lower attitude–behavior relation found in studies using student samples, because studies have found that university students tend to have less crystallized attitudes compared to older individuals (see Sears, 1986; Visser & Krosnick, 1998). Then again, there could be other individual differences that explain this difference. For instance, people with *defensive self-esteem* (high explicit reports of self-esteem but low self-esteem on an implicit measure) exhibit stronger attitudes on different measures across different attitude objects (Haddock & Gebauer, 2011). Also, people who believe that attitudes are stable over time show greater attitude certainty for specific topics, with consequences for their behavioral intentions and resistance to change, than people who believe that attitudes are malleable (Petrocelli, Clarkson, Tormala, & Hendrix, 2010). Defensive self-esteem and beliefs about the stability of attitudes may therefore be additional important factors in understanding between-person differences in the consequences of attitudes.

# When do attitudes predict behavior? It depends on the situation

Perhaps we are more likely to behave in accordance with our attitudes when a situation encourages this consistency. For example, imagine that you are under great time pressure and have to make a decision very quickly. Are you more likely to behave in a way consistent with your attitude when you are under time pressure than when you are not?

This question was addressed in some clever experiments conducted by David Jamieson and Mark Zanna (1989). In one study, university students were asked to play the role of a juror. They read a murder case that was primarily based on circumstantial, ambiguous evidence. After reading information about the case, participants indicated the likelihood that they would vote in favor of finding the defendant guilty of first-degree murder. This decision served as the measure of behavior. Participants' attitudes towards capital punishment were measured in a prior context before they read about the particular case.

Jamieson and Zanna (1989) were interested in how two independent variables might work together in determining when participants' attitudes would be most likely to influence their decision-making behavior. First, Jamieson and Zanna manipulated the amount of time participants had to read about the case and make their decision. Participants in their time pressure condition were given about three minutes to complete the task, whereas participants in the no time pressure condition were not given any time constraints. Second, Jamieson and Zanna measured individual differences in self-monitoring. As we have already seen, individuals low in self-monitoring are more likely to show high attitude–behavior correlations compared to individuals high in this construct. Jamieson and Zanna predicted that participants' decisions would be most likely to be based on their attitudes when they had to make their decision in a hurry *and* when they were low in self-monitoring, compared to the other three combinations. This is precisely what was found. In this study, a situational variable (time pressure) and an individual difference variable (self-monitoring) interacted in understanding the circumstances when attitudes are most likely to guide behavior.

A similar example is relevant to the construct of self-consciousness. People can be very aware of their personal and internal characteristics or they can be highly aware of their public image or both (Scheier & Carver, 1985). Both private and public self-consciousness can be manipulated, because everyone experiences both types of self-consciousness to some degree (Froming, Walker, & Lopyan, 1982). For example, private self-consciousness can be induced by the presence of a mirror, whereas public self-consciousness can be induced by the presence of an audience. In theory, private self-consciousness should cause people to be more likely to use their attitudes as a basis for their behavior, whereas public self-consciousness should cause people to use their audience as a guide to behavior.

To test this hypothesis about situational variation in self-consciousness, Froming et al. (1982) selected participants who held strong pro- or anti-punishment attitudes *and* who believed that most people hold the opposite attitude. Participants were asked to shock a "learner" who gave a series of incorrect and correct responses to various questions. As expected, it turned out that participants' behavior in the mirror condition corresponded to their attitudes better than behavior in the control condition. In contrast, behavior in the audience condition corresponded to partici- pants' beliefs about the audience's attitudes better than did behavior in the control condition. In other words, behavior matched either the internal (attitude) or external (audience) standards that were made salient.

## When does an attitude predict behavior? When does behavior predict an attitude?

So far in this chapter, we have seen attitudes predict behavior. Of course, it is also likely that behavior influences attitudes (see Chapter 7). When is one direction of influence more important? It is likely that the answer to this question depends at least partly on attitude strength.

An ingenious study by Rob Holland, Bas Verplanken, and Ad van Knippenberg (2002) supports this conclusion. They tested the circumstances under which (a) attitudes predict behavior and (b) behavior predicts attitudes. Holland et al. suggested that the concept of attitude strength is crucial to understanding which directional influence (attitudes predicting behavior versus behavior predicting attitudes) would be most important. These scientists postulated that strong attitudes are more likely than weak attitudes to predict behavior, whereas weak attitudes are more likely than strong attitudes to follow from behavior. Given what we have already learned, this prediction makes sense. When our attitudes are strong, they are more likely to influence what we do. However, when our attitudes are weak, it follows that they should be influenced by what we have done.

To test their hypothesis, Holland et al. (2002) had Dutch undergraduates complete an experiment that included two sessions, with an interval of one week. In session 1, participants answered questions assessing the favorability and strength (e.g., certainty, importance) of their attitudes toward Greenpeace. One week later, participants returned for what they thought was an unrelated study. At the end of this second, supposedly unrelated study, they were paid the equivalent of about € 5 (in various coins and bills). Immediately after being paid, participants were told that the experimenter was also conducting a small study for Greenpeace and that they could choose to donate money to Greenpeace. After deciding whether or not to donate, participants were asked to complete a short questionnaire, which included an assessment of their attitude toward Greenpeace. The *attitude–behavior* relation was derived by comparing the favorability of participants' attitude at time 1 with the amount of money they donated at time 2. The *behavior–attitude* relation was derived by comparing the amount of money participants donated at time 2 with the measure of attitude that was taken immediately after the donation behavior.

As shown in Figure 3.4, Holland et al. (2002) found that attitude strength was crucial for understanding when attitudes predict behavior as opposed to when behavior predicts attitudes. With respect to the *attitude–behavior* relation (upper panel), analyses revealed that strong attitudes at time 1 uniquely predicted behavior at time 2, whereas weak attitudes did not. With respect to the *behavior–attitude* relation (bottom panel), weak attitudes were greatly influenced by behavior, whereas strong attitudes were not. On the basis of their findings, Holland and colleagues concluded that strong attitudes guide behavior, whereas weak attitudes follow behavior. This study makes an important contribution to our understanding of the bi-dimensional causal relations between attitudes and behavior by testing both relations in a single experiment.

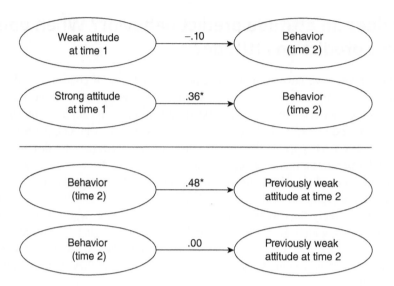

**Figure 3.4**    *Attitudes predicting subsequent behavior and behavior predicting subsequent attitudes (Holland et al., 2002)*

*Note*: The co-efficient over each path indicates the strength of the association between the variables. An asterisk (*) beside a co-efficient indicates that the association was statistically significant.

## KEY POINTS

- Attitudes do a reasonable job of predicting behavior, but the size of the relation between attitudes and behavior depends on a number of factors.
- Attitudes are stronger predictors of behavior when the measures of attitude examine the same actions as in the measures of behavior, relying on a similar level of consciousness in both measures.
- Strong attitudes are more likely to predict behavior than weak attitudes.
- The influence of attitudes on behavior may also depend on the type of behavior (e.g., its difficulty), the functions of the attitude, and the personality of the individual.
- Ironically, situations that make people think about reasons for their attitude undermine the correspondence between the attitude and behavior.

## WHAT WE HAVE LEARNED

- Attitudes influence how we encode, interpret, and remember relevant information.
- Attitudes are significant predictors of behavior.

- The relations between attitudes and behavior depend on a number of factors, including correspondence between the measures of attitude and behavior, the type of behavior, the function of the attitude, personality variables, and situational factors.

# WHAT DO YOU THINK?

- We have seen that attitudes can bias our perceptions of the world around us. This may be useful at times. For instance, our attitudes may help us to quickly spot the brands we like and dislike in a supermarket, without having to inspect every single item. There may be other times when this influence is a "bad" thing – can you think of some situations where this would be true?

- We measure attitudes by looking at a behavior of some type, such as circling answers on a questionnaire. We then look at how the scores from this behavior predict other behaviors. In essence, we are always looking at behavior–behavior correspondence, while assuming that both behaviors reflect a common attitude. Why then do we place special emphasis on the first measure's ability to tap an attitude? Is the first measure (of "attitude") better in some way?

- Policy makers are increasingly interested in discovering how to make attitudes exert a stronger effect on behaviors that are difficult to enact. For instance, health care workers know that people are favorable toward good health and environmentalists know that people want to protect the environment from destruction. Yet people can find it difficult to perform behaviors that fit these attitudes (e.g., exercising more, giving up a car). Given the evidence we described, how would you solve this problem?

# KEY TERMS

*Attitude–behavior measurement correspondence* – the extent to which measures of attitude and behavior refer to the same actions, targets, context, and time.

*Attitude extremity* – an attitude's deviation from neutrality.

*Congeniality effect* – the purported tendency to better remember information that is congruent with our attitudes than information incongruent with our attitudes.

*Deliberative behavior* – actions that are relatively thoughtful.

*Evaluative-affective consistency* – the amount of congruence between an individual's attitude and the person's feelings and emotions.

*Evaluative-behavioral consistency* – the amount of congruence between an individual's attitude and the person's past behaviors.

*Evaluative-cognitive consistency* – the amount of congruence between an individual's attitude and the person's beliefs.

*Impulsive system* – According to the Reflective-Impulsive Model, this system guides and elicits behavior through automatic associative links.

*Need for cognition* – stable differences in the desire to engage in and enjoy effortful cognitive activity.

*Private self-consciousness* – awareness of personal and internal characteristics.

*Public self-consciousness* – awareness of public image.

*Reflective system* – According to the Reflective-Impulsive Model, this system guides and elicits behavior via a reasoned consideration of available information.

*Reflective-Impulsive Model* – proposes that behavior is controlled by a reflective system and an impulsive system.

*Reverse correlation data reduction* – in studies of facial perception, this technique builds a picture of participants' mental image of a face by asking them to choose the most accurate among digitally scrambled images of the face.

*Selective attention* – the tendency to notice and focus on attitude-congruent and attitude-incongruent information to different degrees.

*Selective exposure* – the tendency to seek out different amounts of attitude-congruent and attitude-incongruent information.

*Selective interpretation* – the tendency to be biased in our judgments of the meaning and significance of attitude-relevant information.

*Selective memory* – the effect of attitudes on the types of attitude-relevant information we remember (e.g., attitude incongruent).

*Spontaneous behavior* – actions that are relatively automatic.

# FURTHER READING

## BASIC

Glasman, L. R. and Albarracín, D. (2006) Forming attitudes that predict future behavior: A meta-analysis of the attitude–behavior relation. *Psychological Bulletin, 132*, 778–822.

Payne, B. K., Burkley, M. A. and Stokes, M. B. (2008) Why do implicit and explicit attitude tests diverge? The role of structural fit. *Journal of Personality and Social Psychology, 94*, 16–31.

Richetin, J., Conner, M. and Perugini, M. (2011) Not doing is not the opposite of doing: Implications for attitudinal models of behavioral prediction. *Personality and Social Psychology Bulletin, 37*, 40–54.

Sia, T. L., Lord, C. G., Blessum, K. A., Ratcliff, C. D. and Lepper, M. R. (1997) Is a rose always a rose? The role of social category exemplar change in attitude stability and attitude–behavior consistency. *Journal of Personality and Social Psychology, 72*, 501–514.

## APPLIED

Aubrey, J. S. (2006) Exposure to sexually objectifying media and body self-perceptions among college women: An examination of the selective exposure hypothesis and the role of moderating variables. *Sex Roles, 55* (3–4), 159–172.

Bastardi, A., Uhlmann, E. L. and Ross, L. (2011) Wishful thinking: Belief, desire, and the motivated evaluation of scientific evidence. *Psychological Science, 22,* 731–732.

Morwitz, V., Johnson, E. and Schmittlein, D. (1993) Does measuring intent change behavior? *Journal of Consumer Psychology, 20,* 46–61.

Vargas, P. T., Von Hippel, W. and Petty, R. E. (2004) Using partially structured attitude measures to enhance the attitude–behavior relationship. *Personality and Social Psychology Bulletin, 30,* 197–211.

# 4

---

# HOW DO ATTITUDES INFLUENCE BEHAVIOR?

---

## QUESTIONS TO PONDER

1. How do attitudes predict deliberative behavior?
2. How do attitudes predict spontaneous behavior?
3. What are habits and how do they influence behavior?
4. Do we need attitudes if we have habits?

### PREVIEW

In the previous chapter, we explored the issue of *when* attitudes predict behavior. In addition to addressing when attitudes predict behavior, social psychologists have developed a number of models to explain *how* attitudes predict behavior. In this chapter, we introduce what we perceive to be the most prominent models of attitude–behavior relations: Fishbein and Azjen's (1975) Theory of Reasoned Action (as well as its extension, the Theory of Planned Behavior), Fazio's (1990) MODE Model, and Eagly and Chaiken's (1993, 1998) Composite Model. For each model, we describe the basic tenets of the model and highlight research that has tested it. A lot of this research has focused on trying to predict diverse behaviors that are notoriously difficult to change or controversial in some way (e.g., using condoms to prevent spread of sexually transmitted disease), which testifies to the importance of this research topic.

## THE THEORY OF REASONED ACTION AND THE THEORY OF PLANNED BEHAVIOR

As its name suggests, the Theory of Reasoned Action was developed to predict reasoned, deliberative (i.e., planned) behavior. According to this model (see Figure 4.1), the immediate predictor (or determinant) of individuals' behavior is their *intention*. Put simply, the idea is that if, for example, you intend to recycle empty bottles, you are likely to engage in this behavior. Within the original conceptualization of the model, intentions were determined by two factors: attitudes and subjective norms. The *attitude* component refers to the individual's attitude toward the behavior – whether the person thinks that performing the behavior is good or bad. *Subjective norms* refer to the perceived social pressure to perform or not perform the behavior. To continue our example, we should be more likely to intend to recycle empty bottles if we think it is good to recycle them and we feel that this would help us get along with people who are important to us.

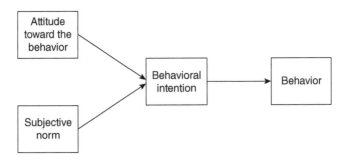

**Figure 4.1**  *The Theory of Reasoned Action*

The Theory of Reasoned Action proposes that attitudes are shaped by the person's *expectancy* that the behavior will produce a desired consequence (e.g., recycling empty bottles helps the environment) and the *value* attached to this consequence (e.g., it is good to help the environment). Consequently, if we are asking participants about their attitude to recycling empty bottles, we might ask people to rate their agreement with different statements describing potential effects of recycling. The examples below focus on consequences for waste reduction:

*Recycling reduces waste.*

| Disagree Strongly | | Neither | | Agree Strongly | | |
|---|---|---|---|---|---|---|
| −3 | −2 | −1 | 0 | +1 | +2 | +3 |

*It is good to reduce waste.*

| Disagree Strongly | | Neither | | Agree Strongly | | |
|---|---|---|---|---|---|---|
| −3 | −2 | −1 | 0 | +1 | +2 | +3 |

Similar items could be generated for other consequences, such as effects on personal time, energy consumption, and climate change. According to the model, an individual's attitude toward the behavior can be measured by multiplying the expectancy score by the value score for each consequence examined (e.g., reducing waste, saving energy), and summing these products across the consequences.

Like the attitude component, subjective norms are determined by two factors. Specifically, the subjective norm component is the product of *normative beliefs* about how people who are important to the individual expect him or her to act and the individual's motivation to comply with these expectations. Returning to our example, subjective norms will be favorable if family and close friends have positive expectations toward recycling empty bottles and you are motivated to comply with their expectations. This would entail agreement with the items below:

*People who are important to me would want me to recycle.*

| Disagree Strongly | | | Neither | | Agree Strongly | |
|---|---|---|---|---|---|---|
| −3 | −2 | −1 | 0 | +1 | +2 | +3 |

*Generally speaking, I want to do what the people who are most important to me want me to do.*

| Disagree Strongly | | | Neither | | Agree Strongly | |
|---|---|---|---|---|---|---|
| −3 | −2 | −1 | 0 | +1 | +2 | +3 |

Using these items, subjective norms can be measured by multiplying the belief scores by the motivation scores.

Researchers have tended to adopt a slightly simpler approach in practice. Dozens of studies have used simpler measures of attitude, like the semantic differential scales described in Chapter 1, and they often do not ask about motivation to comply with others. Also, studies have utilized primarily explicit measures, although implicit measures of attitudes *and* norms are now available (Yoshida, Peach, Zanna, & Spencer, 2012). Despite these simplifications, the measures of attitudes and norms often do a commendable job in predicting intentions and behavior.

Notwithstanding this success, it became clear to Ajzen (1991) that actions are also influenced by whether or not people feel they *can* perform the relevant behavior. Returning to our empty bottles, even if we have a positive attitude and positive subjective norms toward recycling empty bottles, we might feel that it is difficult to do if there is no recycling facility near our house and we do not own a car. These beliefs undermine a sense of self-efficacy, which is the "conviction that one can successfully execute the behavior required to produce the (desired) outcomes" (see Bandura, 1977, p. 193). In light of how these types of self-efficacy factors can influence our actions, the Theory of Reasoned Action was revised to include the idea that behavioral prediction is influenced by whether people believe that they can perform the relevant behavior. This revision is captured by the concept of *perceived behavioral control* – individuals' perceptions about whether they possess the resources and opportunities required to perform the behavior. The inclusion of this concept led Ajzen (1991; see also Ajzen & Madden, 1986) to name the revised model the *Theory of Planned Behavior*.

As shown in Figure 4.2, the Theory of Planned Behavior suggests that perceived behavioral control influences behavior in two ways. First, it has a direct effect on behavioral intentions: individuals' intention to engage in a particular behavior is affected by their confidence in their ability to perform the action. Second, perceived behavioral control has a direct effect on behavior. This effect depends on actual control of the relevant action; that is, whether the behavior can, in reality, be performed. Put simply, while people may believe that they can perform the relevant behavior, their perception may not be accurate. As a result, perceived behavioral control might not predict their behavior. Overall, adding a measure of perceived behavioral control should lead to a better ability to predict behavior than by only considering variables from the Theory of Reasoned Action.

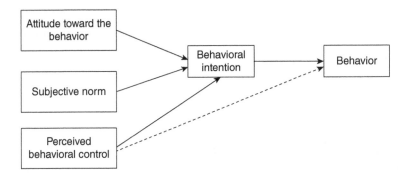

**Figure 4.2**   *The Theory of Planned Behavior*

The Theory of Reasoned Action and Theory of Planned Behavior are the most frequently tested models of attitude–behavior relations. The predictions derived from the models have received strong empirical support. For example, a meta-analysis by Dolores Albarracín, Blair Johnson, Martin Fishbein, and Paige Muellerleile (2001) reviewed the results of studies assessing whether the Theory of Reasoned Action does an effective job in predicting condom use. Averaging across 96 studies, future condom use behavior was significantly related to behavioral intentions to use condoms ($r = 0.45$). People who reported that they intended to use condoms were more likely to use condoms in the future. Consistent with the model, behavioral intentions were predicted by both attitudes toward condom use ($r = 0.58$) and subjective norms about condom use ($r = 0.39$). If people held positive attitudes toward using condoms and felt that significant others viewed condom use as positive, they were more likely to intend to use condoms. Further, attitudes toward condom use were predicted by behavioral beliefs ($r = 0.56$), and subjective norms were predicted by normative beliefs ($r = 0.46$). Thus, the variables from the Theory of Reasoned Action showed the expected pattern of relations.

The Theory of Reasoned Action and Theory of Planned Behavior have been supported by reviews of research in other domains. For example, Chris Armitage and Mark Conner (2001) conducted a meta-analysis based on 185 studies that tested all or parts of the Theory of Planned Behavior in domains such as encouraging people to stop smoking, increasing the prevalence of blood donation, and getting people to take public transportation to work. Averaging across these studies, Armitage and Conner (2001) found strong support for the Theory of Planned Behavior. Basically, the results of these types of meta-analyses provide strong evidence that the Theory of Reasoned Action and Theory of Planned Behavior are effective in predicting "thoughtful" behavior.

## KEY POINTS

- The Theories of Planned Behavior and Reasoned Action both indicate that attitudes are only one of several psychological variables (e.g., subjective norms, perceived behavioral control) that shape behavior.

- The Theories of Planned Behavior and Reasoned Action both propose that the effects of attitudes on behavior are indirect: attitudes shape intentions to act, which in turn determine behavior.

- Numerous studies have obtained correlations supporting the Theories of Planned Behavior and Reasoned Action.

## ISSUES RELEVANT TO THE REASONED ACTION FRAMEWORK

Researchers have considered a number of questions that stem from the Theory of Reasoned Action and the Theory of Planned Behavior. Four questions are particularly interesting. First, the model posits that attitudes are influenced by expectancies about the outcomes of action. Are some types of expectancies more important than others? We will show that this question is directly relevant to two of our attitude witches.

Second, the model posits that behavioral intentions are predicted by attitudes and subjective norms. Is one of these two predictors more important than the other? Both of the meta-analyses we described earlier in this chapter suggest that behavioral intentions are better predicted by attitudes toward the behavior than by subjective norms. However, there may be instances when subjective norms are more important. We will review whether there are particular behaviors and situations where subjective norms are especially important in predicting behavioral intentions, and whether there are individuals for whom subjective norms tend to be the more important predictor of behavioral intentions.

Third, an important part of the model examines how behavioral intentions get translated into behavior. We can all think of times when we intended to do something but did not follow through and carry out the behavior. For instance, one of the authors intended to complete a big cycling trip in France for his 40th birthday. Sadly, and despite his best intentions and urgings from others, that birthday came and went without a cycling trip. He still hasn't made good on his intention years later. We review research that considers how to increase the likelihood that behavioral intentions get translated into actions (and that the trip will eventually happen!).

Fourth, the models' focus on "reasoned" action and "planned" behavior makes it important to wonder what happens when people think about their attitudes more carefully. If we think about our attitudes, should they become more in line with our primary beliefs and, hence, better predictors of our intentions and action? We will describe evidence showing that the effect of thinking about attitudes is more complex than this.

## Are some types of beliefs more important than others?

This question is relevant to Fishbein and Ajzen's (1975) argument that behavior can be changed by identifying the *salient beliefs* that are major determinants of that behavior. People can hold many beliefs about a given object, but they can think about only a small number at any given time. The salient beliefs are those that are easy to recall and link to the behavior. Fishbein and Ajzen (1975) suggested that these salient, easy-to-remember beliefs are the fundamental determinants of people's attitudes and behavioral intentions. To identify our salient beliefs for eating fruit, for example, the researchers would ask us to list all the advantages and disadvantages of eating fruit. They might also ask us to describe what people who are important to us would think about us eating fruit and to list the factors or circumstances that might make it easier (or more difficult) for us to do so.

It turns out that it may be useful to further subgroup these beliefs (Conner & Norman, 2005). Two potentially important dimensions are the extent to which they refer to positive versus negative outcomes and the extent to which they refer to instrumental versus emotional outcomes. The first dimension is similar to our distinction between positive and negative valence in attitude structure, and the second dimension is similar to our distinction between cognition and emotion in attitudes.

To be more specific, the first dimension distinguishes between outcomes that are liked (e.g., increased health from eating fruit) from those that are disliked (e.g., variable quality of taste). These beliefs about positive and negative outcomes may have distinct effects on behavior (Conner & Sparks, 2002). For example, Rebecca Lawton, Mark Conner, and Diane Parker (2007) found that beliefs about negative outcomes were most important in predicting speeding behavior, but beliefs about positive outcomes were most important in predicting the initiation of smoking.

The second dimension distinguishes between material costs and benefits to the self and consequences of an action for feelings and well-being. For example, instrumental outcomes for eating fruit may include better energy levels, easier weight control, and cardiovascular health; emotional outcomes could include feelings of pride and vitality. A large number of experiments support the distinction between instrumental and emotional beliefs (e.g., Crites et al., 1994; Trafimow & Sheeran, 1998; van der Pligt, Zeelenberg, van Dijk, de Vries, & Richard, 1998). This distinction is particularly important for understanding risky behaviors, which frequently conflict with relevant outcome cognitions (Loewenstein, Weber, Hsee, & Welch, 2001). People often know the risks of dangerous behaviors and think the risks are bad, but still perform the behaviors. For instance, people know that skiing is dangerous, but the thrills compel us to ignore the dangers of the spills. According to the "risk as feelings" hypothesis (Loewenstein et al., 2001), emotional reactions often drive behavior when cognitive and emotional reactions conflict (see also Lavine et al., 1998).

## Are there times when attitudes or subjective norms are most important in predicting behavioral intentions?

Usually, behavioral intentions are better predicted by attitudes than by subjective norms. Research has examined relevant differences between people and situations in determining whether attitudes or subjective norms are better predictors of intentions. It turns out that there are differences in the extent to which people and situations emphasize either personal or collective beliefs.

The idea that people differ in the degree that their behavioral intentions are influenced by attitudes and subjective norms was tested by David Trafimow and Kristina Finlay (1996). In their research, university students completed measures of attitudes, subjective norms, and behavioral intentions for 30 behaviors, which ranged from eating vegetables regularly to paying bills on time. When looking separately at each of the behaviors, Trafimow and Finlay (1996) found that, overall, behavioral intentions were better predicted by people's attitudes than by their subjective norms. Subjective norms were more important than attitudes for only one of the 30 behaviors – going into debt on one's credit cards (something familiar to many students!). That said, for most of the 30 behaviors, subjective norms uniquely predicted people's behavioral intentions after their attitudes had been taken into account. This means that subjective norms do predict behavioral intentions separately from attitudes, but not as much as attitudes.

More importantly, because Trafimow and Finlay (1996) collected measures of attitudes, subjective norms, and intentions from every participant for 30 different behaviors, these scientists could also consider whether *every* respondent's personal intentions were better predicted by their attitudes or subjective norms. For each participant, Trafimow and Finlay calculated the correlations among the respondent's own reported attitudes, subjective norms, and behavioral intentions. These analyses found that, when looking across their respondents, about 80% of people had intentions that were better predicted by their attitudes than by their subjective norms. Of course, this means that about 20% of the participants reported intentions that were more closely related to their subjective norms than their attitudes.

It is interesting to think about why some people's behavioral intentions are more strongly related to their attitudes, whereas others' intentions are more strongly related to their subjective norms. Is an individual's cultural background important? Are normative people more conformist in nature? Do they tend to have weaker attitudes? Are they more likely to be aware of the views of others? To start addressing these types of questions, Oscar Ybarra and David Trafimow (1998) explored whether making people think about *private-self cognitions* versus *collective-self cognitions* would influence how attitudes and subjective norms predict behavioral intentions. Private-self cognitions refer to an individual's self-assessment, while collective-self cognitions refer to how the individual feels judged by others. An example of a private-self cognition would be the belief "I am funny." In contrast, an example of a collective-self cognition would be the belief "My family thinks that I am funny." Research has found that people from individualistic cultures (e.g., the United States) can retrieve more private-self beliefs than collective-self beliefs, whereas individuals from collectivist cultures (e.g., China) can retrieve more collective-self beliefs than private-self beliefs (see Trafimow, Triandis, & Goto, 1991; Triandis, 1989).

Ybarra and Trafimow (1998) tested two predictions based on the distinction between private- and collective-self beliefs. First, they tested whether making salient a person's private self would also make their personal attitudes toward a behavior more salient, causing their attitudes to have a greater impact than subjective norms in forming behavioral intentions. Second, they tested whether making salient a person's collective self would make their subjective norms more salient, causing subjective norms to have a greater impact than attitudes in forming behavioral intentions. To test these hypotheses, Ybarra and Trafimow (1998, Study 2) asked one group of participants to think about themselves, their expectations, and how they were different from their family and friends, while another group of participants was asked to think about what they have in common with their family and friends and what these people expect from them. As you might have already guessed, the first manipulation was intended to make personal-self beliefs salient, whereas the second manipulation was designed to make collective-self beliefs salient. After completing this task, participants reported their attitudes, subjective norms, and behavioral intentions toward using a condom when having sex. The results showed that, among participants in the private-self belief priming condition, behavioral intentions were more highly correlated with (and better predicted by) attitudes ($r = 0.64$) than subjective norms ($r = 0.48$). In contrast, among participants in the collective-self belief priming condition, behavioral intentions were more highly correlated with (and better predicted by) subjective norms ($r = 0.67$) than attitudes ($r = 0.54$).

Taken together, the results of these studies have a number of important implications. First, they highlight the conditions under which subjective norms can become more important in predicting behavioral intentions. Second, the effect of this manipulation (making people think about private- versus collective-self beliefs) fits the results of other experiments showing that different ways of thinking about ourselves affect the links between our attitudes and behavior. Third, they are relevant to understanding potential differences in the role of attitudes across cultures, which is a topic we explore further toward the end of the book.

---

**Function Witch:** *Shouldn't the effect of the collective self be greater for attitudes that serve a social adjustment function, while the role of the individual self may be more prominent for attitudes serving other functions (e.g., instrumental, ego-defense)?*

---

# How are behavioral intentions translated into behavior?

Our intentions don't always predict our behavior. Every single one of us has intended to do something that, for one reason or another, did not get done. Sometimes, this can happen because we do not want to perform the intended behavior. Many people go to bed intending to exercise the next morning, but only because they feel they have to exercise and not because they want to exercise. This makes it all too easy to come up with something else to do instead (e.g., sleep longer, do the laundry). Other times, we simply forget to perform the intended behavior. For instance, we may forget to exercise because of distractions (phone calls, kids arguing). The question of how to increase the link between intentions and behavior has received considerable attention in the social psychological literature.

Perhaps the most important development in this area is the concept of *implementation intentions* (Gollwitzer, 1999). At a basic level, implementation intentions are like "if–then" plans that specify behaviors that a person will need to perform in order to achieve a goal (Sheeran, 2002). In other words, implementation intentions take the form of mindsets that focus an individual on specifying where, when, and how a behavior will be enacted. These may occur in the form of "When I encounter situation A, I will perform behavior B" (Gollwitzer & Brandstätter, 1997). Think about an essay that you have to complete two weeks from now. In this case, an implementation intention might take the form of "When I return to university from my weekend at home, I will go straight to the library and start researching the essay topic."

Numerous studies have demonstrated that forming an implementation intention increases the likelihood that an individual will act on the intention. In one study, Sheina Orbell, Sarah Hodgkins, and Paschal Sheeran (1997) considered whether the formation of an implementation intention would increase the likelihood that women would perform breast self-examination (BSE) to help detect tumors in early stages. In Orbell et al.'s study, women randomly assigned to an intervention group were asked to indicate where and when they would perform BSE. Participants read these instructions:

> You are more likely to carry out your intention to perform BSE if you make a decision about where and when you will do so. Many women find it most convenient to perform BSE at the start of the morning or last thing at night, in the shower or bath, or while they are getting dressed in their bedroom or bathroom. Others like to do it in bed before they go to sleep or prior to getting up. Decide now where and when you will perform BSE in the next month and make a commitment to do so.

Following this instruction, participants in this intervention condition were asked to write down where and when they would perform BSE. Women randomly assigned to the control group were not given any instructions about implementation intentions. Orbell et al. (1997) predicted that women in the implementation intention condition would be less likely to report forgetting to perform BSE and more likely to perform it.

The results of the study revealed that the formation of an implementation intention was effective. Indeed, one month after the intervention, 64% of participants in the intervention group reported having performed BSE, compared to just 14% in the control group. The implementation intention instructions had a huge effect on behavior.

The positive effects of implementation intentions have since been documented for many types of health behaviors (see Sheeran, Milne, Webb, & Gollwitzer, 2005, for a review), ranging from healthy eating to participation in cancer screening and psychotherapy. Effects have been found outside of the health context as well. For example, in a sample of more than 287,000 individuals during the 2008 American presidential election, one compelling field experiment found that facilitating implementation intentions helped to increase voter turnout by 4% (Nickerson & Rogers, 2010). Further, a meta-analysis by Gollwitzer and Sheeran (2006) provides strong evidence highlighting the role that implementation intentions can play in enacting behavioral intentions. Across almost 100 studies, they found that forming an implementation intention was very effective in making it more likely for an individual to enact a behavior they intended to perform.

These findings suggest that implementation intentions can serve as useful tools for helping people do as they intend. What's particularly elegant about this approach is its simplicity – it is not that hard to form an implementation intention. Just specify when, where, and how you are going to do something (even when it is something you really do not want to do), and chances are you are more likely to follow through on your intentions. At the same time, forming implementation intentions frees up cognitive capacity for other, different tasks, because goal performance has been placed under automatic control (Masicampo & Baumeister, 2011).

But this does not mean that forming *many* implementation intentions works. It's human nature to think that, when we can do something that is useful and easy, it's good to do lots of it. However, Aujke Verhoeven and colleagues (Verhoeven, Adriaanse, de Ridder, de Vet, & Fennis, 2013) found that forming a single implementation for a single goal (unhealthy snacking) was more effective than forming multiple implementation intentions. Multiple plans were less effective because they elicited different ways to fulfill the intention, rather than allow memory to powerfully focus on one behavior that could be automatically elicited.

## Variables other than attitude, subjective norms, perceived behavioral control, and intentions

If the Theory of Planned Behavior is truly complete, we should not be able to find other variables that predict behavior. Stated more precisely, we should not be able to find other variables that predict behavior intentions or behavior *independently* of attitude, subjective norms, and perceived behavioral control. For example, we might believe that beliefs about the moral correctness of an action is important for whether people will perform the action, but the perceived morality of behavior is not explicitly included in the Theory of Planned Behavior. The Theory of Planned Behavior would suggest that, if moral beliefs do have any effect at all, these effects occur because the moral beliefs influence the attitudes, norms, or perceived behavioral control. Thus, if the Theory of Planned Behavior is correct, moral beliefs should *not* help us to predict a behavior after our analyses take attitudes, norms, and behavioral control into account.

The problem is that moral beliefs do help to predict behavior after analyses control for attitudes, norms, and perceived behavioral control (Conner et al., 2007; Maio & Olson, 1995a). Effects of attitudes on behavior are determined at least in part by moral considerations, though it is not yet clear whether this conclusion is better supported for some types of behavior (e.g., interpersonal behaviors) than for others (Godin, Conner, & Sheeran, 2005; Maio & Olson, 2000a, 2000b; Sparks & Manstead, 2006).

The problem is exacerbated by evidence that other variables also contribute uniquely to the prediction of intentions and behavior, above and beyond attitudes, norms, and perceived behavioral control. These additional variables include the personal need for satisfaction (Hagger, Chatzisarantis, & Harris, 2006), anticipated negative self-conscious emotion (Hynie, MacDonald, & Marques, 2006), and individual differences in self-efficacy (i.e., beliefs that one is capable of action; Manstead & van Eekelen, 1998). Thus, although the variables in the Theory of Planned Behavior are important (Armitage & Conner, 2001), it is clear that they are not enough for explaining behavior.

# The effects of thinking about reasons behind our attitude

Imagine that a friend sends you a web link to a charity running a survey on attitudes to helping the homeless. At your friend's urging, you complete the survey, which asks you to indicate your opinion toward helping the homeless and to write down reasons why you feel the way you do. A few months later, you encounter a homeless individual asking if you could spare some change. Will having thought about the reasons behind your attitude change your attitude in some way, with consequences for your later behavior?

A fascinating line of research by Timothy Wilson and his colleagues has found that analyzing reasons for attitudes actually can cause attitude change, particularly when people lack knowledge about the attitude object and not when people possess a lot of knowledge about the attitude object (Wilson, Dunn, Kraft, & Lisle, 1989; Wilson, Kraft, & Dunn, 1989; see also Wilson et al., 1993). According to Wilson and colleagues, individuals who lack cognitive support for an attitude tend to access randomly a subset of their most accessible and easy to verbalize reasons when they are asked about their reasons, and these reasons often imply a slightly more unfavorable or favorable view than the person normally expresses. This random access occurs because these individuals do not know exactly *why* they feel the way that they do – their attitudes are not strongly associated (in memory) with a set of reasons. Thus, these individuals access reasons that are temporarily accessible and possibly not consistent with their original attitude.

So how well does a person's new, post-reasons attitude predict his or her behavior? Several studies have found that analyzing reasons for an attitude caused lower subsequent attitude–behavior correlations (Wilson, Dunn et al., 1989). Other research found that analyzing reasons for an attitude caused lower subsequent attitude–behavior correlations when the attitude-relevant behaviors were affectively based than when the behaviors were cognitively based (Millar & Tesser, 1986; see also Maio & Olson, 1998a). Presumably, people who analyzed their reasons expressed subsequent attitudes that were based on their cognitions about the attitude object. If, in contrast, the attitude-relevant behavior was based on individuals' feelings about the attitude object, then the mismatch between the basis for the behavior and the basis for the post-reasons-analysis attitude produced low attitude–behavior correspondence. Thus, consistency between the basis for attitudes and behaviors appears to be an important determinant of the extent to which attitudes predict behavior.

According to Wilson, Dunn et al. (1989), analyzing reasons causes participants to access momentarily verbalizable reasons that influence their attitude immediately after reasons analysis, but the influence of these reasons eventually decays, thereby returning the attitude and subsequent attitude-relevant behavior to their original, affective bases. Consequently, the immediate post-reasons analysis attitude is often incongruent with the later behavior. Consistent with this reasoning, post-reasons-analysis attitudes are less incongruent with subsequent behavior when there is a short interval before the measurement of behavior than when there is a long delay (Wilson, Dunn et al., 1989). In addition, analyzing reasons for an attitude increases subsequent attitude–behavior correlations when the instrumental attributes of the attitude object are reconsidered prior to target behavior (Millar & Tesser, 1986; Wilson, Dunn et al., 1989).

## KEY POINTS

- Negative emotional beliefs may have a stronger impact on intentions than positive non-emotional beliefs.
- Relative to the influence of subjective norms, the influence of attitudes may be lower when people's collective self is salient than when their private self is salient.
- Getting people to form detailed plans about when and how they will execute behaviors can increase the likelihood of performing the behavior.
- Although the Theory of Planned Behavior is useful for predicting behavior, its utility can be further improved by considering other predictor variables (e.g., moral beliefs, emotion) and deliberative processes (e.g., effects of thinking about reasons for attitudes).

## THE "MODE" MODEL

We don't always think carefully about our actions. In many situations, we think and act spontaneously, without really thinking of what we intend to do. These spontaneous actions can even contradict our intentions, leaving us at a loss to explain our behavior. As a result, the Theory of Planned Behavior may not provide the most appropriate framework for understanding and predicting spontaneous behavior. In an attempt to uncover how attitudes influence deliberative *and* spontaneous information processing, Russell Fazio (1990) developed the MODE Model of attitude–behavior relations.

MODE refers to *M*otivation and *O*pportunity as *DE*terminants of Behavior. The MODE Model is best characterized as a dual-process model, in that it specifies two different ways in which attitudes can influence behavior. The MODE Model is characterized in Figure 4.3. The model suggests that, if individuals have *both* sufficient motivation and opportunity, they may base their behavior on a deliberative consideration of their attitudes and other available information. However, when either the motivation or the opportunity to make a reasoned decision is low, individuals enter a spontaneous mode of information processing. Under these circumstances, the model states that attitude accessibility is vital. When people have a highly accessible attitude, it becomes automatically activated and elicits behavior that is consistent with the attitude. Conversely, when the attitude is not accessible, it is not automatically activated and is therefore not likely to predict behavior.

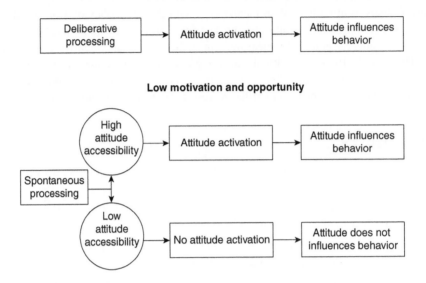

**Figure 4.3**   *The MODE Model*

A number of studies by Fazio and colleagues have supported the MODE Model (e.g., Sanbonmatsu & Fazio, 1990; Schuette & Fazio, 1995). Most of these studies have focused on demonstrating the role of attitude accessibility in the spontaneous route, because this is the portion of the model that differs most from the focus of the Theories of Reasoned Action and Planned Behavior. An excellent example was a study conducted during the 1984 American presidential election. In Chapter 3, we described how Fazio and Williams (1986) measured participants' attitudes toward the incumbent United States President Ronald Reagan, as well as his opponent, Walter Mondale. Approximately five months later (and very soon after the election), Fazio and Williams measured whether their participants voted for Reagan or Mondale. We noted in Chapter 3 that the correlation between voters' initial attitude and their subsequent voting behavior was 0.78 for Reagan and 0.63 for Mondale. This is very impressive, particularly given the relatively long time lag between the measures of attitude and behavior. What we did not say was that the large correlations were not the primary focus of this study. Fazio and Williams were interested in showing that the magnitude of the attitude–behavior relation depended on the *accessibility* of participants' initial attitude. Some participants had very accessible (i.e., strong) attitudes toward Reagan. These participants could report their attitudes very quickly. Other participants' attitudes were less accessible (i.e., weak); these participants could report their attitudes less quickly. Fazio and Williams (1986) found that the correlation between attitudes and behavior was significantly greater among those individuals whose attitude toward Reagan was highly accessible. Specifically, the correlation between attitudes toward Reagan and voting behavior was 0.89 among voters with highly accessible attitudes, compared to 0.66 among voters with less accessible attitudes toward Reagan.

So how does an attitude become accessible and what does this accessibility mean? As indicated in Chapter 1, Fazio (1990) suggested that attitudes become accessible when people have formed a strong association between their evaluation of an attitude object and their mental representation of the object. A general principle in psychology is that associations between any two concepts are strengthened by repeated pairing; thus, the strength of association between an attitude and the attitude object in memory should become stronger when people repeatedly perform behaviors that express the attitude. Consistent with this view, people become faster at reporting an attitude when they have previously been given many opportunities to express the attitude (e.g., on a rating scale) than when they have been given fewer opportunities to express it (Powell & Fazio, 1984).

---

*Structure Witch: There is evidence that people are somewhat quicker to report attitudes when the attitudes are less ambivalent (Bargh, Chaiken, Govender, & Pratto, 1992). Does higher accessibility improve attitude–behavior correspondence even when attitudes remain ambivalent and, therefore, are more complex?*

---

Research by Schuette and Fazio (1995) considers how attitude accessibility and motivation influence the extent to which people process information in a biased way. Schuette and Fazio asked university students to evaluate two research studies on the effectiveness of the death penalty as a deterrent of crime. One study supported the idea that capital punishment is an effective deterrent; the second study reached the opposite conclusion. Before participants looked at the studies, Schuette and Fazio manipulated the accessibility of each participant's attitude toward the death penalty. Some participants expressed their attitude once (low accessibility), whereas others expressed their attitude six times (high accessibility). To manipulate motivation, some participants were told that their conclusions would be compared to those made by an expert panel. Participants in the low motivation condition did not receive this information.

The results revealed that the relation between individuals' prior attitude and their judgment about the study depended on both the accessibility of the participants' attitude and their level of motivation. Evaluations of the articles were consistent with participants' attitude when their attitude was highly accessible and their motivation was low ($r = 0.51$). In this case, their highly accessible attitude served as a cue that biased their perceptions. However, when participants were highly motivated, or when they had expressed their attitude only one time, attitudes were not correlated with evaluations of the studies (the correlations ranged from $-0.06$ to $0.18$). In these conditions, being motivated can lead individuals to overcome the potential biases of their attitude, even if it is accessible. When not motivated, expressing an attitude just once does not make it sufficiently accessible for it to influence their perceptions.

Similar results can occur for implicit measures of attitude. Recall from Chapter 1 that implicit measures of attitude tap evaluations that spontaneously come to mind, without people reporting their attitudes in a conscious manner. In general, spontaneous evaluations may reflect attitudes that are highly accessible (Fazio, Sanbonmatsu, Powell, & Kardes, 1986; cf. Bargh et al., 1992). As a consequence, the MODE Model predicts that the spontaneous evaluations that are tapped by implicit measures should be stronger predictors of judgments and behavior when motivation to deliberate is low than when it is high. In one experiment supporting this hypothesis, Olson and Fazio (2004b) asked university undergraduates to complete a measure of their motivation to control prejudicial reactions and the evaluative priming measure of attitudes described in Chapter 1. Three to five weeks later, participants were shown pictures of Black individuals and White individuals, along with brief descriptions of them. The descriptions of the Black individuals and the White individuals were matched by gender, status, and type of occupation (e.g., a Black repair woman and a White painter). For each photo, participants had to rate the individual on a variety of traits (e.g., intelligent, likeable).

Analyses of these ratings revealed that they varied as a function of participants' motivation to control prejudice and their spontaneous attitudes. When participants were low in the motivation to control prejudice, those who possessed more negative spontaneous attitudes toward Blacks rated the Black individuals more negatively (relative to the White individuals). This effect is straightforward and is consistent with the previously described effects of accessible attitudes on judgment and behavior when motivation to deliberate is low. The story becomes more interesting when we consider the participants who were high in the motivation to control prejudice: those who possessed more negative spontaneous attitudes toward Blacks rated the Black individuals more *positively* (relative to the White individuals). These participants appeared to override and overcompensate for their spontaneous negative attitudes in an effort to appear less prejudiced! In other words, participants' high motivation overrode the effect of participants' spontaneous attitudes, as the MODE Model predicts.

## RESEARCH HIGHLIGHT 4.1

### WHICH DEPARTMENT STORE TO VISIT?

One particularly ingenious study testing the MODE Model gave participants information about two department stores that included camera departments (Sanbonmatsu & Fazio, 1990). Brown's store was described favorably, but its camera department was described negatively. In contrast, Smith's store was described unfavorably, but its camera department was described positively. After a delay, participants were asked where they would shop for a camera. Sanbonmatsu and Fazio (1990) manipulated the conditions under which people made their choice. Some people were motivated to make a good decision, because they were told they would need to justify their choice. Other participants were not given this instruction. Opportunity was manipulated by forcing some people to make their decision under time pressure.

The results of the study indicated that participants were likely to base their decisions on the description of the camera department (that is, to buy a camera from Smith's) when they were *both* motivated and had the opportunity to make their decision without time pressure. Participants were less likely to base their decisions on the description of the camera departments when either (a) the instructions encouraged them merely to form an opinion about the stores (when they were less motivated) or (b) participants had to make their decision under time pressure (when they had limited opportunity).

The MODE Model has become tremendously important in research on attitudes. The model elegantly explains how both deliberative and spontaneous behaviors are influenced by attitudes. This breadth is attained by its focus on motivation and ability as determinants of processing strategy – a focus that is shared with leading models of how attitudes are shaped (see Chapter 5). Nonetheless, its most compelling and unique evidence has helped to understand the effects of attitudes on spontaneous behavior in particular. Across a variety of studies, it is clear that attitude accessibility plays an important role in understanding the effects of attitudes on spontaneous behavior (see Glasman & Albarracín, 2006).

## KEY POINTS

- The MODE Model suggests that attitudes can influence behavior through either a spontaneous or deliberate route.
- In the spontaneous route, the strength of association between people's mental representations of the attitude object and their evaluation of it determines the likelihood that the attitude will influence judgments and behavior.

## THE COMPOSITE ATTITUDE–BEHAVIOR MODEL

The final model we wish to address is Alice Eagly and Shelly Chaiken's (1993, 1998) Composite Model of attitude–behavior relations. Like the Theories of Reasoned Action and Planned Behavior, the Composite Model suggests a link between attitudes, intentions, and behavior. As can be seen in Figure 4.4, the model proposes a number of factors that affect attitudes toward behaviors: *habits* (relevant past behaviors), *attitudes toward targets* (the target of the behavior), *utilitarian outcomes* (rewards and punishments associated with performing the behavior), *normative outcomes* (approval and disapproval from others that might occur from performing the behavior), and *self-identity outcomes* (how performing the behavior might influence the self-concept). Eagly and Chaiken suggest that some of these factors can affect intentions or directly affect behavior.

To date, relatively little research has tested the complete Composite Model. However, the model is well known among scientists who study attitudes, and we believe that it is important to mention the model because it explicitly highlights the role that *habits* can play in determining behavior. As such, we want to devote attention to recent research that has tested how habits influence behavior. Readers interested in a more complete treatment of the model (and especially its treatment of different types of outcomes) should read Eagly and Chaiken's (1993) comprehensive text.

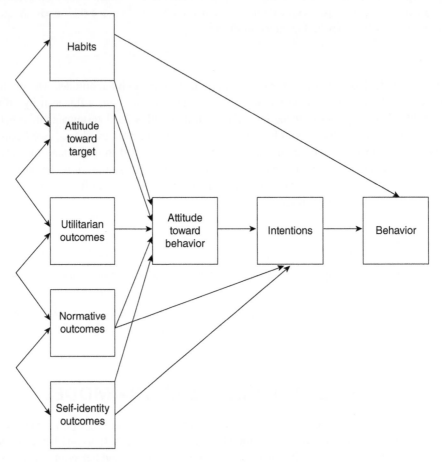

**Figure 4.4**   *The Composite Model of Attitude–Behavior Relations*

## What are habits?

The inclusion of *habits* is an important aspect of Eagly and Chaiken's framework. Many researchers have suggested that habits should be effective in predicting future behavior. From a social psychological perspective, habits are more than just behaviors that we have performed frequently. Of greater relevance is the idea that habits are *automatic* behaviors, in the sense that they can occur without conscious monitoring and are difficult to control (see Verplanken, 2006; Verplanken & Orbell, 2003). Consistent with that view, Bas Verplanken and Henk Aarts (1999, p. 104) defined habits as "learned sequences of acts that have become automatic responses to specific cues, and are functional in obtaining certain goals or end states." These qualities make habits particularly impactful on behavior when willpower (i.e., our ability to control our behavior) is low (Neal, Wood, & Drolet, 2013).

## How do habits influence behavior?

Many studies have demonstrated that habits can play an important role in predicting future behavior. For example, an important field experiment in the Netherlands assessed the degree to which habits and variables from the Theory of Planned Behavior predicted travel behavior (Verplanken, Aarts, van Knippenberg, & Moonen, 1998). The travel behavior included decisions about whether to take a bicycle, bus, car, or train to work. At the start of the study, participants completed measures of habit strength (e.g., frequency of past behavior), attitudes, subjective norms, and behavioral intentions about their travel choice. For the next week, participants kept a diary that recorded how often they drove their car and used other forms of transport. The results revealed that habits were highly predictive of behavior, even predicting behavior after behavioral intentions and perceived behavioral control were taken into account. Further, the study found that behavioral intentions were uniquely predictive of behavior only when participants' habits were weak. When habits were strong, they were enough to be the main predictor of future behavior.

Similarly, in a meta-analytic review of the literature, Judith Ouellette and Wendy Wood (1998) found that the role of habits in predicting future behavior depends upon the stability of the context in which the behavior is performed. These scientists found that behaviors that occur repeatedly in a stable context (e.g., wearing seat belts) are likely to be re-enacted when individuals face that situation in the future. Furthermore, this role of habits was presumably spontaneous, because a large component of this effect was independent of effects of reported intentions on behavior. In contrast, unstable contexts (e.g., using a condom when having sex with a new partner) prevented habits from exerting a powerful role in predicting behavior (see also Albarracín et al., 2001), and the effects of habits in these contexts were more strongly related to the simultaneous influence of intentions.

### RESEARCH HIGHLIGHT 4.2

#### YOU'RE A HARD HABIT TO BREAK: GETTING RID OF UNWANTED HABITS

Don't we all have some habit that we'd like to eliminate? For example, many smokers consider their own smoking as a bad habit they would like to break. While neither author is a smoker, one of them has a bad habit of reaching for a small bag of potato snacks (chips or crisps)

*(Continued)*

*(Continued)*

instead of a piece of fruit when craving a late-night snack; the other author habitually slouches. Research has considered how unwanted habits can be broken and replaced with "good" habits, using techniques such as implementation intentions.

In a demonstration of how implementation intentions can be used to replace bad habits with good ones, Rob Holland, Henk Aarts, and Daan Langendam (2006) conducted a clever field experiment in which they tested whether habit replacement (via implementation intentions) would lead to more recycling in a workplace environment. At the start of the experiment, the researchers unobtrusively measured the amount of paper and plastic cups being recycled in several departments within one company. After emptying garbage cans for a few days (in order to get a good pre-test measure of recycling behavior), different departments within the company were randomly assigned to either a control condition, a facility condition (in which a recycling box was placed near the desk of each participant), or an implementation intentions condition. In the implementation intentions condition, participants were asked to write down when, where, and how to recycle their old paper and used plastic cups. After the departments were randomly assigned to one of the conditions, recycling behavior was measured after one week, two weeks, and two months.

In the implementation intentions conditions of the study, the amount of paper and plastic cups thrown away was reduced by about 75%. This change remained even after two months, suggesting that new habits were leading to a real change in behavior. Similarly, Holland et al. (2006) found that the correlation between recycling behavior before the study and recycling behavior two months after the study was close to zero in the implementation intention conditions, suggesting that participants' bad habits were broken and replaced.

This study, and others like it, have played an important role in helping determine how and when habitual behaviors influence future behaviors. They also have tremendous practical importance. After all, most of us are confronted with behaviors we want to change, but find it very difficult. Whether we are trying to save more money, exercise more regularly, or eat a healthier diet, we experience difficulties jumping the gap from good intentions to good actions. Research is providing strong clues about how these gaps can be overcome.

## KEY POINTS

- The Composite Model indicates that behavior is influenced by a combination of habit, attitudes, and three types of behavioral outcomes (utilitarian, normative, and self-identity).

- The Composite Model's emphasis on the role of habit is supported by a powerful role of habit in predicting behavior.

- Habits may affect behavior more strongly when the behavior is repeatedly performed in a similar context than when the behavior must be performed in different contexts.

# WHAT WE HAVE LEARNED

- Research examining the Theory of Reasoned Action and the Theory of Planned Behavior has found that behavior can be predicted from behavioral intentions, which are based on attitudes, subjective norms, and perceived behavioral control.

- The Theory of Reasoned Action and the Theory of Planned Behavior do not effectively account for unique effects of different types of belief or for other variables that affect behavior independently of attitudes, subjective norms, and perceived behavioral control (e.g., moral norms, habit).

- According to the MODE Model, attitude accessibility is an important determinant of attitude–behavior correspondence when there is low motivation and/or opportunity to carefully consider available information.

- The Composite Model uniquely emphasizes the role of habit in predicting intentions and behavior.

# WHAT DO YOU THINK?

- The Theory of Planned Behavior predicts that stronger perceptions of behavioral control lead to greater intentions to perform the action and a greater likelihood of performing the action. Should this be true for all behaviors? Are there behaviors that you can easily control, but would never intend to enact? How would the Theory of Planned Behavior look at those behaviors?

- How often are behaviors truly spontaneous or truly deliberate? Can you think of cases where behavior is a mixture of spontaneous processes and deliberate ones? For instance, how would attitudes toward gender and ethnicity influence judgments of a job candidate?

- Can you think of any barriers to the successful use of implementation intentions? The wife of one of the authors suggested that he can correct his slouching habit by thinking "Every time I see a door frame, I will stand up straight." Two years later, his habitual vertical orientation remains curved, though perhaps a bit straighter than before. How would you help him?

- How well do the existing models help to predict the performance of complex behaviors, such as healthy eating, which entails different foods, situations, and repetition over time? These behaviors involve plans, abilities to overcome obstacles, goals, social influences, and adaptation to competing needs. Is it a simple matter to expand current models of attitude–behavior relations to explain such behavior?

# KEY TERMS

*Behavioral intentions* – a pre-behavior decision to perform or not perform the action.

*Collective-self cognitions* – how the individual feels judged by others.

*Emotional beliefs* – those that refer to the consequences of an action for feelings and well-being.

*Expectancy* – belief that a behavior will produce a desired consequence.

*Habits* – automatic behaviors that occur as a response to cues and are capable of being enacted without conscious monitoring, while being difficult to control.

*Implementation intentions* – "if–then" plans specifying behaviors that a person will need to perform in order to achieve a goal.

*Instrumental beliefs* – those that refer to the personal, material costs and benefits of an action.

*Normative beliefs* – beliefs about how people who are important to us expect us to act.

*Normative outcomes* – approval and disapproval from others that might occur from performing a behavior.

*Perceived behavioral control* – individuals' perceptions about whether they possess the resources and opportunities required to perform a behavior.

*Salient beliefs* – those that are easy to recall and link to the behavior.

*Self-efficacy* – individuals' belief that they can successfully execute a behavior.

*Self-identity outcomes* – effects of a behavior on the self-concept.

*Subjective norms* – perceived social pressure to perform or not perform a behavior.

*Utilitarian outcomes* – rewards and punishments associated with performing a behavior.

*Value* – the perceived importance of a consequence of a behavior.

---

# FURTHER READING

## BASIC

Ajzen, I., Brown, T. C. and Carvajal, F. (2004) Explaining the discrepancy between intentions and actions: The case of hypothetical bias in contingent valuation. *Personality and Social Psychology Bulletin*, *30*, 1108–1121.

Fazio, R. H. (1995) Attitudes as object-evaluation associations: Determinants, consequences and correlates of attitude accessibility. In R. E. Petty and J. A. Krosnick (eds), *Attitude Strength: Antecedents and Consequences* (pp. 247–282). Hillsdale, NJ: Erlbaum.

Strack, F. and Deutsch, R. (2004) Reflective and impulsive determinants of social behavior. *Personality and Social Psychology Review*, *8*, 220–247.

## APPLIED

Albarracín, D., Gillette, J. C., Earl, A. N., Glasman, L. R., Durantini, M. R. and Ho, M. H. (2005) A test of major assumptions about behavior change: A comprehensive look at the effects of passive and active HIV-prevention interventions since the beginning of the epidemic. *Psychological Bulletin, 131*, 856–897.

Finlay, K. A., Trafimow, D. and Villareal, A. (2002) Predicting exercise and health behavioral intentions: Attitudes, subjective norms, and other behavioral determinants. *Journal of Applied Social Psychology, 32*, 342–358.

Maio, G. R., Verplanken, B., Manstead, A. S. R., Stroebe, W., Abraham, C. S., Sheeran, P. and Conner, M. (2007) Social psychological factors in lifestyle change and their relevance to policy. *Journal of Social Issues and Policy Review, 1*, 99–137.

Verplanken, B. and Orbell, S. (2003) Reflection on past behavior: A self-report index of habit strength. *Journal of Applied Social Psychology, 33*, 1313–1330.

# SECTION 3

## INTRODUCTION: WHAT SHAPES ATTITUDES?

Can you remember meeting other students for the first time during your first days at school, college, or university? Some of them may have smiled when you greeted them; others may have seemed indifferent or even a little insincere. As the initial weeks progressed, you may have found it easy to warm up to some people more than others: you ended up liking some and disliking others. We seem to form impressions of people almost instantly. We develop intuitions that some people are nice and others are not, and we then hear good things or bad things about them. These intuitions and information can merge to form relatively long-term attitudes, which easily jump into mind whenever we encounter the individuals.

The process of getting to know people provides an example of how attitudes are shaped and changed, and the chapters in this section describe theories and research that explain how we form and change attitudes more generally. To address these issues, the chapters build on differences in attitude content. In Chapter 2, we noted that most research has dealt with the three different types of content, which we called the taxi CAB of attitudes: *cognition*, *affect*, and *behavior*. Each type of content can be used to describe attitude formation and change.

Chapter 5 focuses on cognitive processes. We will see that the dominant models of attitude change have focused on how cognitions shape attitudes and that these models have been tested by a number of clever experiments. Chapter 6 focuses on affective processes. This chapter describes a diverse array of fascinating ways in which affect plays a role in attitude – effects that have each led to interesting speculations about how they occur. Chapter 7 focuses on behavioral processes. We will see that behavior has subtle, counterintuitive, and powerful effects on our attitudes and that these effects have led to major theories and programs of experiments to discover their origins. Chapter 8 rounds off the section by highlighting some basic principles that are common across the cognitive, affective, and behavioral processes that shape attitudes.

# 5

---

# COGNITIVE INFLUENCES ON ATTITUDES

---

## QUESTIONS TO PONDER

1. What motivates people to change their attitudes rather than stick with the ones they have?

2. What are the key factors for understanding the success or failure of persuasive messages?

3. How do the effects of messages depend on people's cognitive responses to them?

4. When are cognitive responses to message arguments important for attitude change?

5. Does a complete explanation of attitude change require more than one psychological process?

6. Do beliefs *about* one's own beliefs shape attitudes?

## PREVIEW

This chapter examines cognitive influences on attitudes. It does so by touring ideas and evidence across a number of cognitively focused theories of attitude change. These theories reveal the importance of understanding motivations to accept new beliefs about an attitude object, the stages through which we respond to persuasive information, the extent to which we think about persuasive information, differences in the types of information we consider, and our own beliefs about the types of information we are using. We will see how each of these variables has important consequences for how attitudes are shaped and changed.

# THE CLOSE CONNECTION BETWEEN BELIEFS AND ATTITUDES

Have you ever tried eggnog? This creamy beverage somehow manages to combine the flavors of nutmeg, cinnamon, vanilla, and custard, and it is very popular at Christmas in several countries. Some people like it a lot, but try asking someone what is in eggnog. The odds are that you will get a range of answers. Some people think it is a healthy egg drink, and others think it is an oil-based concoction that might kill you unless you exercise immediately afterward. (A lot of people just don't know if the beverage even contains eggs.) The person who thinks eggnog is a healthy egg drink probably likes it more than the person who thinks it is a horrible oil-based beverage, as long as there aren't stronger feelings (e.g., disgust at its taste) or behavioral experiences with the drink (e.g., working for the International Eggnog Producer Association). In other words, as we learned in the prior section, an individual's beliefs about eggnog's health value should help to predict their overall evaluation of the drink.

Beliefs may be even more important for attitudes toward a variety of important issues. For instance, people's attitudes toward car use can be influenced by their beliefs about climate change; people's attitudes toward different politicians may be based on their beliefs about a politician's integrity and intelligence; and people's attitudes toward the death penalty might be based on their beliefs about its fit with personal values. The wealth of important topics pertinent to people's beliefs may be the reason why scientists who study attitudes have been particularly focused on the role of beliefs.

Abundant research has studied the effects of cognitive information about an object on attitudes toward it. There are so many experiments that have taken this cognitive approach that major models of attitude change in general have concentrated on the role of cognitions in persuasion. These theories also can help to understand affective and behavioral influences, as we will show in subsequent chapters. At the same time, these later chapters will show that there are theories about affective and behavioral influences that have nonetheless included a focus on cognition (e.g., Cognitive Dissonance Theory). Thus, we think that the first step for understanding the impact of all types of information is to consider models of persuasion in the past century, which have focused on the role of cognitions.

Scientific research on persuasion is well summarized by eight models: the Yale Model of Persuasion (Hovland et al., 1953), the Information Processing Paradigm (McGuire, 1968), the Cognition-in-Persuasion Model (Albarracín, 2002), the Social Judgment Model (Sherif, 1980; Sherif & Sherif, 1967), the Elaboration Likelihood Model (Petty & Cacioppo, 1986), the Heuristic-Systematic Model (Chaiken et al., 1989), the Unimodel (Kruglanski, Fishbach, Erb, Pierro, & Mannetti, 2004), and the Meta-Cognitive Model (Briñol & Petty, 2009). This chapter looks at cognitive aspects of persuasion that are highlighted by these models, focusing on the models that have had the biggest impact so far.

# INCENTIVES TO CHANGE

No doubt, you have encountered people who seem totally unwilling to accept evidence that contradicts their views. You might think that this is some sign of their own dogmatism or even psychopathology, but this type of resistance is actually quite common. This may be why the first models of persuasion focused on understanding what types of factors would make people *motivated* to accept cognitive information about an object and change their attitude.

After leading research on the effects of war propaganda in World War II (Hovland, Lumsdaine, & Sheffield, 1949), Carl Hovland and his colleagues established the *Yale Communication Research Program*. This program was the first modern attempt to examine the factors that determine whether persuasive messages cause attitudes to change. In what became known as the Yale Model of Persuasion, Hovland et al. (1953) suggested that messages change people's attitudes by presenting an *incentive* for attitude change. For example, an advertisement might describe the utilitarian benefits of buying a particular model of mobile phone (e.g., inexpensive, large memory), or the ad might describe the social benefits of the phone (e.g., fashionable, sleek).

---

**Function Witch:** *Would you be persuaded by an ad saying that a mobile phone is inexpensive if you were actually after something glamorous (see Chapter 8)?*

---

Hovland and colleagues focused on how these incentives can be influenced by three factors identified in Lasswell's (1948) famous statement that, to understand the effect of a communication, we must know "*Who* says *what* in which channel to *whom* with what effect" (own italics; p. 37). Hovland et al.'s (1953) classic monograph, *Communication and Persuasion*, emphasized the importance of considering how the incentive for attitude change is influenced by the *source* of the persuasive communication (who), its *content* (what), and the *audience* (whom).

Each of these factors can vary in many ways. For instance, the source of a message might be an expert on the topic, physically attractive, trustworthy, high in status, or low on these attributes (among others). Would you be more persuaded by a message in favor of a new brand of toothpaste if it came from a famous, rich dentist who is attractive and looks trustworthy? The source could also be a group of friends, a government agency (e.g., in safe driving campaigns), a group of people from a political party, or anonymous. Would an argument in favor of a new tax policy be more compelling from a large political party than from a single politician? The source may also have a low or high vested interest: it may make a big difference whether one inadvertently overhears great things about Nike running shoes during a conversation between running enthusiasts, rather than hearing these things from a Nike salesperson.

At the same time, a message can be short, clear, strongly argued, and convey arguments on both sides of the issue, or the message can have the opposite characteristics. The context can include a large audience and beautiful weather, or it could be a simple one-on-one conversation in a downpour. At the same time, the people receiving the message might be happy, intelligent experts who are full of energy and enthusiasm, or they could be gloomy simpletons who don't understand the topic and are uninterested.

The Yale Model inspired researchers to look at these variables. It would take too long to describe the effects of all of these variables fully, but a couple of early examples merit mention. One well-known experiment found that participants evaluated articles from sources who are believable and trustworthy (e.g., a reputable journal) more favorably than articles from low-credibility sources (e.g., a politically biased columnist) across several topics (e.g., atomic submarines, steel shortage; see Hovland & Weiss, 1951). Another influential experiment (Janis & Feshbach, 1953) found that a message advocating frequent tooth-brushing was more effective if it elicited moderate fear about the effects of failures to brush (e.g., discoloration and decay) than if it gorily depicted severe effects (e.g., serious infection and death!). You will see other examples of simple source, message, context, and audience effects as we describe subsequent models of attitude change in this chapter. It's also worth noting that Robert Cialdini's (2008) wonderful text on tricks to persuasion offers numerous remarkable examples.

## KEY POINTS

- The effects of cognitive content can depend on whether a message presents powerful motives to change an attitude.
- Motives to change an attitude may be influenced by the source, content, audience, and mode of information presentation.

## PROCESSING STAGES

Hovland et al. (1953) also suggested that the effects of persuasion variables depend on a sequence of message processing stages. People must first *notice* and pay *attention* to the message, then *comprehend* it, and, finally, *accept* the message's conclusions. Incentives can influence attitudes at the acceptance stage, but only if people have actually paid attention to the message and understood it.

A brilliant critical thinker, William McGuire (1968), broke down these stages further. McGuire proposed that a successful message must be presented (presentation stage) and then draw attention (attention stage). Next, it must be understood (comprehension stage), and change the recipient's attitude (yielding stage). Finally, people must remember their new attitude at a later time (retention stage), so that the new attitude can actually influence their behavior (behavior stage).

McGuire's (1968) six stages make it seem that the chances of success for most persuasive messages are bleak. Consider the potential effects of a television advertisement attempting to sell a new brand of orange juice, using a cute cartoon character and a memorable slogan. Even if the advertisement's odds of passing each stage are good, the chances of it completing *all* of the stages may be low. For example, we might be optimistic and assume that the ad has a 70% chance of success at each stage. That is, 0.70 may be the probability of exposure, the probability of attention, the probability of comprehension, and so on. These probabilities must be multiplied to discover the odds of successfully completing all of the stages. This calculation would result in a probability of only 0.12 (0.7 x 0.7 x 0.7 x 0.7 x 0.7 x 0.7). In other words, the ad might have only a 12% chance of getting a person to buy the beverage. In the real world, however, many ads and products would compete for our attention (see Chapter 10). So the odds of completing each stage (especially yielding and behavior) may be far lower, creating much lower chances of success.

McGuire (1968) developed his ideas about these stages in a second way that is very important: he focused on the idea that a variable can have different effects on different stages during message processing. That is, one probability can be high while the other is low. For example, audiences with high self-esteem may have a higher chance of attending to a message and understanding it (e.g., due to greater confidence), but may feel less driven to agree with the message after it is understood. If these opposing effects occur, then the mathematics of McGuire's model suggest that self-esteem should produce curvilinear (U-shaped or inverted-U-shaped) effects on persuasion: persuasion may increase from low to moderate levels of self-esteem but then show little change from moderate to high levels. A meta-analytic review of past studies found modest evidence in support of this idea (Rhodes & Wood, 1992).

A more recent stage model is Dolores Albarracín's (2002) Cognition-in-Persuasion Model. In this model, people who receive a message start with their interpretation of a persuasive message and any other information (e.g., source characteristics, their own affect) that is available at the time. Their interpretation of the message cues the recall of relevant prior knowledge from memory, and then they identify, select, and use some of this information for the basis of their final attitude and subsequent behavior. This sequence brings us back to the kinds of curvilinear predictions offered by McGuire (1968). Curvilinear predictions arise from the Cognition-in-Persuasion Model because it suggests that decreases in motivation and ability affect people's chances of first identifying potential information and then selecting information on the basis of its relevance.

Unlike earlier stage models (e.g., McGuire, 1968), Albarracín's (2002) model posits that message processing can occasionally bypass early stages. This acknowledgment is important because of evidence that people can skip processing stages or use them in a different order. We come back to this point in Chapter 8, where we discuss unconscious influences on attitudes. For now, it is enough to say that the Cognition-in-Persuasion Model takes a step toward addressing the role of processing stages on attitude change. Time will tell whether this model yields enough new findings to make it more compelling than other successors to McGuire's model, which we describe in the next section of this chapter.

## KEY POINTS

- Information might influence people through six stages: presentation, attention, comprehension, attitude change, attitude retention, and behavior change. The odds of any single message passing through all six stages may be very low.

- Attitudes may also be shaped by a sequence of selecting, identifying, and integrating relevant information, and later processing stages may occur before earlier ones.

- Stage models predict that there can be curvilinear effects of variables on attitude change.

## COGNITIVE RESPONSES

A new perspective quickly emerged to tackle a crucial weakness evident in McGuire's stage model: it offered little information about *how* message acceptance would actually emerge. It simply predicted that messages should have a higher impact when the message is more likely to be processed, comprehended, and remembered, but this prediction does not make sense for obviously weak messages. If someone offers stupid arguments to convince you to change your attitude, then deeper processing, comprehension, and memory will surely not help to change your attitude. The attitude could even become *more* negative. (The Cognition-in-Persuasion Model is not prey to this weakness.) As such, in addition to considering *when* messages influence evaluations, researchers started to more comprehensively address *how* messages influence evaluations.

In a volume that marked a turning point for research on attitudes, Tony Greenwald (1968) argued that persuasion must be understood by considering people's *cognitive responses* (i.e., message-relevant thoughts) following a persuasive message. (This point had previously been made in different ways made by a number of scientists studying attitudes, but had not yet been outlined cogently.) According to Greenwald, these cognitive responses are a function of the beliefs that people have before receiving the message, the communication itself, and other factors outside of the message. Regardless of their origin, these cognitions should affect attitudes following the message. Put simply, the framework suggests that attitude change should be more likely among people who generate positive cognitive responses to the message than participants who generate negative responses to the message.

Tests of this reasoning began to emerge in the mid-to-late 1970s, when studies examined the role of cognitive responses by asking people to describe their thoughts about a message after reading or hearing it. These experiments found that people who listed more favorable cognitive responses expressed more agreement with the message (Brock, 1967; Osterhouse & Brock, 1970; Petty, Wells, & Brock, 1976). Later experiments found that subtle manipulations of people's thoughts about a persuasive message can shape the attitudes formed after the message (Killeya & Johnson, 1998). Thus, there is both correlational and experimental evidence supporting the importance of cognitive responses in shaping attitudes.

Based on this evidence, Martin Fishbein and Icek Ajzen (e.g., Fishbein & Ajzen, 1981) proposed the first major model to emphasize cognitive responses. Their Acceptance-Yielding-Impact Model nicely integrates their perspective on attitude–behavior effects with the stages of persuasion approach that was favored by the earlier investigators of attitude change. The model is based emphatically on the assumption that beliefs are an important basis of attitudes. If this is true, then messages should cause attitude change when they change the beliefs underlying people's attitudes, their evaluations of these beliefs, or both. As described in the previous chapter, many people refer to this model as a "belief X evaluation" perspective on attitudes.

Nonetheless, Fishbein and Ajzen (1981) argue that not *all* beliefs are important in determining attitudes. What are your attitudes toward the Canadian pop singer Justin Bieber? We might have many beliefs about him, but not all of them would be highly relevant to our attitudes. For example, the singer was criticized by some for hoping that Anne Frank would have been a fan (if she had not died from Nazi persecution). But this belief may hardly matter in determining the final attitude of one of the authors of this text, because this author knows that, although Justin Bieber's music isn't to his taste, (a) his daughters are huge fans, and (b) the musician has shown precocious talent. These beliefs are seen as more immediately come to mind, and, according to Fishbein and Ajzen, the beliefs that immediately come to mind when people are asked to describe an attitude are the ones that count. These are seen as being *modally salient* or *primary*. To change attitudes, we should change these salient, primary beliefs.

According to the Expectancy X Value perspective, belief change can occur by altering either the expectancies associated with the beliefs or the values associated with them. Few studies have attempted to test the effectiveness of attempts to change the evaluation component, perhaps because this may be difficult. For example, if we (the authors of this text) think that a particular music CD is expensive, it would be hard to convince us that "expensiveness" is a good thing. (We consider ourselves "cautious" consumers; our spouses prefer to say we are "cheap.") It could be much easier to convince us that the CD is not really expensive in the first place, perhaps using comparisons to other CD prices or to the CD's known market value.

Perhaps unsurprisingly, the few studies that have attempted to change evaluations have found little effect. Yet you can easily change beliefs, even for well-known truisms. For instance, if an expert tells you that tooth-brushing three times a day is now bad for you, you will probably believe him or her (McGuire & Papageorgis, 1961). It may be even easier to *add* beliefs. This addition is prompted when companies advertise new products. People may not know much about the features of the newest iPhone model, except that it looks sleek and colorful. Here, the advertiser can *form* people's beliefs about the product, rather than attempt to change beliefs. They can say that its new phone is twice as powerful as before and that it includes new capabilities (e.g., digital payment, voice command). These new pieces of information can add to prior beliefs about iPhones, creating a new total attitude.

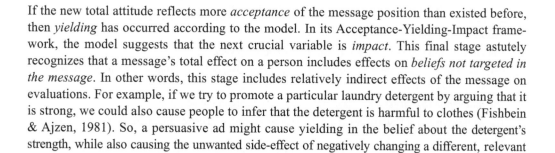

**Structure Witch:** *Does adding beliefs make it more likely that attitudes will assume a complex, ambivalent structure?*

If the new total attitude reflects more *acceptance* of the message position than existed before, then *yielding* has occurred according to the model. In its Acceptance-Yielding-Impact framework, the model suggests that the next crucial variable is *impact*. This final stage astutely recognizes that a message's total effect on a person includes effects on *beliefs not targeted in the message*. In other words, this stage includes relatively indirect effects of the message on evaluations. For example, if we try to promote a particular laundry detergent by arguing that it is strong, we could also cause people to infer that the detergent is harmful to clothes (Fishbein & Ajzen, 1981). So, a persuasive ad might cause yielding in the belief about the detergent's strength, while also causing the unwanted side-effect of negatively changing a different, relevant belief. Of course, this would be something to definitely avoid in a marketing campaign for the detergent!

## KEY POINTS

- Stage models cannot easily explain *how* attitude change occurs, especially in response to weak arguments.
- Cognitive responses to messages predict attitudes afterward, making these responses appear to be important potential precursors to persuasion.
- Attitude change is more likely when we change the modally salient, primary beliefs underlying an attitude.
- It may be easier to add beliefs about an object than to change them.
- The total impact of a message includes important effects on beliefs not targeted by the message.

# DIFFERENT PROCESSES: TO THINK OR NOT TO THINK

Despite the interesting insights offered by the Acceptance-Yielding-Impact Model, the most influential models to build on the cognitive response view are the Elaboration Likelihood Model (ELM; Petty & Cacioppo, 1986) and the Heuristic-Systematic Model (HSM; Chaiken et al., 1989). Their foundation is the idea that the role of cognitive responses to a message varies across people and situations – an idea that separates them from the Acceptance-Yielding-Impact framework. This section shows how this novel idea plays a vital role in both models and provides an important step for understanding attitude change.

## Basic assumptions

The core postulates of the Elaboration Likelihood Model are shown in Table 5.1. Two important postulates are its prediction that people's primary aim is to attain an accurate or correct attitude (Postulate 1) and that persuasion variables can act as arguments, cues, or factors that affect the

**Table 5.1**  *Postulates of the Elaboration Likelihood Model*

1.  People are motivated to hold correct attitudes.
2.  The amount and nature of issue-relevant elaboration can vary.
3.  Variables can affect attitudes by serving as arguments, cues, or factors that affect the nature and amount of elaboration.
4.  The motivation to process a message objectively elicits argument scrutiny.
5.  The motivation and ability to process arguments causes increased use of arguments and lower use of cues.
6.  Biased processing of a message leads to biased issue-relevant thoughts.
7.  Elaborate processing of a message causes new, strong attitudes.

nature and amount of elaboration of a persuasive message (Postulate 3). The assumption that variables can play multiple roles is relevant to understanding the effects of variables like mood and source expertise, as will become clearer in this chapter and the next one.

The core predictions of the Heuristic-Systematic Model are shown in Table 5.2. The Heuristic-Systematic Model (Chaiken et al., 1989; Chen & Chaiken, 1999) shares the Elaboration Likelihood Model's emphasis on motivation and ability as determinants of the depth of message processing. Like the Elaboration Likelihood Model, the Heuristic-Systematic Model proposes that people expend more effort to assess the quality of message arguments when the motivation and ability to process the message are high rather than when they are low, and this type of processing is labeled as "systematic." In addition, the Heuristic-Systematic Model predicts that people will be more likely to utilize simple persuasive cues, or heuristics, when the motivation and ability to process a message are low (Chaiken, 1987). Thus, both models share an emphasis on two distinctly different routes to persuasion and are consistent with the notion that people will be more greatly affected by less relevant persuasive information when their motivation and ability to be correct is low rather than high.

The strongest feature of these dual-process models is their use of *motivation* and *ability* as determinants of the way in which people process persuasive messages. This approach overlaps

**Table 5.2**   *Key Assumptions of the Heuristic-Systematic Model*

1. People may desire a *correct* attitude, an attitude that expresses their *values*, or an attitude that helps their *social image*.

2. *Heuristic processing* entails the retrieval and application of judgmental rules (e.g., experts can be trusted, consensus is correct), whereas *systematic processing* involves an analytic and thorough examination of attitude-relevant information.

3. According to the *least effort and sufficiency principles,* people use as much cognitive effort as is necessary and possible to reach their desired attitudinal goal (i.e., an accurate attitude, a value-expressive attitude, or an image-maintaining attitude), depending on their actual confidence that the desired attitudinal goal has been achieved while processing the information (relative to their desired level of confidence).

4. The *ability hypothesis* predicts that heuristic processing requires less cognitive effort than systematic processing.

5. The *additivity hypothesis* predicts that heuristic and systematic processing can co-occur and exert independent effects.

6. The *bias hypothesis* predicts that heuristic cues may influence attention, examination, and interpretation of information within systematic processing.

7. The *attenuation hypothesis* predicts that systematic processing will reduce use of heuristic processing when the judgments derived from systematic processing contradict conclusions from heuristic processing.

8. The *enhancement hypothesis* predicts that people will use more heuristic processing when they feel unable to perform systematic processing, but the desired level of confidence in their attitudinal goal remains high.

with abundant evidence of differences between shallow, quick processing and deeper, elaborate processing in research on basic cognitive processes (Craik, 2002; Craik & Lockhart, 1972; Moscowitz, Skurnik, & Galinsky, 1999). Put simply, if people are highly motivated and able to process a persuasive message, they should be heavily influenced by the strength of the arguments contained in a persuasive message.

The strength of the arguments influences attitudes by changing cognitive responses to the message (Petty & Cacioppo, 1986; Petty & Wegener, 1999; see Petty & Briñol, 2012, for a review). Strong arguments elicit positive cognitive responses, like "Good point – Right on!", whereas weak arguments elicit negative cognitive responses, like "What utter nonsense!" These cognitive responses, in turn, shape attitudes, causing more favorable attitudes when the cognitive responses are more positive, and less favorable attitudes when the cognitive responses are more negative. In short, high motivation and ability should cause strong arguments to influence attitudes more powerfully than weak arguments, in the same way that "My dog ate my homework" shouldn't be persuasive to a teacher who cares and is paying attention.

In contrast, if people are less motivated or able to process a message, they should be strongly affected by simple cues within the message. For example, people might be persuaded by a message because it is long and possesses many arguments (Petty & Cacioppo, 1984), or because the communicator looks trustworthy (Petty et al., 1981) or physically attractive (Chaiken, 1979). The common feature of these effects is that people do not need to process the message carefully in order to form their attitude: they can base their attitude on easy-to-use information (heuristics) without scrutinizing the content of the message.

The Elaboration Likelihood Model and Heuristic-Systematic Model both suggest that many variables influence motivation and ability. Motivation is high when people receiving the message have goals that are relevant to the message (Petty & Cacioppo, 1984) or when they have a personality that makes them enjoy effortful thinking (Cacioppo, Petty, Feinstein, & Jarvis, 1996). For instance, the person may be a student who wants to graduate with good grades, and the message may be presenting arguments in favor of a new exam, which may or may not be good for the student. In this case, there may seem to be a lot at stake in the issue, and it would be important to form an accurate, valid assessment of the message.

Both of these dual-process models also predict that ability is high when people are not distracted from the message (Petty et al., 1976) and when they possess all of the cognitive skills needed to understand it (Wood, Kallgren, & Preisler, 1985). To continue our example, the student receiving the message about the new exam might be asked to read the message while also listening to some distracting music, or the message may present complex statistics that the student has no hope of understanding. In these cases, ability to process the message would be reduced, and it would be difficult for the person to form an accurate, valid assessment of the exam.

Given these descriptions of the factors that affect motivation and ability, we can consider whether research has supported the models' shared assumption about the importance of motivation and ability as factors that shape reactions to messages. Many experiments have examined this assumption (see Petty & Briñol, 2012, for a recent review). Much of this research has focused on the effects of motivating message scrutiny by increasing the *personal relevance* of the message.

Richard Petty, John Cacioppo, and Rachel Goldman (1981) conducted one of the most elegant experimental examinations of the effects of personal relevance. Participants were undergraduate university students who were told that their university was re-evaluating its academic policies. They were told that the chancellor had asked several groups to prepare policy recommendations for broadcast on the campus radio station. Participants then heard a recording that advocated the implementation of new comprehensive examinations of students' knowledge in their area of specialization (e.g., psychology) before graduating. These proposed exams would be taken in addition to the exams already taken for each course.

The researchers then manipulated three variables. First, the personal relevance of this issue was manipulated by telling half of the participants that the new exams would be implemented in the next year (high relevance), whereas other participants were told that the exams would be implemented 10 years later (low relevance). Second, Petty and colleagues manipulated the expertise of the group recommending the new exam. Half of the participants in each personal relevance condition were told that the proposal was formed by the Carnegie Commission on Higher Education (high expertise), and the remaining participants were told that the proposal was formed by a class at a local high school (inexpert source). The third variable manipulated was the content of the exam message itself. This message contained either strong or weak arguments for the new exam. The strong arguments provided substantial, compelling statements, including evidence that the exams produced better scores on standardized achievement tests. In contrast, the weak arguments relied on specious anecdotes and little evidence. For example, they claimed that undergraduate students should take comprehensive exams in order to avoid irritating the *graduate* student union, because graduate students are forced to take the exams.

After reading the proposal, participants were asked to rate their attitude toward the comprehensive exams. Petty and Cacioppo's (1986) Elaboration Likelihood Model predicts that attitudes should be influenced by the strength of the message when the issue is personally relevant, whereas attitudes should be influenced by source expertise when the issue is made to seem irrelevant. These predictions were supported by the data, as shown in Figure 5.1.

In understanding these results, let's start by considering the way in which personal relevance influenced the impact of message strength on attitudes. When the issue was personally relevant, students who read the strong arguments became more favorable toward the exams than participants who read the weak arguments. Conversely, when the issue was of low relevance, students who read the strong arguments did not become more favorable toward the exams than participants who read the weak arguments.

In contrast, personal relevance affected the impact of source expertise in a completely different way. When the issue was personally relevant, the expertise of the people advocating the new exam did not affect attitudes toward it. However, when the issue was not personally relevant, the message caused more favorable attitudes when it came from the expert source than from the inexpert source.

Petty et al.'s (1981) pattern of data perfectly fit both the Elaboration Likelihood Model and the Heuristic-Systematic Model. Since this experiment, many other experiments have replicated this pattern in a variety of settings (Chen & Chaiken, 1999; Eagly & Chaiken, 1993; Perloff, 2003; Petty & Wegener, 1998a).

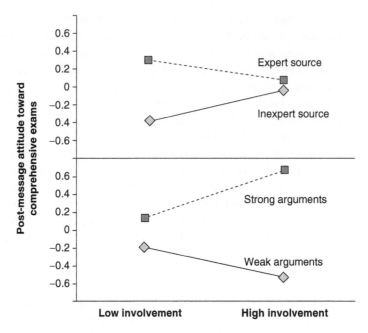

**Figure 5.1** *Effects of personal relevance, argument strength, and source expertise on attitudes (Petty et al., 1981)*

More recent evidence has shed more insight into *why* motivation and ability are important. Specifically, motivation and ability are important because thinking about a message is an effortful, energy- and time-consuming process. If thinking about a message is effortful, then we should be less likely to scrutinize a message when we are mentally fatigued from some prior task. For example, we might have been asked to cross out the letter "e" in an essay using a specific complex rule (only when another vowel follows or precedes two letters before) after having previously learned the habit of crossing out *all* instances of "e." Learning to override habits takes effort and weakens our subsequent ability for effortful mental tasks. Thus, if message scrutiny is effortful, it should be decreased by this type of task. Indeed, a study by Wheeler, Briñol, and Hermann (2007) predicted and found this effect.

## RESEARCH HIGHLIGHT 5.1

### DO WE BLINDLY FOLLOW TRUSTWORTHY ENDORSERS?

Companies often use credible sources to help sell their products. One component of credibility is trustworthiness – the degree to which a source is thought to be transmitting accurate and honest information. Does the trustworthiness of a communicator influence the extent to which a recipient scrutinizes the contents of an advertisement? This question was addressed in a series of experiments by Joseph Priester and Richard Petty (e.g., Priester & Petty, 1995, 2003). These researchers hypothesized that when a recipient is not highly motivated to elaborate on the content of an ad, they would be more likely to carefully scrutinize a message delivered from a low trustworthy source, because people would be sufficiently confident that a high trustworthy source was not trying to deceive them. From the perspective of the ELM Model, this suggests that argument quality should have a greater effect on recipients' attitudes when the message is delivered from a low (compared to high) trustworthy source.

In one study testing this hypothesis (see Priester & Petty, 2003), American undergraduate participants were presented with an ad for a supposedly new brand of roller blades. The product was endorsed by one of two rival American Olympic figure skaters – Nancy Kerrigan or Tonya Harding. Back in 1994 (when the research was conducted), Kerrigan was struck in the knee while getting ready to practice for the United States Figure Skating Championships. It turned out that acquaintances of Tonya Harding (including her ex-husband!) were implicated in the attack, and Harding herself pleaded guilty to hindering the police investigation into the attack. As a result of the incident, Kerrigan was perceived as a source high in trustworthiness, whereas Harding was perceived as a source low in trustworthiness.

In addition to manipulating source trustworthiness, the researchers also varied the quality of the arguments contained within the ad. Some participants read an appeal that contained strong arguments. This appeal noted that the roller blades were designed to fit any shape of foot, came in 12 exciting colors, and were rated Number 1 in safety in a consumer survey. In contrast, other participants read an appeal that contained weak arguments. This appeal noted that the roller blades were designed to fit very small and hard-to-fit feet, came in 12 shades of grey, and were rated Number 6 in safety in a consumer survey. After reading the appeal, participants indicated their attitude and cognitive responses about the product.

The results of the study were consistent with the authors' predictions. The argument quality effect was significantly greater when Tonya Harding was endorsing the roller blades compared to when Nancy Kerrigan was endorsing them. The researchers also found that the correlation between the favorability of participants' attitudes and cognitive responses was higher for the source low in trustworthiness than for the source high in trustworthiness. Taken together, the findings of this study suggest that greater scrutiny is allocated when a product endorser is low in trustworthiness.

Nonetheless, an interesting issue is whether message scrutiny causes attitudes to be affected *equally* by strengths and weaknesses in messages. Sometimes it seems that people are quick to seize on strong arguments that favor their view, while being quick to ignore weaknesses in arguments that support their view. The Elaboration Likelihood Model proposes that people can weigh the strengths or weaknesses more strongly when any of several "biasing" factors are present. Similarly, the

Heuristic-Systematic Model's "bias" hypothesis indicates that heuristic processing can affect the nature of people's reactions to message content. Evidence fits both views. For instance, factors like prior knowledge about a topic and source expertise can cause people to emphasize the strengths or weaknesses in a message more strongly (e.g., Chaiken & Maheswaran, 1994; Clark, Wegener, Habashi, & Evans, 2012; Wood et al., 1985).

Another common feature of the Elaboration Likelihood Model and the Heuristic-Systematic Model is that they both permit multiple roles for variables in the persuasion context. According to the Elaboration Likelihood Model, the role that any variable takes depends on the likelihood of elaboration (which is determined by motivation and ability). For example, the level of expertise of a message source should (1) act as a cue when thinking is low, (2) be scrutinized as an argument when thinking is high, and (3) affect the amount of thinking when elaboration is not already determined by other variables (Heesacker, Petty, & Cacioppo, 1983). Similarly, the Heuristic-Systematic Model allows for cues such as expertise to act as a heuristic, a biasing factor, or as a partial trigger for more processing (when they contradict the gist of a message; see Chaiken & Maheswaran, 1994).

The shared emphasis of both theories provides remarkable testimony to the gains that have been made in understanding how attitudes are shaped. The fact that major explanations agree on key principles suggests that we are closer to understanding basic "laws" in how attitudes change. Nonetheless, the similarities between the theories might make you wonder what should influence your preference for one or the other. One important criterion is *parsimony*: Which model offers the simplest explanation of the data? Another criterion is *power*: Which model explains a wider range of effects? Rather than advocate particular answers, we recommend that readers form their own views on these questions. It may help to consider some of the differences between the models, below.

## Different perspectives

The shared assumptions described above are just the beginning for understanding the Elaboration Likelihood Model and the Heuristic-Systematic Model. There are several unique features of each model that have attracted the most attention so far. First, while the Elaboration Likelihood Model focuses on the motivation to attain correct attitudes, the Heuristic-Systematic Model predicts that people can be motivated to attain a *correct* attitude, an attitude that is *socially desirable*, or an attitude that expresses *personal identity and values*. As you might have noticed, these three motives largely reflect the knowledge, social-adjustive, and value-expressive functions described in Chapter 2. The Heuristic-Systematic Model suggests that the motives to achieve a socially acceptable attitude and a value-expressive attitude elicit more biased thinking about a message than the accuracy motive, and this hypothesis has been supported by several experiments (Johnson & Eagly, 1989; Johnson, Lin, Symons, Campbell, & Ekstein, 1995). This multiple motive approach also fits abundant research suggesting that social behaviors in general serve numerous motives (Chaiken, Duckworth, & Darke, 1999; Maio & Olson, 2000c). Nevertheless, advocates of the Elaboration Likelihood Model argue that the alleged effects of these motives on persuasion can be explained by flaws in past studies, causing the multiple-motive hypothesis to remain somewhat controversial (Petty & Cacioppo, 1990; cf. Johnson & Eagly, 1990).

Another difference between the models is the Elaboration Likelihood Model's greater attention to the strength of the attitudes that participants form after receiving a persuasive message (Petty & Briñol, 2012; Petty & Cacioppo, 1986; Petty & Wegener, 1999). This issue is particularly interesting because it is intuitively plausible that people sometimes form very weak unimportant attitudes after hearing a message, while forming very strong opinions on other occasions. Because the stronger attitudes should have a greater influence on relevant judgments and behaviors (Krosnick & Petty, 1995; see Chapter 3), it is important to discern when the post-message attitudes will be strong or weak. According to the Elaboration Likelihood Model, persuasion in the more elaborate, central route occurs through its impact on cognitive responses to the message content (Petty & Cacioppo, 1986; Petty & Wegener, 1999). The bases of the post-message attitude in elaborate cognitive responses should make them stronger than if the attitudes would have been formed through the peripheral route, because links to *many* cognitive beliefs help attitudes withstand persuasive attack and predict behavior (Petty et al., 1995).

Third, the models differ in how they describe the variables that influence attitudes when motivation and ability to process information are low. The Elaboration Likelihood Model proposes that a variety of psychological processes can influence persuasion in the low elaboration route. Some of these processes involve effects of emotion (e.g., mood, emotional conditioning) and behavior (e.g., self-perception). In contrast, the Heuristic-Systematic Model focuses on heuristic "rules of thumb," which work as "if–then" rules and guides. Examples of such heuristics are "If a communicator is an expert, then he or she is likely to be correct," and "If most people say so, it must be right." However, can most of the processes in the low elaboration route of the Elaboration Likelihood Model be restated *as* heuristic rules? This question is worth pondering as you learn more about affective and behavioral influences on attitudes in the next chapters.

Fourth, the Heuristic-Systematic Model's additivity hypothesis may distinguish the two models by suggesting that personal relevance should not *always* lead to lower use of cues, such as whether the model for a new hair spray looks stunning or ordinary (see the enhancement hypothesis in Table 5.2). The reason is that even a lot of processing will not always be enough to attain confidence that the desired (e.g., accurate) attitude has been reached. For example, imagine that a model speaking for a shampoo says contradictory things about it: "My husband doesn't like the smell when I apply it, but what does he matter when it leaves my hair this beautiful!" No amount of thought about this message will make you confident that, yes, this shampoo is wonderful (see Reich & Tormala, 2013). Confidence may build only after noticing that the model's hair *is* gorgeous, while optimistically believing that this is due to the product – because why would advertisers lie?! Experiments have found that high-status sources are more influential when a message is difficult to comprehend (Hafer, Reynolds, & Obertynski, 1996). When these effects are not driven by changes in thoughts about the message, then they are more supportive of the Heuristic-Systematic Model than the Elaboration Likelihood Model (see Research Highlight 5.2).

## RESEARCH HIGHLIGHT 5.2

## DOES THE TYPE OF MESSAGE MATTER?

Shelley Chaiken and Durairaj Maheswaran (1994) conducted an ambitious experiment testing whether cues might be used in conditions of high personal relevance. As part of an ostensible consumer survey, participants in this experiment were given information about a new product – the XT-100 telephone answering machine. The machine was made to seem personally relevant to some participants, by telling them that their attitudes would be an important guide for the decision to market the product in their area. In contrast, other participants were told that their attitudes would be a minor guide for the decision to market the product in a distant region. Chaiken and Maheswaran also manipulated the credibility of the information about this product. In the high credibility condition, participants read a description of the product that allegedly came from *Consumer Reports* magazine, a well-known assessor of consumer products. In the low credibility condition, participants read a description that merely came from a small department store's promotional pamphlet. Participants then read a description that supported the product strongly, weakly, or neither strongly nor weakly. The addition of the mixed message was the key novel feature of their design. For this message, systematic processing should not help people to become confident in their attitude; people may have no choice but to also consider the credibility of the source.

Chaiken and Maheswaran's results were provocative. The effects of personal relevance on use of source credibility and argument strength were identical to those obtained in past tests of the Elaboration Likelihood Model when using clearly strong and weak arguments. For these arguments, when the topic was of low personal relevance, participants' attitudes toward the XT-100 were more positive following the highly credible source than the less credible source, while the strength of the message had no impact. In contrast, when the topic was of high personal relevance, participants were more persuaded by the stronger arguments and source credibility had no impact.

The effects of source credibility in the high relevance condition were different when the message was mixed, however. In this condition, the high credibility source led to more positive attitudes than the low credibility source when the issue was personally relevant. Of interest, this effect was partly driven by a change in thoughts about the message. As predicted by the Heuristic-Systematic Model and the Elaboration Likelihood Model, participants' thoughts about the message were more positive when the source was higher in credibility. This change in thoughts correlated with the similar change in attitudes, indicating that source credibility biased participants' thinking. At the same time, however, source credibility also affected attitudes *independently* of this change in thoughts. This independent effect fits the Heuristic-Systematic Model's prediction that people can use heuristics per se under high relevance conditions, particularly when deep thought alone cannot yield a confident attitude (Table 5.2).

# ONE PROCESS OR TWO?

The dual-process models converge with a lot of evidence of differences between shallow, quick processing and deeper, elaborate processing in basic cognitive tasks (Craik, 2002; Craik & Lockhart, 1972; Moscowitz et al., 1999). Ironically, however, this joint asset has become a focus of debate when understanding persuasion. An influential and integrative thinker in the study of social cognition, Arie Kruglanski, has questioned whether this difference in processing needs to be modeled using two distinct routes to persuasion. He and his colleagues proposed that persuasion involves a *single* process (Kruglanski & Thompson, 1999; Thompson, Kruglanski, & Spiegel, 2000; for a more general perspective, see Kruglanski, 2013; Kruglanski & Gigerenzer, 2011). The idea is that *any* information that is relevant to the attitude judgment can be used as compelling evidence to form an attitude, even when the information is a so-called cue. For instance, if an anti-abortion message told you that a fetus suffers during an abortion at 20 weeks, then it would be reasonable to believe the content more strongly if it came from a widely acknowledged expert on fetal development than if it came from a priest with no medical knowledge. The source of the information is relevant as its own argument, because you have no independent way of assessing the validity of the message. Thus, Kruglanski suggests that there is no *fundamental* difference between a cue and message content.

Kruglanski suggests that past studies testing the dual-process models presented the "cues" early and briefly in the messages. In contrast, the message arguments appeared later, were longer, and more complex. As a result, people did not need to think a lot to understand and use the cues in these experiments, but they did need higher levels of processing to understand and use the message arguments. According to Kruglanski, the apparent differences between cues and arguments should disappear when cues are made more complex and the arguments are made simple. For example, source expertise can be presented in a complex way through a lengthy résumé of the message source. This format would require a high level of attention in order for the résumé to be understood and used as a "cue."

An impressive number of experiments have supported this perspective (Pierro, Mannetti, Kruglanski, & Sleeth-Keppler, 2004; Thompson et al., 2000). Nonetheless, it remains a matter of debate whether this perspective is truly incompatible with the dual-process models (Chaiken et al., 1999; Petty, Wheeler, & Bizer, 1999). One argument against its validity is that prior experiments have found differences between message cues and message content even when the cue is bound up *with* the arguments. For instance, people are more persuaded by nine weak arguments than by three weak arguments when the motivation to process is low (Petty & Cacioppo, 1984). An argument against its divergence from the dual-process models is that the dual-process models explicitly state that any variable can serve multiple roles depending on how it is processed (e.g., as a cue under low relevance conditions or as an argument under high relevance conditions). More is said about this debate in special issues of the journal *Psychological Inquiry* (Vol. 10, 1999) and the journal *Perspectives on Psychological Science* (Vol. 8, 2013); they are engaging reading for anyone interested in a deeper understanding of the dual-process versus single-process models and views on them.

## KEY POINTS

- Dual-process models predict that the effects of persuasive information depend on the motivation and ability to scrutinize the information.

- Lower motivation and ability cause cues or heuristics to exert a greater effect on attitudes, whereas high motivation and ability cause message content to exert a greater effect.

- Complex information may increase reliance on cues even when personal relevance is high.

- Cues and message arguments may have similar effects if they are made equally relevant and easy to process.

# META-COGNITIONS

The success of the dual-process models shows how a lot has been gained by focusing on cognitive responses to messages. In some ways, however, these models may not yet have fully appreciated the role of cognitive responses. They have focused on the number and valence of cognitive responses to a message, but people also *think* about their thoughts. In psychology, "thoughts about thoughts" are called *meta-cognitions*. The Meta-Cognitive Model was developed to describe the role of these meta-cognitions in attitude formation and change (see, e.g., Petty & Briñol, 2006; Petty et al., 2007). By tackling this issue, the model helps to address one fascinating question about the effects of persuasive interventions: When an attitude is changed, does the old attitude disappear completely or does some trace of it remain?

The Meta-Cognitive Model proposes that a persuasive intervention can (1) introduce a *new* evaluative association with the attitude object, or (2) try to re-shape an *old* association. For example, a film critic might try to convince us that Disney films have included child role models who are too disrespectful of others. Before hearing this argument, we might have generally enjoyed Disney films, as shown in the upper panel of Figure 5.2. If we receive the new argument about child role models, it suddenly *adds* a negative perspective that was not there before. This addition could change attitudes, as specified in the earlier Acceptance-Yielding-Impact Model, but is that its only effect?

According to the Meta-Cognitive Model, a crucial consideration is what happens next with the added information. In one case, we might scrutinize the researcher's evidence and conclude that we disagree with it. In this instance, we may be left with an attitude that is still connected in memory with the new negative idea, because we still *remember* the researcher's argument. At the same time, we may add a "tag" to the memory, indicating that this negative idea is invalid. This tag is shown in the middle panel of Figure 5.2. We would be left with the negative evaluative association (idea) and a tag warning us not to believe the negative association. Alternatively, we might *not* critically evaluate this new idea because we are uninterested in the topic or distracted. In this case, we would form the new association without the negative tag (see Figure 5.2, lower panel).

This process is interesting because it may cause us to experience ambivalence due to the offsetting positive and negative associations with the issue. When new information is added but *not* believed, the ambivalence remains at the level of our memory's quick associations with the attitude object, but is negated by the tag when it is consciously recalled. In this situation, the

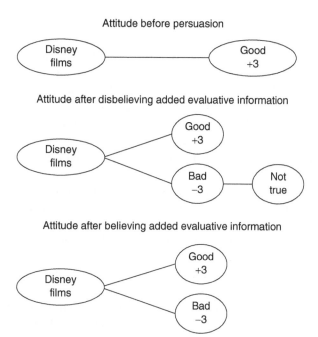

Attitude before persuasion

Attitude after disbelieving added evaluative information

Attitude after believing added evaluative information

**Figure 5.2** *The Meta-Cognitive Model's predictions for responses after receiving novel negative information about an attitude object*

attitude may appear unchanged at a conscious level, because people can retrieve the warning label that they attached to their memory of the new argument. At a nonconscious level, however, the attitude would look decidedly ambivalent. In this case, the old attitude appears using explicit measures, while the new one appears using implicit measures. In contrast, when the new information is added *and* believed, an ambivalent attitude should appear using both types of measure.

Several elegant experiments have tested and supported this model (e.g., Petty, Tormala, Briñol, & Jarvis, 2006). In one of these experiments, students at the Universidad Autónoma de Madrid were given information about the personality traits possessed by two fictitious people, José Luis Martin and Juan Antonio Perez. For each student, either José Luis or Juan Antonio was described positively, while the other was described negatively. Next, some participants were told something like "Wait, your beliefs about these people are wrong!" (p. 32):

"Our apologies … We recently discovered that due to errors in copying the information, the files describing Juan Antonio Perez and José Luis Martin were transposed. That is, the information you just read about these individuals was reversed, so you received incorrect information for each person. As a result, what you just learned about them needs to be reversed. Everything you learned about Juan is, in fact, the information about José. Conversely, everything you learned about José actually corresponds to Juan."

According to the Meta-Cognitive Model, this information should cause people to correct their judgments and consciously form more positive attitudes toward the person who should have been paired with the positive information. The researchers found that the participants did indeed form the correct judgments after the apology, using an explicit measure of attitudes.

More important, the Meta-Cognitive Model also predicts that the participants should show evidence of conflict at the nonconscious level, because they still remember the trait information about each person, even though they have attached an invalidity tag to it. Thus, using implicit measures, there should be evidence of some degree of conflict between the recalled information and the invalidity tag. This is exactly what the researchers found using an implicit measure of this ambivalence.

These results provide only a glimpse of the potential role of meta-cognitions. The Meta-Cognitive Model also makes predictions for the effects of messages that attempt to change our pre-existing beliefs (e.g., if we receive an argument that instead tries to contradict our prior belief that Disney films are highly entertaining) and, in general, it allows for a role of meta-cognitions any time something affects our confidence in our thoughts. In subsequent chapters, we will consider many variables that can influence thought confidence, including mood and body actions (e.g., Chapter 9). More generally, researchers have considered the role of meta-cognitive processes across a number of domains relevant to evaluation, such as minority influence processes and message framing (Rucker, Petty, & Briñol, 2008; Tormala, DeSensi, & Petty, 2007). Researchers have also started to apply neuroscientific approaches to the study of meta-cognition (Luttrell, Briñol, Petty, Cunningham, & Diaz, 2013).

## KEY POINTS

- A persuasive intervention can (1) introduce a *new* evaluative association with the attitude object, or (2) try to re-shape an *old* association.

- Persuasive information can have different effects on explicit and implicit measures of attitude: explicit measures of attitude can tap information about an object that is present and believed, whereas implicit measures tap information that is present but may or may not be believed.

## WHAT WE HAVE LEARNED

- Attitudes are influenced by the information we have about an attitude object's attributes and properties.

- Reactions to message information depend on the source of the message, the content of the message, the audience, the context of the message, and the way in which it is delivered.

- Theories that emphasize an information processing sequence show how persuasive messages can potentially have very little impact; it may be difficult to engineer a message that is successful at all stages.

- People's cognitive reactions to persuasive information are vital determinants of their subsequent attitudes.

- Cognitive responses to persuasive information are more likely to shape attitudes when people are motivated and able to process the information.

- There is debate about whether two qualitatively different psychological processes are required to predict attitude change.

- Attitudes can be influenced by meta-cognitions: beliefs about one's beliefs.

## WHAT DO YOU THINK?

- The Elaboration-Likelihood Model and the Heuristic-Systematic Model both note occasions when source and context information will not be confined to their lower processing routes (Chaiken et al., 1999; Petty et al., 1999). The Elaboration Likelihood Model's third postulate predicts that there will be times when a variable that would normally act as a cue instead acts as an argument. For example, the attractiveness of a spokesmodel's hair is relevant to her claims about the shampoo that she promotes. Also, the Heuristic-Systematic Model describes cases when a cue will be used in high processing conditions. However, Kruglanski et al. (2004) propose that the Unimodel offers a simpler explanation of these effects. Is this true?

- We have described how manipulations of the personal relevance of an issue have been repeatedly used to manipulate the motivation to form a correct attitude. It is important to note its ability to activate quite diverse motives. Any need that is strong and salient for the individual could be activated by personal relevance, and research on personality and social processes has identified a plethora of such needs (Murray, 1938). Personal relevance may also have a strong effect on basic self-motives, such as needs to protect self-esteem, assess the self accurately, verify self-conceptions, and improve the self (Sedikides & Strube, 1997). Does personal relevance activate different motives for different people?

## KEY TERMS

*Acceptance-Yielding Impact Model* – a framework stating that messages should cause attitude change when they change the beliefs underlying people's attitudes, their evaluations of these beliefs, or both.

*Beliefs* – thoughts or attributes associated with an attitude object.

*Central route* – attitude change that occurs through its impact on cognitive responses to the message content.

*Cognition-in-Persuasion Model* – a stage model stating that interpretation of a message cues the recall of relevant knowledge, which is used to determine our evaluation.

*Elaboration Likelihood Model* – a dual-process model that distinguishes between central and peripheral routes to attitude change.

*Heuristic processing* – the use of simple judgmental rules.

*Heuristic-Systematic Model* – a dual-process model that distinguishes between heuristic and systematic routes to attitude change.

*Information Processing Paradigm* – A model proposing that a message must navigate a series of stages to elicit attitude change.

*Meta-Cognitive Model* – a model that considers how "thoughts about thoughts" influence persuasion.

*Peripheral route* – attitude change that occurs by considering simple characteristics of a message.

*Salient beliefs* – the beliefs that immediately come to mind when people are asked to describe beliefs that are relevant to their attitude.

*Social Judgment Model* – a model in which individuals weigh new information and compare it to their attitude.

*Systematic processing* – analytic and thorough examination of attitude-relevant information.

*Unimodel* – a single-process model of persuasion.

*Yale Model of Persuasion* – a program of research that examined the factors that determine when persuasive messages cause attitudes to change.

# FURTHER READING

## BASIC

Chaiken, S., Duckworth, K. L. and Darke, P. (1999) When parsimony fails . . . *Psychological Inquiry, 10,* 118–123.

Kruglanski, A. W. (2013) Only one? The default interventionist perspective as a unimodel: Commentary on Evans and Stanovich. *Perspectives on Psychological Science, 8,* 242–247.

Petty, R. E. and Briñol, P. (2012) The Elaboration Likelihood Model. In P. A. M. Van Lange, A. Kruglanski and E. T. Higgins (eds), *Handbook of Theories of Social Psychology* (Vol. 1, pp. 224–245). London: SAGE.

## APPLIED

Bradley, S. D., III and Meeds, R. (2004) The effects of sentence-level context, prior word knowledge, and need for cognition on information processing of technical language in print ads. *Journal of Consumer Psychology, 14,* 291–302.

Clark, J. K., Wegener, D. T., Habashi, M. M. and Evans, A. T. (2012) Source expertise and per-suasion: The effects of perceived opposition or support on message scrutiny. *Personality and Social Psychology Bulletin, 38,* 90–100.

Kumkale, G. T., Albarracín, D. and Seignourel, P. J. (2010) The effects of source credibility in the presence or absence of prior attitudes: Implications for the design of persuasive communica-tion campaigns. *Journal of Applied Social Psychology, 40,* 1325–1356.

Werner, C. M., Stoll, R. B., Birch, P. and White, P. H. (2002) Clinical validation and cognitive elaboration: Signs that encourage sustained recycling. *Basic and Applied Social Psychology, 24,* 185–203.

# 6

---

# AFFECTIVE INFLUENCES ON ATTITUDES

---

## QUESTIONS TO PONDER

1. What are some affective, emotional influences on attitudes?

2. What types of affect influence people most strongly when they are forming attitudes in a new environment?

3. What is the "mere exposure effect" and what does it potentially mean for our attitudes toward other individuals and groups?

4. What are some ways in which attitudes are shaped by emotion learning processes?

5. How does mood affect our attitudes?

6. How does emotion affect the way we process information?

## PREVIEW

This chapter examines a variety of ways in which affect shapes attitudes. After considering the influence of merely exposing people to attitude objects, *without* any direct affective information, this chapter will show how attitudes can be shaped by affective information in the presence of an attitude object (exposure conditioning), relevant behavior (behavior conditioning), or role model (observational conditioning). The second half of the chapter will examine diverse roles of affect in people's use of persuasive information, showing how current mood can act in different ways to shape attitudes. Interesting implications of this evidence for understanding the effects of fear-eliciting messages will also be considered.

# THE CLOSE CONNECTION BETWEEN FEELING AND ATTITUDES

"Feelings, woo-o-o feelings; woo-o o feelings, for all my life" (Morris Albert, "Feelings," 1975)

Emotion is a major part of everyday life. On a daily basis, we experience different emotions in response to everything from popular (or unpopular, depending on your tastes!) songs by Morris Albert to things that other people do or say. Musicians, poets, and writers go to great effort to sway our emotions, and we all love to be in a good mood.

The persuasiveness and power of emotion is pervasive. Both of us are parents. We both noticed that from an early age our children were wary of approaching us with requests (Daddy, can I stay up extra late to watch a movie?) when they perceived that we might be in a bad mood (which is pretty rare!). They seemed to understand that we are likely to dislike *anything* at that moment in time and that they would be better off waiting for the negative mood to change. Even from an age when they couldn't tie their shoe laces, they had grasped that people in a good mood seem easier to persuade than people in a bad one.

In this chapter, we will show that emotion influences attitudes in a variety of ways. Some of these influences are subtle and indirect, whereas others are more powerful and direct. This variety is useful, but it also makes it difficult for researchers to integrate the research in single models. Unlike the research on cognitive factors described in Chapter 5, there is no clear lineage of models encompassing the diverse effects of emotion that we describe in this chapter. As a result, this chapter is more like a fan-shaped set of ideas with a common emphasis than a single line of developments.

## EXPOSURE

Early studies of friendship revealed that physical proximity to another person makes it more likely that we will like them (Bossard, 1932; Festinger, 1951; Festinger, Schachter, & Back, 1950). It was thought that this effect may occur because proximity encourages *positive* interactions with others (Newcomb, 1956). But we all encounter some things or people frequently, without any strong positive or negative experience of them. They might be food items you always see in the supermarket or the newspaper vendor you pass on the way to work each day. Does such mere familiarity breed contempt or does it encourage affection?

## The original evidence: Turkish words, Chinese ideographs, and human faces

In a landmark paper, Robert Zajonc (1968) suggested that mere exposure to a stimulus may be sufficient, even without direct interaction, to evoke a positive attitude. In theory, this *mere exposure effect* occurs when repeated, simple exposure to an object leads to more favorable feelings toward it. For example, an abstract painting that initially evokes no reaction might become liked over time.

Zajonc (1968) conducted several clever experiments to demonstrate the mere exposure effect. In these experiments, participants were exposed to sets of novel foreign words (Experiment 1), Chinese ideographs (Experiment 2), or human faces (Experiment 3). Each stimulus was shown 0, 1, 2, 5, 10, or 25 times. Participants then evaluated each stimulus using a good–bad scale. Analyses of these ratings revealed that participants formed more positive evaluations of the stimuli that they had been shown more frequently. The effect of repeated exposure diminished somewhat at higher exposure levels (e.g., 10 vs. 25), but the overall effect was powerful. It is also remarkable that the effect occurred across diverse stimuli. Since Zajonc's landmark study, the mere exposure effect has been found for many types of attitude object, including colors, nations, cities, food, flavors, share purchases, academic journal evaluations, and geometric figures; in addition, the effects have been shown among nationals of many countries, amnesiacs, new-born babies, and even ducklings (see Huberman, 2001; Moreland & Topolinski, 2010; Murphy, Monahan, & Zajonc, 1995; Serenko & Bontis, 2011). European readers will be interested to know that mere exposure has even been shown to influence voting preferences in the Eurovision Song Contest (Verrier, 2012)!

Richard Moreland and Scott Beach (1992) provided a particularly interesting application of the mere exposure effect. These scientists arranged to have four women of similar appearance attend a class of 130 students at the University of Pittsburgh. These women did not interact with any of the students, and attended the class 0, 5, 10, or 15 times. At the end of term, the students were shown pictures of each woman and rated them on a series of trait dimensions (e.g., interesting vs. boring, unattractive vs. attractive, unselfish vs. selfish, warm vs. cold). In addition, participants rated the probability that they would like the woman and become friends with her, enjoy spending time with her, and work with her on a collaborative project. As can be seen in Figure 6.1, even despite the lack of interaction with the four individuals, the students more strongly liked the women whom they had seen more often. This is interesting evidence about the interpersonal, "real world" implications of repeated exposure.

At one level, these findings might seem a bit counter-intuitive, because it may be hard to imagine it working when people repeatedly see someone or something they *dislike*. Brickman, Redfield, Harrison, and Crandall (1972) tested whether an individual's initial attitude matters when it comes to repeated exposure. These researchers measured participants' attitudes toward 20 abstract paintings and then varied the number of times that participants subsequently viewed four of the paintings that they liked, disliked, or neither liked nor disliked. Participants then rated their attitudes toward the four paintings after the exposure manipulation. Analyses of these ratings revealed that attitudes were more positive after frequent exposures to the paintings that were affectively neutral or positive than after infrequent exposures to the paintings. In other words, the mere exposure effect was replicated for the neutral and liked stimuli. In contrast, following exposure to the disliked paintings, participants tended to exhibit *lower* liking of the disliked paintings after high exposure to them than after low exposure to them. This result and similar evidence for negative effects of exposure to objects with negative meaning (Perlman & Oskamp, 1971) suggest that mere exposure may have quite different effects when trying to change an existing attitude than when trying to shape a new attitude. Unfortunately, however, there is no firm consensus on this issue, because of evidence that mere exposure can also facilitate increased liking for disliked objects (e.g., snakes; Litvak, 1969). At present, it seems safest to conclude that the effect can occur for liked and disliked objects, though it may be weaker for disliked ones.

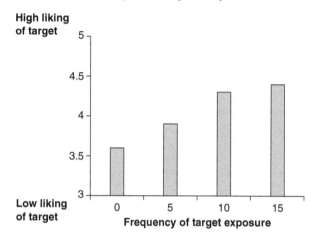

**Figure 6.1**   *The effects of differential exposure on liking toward a female confederate (Moreland & Beach, 1992)*

The mere exposure effect also has interesting implications for the processing of persuasive messages. Weisbuch, Mackie, and Garcia-Marques (2003) obtained provocative evidence that mere exposure to the source of a persuasive message increases agreement with the message, but only when people are not made aware of their prior exposure. In their experiments, participants received a 200-word essay in favor of tax hikes to repair roads. The (alleged) author of the message was shown in a small photograph in the upper left corner of the essay. Before reading the essay, participants' prior exposure to this photo was manipulated. Some participants saw the individual in a series of photos for another experimental task; other participants were subliminally exposed to the individual (interspersed among the others), and a third group of participants were never shown the photo beforehand. Analyses of participants' attitudes following the essay indicated greater agreement when the source was shown previously. However, after having seen the photo consciously, this effect was eliminated if participants were asked whether they had seen a photo of the author (prior to rating their attitudes); subliminal prior exposure continued to cause more agreement with the message even after answering this question.

## How mere exposure works: familiarity and boredom

It turns out that the effect of mere exposure depends on several factors. For instance, the effect is strongest when the stimuli are complex, presented a limited number of times (and for short durations), when the presentation and evaluation of stimuli are completed in the same context, and when stimulus presentation includes both repeated and non-repeated stimuli (see Bornstein, 1989; de Zilva, Mitchell, & Newell, 2013; Dechêne, Stahl, Hansen, & Wänke, 2009). Perhaps not surprisingly, these types of findings have led to many explanations for the effect, with one investigator concluding that "a parsimonious explanation for this phenomenon is lacking" (Lee, 2001).

The best-known early explanation for mere exposure effects is the two-factor model (Berlyne, 1966, 1970; Stang, 1974a, 1974b; see Figure 6.2). The first factor, *habituation*, arises from an instinctive tendency to perceive new stimuli as threatening. Consequently, new stimuli automatically elicit a negative affective reaction. After repeated exposure, however, habituation occurs; that is, people get used to the stimulus. Habituation makes the stimulus seem less threatening, and affective reactions to it become more positive. Thus, habituation to "threatening" novel stimuli may help create the mere exposure effect.

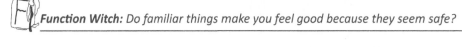

**Function Witch:** *Do familiar things make you feel good because they seem safe?*

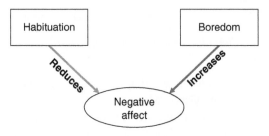

**Figure 6.2**   *Two-Factor Model of Exposure Effects (Berlyne, 1970)*

The second factor is *boredom*. Over time, people can become bored with the stimulus. As a result, its repeated presentation begins to cause a *negative* affective reaction. This boredom should be more likely to arise when stimuli are simple, presented many times, isolated from other stimuli, and presented for long durations. Thus, boredom may explain the negative impact of these factors, as discovered in Bornstein's review.

This model fits evidence that people who score higher on a measure of "boredom proneness" are less likely to show an exposure effect (Bornstein, Kale, & Cornell, 1990). The model also fits evidence that the mere exposure effect is evident only among people who are low in tolerance for ambiguity (Crandall, 1968). High tolerance of ambiguity involves being accepting of things that are unknown or unclear. Thus, high tolerance of ambiguity should make *novel* stimuli less threatening, and the moderating effect of this variable fits the suggestion that habituation drives the mere exposure effect.

Nonetheless, the model does not easily fit other evidence relevant to the habituation factor. If habituation occurs, then mere exposure effects should be stronger when people become more familiar with the stimulus and more able to recognize it. Yet many studies have found mere exposure effects using subliminal presentation procedures that prevent participants from consciously seeing the stimulus (Bornstein, Leone, & Galley, 1987; Kunst-Wilson & Zajonc, 1980). Participants in these studies are shown the stimuli very quickly, perhaps in peripheral areas of vision, and with subsequent pattern masks that make it difficult to consciously detect the stimuli. Despite being unable to recall seeing these subliminal stimuli, participants report liking them more than subliminal stimuli that they have seen less frequently. In fact, some studies using subliminal stimuli show the largest effects (cf. Lee, 2001).

## How mere exposure works: conscious and nonconscious habituation

The evidence for subliminal mere exposure effects led Bornstein to propose a modified two-factor model (Bornstein, 1989; Bornstein & D'Agostino, 1992, 1994). The modified model allows for habituation via both conscious deliberate processing *and* nonconscious processing of stimuli. At the conscious level, recognition of a stimulus reduces uncertainty about the stimulus. At the nonconscious level, people may find it easier to process an object that has been the object of implicit learning through subliminal exposure. This new "perceptual fluency" may create positive affect automatically, because feelings of certainty and familiarity are generated by easy processing. Thus, perceptual fluency may be *intrinsically* pleasing (see also Hansen & Wänke, 2009; Lee, 2001; Reber, Winkielman, & Schwarz, 1998).

Since Bornstein's review, a range of evidence has supported the hypothesis that perceptual fluency elicits positive affect (Winkielman & Cacioppo, 2001). Support for a role of perceptual fluency comes from evidence that beliefs about previously seeing an object predict liking, independent of actual past exposure to it (Lee, 2001). That is, people like an object that they *think* they have seen many times before, even if they have not actually seen it (Murphy & Zajonc, 1993).

Additional support comes from experiments indicating that the mere exposure effect is stronger among people who tend to experience high levels of negative affect and low levels of positive affect (Harmon-Jones & Allen, 2001). This result matches what would be expected if people automatically link negative affect to new stimuli. This linkage should be more common among people who are more inclined to experience negative affect. More interesting, Harmon-Jones and Allen did not find a reduction in negative feeling after mere exposure; instead, they found an increase in positive feeling.

Two experiments conducted by Jennifer Monahan, Sheila Murphy, and Robert Zajonc (2000) provided further support for this perspective. In one experiment, the scientists found that repeated subliminal exposure elicits more positive mood during a subsequent presentation of similar stimuli. In a second experiment, they found that this repeated subliminal exposure caused more liking for new stimuli that were similar to the old ones (e.g., both were Chinese ideographs) than for new stimuli that were of a different category (e.g., different shapes). This result suggests that exposure creates some *general* positive affect, which can then be attached to new objects that are similar to the old ones. Overall, then, an automatic familiarity–positivity link is a simple and interesting explanation for the mere exposure effect.

# KEY POINTS

- We form more positive attitudes toward people or things we have seen many times, especially when we cannot remember the past encounters.

- Mere exposure may elicit positive attitudes by increasing a sense of certainty and familiarity with the attitude object.

- The generation of boredom from mere exposure works against the effects of habituation that can occur at conscious and nonconscious levels.

- Nonconscious habituation occurs when subliminal exposure makes it easier to process similar stimuli, enhancing feelings of familiarity and positive mood.

---

## RESEARCH HIGHLIGHT 6.1

### "MIRROR, MIRROR ON THE WALL . . . WHO ARE THE FAIREST PEOPLE OF THEM ALL?"

Pamela Smith, Ap Dijksterhuis, and Shelley Chaiken (2008) noticed that Monahan et al.'s (2000) discovery of a generalized mere exposure effect may help to understand prejudice. Prior research had speculated that mere exposure to people from other ethnic groups might be a good way to reduce prejudice, but this conclusion was weakened by a lack of rigorous experiments on the issue (Bornstein, 1993). Smith and colleagues pointed out that Monahan et al.'s findings actually reveal an interesting problem for seeing mere exposure as a reducer of prejudice: exposure to people from one's *own* ethnic category might increase liking for people from this group over people from other groups.

In one study testing this prediction, White undergraduate students at the University of Amsterdam were first shown either subliminal presentations of White faces or a blank screen. Subsequently, participants indicated their attitudes toward Whites and Blacks. Smith and colleagues found that repeatedly exposing White participants to subliminal photos of White faces made participants exhibit more positive attitudes toward Whites than toward Blacks.

More surprising, this effect occurred because it increased the negativity of attitudes toward Blacks. These effects occurred on both explicit and implicit measures of prejudice, and they were stronger among people with especially positive attitudes toward Whites. Thus, it is possible that everyday, brief exposure to people from one's own ethnic group might powerfully increase negativity toward other groups, especially when attitudes toward one's own group are strong.

---

# EMOTION LEARNING

People around the world recognize the Nike swoosh symbol, the Coca-Cola insignia, and the golden arches of McDonalds, because each of these companies has spent enormous amounts of money to ensure that its brand is recognized. While these companies count on mere exposure to ensure recognition of their products, they also go a step further by trying to *pair* these symbols with something positive. Consider that they often don't pair the brands with detailed information about their products' quality (e.g., shoe longevity, food nutritional value), perhaps because many people would see through this information and be skeptical. Instead, the companies attach their products to popular celebrities and athletes, attractive models, and people singing upbeat songs. For example, in perhaps the most successful Coca-Cola ad, people were filmed on hilltops around the world joyfully singing "I'd Like to Buy the World a Coke." In short, these ads seek to pair "happiness" with the products.

*Content Witch: Is emotion more powerful and more basic than belief?*

Let's take these examples a step further. Suppose the female volunteers in Moreland and Beach's experiment (described earlier) did not just come to class a lot of times or few times. Suppose that some of them wore drab and dull clothing, and others wore lively, happy clothing. Would the students have liked the pictures of the faces of the women who wore happy clothing more than the pictures of the women who wore drab clothing?

If this experiment were to be done – to our knowledge it has not been done yet – then it would be examining one type of *emotion learning*. Whereas mere exposure effects occur through repeated presentation of an object on its own, emotion learning involves exposure to an attitude object that is accompanied by events that have emotional consequences. Past research has focused on three broad types of emotion learning, which we label *exposure conditioning*, *behavior conditioning*, and *observational conditioning*. Researchers have proposed that all three types of conditioning processes share a lot in common, and distinctions among them may be somewhat arbitrary. Nonetheless, we will focus on their most important common characteristic: all three work primarily by shaping emotional responses to an attitude object or to a behavior.

## Exposure conditioning: attitudes and the free lunch

Exposure conditioning describes the repeated presentation of an attitude object paired with an affective sensation. As a result, this process has also been labeled as affective or evaluative conditioning (De Houwer, Thomas, & Baeyens, 2001). Our examples above describe this type of conditioning, which differs from mere exposure because exposure conditioning involves pairing the object with an emotional stimulus, rather than simply repeating exposure with no accompanying emotion. The pairing of an attitude object with a positive emotion causes the feeling to be experienced automatically in subsequent exposures to the object.

This process resembles the well-known *classical conditioning* process described by Ivan Pavlov, who is famous for describing how this process could cause a dog to salivate in response to a bell that rang at mealtime. In his experiments, the sound of the bell was a *conditioned stimulus* (CS). A conditioned stimulus is paired with something else that produces a response (e.g., salivation). In his experiments, the CS was paired with food, which can be labeled an *unconditioned stimulus* (US). An unconditioned stimulus evokes a response on its own, without training. Over time, a dog can learn that the CS accompanies the positive US, causing the CS to elicit the same response as the US. In this terminology, the US evokes a response that is mapped onto the CS.

Exposure or evaluative conditioning is very similar to classical conditioning. The key difference is that the US in exposure conditioning is presumed to evoke an internal affective response, rather than a specific behavioral response such as salivation. Evidence for exposure conditioning in humans has been around for decades. Before World War II, Gregory Razran illustrated the idea in experiments examining the effects of the business "free lunch" on attitudes. In one study, participants rated their agreement with many political statements, such as "Workers for the World Unite!" and "America for Americans!" A subset of these slogans was then presented while participants were given a free lunch or while they were exposed to a number of unpleasant odors (Razran, 1940). After five to eight of these sessions, participants rated their approval of each slogan again.

Razran expected that a free lunch would elicit a more positive emotional response in people than foul odors. Consequently, people should come to associate a positive affective response to the statements that had been presented while eating (a positive US) and a negative affective response to the statements that were seen while experiencing the foul odors (a negative US). The results revealed that participants rated the statements that had been presented while eating more positively than the statements that had been presented with the foul odors: participants appeared to map their affective reactions to the free food or foul odors onto their reactions to the statements. More impressive, participants could not remember exactly which statements they had seen while eating or smelling the odor. Thus, the pairing of the political ideas with the positive and negative stimuli might have affected opinions unconsciously. Another interesting feature of exposure conditioning is that it may help to explain how different evaluative words, such as "good" and "bad," come to imply particular attitudes. From the perspective of conditioning theory, children come to learn that the word "good" is uttered during positive acts and experiences, while the word "bad" is uttered during negative acts and experiences. (Sometimes children come to believe that other words, such as "puck" and "ship," are associated with bad things, after their parents have been caught swearing.) This repeated pairing enables children to learn an affective response to "good" and "bad." These words then develop the power to shape attitudes toward other things that are labeled "good" and "bad." A series of experiments in the 1950s (Staats & Staats, 1958) and a particularly robust demonstration by Zanna, Kiesler, and Pilkonis (1970) showed that people could learn positive or negative associations to words in this way.

Sophisticated experiments have continued to reveal conditioning effects on attitudes (e.g., Cacioppo, Marshall-Goodell, Tassinary, & Petty, 1992; see Jones, Olson, & Fazio, 2010, for a review). In one such study, Jon Krosnick and colleagues (1992) showed participants a series of pictures of an unfamiliar person. Each picture was preceded by an affect-arousing image that was presented at a subliminal level. For some participants, the subliminal images were negative (e.g., a bloody shark, a bucket of snakes); for other participants, the subliminal images were positive (e.g., a couple getting married, a pair of kittens). Participants were then asked to evaluate the unfamiliar person. As can be seen in Figure 6.3, Krosnick, Betz, Jussim, and Lynn (1992) found that participants who were subliminally presented with the positive images liked the individual more than participants who were subliminally presented with the negative images. Not only were participants' attitudes affected by the subliminal presentations, so too were their perceptions of the target's personality characteristics and physical attractiveness. Interestingly, this type of effect can also be observed using implicit measures of post-conditioning attitudes, as Michael Olson and Russell Fazio (2001) demonstrated in a clever study that conditioned attitudes toward Pokémon characters.

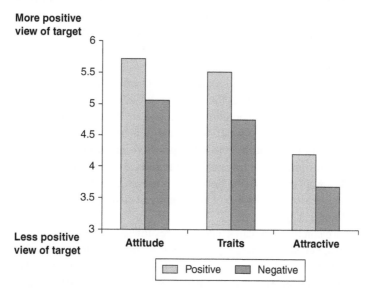

**Figure 6.3** *The effects of negative and positive primes on evaluations of an unfamiliar target (Krosnick et al., 1992)*

Such evidence has important implications for the formation of attitudes toward members of socially stigmatized groups. For example, if members of an ethnic group are often shown on television with negative images of crime, then this repeated pairing could shape negative attitudes toward ethnic minorities. Michael Olson and Russell Fazio (2006) demonstrated this type of influence in a clever experiment. They repeatedly flashed photos of eight Black and eight White people on a computer screen, and each photo of a Black person was repeatedly presented with images and words that were positive (e.g., a picture of puppies, "wonderful"), while photos of White people were paired with images and words that were negative (e.g., garbage in the sand, "horrible"). Participants' task was to respond to a separate, pre-specified target item (e.g., a woman jogging) appearing at random in the sequence of photos. Later, they completed the evaluative priming measure of attitudes that was described in Chapter 1.

Results indicated that participants who had been exposed to the White–bad and Black–good pairings exhibited more favorable attitudes toward Blacks than participants in a control condition, who completed the exposure task using the same photos, words, and images, but with no systematic pairing of them. Remarkably, this conditioning effect was also evident in an evaluative priming measure administered two days after the intervention.

Olson and Fazio's evidence is interesting for another reason. Specifically, these researchers found that evaluative conditioning influences attitude *change* and not just attitude *formation*. That is, their procedure did not merely cause people to form attitudes toward Black people and White people; it altered associations that existed before the experiment. Most other work on conditioning has examined attitudes toward unfamiliar objects or people, rather than a familiar object or person. The prior focus on unfamiliar things was justified by evidence that effects of evaluative conditioning are stronger when people possess low knowledge about the attitude object (Cacioppo et al., 1992). Notwithstanding this pattern, Olson and Fazio showed that exposure conditioning can also cause attitude change.

Research has also sought to better understand the mechanisms underlying evaluative conditioning effects. Jones, Fazio, and Olson (2009; Jones et al., 2010) reviewed a number of potential mechanisms relevant to evaluative conditioning. In one set of studies, these researchers offered interesting evidence that implicit misattribution plays a role within evaluative conditioning. According to Jones and colleagues' Implicit Misattribution Model, a response elicited by a US is unconsciously (or implicitly) misattributed to the CS, which subsequently influences the individual's attitude toward the CS. At the same time, however, other researchers argue that additional evidence is required to understand the role of awareness and memory in evaluative conditioning (see Gawronski & Walther, 2012).

Overall, exposure conditioning can shape attitudes toward a range of things, including faces, sculptures, paintings, slogans, foods, shapes, sounds, animated characters, and even objects that are merely touched. That said, researchers have argued that there are boundary conditions to these effects (see De Houwer, Baeyens, & Field, 2005; Jones et al., 2010). An insightful review by Jan De Houwer and colleagues (2001) describes several other important features of evaluative conditioning. First, attitudes formed from evaluative conditioning are resistant to change from *extinction* procedures, which present the objects repeatedly without the US. Second, evaluative conditioning is more dependent on the absolute *number* of presentations of the CS with the US (e.g., 10 CS–US pairings) than on the *proportion* of times they are together (e.g., 10 CS–US pairings with 10 CS only and 10 US only); in other words, evaluative conditioning is effective even when the CS and the US occur together only a fraction of the time. Third, the effects do not appear to depend on conscious awareness of the link between the CS and the US (De Houwer, 2001b). Fourth, evaluative conditioning can occur in conditions where classical conditioning does not normally occur. Together, the evidence suggests that evaluative conditioning is a vital emotional process for understanding attitude formation and change.

## Behavior conditioning: effects of being pleasant or silent

The key feature of behavior conditioning is that it provides an emotional reinforcement for a specific behavior. For example, a child who says "please" and "thank you" will be met with smiles from encouraging adults. The smiles trigger positive feelings that increase the chance of the behavior occurring again. Put simply, behavior conditioning pairs an emotion with a behavior that has been performed.

Emotional learning is not the only process that is taking place when a parent subtly reinforces the behavior of a polite child. In this example, the child may also be *aware* of the way in which polite responses are being reinforced, despite the parent's subtlety. As a result, the child might see how a parent is attempting to alter the child's behavior and react in such a way as to please the parent. Early research attempting to demonstrate reinforcement for attitudes was confronted with the same issue (Dulany, 1961). These experiments possessed *demand characteristics*, which are features of an experiment that convey the experimental hypothesis and can motivate participants to behave in a manner supporting it (Orne, 1962). Knowledge that one is in an experiment may motivate participants to attempt to deduce the true purpose of the experiment.

In an attempt to avoid these concerns, Insko and his colleagues (Insko, 1965; Insko & Cialdini, 1969) conducted several clever examinations of behavioral conditioning of attitudes outside of a lab environment. In one study (Insko & Cialdini, 1969), a researcher dialed phone numbers at random from a telephone directory of university students. The students were asked to answer a number of survey questions about pay television. In one experimental condition, the researcher said "good" after students gave a response that supported pay television, and the researcher gave no statement after each response that opposed pay television. In another experimental condition, the researcher said "good" after each response that opposed pay television and gave no statement after each supportive response. This subtle manipulation affected participants' responses to subsequent questions about pay television: participants indicated more positive attitudes after positive responses had been reinforced than after negative responses had been reinforced.

This result occurred even though participants reported no awareness of a connection between their responses and the researcher's statements. Also, the influence on attitudes was detectable even a week after the reinforcement procedure took place, and the effect was even stronger when the experimenter opened the "survey" in a way that established positive rapport with the interviewee (Insko & Butzine, 1967). The effect of rapport is consistent with the notion that we care more about agreeing with people whom we like (Heider, 1958), making "good" responses from a likeable experimenter especially reinforcing.

These studies are pretty neat – they showed effects of subtle reinforcements that might operate outside of people's *conscious* awareness. Most studies of reinforcement have examined the effects of reinforcements when people *know* that the reinforcements are present. This high level of awareness can produce a different kind of result. For example, many experiments have found that offering blatant, strong rewards (e.g., treats) to children causes better performance of the activities while the rewards are in place, but worse performance after the rewards have been removed (e.g., Freedman, Cunningham, & Krismer, 1992). This *overjustification* effect has been explained through the suggestion that rewards decrease the inherent, intrinsic attractiveness of the task – it becomes less *pleasing* on its own merits, without the reward being in place (Lepper,

Greene, & Nisbett, 1973; see also Heyman & Ariely, 2004). Consistent with this hypothesis, there is evidence that the effect occurs because negative emotions become associated with the behavior (see also Freedman et al., 1992; Pretty & Seligman, 1984).

Another explanation is relevant to one of our three witches: attitude structure. Specifically, Crano and Sivacek (1984) proposed that high rewards can increase ambivalence toward a behavior because the excessive reinforcement makes people wonder if the behavior is legitimate. If someone offered us a paid holiday in Italy just for crossing a road, we'd probably think "something is up." Is it illegal to cross that particular road at this time of day? Is there a hidden trap, a secret camera taking photos, a car waiting to startle us? Large rewards evoke suspicion because we have heard that nothing comes free. When the context makes this suspicion important, it can influence attitudes.

## Observational conditioning: scenes that make us cringe

Observational (vicarious) conditioning occurs when someone sees *and* experiences or empathizes with the emotional response that happens to another person who has performed a particular behavior (Bandura & Rosenthal, 1967; Bandura, Blanchard, & Ritter, 1969). In vicarious conditioning, a person learns about a behavior and an emotional response that goes with it. For example, in one experiment, mothers were asked to display a fearful reaction to one rubber toy (e.g., a snake) and a happy reaction to another rubber toy (e.g., a spider), while showing each toy to their toddler. The toddlers later expressed a significantly more fearful reaction to the toy that had been paired with the mother's fearful emotional expression than to the toy that had been paired with the positive emotion (Gerull & Rapee, 2002). The toddlers *acquired* the mother's (manipulated) emotional response to the toy.

Similarly, people respond emotionally to a neutral sound tone after seeing another person show painful reactions after hearing the tone, even though they never experienced the (actually feigned) pain themselves (Berger, 1962). Further, experiments have revealed that people learn attitudes toward novel foods by watching other people's emotional reactions to the foods and that others' facial expressions function like an unconditioned stimulus, *automatically* eliciting the liking or disliking without altering conscious, cognitive inferences (Baeyens, Eelen, Crombez, & De Houwer, 2001).

This type of evidence fits Bandura's conclusion that vicarious conditioning involves more than learning a modeled behavior: it involves learning the model's emotional responses to the behavior. This adoption of the model's emotional response is important – we learn many behaviors simply by observing the emotional consequences of things that happen to other people's actions. Parents of siblings often see one of them become an "angel" after rebuking or punishing another sibling. Bandura's model suggests that this change in attitude is even more likely when the sibling exhibits other signs of sympathy with the child who has misbehaved. When a person *feels* another's distress, it is natural to avoid experiencing the same fate. Vicarious learning facilitates this process.

## KEY POINTS

- Explicit and implicit measures of attitudes can be influenced by the repeated presentation of an attitude object with an affective sensation.
- Subtle reward following a behavior tends to elicit more favorable attitudes toward the behavior than when punishment or no reward occurs.
- People may acquire a model's emotional responses to a behavior through vicarious conditioning.

## MOOD EFFECTS ON ATTITUDE JUDGMENT

Earlier in the chapter, we noted that children may expect more success at influencing a parent when the parent is in a good mood than in a bad one. Children may even hope that their parents are not aware of any positive influence that a good mood is having, or the parents could reconsider their position! These intuitions about the attitudes formed while people are in different moods have been tested in a variety of experiments.

Research has suggested that moods have a powerful effect on attitude. The bulk of the evidence reveals a *mood-congruence effect*, which is the tendency for people to express attitudes that match their current mood. In research on the mood-congruence effect, the current mood is shaped by something unconnected to the attitude object. For example, the mood may be elicited by the weather (like rain in Wales!), rather than being a specific feeling repeatedly paired with the object. Research illustrating this effect has used a variety of methods to induce positive or negative moods, including hypnosis, music, or manipulated feedback about participants' performance in a prior task (Forgas & Bower, 1987). Mood-congruence effects have also been obtained in interesting field settings, such as studies examining judgments after watching a happy or sad movie (Forgas & Moylan, 1987), finding change in a phone booth, or after receiving a free gift (Isen, Shalker, Clark, & Karp, 1978).

One well-known study capitalized on prior evidence that receiving a free gift puts people in a good mood (Isen et al., 1978). People walking alone in a shopping mall were approached and given a free pocket-sized notebook or nail clippers. About 50 metres after receiving this gift, the shoppers were approached by a different person claiming to conduct a consumer opinion survey. The survey researcher asked participants to rate the performance and reliability of their automobiles and television sets (if they had them). Analyses of responses to these questions revealed that the automobiles and television sets were evaluated more positively by people who had received the free gift than by people who had not been offered a gift. It is amazing that a little notebook or nail clippers could have such a big effect: people who are likely to be feeling good from these small gifts have a more positive outlook; they seem to see the brighter side of things.

*Function Witch: How useful is it to have attitudes that get pushed around by mood? Shouldn't useful attitudes be relatively stable?*

# Moderators of mood congruence: the weather made me do it

Despite the wide range of supporting evidence, mood does not *always* elicit matching attitudes. Mood is less likely to influence attitudes when people's attention is explicitly drawn to the cause of their mood. This idea was nicely illustrated in a clever experiment by Norbert Schwarz and Gerry Clore (1983). They called people on the telephone and asked them to rate their satisfaction with their life and to rate their current mood. Consistent with the mood-congruence effect, respondents' ratings were associated with the weather on the day they were called: their life and their mood seemed better on sunny days than on rainy days. However, this effect was eliminated when the weather was casually mentioned *before* asking for ratings. This pattern fits a *mood-as-information* view of mood-congruence effects. This perspective suggests that mood may merely be a source of data that people use when figuring out how they feel about things. Mood acts as information when we fail to realize that the mood comes from some irrelevant source (e.g., the weather). In contrast, when we realize that the mood comes from an irrelevant source, we can treat it as useless information for our current judgments.

A number of additional factors may determine whether mood elicits matching attitudes. For instance, mood congruence effects are more likely when circumstances enable people to *select* information that fits their current mood (Bower, 1991). These situations arise when we can shift our attention across different pieces of information (perception), study some of the information more closely (encoding), remember portions of the information better than others (recall), and construe the information in different ways (interpretation). Although these selective perception, encoding, recall, and interpretation processes are different from the mood-as-information process, they appear to be stronger for global evaluative judgments than for tasks that rely on more basic memory and reasoning processes (Forgas, 1995). It appears that the general evaluations that we call "attitudes" are vulnerable to effects of mood in many ways.

Scientists have also discovered that mood has more powerful effects when judgments are constructed on the spot, rather than retrieved from memory (see Chapter 2). Judgments have to be constructed when the things being judged are unfamiliar, but they can be retrieved when people have a lot of experience with them. This difference is supposed to explain why evaluations of familiar consumer products show less mood-congruent bias than highly unfamiliar items (Srull, 1983, 1984). Presumably, this difference occurs because people can merely recall their prior attitude toward products they know well, but they must construct attitudes for products that are unfamiliar.

Similarly, judgments about atypical or unusual people are more strongly affected by mood than are judgments about typical people, perhaps because we don't tend to think about "typical" people as deeply (Forgas, 1992). These results converge with other evidence that judgments requiring the production of new information are more likely to match induced moods than do judgments that rely merely on the reproduction of information (Fiedler, 1991).

# Mood and persuasion

The role of mood is relevant to several models of persuasion described in Chapter 5, such as the Elaboration Likelihood Model (Petty & Cacioppo, 1986; Petty & Wegener, 1999). This model emphasizes the importance of knowing when people will think about persuasive information carefully. One important prediction from the Elaboration Likelihood Model is that the effects of mood on persuasion depend on whether people are low or high in the motivation and ability to think carefully about the persuasive message. According to this model, positive mood acts as a simple cue to accept a message when motivation and ability are low, perhaps because of low personal relevance or distractions. In contrast, positive mood biases the processing of message content when motivation and ability are high, perhaps due to high personal relevance and high knowledge about the issue (Petty, Schumann, Richman, & Strathman, 1993). Biased processing causes people to be more influenced by content that matches their current goals, such as the goal of maintaining a good mood, than by content that mismatches their current goals. In short, the mood-as-cue route and the mood-as-bias route can both produce mood-congruent judgments.

The effects of mood are not so straightforward when motivation and ability are moderate, however. According to the Elaboration Likelihood Model, this circumstance causes mood itself to influence the extent to which people think about the content of a message (Petty, Gleicher, & Baker, 1991). Indeed, one finding in the literature is that people in a positive mood are often less likely to carefully study information about an attitude object than are people in a negative mood (e.g., Bless, Mackie, & Schwarz, 1992; Schwarz, Bless, & Bohner, 1991; though see below). Remarkably, the effects of mood on amount of processing occur even when the mood is created by subtle manipulations that subliminally flash emotional words on a screen faster than people can read (Chartrand, van Baaren, & Bargh, 2006).

The effect of mood on message processing was nicely illustrated in an experiment reminiscent of Schwarz and Clore's (1983) study of the effects of good and bad weather on judgment. Robert Sinclair, Melvin Mark, and Gerry Clore (1994) asked students to read arguments in favor of new comprehensive examinations on days when there was good weather or bad weather, and these researchers manipulated the strength of the arguments. As can be seen in Figure 6.4, the results indicated that the students were more influenced by argument strength on bad weather days than on good weather days, provided that the experimenter did not first draw students' attention to the weather. When the experimenter did draw attention to the weather, there were no effects of the weather on persuasion.

Other research has shown that the effect of mood on message processing depends on the nature of the information in the message. According to the Hedonic Contingency Model (HCM; Wegener & Petty, 1995; Wegener, Petty, & Smith, 1995) message recipients in a good mood are likely to devote substantive attention to persuasive appeals that help them maintain their positive affect, on the basis that people in a positive mood are more tuned in to the hedonic consequences of their actions. Consistent with this perspective, Wegener et al. (1995) found that, compared to people in a sad mood, people in a positive mood (a) devoted greater attention and scrutiny to uplifting persuasive appeals (e.g., a message advocating reduced tuition fees in exchange for assisting the

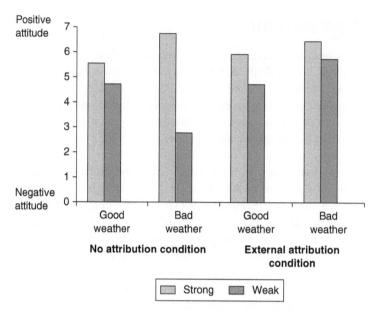

**Figure 6.4**   *The effects of argument strength, affect, and attribution on evaluations (Sinclair et al., 1994)*

university), and (b) devoted less attention and scrutiny to depressing persuasive appeals (e.g., a message advocating that students undertake additional work while at university to avoid higher tuition fees). In essence, the happy mood is thought to lead people to think more carefully about uplifting information and avoid mood-threatening information. This evidence is consistent with a mood-as-goal perspective, wherein moods function like goals that people strive to maintain.

Building upon the HCM, the more recent Mood-Congruent Expectancies Approach (MCA; Ziegler, 2010, 2013) argues that there is a cognitive mechanism that influences message processing in positive *and* negative moods. According to the MCA, people in a good mood or a bad mood are more likely to engage in enhanced processing of a message when mood-congruent expectancies are disconfirmed. That is, people in a happy mood should process information more deeply when positive expectations are disconfirmed by negative information compared to when expectations are confirmed with positive information, and that people in a bad mood should process information more deeply when negative expectations are disconfirmed by positive information compared to when expectations are confirmed with negative information.

 ***Content Witch:*** *It's one thing to describe how affect influences reactions to cognitive information, but what about behavioral information? Affect should influence how people respond to their own behaviors too.*

Thus far, then, we have seen that mood can function as a source of information and as a goal. Raghunathan and Trope (2002) have suggested that mood can also function as a resource. In their view, positive mood gives people the energy to be open-minded about information that contradicts their views. For instance, while in a positive mood, people who are high consumers of caffeine should be able to tolerate and process information about the dangers of high caffeine consumption more than low consumers of caffeine. This function of mood as a resource causes people in a positive mood to process the information in more of an unbiased fashion than people in a negative mood. In contrast, people in a negative mood focus on finding information that supports their prior attitude and are less influenced by information that contradicts their attitude. Results across several experiments supported this mood-as-resource perspective, while also showing when mood might alternately function as information or as a goal.

An important aspect of these perspectives is that mood almost always has an impact on attitude, albeit in different ways. Whether mood functions as a cue, source of bias, motivator of information processing, or a resource appears to depend on motivation, ability, and prior attitude. But across these variables, mood tends to influence judgments.

Some findings reveal potential limitations to this influence, however (e.g., Albarracín & Kumkale, 2003). For instance, it is not clear that *everyone* shows mood-congruent judgment effects. Personality differences may determine whether people's attitudes are swayed by mood. In one study, Haddock, Zanna, and Esses (1994) found that mood-inducing music affected English Canadian participants' attitudes toward French Canadians, replicating the mood-congruent bias. More relevant, they found that these effects were stronger among people who habitually experience stronger emotions, as assessed through a personality scale assessing affect intensity (Larsen & Diener, 1987). In other words, people who experience emotions more weakly may not show much of a mood-congruent bias (see also Strack, Schwarz, & Gschneidinger, 1985). As we will show later in the book (Chapter 8), some personalities may also be more influenced by affective information and others by cognitive information.

**Structure Witch:** *What happens to attitudes when people feel happy and sad at the same time?*

## KEY POINTS

- A variety of research methods have found that people tend to form attitudes that match their current mood.

- Mood congruence depends on a variety of factors, including salient causes of the mood, the extent to which the target of judgment is abstract or typical, and biases in perception, encoding, recall, and interpretation.

- Mood can function as a cue, source of bias, motivator of information processing, or as a resource.

- There may be individual differences in the extent to which mood influences judgment.

# EMOTION EFFECTS ON ATTITUDE JUDGMENT

Until now, we have focused on the effects of general positive or negative moods, such as those arising from the weather. Moods are diffuse and unfocused feeling states that may have no clear source. Emotions, such as anger or disgust, are affective reactions to specific things or events. A sunny day may import a skip to your step, but the mood from a sunny day is quite different from anger at rush hour traffic or disgust at the sight of feces on the pavement (or the bottom of your shoe!).

Specific emotions can be different from each other in many ways. Researchers have therefore tried to identify basic categories of emotion, but these attempts have led to lists of different numbers of basic emotion categories. Studies examining cross-cultural similarities in facial expressions proposed that there are seven basic emotions (Ekman & Friesen, 1986). In contrast, research examining cognitive processing of emotion found evidence for many more basic emotions (Ortony, Clore, & Collins, 1988), and research examining physical patterns of arousal found fewer basic emotions (Ekman, Levenson, & Friesen, 1983). Despite this divergence in number, most models tend to include happiness, sadness, anger, fear, and disgust as basic emotions (for a comprehensive review on the structure of emotions, see Keltner & Lerner, 2010).

## Effects of emotion on attitude: specificity and uncertainty

Happiness and sadness are the emotions most often induced in studies of the effects of emotion on attitudes. When these feelings run deep because of a strong recent trigger, such as winning the lottery or the death of a close friend, then they are experienced as specific emotions rather than mere diffuse moods. Schwarz and Clore (1997) point out that this specificity may make emotions less malleable as sources of information than moods; for instance, it may be harder to interpret happiness from one source, such as winning the lottery, as evidence for a positive attitude toward something else, such as nuclear power plants.

The effects of emotions may also depend on the amount of uncertainty that they elicit (Smith & Ellsworth, 1985). Emotions like surprise, worry, and fear involve uncertainty about past or future events. In contrast, emotions like happiness, disgust, and anger occur with a sense of certainty. Across two experiments, Tiedens and Linton (2001) found that certainty-related emotion causes people to process persuasive information less carefully than uncertainty-related emotion. As a result, people experiencing a certainty-related emotion are more likely to agree with an expert than a non-expert, without as much scrutiny of their arguments (cf. Moons & Mackie, 2007). Specific emotions can also be linked with particular moral concerns. For example, anger has been associated with retributive justice, whereas gratitude has been associated with equality (Keltner & Lerner, 2010). As such, experiencing these emotions can influence how individuals evaluate groups and social policy issues.

*Function Witch:* Do uncertainty-related emotions activate the knowledge function of attitudes and make it more influential?

## Incidental versus integral emotion and scary messages

To this point, we have been focusing on the effects of affect that are *incidental* to the attitude topic, rather than being *integral* to it (Bodenhausen, 1993). For example, the fear created by seeing a scary movie about a serial killer presumably has no logical connection with the viewer's subsequent attitude toward driving within the speed limit. It may be quite different for the viewer to experience fear about speeding and then express an attitude toward it.

A lot of research has examined the effects of emotions that are induced by the attitude topic or a message on it. This issue has been the focus of extensive research on fear messages – messages that make people afraid of some consequence if they do not change their views or actions. Interest in the effects of fear messages has been inspired by the practical need to get people to stop performing dangerous behaviors, such as drinking-and-driving, smoking, unsafe sex, speeding, failing to wear a seat belt, and taking illegal drugs.

Naïve campaigners tend to think that people will stop performing these behaviors if *only* they just learned how the behaviors are dangerous. It turns out that this expectation is unrealistic, although it is not *entirely* naïve either (Petty, Fabrigar, & Wegener, 2003; Stroebe, 2000). The biggest problem with fear appeals is that they emphasize the severity of negative consequences so much that people often deny their vulnerability in order to avoid feeling threatened by the fear (Ditto, Munro, Apanovitch, Scepansky, & Lockhart, 2003). That is, people don't see *themselves* as being in danger. Fear appeals generate favorable cognitive responses and attitude change only if people feel vulnerable (Das, DeWit, & Stroebe, 2003).

Even if people accept that they are vulnerable, they need to be told about specific behaviors that help lower their vulnerability. Without specific, useful recommendations, their attitudes and behaviors will not change (Maddux & Rogers, 1983). Fear can even *backfire* by causing attitudes to become more negative toward the advocated action (Rogers & Prentice-Dunn, 1997).

## KEY POINTS

- There are several basic emotions, which are more specific than moods.
- Uncertainty-related emotion may cause deeper processing of attitude-relevant information.
- Depending on a number of factors (e.g., personal vulnerability to a threat), messages that elicit fear may cause more persuasion, no persuasion, or less persuasion.

## RESEARCH HIGHLIGHT 6.2

### DO OUR EMOTIONS INFLUENCE THE MONETARY VALUE WE ATTACH TO CONSUMER PRODUCTS?

Do our experienced emotions influence our evaluations of how much we like consumer products? In an interesting application of the link between emotions and decision-making, Jennifer Lerner, Deborah Small, and George Loewenstein (2004) studied how disgust and sadness influence individuals' assessment of the monetary value of consumer products. While disgust and sadness are core negative emotions, research has shown that they elicit different reactions within people. Lerner and colleagues note that disgust is thought to evoke feelings of being too close to an indigestible object or idea, leading individuals to want to avoid acquiring anything new. In contrast, sadness is described as being linked with feelings of loss and helplessness, and would have the effect of increasing individuals' desire to change their personal circumstances. Applying this reasoning to consumers' perceptions of value, Lerner and colleagues tested the hypothesis that experiencing disgust or sadness would have opposite effects on "choice prices" – the amount of money individuals would forego in order to receive a commodity. Specifically, it was expected that disgust would lower participants' choice prices, whereas sadness would increase participants' choice prices (relative to a baseline condition).

To test this idea, Lerner and colleagues randomly assigned participants to a neutral, disgust, or sadness emotion condition (this was done by having participants watch one of three films). Next, participants were given the chance to acquire a set of highlighters or to forego the highlighters and instead receive cash. Consistent with predictions, the results revealed that disgusted participants wanted less money (approximately around $3) to forego the highlighters compared to sad participants (who wanted approximately $4.50). In other words, the sad participants desired the highlighters more than the disgusted participants.

These results offer compelling evidence of how emotions influence consumers' perceptions of monetary value. In a subsequent study, these findings were extended by demonstrating that sad participants were willing to pay almost four times as much to purchase a water bottle compared to participants in a neutral mood (Cryder, Lerner, Gross, & Dahl, 2008). Taken together, these (and other) studies offer a fascinating perspective on how emotions influence everyday thinking and decisions.

# WHAT WE HAVE LEARNED

- Mere exposure elicits positive attitudes.
- Attitudes are influenced by pairing objects or behaviors with emotional experiences and subtle rewards and punishments, even when the associations are formed merely by observing another individual.
- People in a positive mood like things more than people in a negative mood, but this mood-congruence effect can vary across people and situations.

- Mood can function as a cue, source of bias, motivator of information processing, or as a resource.
- Basic emotions (e.g., fear) are more specific than moods and may exert less powerful mood congruence, but they may still affect processing of attitude-relevant information.

# WHAT DO YOU THINK?

- Does happy people's tendency to use less effort in message processing make their attitudes reflect reality less accurately (Taylor & Brown, 1994)? Scientists studying depression have suggested that chronically happy people over-estimate themselves compared to people experiencing lower mood or full blown depression, and the general pattern of most of the evidence reviewed here supports the conclusion that happiness may, in general, make it easier to hold desired attitudes, rather than accurate ones.

- According to a bidimensional view on emotion, emotions vary in their intensity and in their valence (Watson, Wiese, Vaidya, & Tellegen, 1999). For instance, fear can be high or low in intensity, and it can be high or low in negativity. Some evidence indicates that greater arousal in fear increases persuasion, whereas greater negativity decreases influence (Celuch, Lust, & Showers, 1998; LaTour & Rotfeld, 1997). This evidence fits suggestions that arousal is a signal of the urgency or importance of an issue, whereas valence is about goodness versus badness (Clore & Schnall, 2005). Do arousal and valence have different effects for other emotions as well?

- Do emotions differ in the extent to which they are spontaneously activated by attitude topics? Roger Giner-Sorolla (1999, 2001) proposes that the affect associated with an attitude object varies along a continuum ranging from immediate to deliberate. Immediate affect occurs in bipolar feelings and emotions that are activated quickly and effortlessly, whereas deliberate affect involves qualitatively different, discrete emotions that arise gradually. For example, a person waiting for a medical surgery might experience dread and anxiety immediately upon seeing a masked surgeon; different cognitively elaborate emotions might arise after having a chance to think about the situation, including feelings of trust (in the medical profession) and pride (in modern technology). In general, immediate emotions might be more readily activated by attitude topics and may be more likely to influence the attitudes that are formed.

- How much does the evidence in this chapter apply better to understanding attitude formation than to attitude change? The subtle processes of mere exposure and exposure conditioning, for instance, may be less likely to produce attitude change than attitude formation (Cacioppo et al., 1992; Walther, 2002), notwithstanding the aforementioned research by Olson and Fazio (2006). This is an important issue for real-world applications that attempt to change attitudes. For example, campaigns that attempt to persuade people to stop unhealthy behaviors (e.g., smoking, eating fatty foods) by presenting the behaviors with positive, attractive role models and stimuli might merely reinforce people who already possess positive attitudes toward the behaviors, without actually converting someone who is dead-set against them. Because most of the past research has focused on issues that are new to the participants, it is uncertain whether these results apply precisely the same way when attitude change is considered.

# KEY TERMS

*Behavior conditioning* – pairing an emotion with a behavior that has been performed.

*Classical conditioning* – learning that occurs based on the repeated pairing of a conditioned stimulus and an unconditioned stimulus.

*Emotion learning* – exposure to an attitude object that is accompanied by events that have emotional consequences.

*Exposure (evaluative) conditioning* – the repeated presentation of an attitude object paired with an affective sensation.

*Habituation* – after repeated exposure, individuals get used to a new stimulus and see it as less threatening.

*Hedonic Contingency Model* – a model arguing that message recipients in a good mood are likely to devote substantive attention to persuasive appeals that help them maintain their positive affect.

*Incidental affect* – an affective state that influences judgment of an attitude object, but is not linked to the object (e.g., mood).

*Integral affect* – feelings associated with an attitude object.

*Mere exposure effect* – the notion that the more we are exposed to an attitude object, the more we tend to like it.

*Mood-as-information* – a perspective that states that mood may be a source of data that people use when figuring out how they feel about objects.

*Mood-congruence effect* – the tendency for people to express attitudes that match their current mood.

*Mood-Congruent Expectancies Approach* – a model arguing that people in a good mood or a bad mood are more likely to engage in enhanced processing of a message when mood-congruent expectancies are disconfirmed.

*Observational learning* – learning that occurs through watching others.

*Overjustification effect* – when rewards decrease the intrinsic attractiveness of an activity or object.

*Perceptual fluency* – the ease with which information is processed. Greater ease represents greater fluency.

*Tolerance for ambiguity* – individual differences in being accepting of things that are unknown or unclear.

## FURTHER READING

### BASIC

Gawronski, B. and Walther, E. (2012) What do memory data tell us about the role of contingency awareness in evaluative conditioning? *Journal of Experimental Social Psychology, 48,* 617–623.

Olson, M. A. and Fazio, R. H. (2001) Implicit attitude formation through classical conditioning. *Psychological Science*, *12*, 413–417.

Tiedens, L. Z. and Linton, S. (2001) Judgment under emotional certainty and uncertainty: The effects of specific emotions on information processing. *Journal of Personality and Social Psychology*, *81*, 973–988.

Zajonc, R. B. (2001) Mere exposure: A gateway to the subliminal. *Current Directions in Psychological Science*, *10*, 224–228.

Ziegler, R. (2013) Mood and processing of proattitudinal and counterattitudinal messages. *Personality and Social Psychology Bulletin*, *39*, 482–495.

## APPLIED

Cryder, C.E., Lerner, J.S., Gross, J.J. and Dahl, R.E. (2008) Misery is not miserly. *Psychological Science*, *19*, 525–530.

LaTour, M. S. and Ford, J. (2006) Retrospective and prospective views of 'fear arousal' in 'fear appeals'. *International Journal of Advertising*, *25*, 409–413.

Ottati, V., Terkildsen, N. and Hubbard, C. (1997) Happy faces elicit heuristic processing in a televised impression formation task: A cognitive tuning account. *Personality and Social Psychology Bulletin*, *23*, 1144–1156.

Soldat, A. S., Sinclair, R. C. and Mark, M. M. (1997) Color as an environmental processing cue: External affective cues can directly affect processing strategy without affecting mood. *Social Cognition*, *16*, 55–71.

# 7

---

# BEHAVIORAL INFLUENCES ON ATTITUDES

---

## QUESTIONS TO PONDER

1. How do experiences influence attitudes?

2. Are there patterns in the way that an attitude is shaped by exploring a new environment?

3. When do we guess our own attitudes, rather than simply "knowing" them?

4. Do we change our attitudes to justify things we have done, perhaps things we have done spontaneously without thinking?

## PREVIEW

This chapter describes behavioral influences on attitude. To explain these influences, we consider diverse behaviors (e.g., exploring our environment, role playing) and two major theories (Self-Perception Theory and Cognitive Dissonance Theory). Ultimately, these theories suggest that behaviors work by shaping beliefs and feelings relevant to our attitude. Thus, these theories are deeply interconnected with those described in the previous two chapters on cognitive and affective influences, but with a greater focus on the causal role of behaviors.

## WHY DID I DO THAT?

One of the authors has trouble deciding between two things that he likes. When he was a young graduate student in Canada, he frequently had trouble deciding which scrumptious entrée to eat at the local cafeteria, so he'd eat them all. He had the same trouble choosing between films he'd like to see or books he'd like to read. When it came to films, he would choose between two liked choices by asking his girlfriend to hide them behind her back, move them around, and then he would pick one at random. This hands-behind-the-back routine would be on display almost every week at the video store.

One month, he noticed an odd thing happen. By pure chance, he had happened to *not* pick one film, *The Fugitive* (starring Harrison Ford and Tommy Lee Jones), a few weeks in a row. Week after week, he never chose the hand holding this film. Finally, after six weeks, he chose the hand that held *The Fugitive*. Was he excited about finally seeing this film? No. To his own surprise, he stood there holding the film in his hands and realized that he no longer wanted it. It had gone from seeming great to becoming totally uninteresting. He wondered what had happened in six weeks to change his attitude so dramatically. Reviews of the film were great, it had received seven Oscar nominations, and he knew it was just dumb luck that caused him to miss the film before. Yet he had to force himself to carry the film home and watch it, and he barely managed to enjoy the film. It seemed to possess many attributes of a good film, but it just didn't do anything for him. (And how did Tommy Lee Jones win an Oscar against Ralph Fiennes' disturbing reprisal of a Nazi commander in *Schindler's List* that same year?!)

One explanation for this change in attitude is that his prior acts of choice altered his opinion about the movie. Despite all of his better knowledge about luck, randomness, and chance selection, he *knew* that he had passed up the chance to see the film several times. Some part of his brain thought that he must not really like the film after all. If some other film had been missed by chance, it would have been disliked instead. (He has since avoided the random hands method.)

This example is just one of many ways in which behavioral information can shape attitudes. This effect can happen because behavior can be driven by many factors other than our attitudes (see Chapters 1 and 4), including random events, demands made on us, social norms, and habits. Because of such factors, we may find ourselves doing something and wondering why we did it. Our behavior can then influence our thoughts and subsequent attitudes.

This chapter explores diverse ways in which behavior can guide attitudes. Here, we focus on relatively complex actions like exploration, role playing, and arguing against our own attitude. We first consider the roles of exploration and role playing. Next, we consider two broad theories about how attitudes are shaped by behavior: Self-Perception Theory and Cognitive Dissonance Theory.

# BEHAVIORAL EXPLORATION

Perhaps the best way to begin to describe the effects of behavior on attitudes is by considering studies that have shown substantively *different* ways in which people learn from direct behavioral experiences with attitude objects. In a provocative experiment demonstrating the effects of behavior on attitudes, Dennis Regan and Russell Fazio (1977) asked participants to learn about five interesting new puzzles. In one experimental condition, participants were asked to spend 20 minutes playing with the puzzles and getting familiar with them. In another condition, participants were asked to read a sheet containing information about the puzzles. All participants then indicated their attitudes toward the puzzles, after which the experimenter left the lab to perform a task. During the experimenter's absence, a hidden camera recorded the amount of time that participants spent with the puzzles. Analyses of these recordings revealed that participants who had formed attitudes based on *direct experience* with the objects subsequently reported attitudes that were good predictors of the actual amount of time that they played with the puzzles; participants who had formed attitudes based on the written information subsequently reported attitudes that were weak predictors of the actual amount of time that they played with the puzzles.

More recent experiments have looked at *how* people form attitudes from direct experience. Russell Fazio, Dick Eiser, and Natalie Shook (2004) tackled this issue by developing a videogame called "BeanFest." Participants were told to explore a map that contains good beans, which give energy, and bad ones, which take away energy. Randomly selected patterns of shape and speckling are used to determine which beans are good and which beans are bad. Crucially, each move along the map costs energy, and the player dies when zero energy is reached. So it is important that the player learns to like and frequently visit areas that contain many good beans, while disliking and avoiding places that have bad beans. Repeated exploration is necessary to determine which shapes and patterns indicate good beans versus bad beans.

Analyses of participants' explorations revealed an important result: participants learned significantly better about which beans were bad than about which beans were good. In addition, participants were more likely to assume that *new* beans were negative when they looked similar to "bad" beans than to assume that the new beans were positive when they looked similar to "good" beans. Overall, participants' feelings about their own performance depended more on how many bad objects they encountered than how many good ones they found (Eiser, Shook, & Fazio, 2007). Not surprisingly, the magnitude of this *weighting bias* for negative information varies across people. In more recent research using the Beanfest paradigm, Fazio and colleagues have found that there are meaningful differences across people in the degree to which they have a weighting bias for negative and positive information. While some people weigh negative information very heavily in generalizing their existing attitudes to novel stimuli, other people have a bias toward positive information. Furthermore, these researchers have demonstrated that these individual differences in weighting tendencies have meaningful effects on how people behave (Pietri, Fazio, & Shook, 2013; Rocklage & Fazio, 2014).

Fazio et al. suggest that the difference between effects of positive and negative information is based on a simple fact of life: people tend to learn a lot from trying new things, but not from avoiding them. If we suspect (but do not know for sure) that something is bad, we will avoid it and never discover whether it actually is bad or quite good. In contrast, if we think it is good, we will approach it and find out either way. Avoidance behavior yields less information, so we remain vulnerable to over-generalizing the negative experiences that we have. Perhaps this is the deep reason why parents so often say, "If you don't try it, how do you know you won't like it?"

*Structure Witch: Are we doomed to possess fewer cognitions about things and people we don't like?*

---

## KEY POINTS

- Attitudes based on direct experience are stronger predictors of subsequent behavior than attitudes based on indirect experience.
- We may incorporate negative experiences into our attitudes more quickly and strongly than positive experiences.
- Avoidance behavior causes us to learn less about an attitude object than approach behavior.

# ROLE PLAYING

Some of the earliest experiments about the effects of behavior on attitudes examined the impact of role playing. For example, one clever experiment examined the effect of pretending to be a person who had been diagnosed with terminal lung cancer, in a brief sketch or scene. Smokers who were randomly assigned to play this role later reported more negative attitudes toward smoking than did smokers who had merely been asked to listen to an audiotape of this role play (Janis & Mann, 1965). Similarly, other studies found that people who were randomly assigned to argue in favor of a particular stance on an issue (e.g., legalized abortion) subsequently became more favorable toward the position that they had supported (Janis & King, 1954). Something about their behavior, which was manipulated at random by the experimenter, *caused* the change in attitudes.

What is it about the smokers' role-playing behavior that caused the change in attitudes? Janis and King (1954) suggested that role players search their memory for prior knowledge that supports their role. This search leads them to explore arguments that support the position that they are advocating, ignoring arguments that contradict the position. They may then base their subsequent attitude on these arguments. Although early experiments supported this hypothesis weakly (e.g., Janis & Gilmore, 1965), later research using better methods revealed stronger support (e.g., Greenwald, 1969). In addition, biased scanning plays a stronger role when people can thoughtfully consider the topic than when they are distracted (Albarracín & Wyer, 2000).

Role-playing and the biased scanning mechanism in general have enormous practical implications. If you are using this book in a course on attitudes, your instructor might have asked you to give a presentation on a particular topic (e.g., the strengths and weaknesses of implicit measures of attitude), generating your own arguments for or against the topic. This kind of active learning is often considered more useful than passively sitting and rehearsing information. This method is also used by marketing campaigns that ask the public to take part by letting a company know what is great about a product. In all these cases, people are subtly encouraged to teach themselves, rather than merely let themselves be convinced by others.

## KEY POINTS

- The biased scanning hypothesis indicates that role players search their memory for prior knowledge that supports their role.
- Biased scanning is more likely to predict attitude change when people can consider the topic more thoughtfully.

# SELF-PERCEPTION

The process of operant conditioning inspired a theory of attitude formation and change that emphasizes the way in which people can *infer* attitudes from their own behavior. From the perspective of Self-Perception Theory (Bem, 1965, 1972; see also Olson, 1990), there are many cases when our attitude is weak and we don't really know what it is. In these cases, we are in the same position as anyone else observing the behavior. An observer would rely on another person's actions to guess the person's attitudes. Therefore, according to Bem (1972, p. 2), so must the actor him or herself: "to the extent that internal cues are weak, ambiguous, or uninterpretable, the individual is functionally in the same position as an outside observer." If the actor is essentially in the same position as anyone else, then it is argued that the actor must deduce his or her attitude by considering the behavior and the situation that produced it:

> Individuals come to "know" their attitudes, emotions, and other internal states partially by inferring them from observations of their own overt behavior and/or the circumstances in which this behavior occurs. (Bem, 1972, p. 2)

 *Function Witch: Is self-perception all about the knowledge function of attitudes? Could we also self-perceive in a way that fits needs to defend our ego, our values, or self-image?*

# The basic effect: are cartoons funny because we laugh?

Self-Perception Theory provides a useful perspective on how attitudes can be shaped. In a clever experiment, Bem (1965) trained participants to lie about the funniness of different cartoons when one color of light was flashed (e.g., green), but tell the truth when a different color was flashed (e.g., amber). Then, the participants were instructed to say "This cartoon is very funny" or "This cartoon is very unfunny" for another set of cartoons, while the lights remained flashing, ostensibly because of an equipment malfunction. Participants were then asked to rate their true attitudes toward each cartoon on an attitude scale, and their ratings served as the key dependent variable.

Theoretically, participants should have learned to trust their statements more when the truth light was on than when the lie light was on. As expected, participants' attitudes were affected by the "accidental" exposure to the truth and lie lights. For example, if a participant said, "This is a very funny cartoon" in the presence of the "truth" light, then the participant subsequently rated this cartoon as funnier than if he or she had made this statement in the presence of the "lie" light.

Consistent with Self-Perception Theory, participants inferred the funniness of the cartoons from their behavior and the context in which it occurred.

**Content Witch:** *Does this result reflect an attitude toward the cartoons or simply an emotional response to them or both?*

Some ingenious studies have demonstrated the same type of effect by manipulating the structure of questionnaires asking people about their relevant behavioral experiences. Gerald Salancik and Mary Conway (1975) used a questionnaire with biased wording to elicit responses supportive of religiosity. In this biased questionnaire, some items described pro-religious behaviors and asked whether the respondent performed them "on occasion" (e.g., "On occasion I attend a church or synagogue"). Other items described anti-religious behaviors and asked whether the respondent performed them "frequently" (e.g., "I frequently refuse to donate money to religious institutions"). This bias in phrasing was used because people are more willing to agree that they perform a behavior "on occasion" than they are to say that they perform it "frequently." As a result, participants who answered this version of the questionnaire ended up agreeing with more pro-religious items (paired with "on occasion") than anti-religious items (paired with "frequently"), making participants' pro-religious behaviors salient. In contrast, participants who answered a different version of the questionnaire that reversed this pairing ended up agreeing with more anti-religious items (paired with "on occasion") than pro-religious items (paired with "frequently"), making their anti-religious behaviors salient.

As the key dependent measures, participants then responded to non-biased questions asking them to rate the extent to which they are religious. Responses to these items revealed that participants saw themselves as being more religious after their pro-religious behaviors were made salient than after their anti-religious behaviors were made salient. In other words, participants inferred their religious attitudes from their questionnaire responses, which had been subtly biased by the question wording.

Remember that Self-Perception Theory states that this type of inference should occur when attitudes are being formed, weak, or ambiguous. When our attitudes are held strongly beforehand they should be uninfluenced by simple perception of our overt behavior. Experiments have supported this part of Bem's reasoning. For example, Shelley Chaiken and Mark Baldwin (1981) asked participants to complete a questionnaire containing items that were framed in a way to remind people of either their pro-environment behaviors (e.g., picking up litter) or their anti-environment behaviors (e.g., leaving on lights). After completing this task, participants indicated their attitude toward the environment. The results strongly supported Self-Perception Theory. As can be seen in Figure 7.1, when participants had been reminded of their positive behaviors, they reported more favorable environmental attitudes than participants who had been reminded of their negative behaviors. More important, this effect was obtained only among those individuals who, prior to the experiment, had weak attitudes about protecting the environment. Participants who possessed stronger attitudes were not influenced by the manipulation of behavior salience.

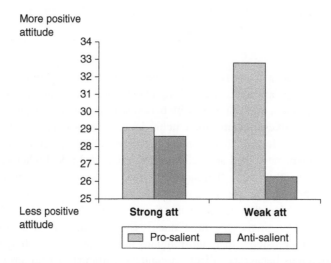

**Figure 7.1**    *Attitudes toward the environment as a function of framing of past behavior and pre-experimental strength of attitudes toward the environment (Chaiken & Baldwin, 1981)*

Other research has shown some unique ways in which self-perception effects can occur. In one line of work, Dolores Albarracín and Robert Wyer (2000) tested whether the mere *belief* in having performed a behavior is sufficient to shape attitudes. These researchers reported several studies where they cleverly tested the effects of knowledge about past behavior by leading participants to believe that, without being aware of it, they had expressed either support for a particular position or opposition to it. Because participants had not actually engaged in such behavior, the research tested directly the effects of merely *believing* that one has behaved in a certain way. As expected, participants reported attitudes that were consistent with the alleged past behavior. In addition, subsequent behavior was more consistent with the alleged prior action. Thus, mere beliefs about past behavior had a direct effect on attitudes and on subsequent behavior.

In a somewhat similar vein, research has considered the role of mindwandering in relation to self-perception. In one clever study, Critcher and Gilovich (2010) asked participants to imagine going to the cinema and having their mind frequently wander while watching the film. Some participants were asked to imagine their mind wandering about three things, while others were asked to imagine their mind wandering about one thing. Afterwards, participants indicated how much they thought they'd have liked the movie. The results revealed that participants liked the film more when they imagined their mind wandering about one thing rather than three. This suggests that the contents of individuals' mindwandering while imagining an action were sufficient to influence their attitude toward the action.

Importantly, research has also demonstrated that self-perception effects can occur even when we watch *others* perform a behavior. In a set of fascinating studies, Noah Goldstein and Robert Cialdini (2007) found evidence in support of *vicarious self-perception* – the idea that people might sometimes infer their own attributes by observing the actions of others. Goldstein and Cialdini found that the occurrence of vicarious self-perception was dependent upon two conditions: (a) when participants had a sense of merged identity with the target performing the behavior, and (b) when the target's actions seemed freely chosen. When people observe a close other (e.g., an ingroup member) engage in a freely chosen behavior, they might infer their own attributes based on the target's actions.

## Practical demonstrations: sales tricks and turning play into work

Self-Perception Theory has guided experiments on diverse topics, ranging from perceptions of personality traits (Fazio, Effrein, & Falender, 1981) and humor in jokes (Olson, 1992) to interpersonal attraction (Seligman, Fazio, & Zanna, 1980) and sexual anxiety (Haemmerlie & Montgomery, 1982). For instance, self-perception may help to explain an intriguing effect that is a favorite among salespeople: the foot-in-the-door technique. This name comes from times when people used to sell products door-to-door (rather than via the phone or the internet), and a salesperson would have a greater chance of success simply by subtly getting a foot in the door so the homeowner could not easily slam it without listening to the sales pitch. This name reflects the idea that a slight act of compliance (leaving the door open to listen) increases the likelihood of complying with a larger request (buying the product).

Freedman and Fraser (1966) nicely demonstrated this effect (see also Burger, 1999; Gorassini & Olson, 1995). The researchers went door-to-door to randomly selected houses in Palo Alto, California and asked homeowners to grace their front gardens with a large, ugly sign urging people to "Drive Carefully." Two weeks earlier, some of these homeowners had been asked to sign a petition (or use a window sticker) supporting a campaign for safe driving or for keeping their state beautiful. Agreement with the first request was high regardless of the topic of the petition; most people were happy to comply. More important, agreement with the second, larger request (to hoist the ugly sign) was significantly higher among homeowners who had received the first request than among homeowners who had not been given the first request.

Self-Perception Theory has also inspired teachers and parents to re-think the use of rewards for teaching children. If children infer their attitudes from their past behavior and their perception of the circumstances that produced it (as Self-Perception Theory suggests), then rewarding children for some behaviors may cause them to infer that they actually dislike the behaviors. This problem should arise particularly when children are rewarded for behaviors that they already *like* to perform. Some evidence indicates that rewarding children for performing a liked behavior subsequently makes the behavior less likeable on its own (rather than for the reward). This line of thinking has also been applied to the costs and benefits of parents offering rewards to influence their children's eating behavior (Cooke, Chambers, Añez, & Wardle, 2011). This loss of intrinsic reinforcement from the behavior is called an *overjustification effect* (Lepper et al., 1973; see Chapter 6). In essence, this effect reflects a reinforcement approach that turns play into work, reversing Mary Poppins' sage advice to turn "work" into play.

## KEY POINTS

- Self-Perception Theory indicates that we use our actions and the environment in which the actions occur to infer our attitudes.

- Self-perception is more likely for weaker attitudes, even when we merely believe that we have performed a particular behavior (which we may have not performed).

- Self-perception processes may help to understand many practical/applied issues, including the use of small commitments to elicit greater compliance with requests and the effects of over-rewarding children for participating in enjoyable activities.

### RESEARCH HIGHLIGHT 7.1

### THE DIFFERENT EFFECTS OF CANNED LAUGHTER

Have you ever watched a television sitcom where it was obvious that the show used a laugh track (e.g., canned laughter)? How did you react – did the canned laughter make the show seem more or less funny? Perhaps it depends on your expectations of its effects. An experiment by James Olson (1992) used Self-Perception Theory to test the effects of (falsely) telling participants that a laugh track increases or decreases our perception of humorous material.

In the study, 60 undergraduate students were presented with two sets of jokes that were equally funny. Participants listened to one set of jokes that were accompanied by a continuous laugh track, while the second set of jokes were unaccompanied. One group of participants was told that a laugh track tends to increase smiling and laughter (the increase group), while a second group was told that a laugh track tends to decrease smiling and laughter (the decrease group). A third, control group was told that a laugh track has no effect on smiling and laughter. After having listened to the two sets of jokes, participants were given the chance to read the books from which the jokes came, and their responses were videotaped.

Olson predicted that participants in the increase group would spend more time reading the book that had not been accompanied by the laugh track. This is because participants would have assumed that that their response to the first set of cartoons was due to the laugh track. In contrast, it was expected that participants in the decrease group would spend more time reading the book that had been accompanied by the laugh track. This book should have appeared funnier, as these participants were told that the laugh track would decrease smiling and laughter.

The results supported the author's predictions. Participants who were led to believe that a laugh track increases smiling and laughter spent almost twice as much time reading the book that was unaccompanied by the canned laughter. In contrast, participants who were led to believe that a laugh track decreases smiling and laughter spent more than twice as much time reading the book that was accompanied by the canned laughter. From a self-perception perspective, participants discounted or augmented their reactions to the jokes as a function of what they had been led to believe about the situation (i.e., the canned laughter).

# COGNITIVE DISSONANCE

## The basic idea: when cognitions go to war

Cognitive Dissonance Theory (Festinger, 1957, 1964) suggests that people feel an aversive tension or "dissonance" from having a set of two or more beliefs that do not seem to fit together. Such discrepant beliefs can occur when people find that they have acted against their own prior attitudes without sufficient reason. In this situation, people can end up with one belief indicating that they don't like the behavior, and another belief saying that they did it for no apparent reason. This inconsistency creates a discomfort, which people try to reduce by changing their attitude toward the behavior.

*Structure Witch: Is cognitive dissonance similar to ambivalence between positive and negative beliefs about an object?*

This process can be illustrated by considering a person who ends up going to a party she did not want to attend. She knows that (a) she did not want to go, and (b) she went anyway. Cognitive dissonance theory suggests that people in this situation feel uncomfortable and attempt to reduce this discomfort in one of several ways. For example, the partygoer may bizarrely attempt to convince herself that she did not actually go to the party. This would require a break from reality that is impossible for most people – so a simpler alternative may involve explaining the discrepancy by adding a relevant belief, such as "My friends forced me to go to the party." This belief would help to explain the gap between her behavior and her attitude, making her beliefs about the behavior and the attitude less discrepant or dissonant.

In some cases, it is easier to dismiss the importance of the inconsistency. The partygoer might realize that no one actually carried her to the party. As a result, it may be psychologically easier for her to simply dismiss her behavior and see its discrepancy from her attitude as *unimportant* in the larger scheme of things. This trivialization should help to reduce the discomfort from dissonance.

Cognitive Dissonance Theory describes another psychological option – one that is most relevant to the effects of behavior on attitude. This option involves assuaging discomfort by changing the attitude toward the behavior. The woman in our example might decide that she was actually happy to go along to the party or at least happy enough not to stay home, and may even decide that the party was worth attending. According to dissonance theory, this change would eliminate the discrepancy between her beliefs about her attitude and behavior, *and* cause great relief.

Abundant evidence supports the basic idea that such counter-attitudinal behavior shapes attitudes. This research has used four major effects: effort justification, post-decision spread, counter-attitudinal advocacy, and hypocrisy. Each of these effects is described in the sections below.

## Effort justification: "Let's talk about sex, baby . . . Let's talk about you and me . . ."

Most people feel anxious when they change schools, join a new club, or become a new employee. Sometimes, people in these places have elaborate rituals for new group members. These initiation rites hit new members at a time when they are least confident and most eager to please. Infamous examples occur in military squads and college fraternities and sororities. These groups are known for welcoming new members by asking them to perform embarrassing acts, such as streaking nude or dressing in a bizarre outfit in a public place. People outside the groups often shake their heads and either laugh or frown at this odd behavior. They wonder at the ills of youth and the perversity of each new generation.

Social psychologists instead wonder *why* groups use such ordeals. Confronted by these bizarre initiations, one group of researchers came up with what seems like a bizarre explanation: new members' performance of these embarrassing behaviors actually *increases* their liking for a group and helps the group's long-term cohesiveness and success (Aronson & Mills, 1959). For example, following initiation rituals, new members can reduce their guilt by convincing themselves that the behavior is not so bad and that the group requesting it is very much worth joining. Thus, initiation rituals may use cognitive dissonance to make the new members more amenable to group demands and more committed to the group.

Elliot Aronson and Judson Mills (1959) devised a famous experiment that tested this reasoning. Female participants were recruited for a discussion group study on the topic of sex (our reason for using the Salt 'N' Pepa lyric in this section's subtitle). There was a catch, however. The women were told that they must first undergo a "screening test" before entering the discussion group, in order to prove their ability to join the discussion. The experimenters manipulated the emotional difficulty of this test. In the *severe* initiation condition, the test involved reading aloud a graphic description of sexual activity that was replete with uncommon, obscene words. In the mild initiation condition, the women merely read a list of "polite" sexual words (e.g., virgin, prostitute).

All of the women were then told that their screening had taken too long. They could no longer actively take part in the discussion group, as it would ruin the flow of the discussion. Now, all they could do was merely listen to the discussion through headphones. The discussion they heard did not cover human sex, however; it was merely a boring and incoherent discussion about the secondary sex characteristics of lower animals. Participants' initiation had been for nothing but a *very* boring and unworthy outcome.

In the severe initiation condition, the discussion task presumably left the participants with inconsistent cognitions, such as "The discussion was *so* awful" and "I underwent a lot of embarrassment to listen to this discussion." How could the initiates reconcile this discrepancy? The most visible option would have been to decide that the discussion group was not so bad after all. Indeed, this is what Aronson and Mills found: participants' attitudes toward the post-initiation discussion group were more positive in the severe initiation group than in the mild initiation group (or a control group that completed no prior initiation before hearing the discussion). The act of completing the prior initiation led participants to like the group for which they had suffered so much. Because this study shows how hardship can influence attitudes, this finding has been labeled the *effort justification effect*.

The effort justification effect is relevant to understanding the effects of a variety of behaviors, including even therapeutic interventions. This relevance to therapeutic interventions is nicely illustrated in an experiment that is one of our all-time favorites. It used a real-world sample (i.e., not just psychology undergraduates!) and measured a behavior that is notoriously difficult to shift. Danny Axsom and Joel Cooper's (1985) experiment involved participants who were 10–20% over the desirable body weight. Participants had signed up for an experiment on possible methods of weight reduction. Accordingly, all participants completed a questionnaire about eating and exercise, and they received a booklet to help them monitor their diet over a three-week training period. During this period, the participants took part in five training sessions.

Each training session was designed to increase "neuropsychological arousal" and thereby increase "emotional sensitivity," which the researchers (falsely) claimed was associated with greater weight loss. To increase this "neuropsychological arousal," participants completed two difficult cognitive tasks. One task involved judging the vertical orientation of lines flashed quickly on a screen, and the second task involved reciting text (e.g., nursery rhymes) while hearing their voice and another voice echoed back to them. Participants in a high-effort condition were asked to do these tasks for 50 minutes, while participants in a low-effort condition performed them only for 10 minutes. Participants in a control condition simply completed a brief, irrelevant questionnaire in each session and had their weight recorded.

At a weigh-in after the three weeks of training, participants in the high effort condition had lost significantly more weight than participants in the low effort condition. This result was interesting, but the real, tough test was whether the weight loss persisted over time. As most ex-dieters are aware, well-developed, medically designed weight-loss and exercise regimes are notorious for failing to alter weight after a year. For this reason, the researchers called participants for another, surprise weigh-in six months later and then re-assessed their weight a year after the sessions had begun.

Figure 7.2 displays the principal results of this experiment. Amazingly, the weight loss among participants in the high effort group was significantly *higher* six months later and remained for the full year. This example of effort justification shows how people may not only adjust their attitudes to justify their behavior – the behavior related to the attitude also changes. That is, participants must have dieted and exercised more effectively, because the cognitive tasks had absolutely nothing to do with losing weight.

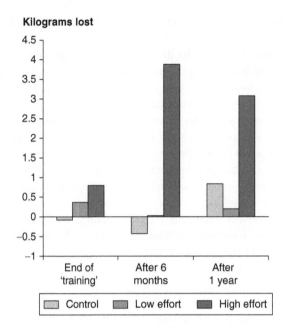

**Figure 7.2**   *Kilograms lost by participants as a function of effort justification (Axsom & Cooper, 1985)*

The potential practical value of effort justification is considerable, and Chapter 11 describes evidence that even non-human species have also been shown to exhibit behavior that is consistent with effort justification effects. People and animals don't feel comfortable with the idea that they have put in a lot of effort for nothing, perhaps especially when the effort seems to make little sense or comes at great personal cost. People often seem completely unaware that initiation rites may increase group commitment or that the value of therapy partly resides in the effort that people use to complete it. Suffering for something is better than suffering for nothing.

## Post-decision spread: Would you like the toaster or the teapot?

Effort justification is one way in which cognitive dissonance has been examined. A second type of effect occurs when people choose between two options that are equally liked or disliked, as when one of the authors struggles to choose between two films. In an important study, Jack Brehm (1956) asked participants to rank their preferences among a set of household items (e.g., a toaster, a radio), ostensibly as part of a study of consumer preferences. He later asked the participants to choose one of two equally liked items as a reward for participating in the study. He found that, over time, participants grew to like the chosen item *much* more than the unchosen item. That is, the difference in preference grew larger and larger after one item had been selected over the other.

This difference between the post-decision appraisal of the chosen and unchosen alternatives is often called a *spreading apart of choice alternatives*. This spreading effect is often regarded as evidence of *post-decisional dissonance*. It occurs when a decision is made between alternatives that are close in overall value, and the decision cannot be changed. The choice presumably causes dissonance from competing cognitions, including "I did not choose Object B" and "Object B is pretty amazing." Even though the chosen object is very appealing, this appears insufficient to reduce the dissonance, and a spread in subsequent attitudes helps people to feel better about their choice.

Research has considered a number of factors or situations that influence the spreading effect. From our perspective, perhaps the most interesting research has addressed how the effect might depend on whether people have the option to change their mind once a decision has been made. In Brehm's original study, participants could not change their mind after they chose between the two equally liked alternatives. What happens if people have the option to change their mind after making their original choice? This was addressed in research by Gilbert and Ebert (2002). In one study, all participants were asked to select one of two art posters that had been rated as equally liked. At that point, some participants were told that their decision was final, whereas others were told that they could reverse their decision (and take the other poster) anytime in the following four weeks. When they re-rated the prints 15 minutes later, people in the irreversible condition showed the classic spreading effect – they came to like the chosen print *much* more than the unchosen print. However, people who could reverse their decision showed the opposite effect – they evaluated the chosen print more *negatively* than the unchosen print. In explaining the impact of reversibility, Gilbert and Ebert speculated that having the chance to change one's mind makes people more likely to think about the flaws in the selected item. Consistent with this explanation, research has shown that reversibility increased the accessibility of negative thoughts about the chosen alternative as well as increasing the accessibility of positive thoughts about the unchosen alternative (Bullens, van Harreveld, Förster, & van der Plight, 2013).

In addition to addressing when the effect might be more or less likely to occur, research has also examined the reasons for this effect. Eddie and Cindy Harmon-Jones (2002) proposed that the spreading effect reflects an action orientation in people: the effect helps people get on with things (see also Harmon-Jones, Amodio, & Harmon-Jones, 2009). For instance, if Maxine has just decided which of two jobs to pursue, she can no longer afford to sit around and muse about whether her decision was right or not; she must do the job she chose and do it well. This requires that she focus on her actions or implementation of her decision. The spreading effect can help her to finish the decision-making stage and get on with the task at hand.

Support for the Action-Based Model of cognitive dissonance comes in a variety of forms. Harmon-Jones, Schmeichel, Inzlicht, and Harmon-Jones (2011) assessed whether approach-relevant personality attributes would be linked with greater dissonance reduction in a spreading of alternatives paradigm. Based on Corr's (2008) Revised Reinforcement Sensitivity Theory, Harmon-Jones and colleagues tested the hypothesis that individuals with a greater behavioral approach sensitivity (i.e., people who show a larger tendency to engage in goal-directed behavior) would be more likely to show more pronounced dissonance reduction effects, which would allow them to proceed with the engagement of goal-directed behavior. Using the Brehm (1956) paradigm, the researchers found evidence in support of the action-based model.

The Action-Based Model of cognitive dissonance has also been tested in an impressive set of experiments that used neuro-feedback training to increase or decrease activity in a portion of the brain that is closely tied to action orientation: the left frontal cortex (Harmon-Jones, Harmon-Jones, Fearn, Sigelman, & Johnson, 2008; see also Harmon-Jones, Harmon-Jones, Serra, & Gable, 2011). As expected, participants who received training that boosted activity in the left frontal cortex subsequently showed the spreading effect to a greater extent. These results support the idea that post-decision spreading occurs in order to support future action.

## Counter-attitudinal advocacy: effects of saying what we don't believe

Our next major demonstration of cognitive dissonance is perhaps the best known. Its genesis lays in the role-playing experiments mentioned at the start of the chapter. Often, the role-playing task explicitly required *counter-attitudinal advocacy*, which involves presenting an attitude or opinion that opposes the person's initial attitude. For example, university students might be asked to write an essay arguing for increased tuition fees.

### Seminal experiments

Festinger and Carlsmith (1959) showed that the effects of counter-attitudinal advocacy depend on the incentive that is offered. Their clever experiment consisted of three stages. The first stage was presented as a study of "Measures of Performance." Participants were asked to put 12 spools on a tray, empty the tray, and refill the tray. The experimenter madly pretended to record their performance while participants repeated this task with one hand for half an hour. Next, participants were asked to use one hand to quarter-turn 48 square pegs on a board (one way and then the other way) for half an hour, while the experimenter continued recording performance. The researchers expected that participants would loathe the experiment after an hour of these dull tasks.

In the second stage, participants were asked to do something that totally contradicted the experience they just had: they were asked to tell a new participant that the tasks were interesting and enjoyable. The experimenter explained this request by saying that he was actually looking at the effects of expectations on performance and that he was comparing the performance of participants who had been told nothing with the performance of participants who had been given positive expectations. He said that the next participant was due to receive positive feedback about the tasks, but a colleague who usually gives this information had not arrived. The experimenter then asked whether the participant could temporarily fill in, and virtually all of the participants agreed. The participant then attempted to persuade the next participant (who was actually a confederate of the experimenter) that the tasks were interesting, enjoyable, and exciting. In fact, they even argued with the confederate when the confederate said that someone else had said the tasks were dull!

In the third stage, participants were asked to meet an interviewer who was studying people's feelings about psychological experiments. Some of the interviewer's questions asked whether participants enjoyed the tasks from their experiment. This attitude measure was the key dependent variable.

The key independent variable was the amount of financial incentive that the experimenter offered for lying about the tasks: participants were offered either U.S.$20 or $1 to describe the dull tasks favorably to the next "participant"; $20 was a large amount of money in the 1950s. Indeed, this amount is equivalent to about $150 today (U.S. Bureau of Labor Statistics' Consumer Price Index Calculator), enough to enjoy a nice dinner for two and a show! In contrast, $1 was probably enough to buy some greasy onion rings and a small drink at the local burger joint. Basically, $20 provided a *very* large justification for lying by saying that the tasks were interesting, while $1 was paltry justification for this behavior.

Classic reinforcement theory suggests that people will be more likely to repeat a behavior that gets associated with a larger reward; this could happen by linking the behavior in memory with a strong positive emotional response. On these grounds, you might think that the large reward would also generate a more positive attitude. But this is not what Festinger and Carlsmith expected. Instead, they predicted that the larger reward would help to explain participants' dissonant cognitions about their behavior: "I said the tasks were interesting" but "the tasks were super dull." If they had also been offered $20 to say the tasks were interesting, then they could add another cognition to this mix: "I was offered $20!", which would provide ample explanation for the two inconsistent cognitions. But think about the scenario when only $1 is offered. In this case, "I was offered one measly dollar" would not be enough to resolve the discrepancy (i.e., explain their lie). They have to resolve their dissonance in other ways, but only one option will work easily: they can decide that the tasks were not so bad after all.

That is exactly what Festinger and Carlsmith found. As expected, participants were more favorable toward the tasks if they had been offered $1 than if they had been offered $20 or had not been asked to lie about the tasks (in a separate control condition). Thus, the presence of *lower* justification for the behavior led to more favorable attitudes.

This effect has been replicated many times and in diverse ways. For example, rather than merely asking participants to write a counter-attitudinal essay, Zimbardo, Weisenberg, Firestone, and Levy (1965) asked American college students and army reservists to eat fried grasshoppers! Of course, most of the participants would have been disgusted by these bounding insects. Yet, among participants who actually ate the grasshoppers (almost 50%), those who were asked by an unattractive experimenter (low incentive condition) were subsequently more favorable toward grasshoppers as food than were those who received the request from an attractive experimenter (high incentive condition).

## Self-presentation

Numerous researchers have looked at the mechanism that produces the effect of counter-attitudinal advocacy. One early explanation was that participants merely wanted to appear consistent in front of the experimenter (Gaes, Kalle, & Tedeschi, 1978; Tedeschi, Schlenker, & Bonoma, 1971). That is, they didn't wish to look like people who act differently from how they feel.

Many experiments had taken special precautions to avoid this bias. The Festinger and Carlsmith (1959) experiment used separate experimenters and an elaborate cover story to make participants comfortable assuming that any consistency or inconsistency would not be visible to anyone. Nonetheless, some experiments found that attitude change from counter-attitudinal behavior is reduced or completely eliminated when elaborate procedures make the behavior seem truly anonymous (Gaes et al., 1978). In addition, there is evidence that the effect is stronger among people who tend to be concerned about their impression on others (Paulhus, 1982; Scheier & Carver, 1980).

But do these effects happen because people are *consciously* trying to manipulate the perceptions of others? It could be the case that people may believe in their changed attitude and are unaware that it reflects an attempt to save face. It is difficult to address this question. It is also difficult to see how this explanation accounts for experiments showing that dissonance-induced attitude change can persist for many days (Freedman, 1965; Staw, 1974). In addition, there is evidence that impression management does not account for the "dissonance" effect in the effort justification paradigm (Rosenfeld, Giacalone, & Tedeschi, 1984). On balance, then, the current evidence supports dissonance theory, while suggesting that we also cannot ignore the social consequences of attitude expression when explaining the effects of counter-attitudinal behavior.

**Function Witch:** *After we lie about our attitude, does the new attitude express our personal values or social concerns?*

## Freedom and aversive consequences

The importance of social consequences broadly fits an influential review of experiments that examined the effects of counter-attitudinal advocacy. Joel Cooper and Russell Fazio (1984) summarized these experiments by suggesting that counter-attitudinal advocacy causes attitudes to change only when people feel entirely *free* to commit the counter-attitudinal act, despite *foreseeing* that the act will produce negative *consequences* for which they feel *responsible*. These negative consequences can potentially include negative impressions given to others. Since Cooper and Fazio's review, however, there has been controversy over whether the dissonant act needs to yield aversive consequences (Harmon-Jones & Mills, 1999). Some experiments suggest that they at least contribute to the effect (Johnson, Kelly, & LeBlanc, 1995) and others indicate that they are not needed (Harmon-Jones, Brehm, Greenberg, Simon, & Nelson, 1996; Prislin & Pool, 1996).

## Threat to the self

It may be the case that counter-attitudinal advocacy produces one particular type of negative consequence that is vital: a threat to the self-concept (Aronson, 1969; Heine & Lehman, 1997;

Steele & Liu, 1983). People want to believe that they are good, honest individuals, but lying about their attitude threatens this belief about themselves. It could be this threat to the self-concept that is most disconcerting, especially when there are aversive consequences of the counter-attitudinal advocacy.

This hypothesis fits evidence that the effects of counter-attitudinal advocacy are reduced after people have been given an opportunity to re-affirm their self-integrity (Steele, 1988). Steele and Liu (1983) pointed out that this *self-affirmation* of integrity can be achieved easily, simply by getting people to express values that are important to them. They showed that subtly induced counter-attitudinal advocacy exerted no effects on attitude when participants had an opportunity for such self-affirmation between the time they wrote a counter-attitudinal essay and the time that they reported their attitude toward the topic. More important, this effect happened even though the participants' self-affirmation involved rating the importance of values (e.g., on aesthetics) that had little to do with the topic at hand (e.g., funding research).

## Arousal is futile?

Another major challenge to the dissonance interpretation of the effects of counter-attitudinal advocacy was posed by Bem's (1972) Self-Perception Theory. According to Self-Perception Theory, the presence of small incentives causes people to *guess* that their attitude actually matches the position that they advocated, because they can see no *external* reasons why they performed the behavior. Participants who argue against their own attitude might simply guess their attitude from their behavior, without feeling any dissonance or arousal whatsoever.

Bem's perspective raises two important questions. First, does counter-attitudinal advocacy cause people to feel an *aversive* arousal? Second, does this arousal account for attitude change? Answers of "yes" to both questions would provide more compelling support for the cognitive dissonance theory explanation.

Several famous studies of the effects of *misattributing* arousal help to answer these questions. In one ingenious experiment, Mark Zanna and Joel Cooper (1974) gave participants a placebo pill and said that this pill would make the participant relaxed, aroused, or have no effect. Later, in an ostensibly unrelated study, participants were asked to write an essay arguing that inflammatory speakers should be banned from college campuses. (This was not a popular position.) To manipulate the experience of dissonance, participants were either reminded about their choice in writing a counter-attitudinal essay or not reminded of this choice. In theory, dissonance should be higher when choice is salient (thereby removing any explanatory cognitions, such as "they made me do it").

If participants experience arousal after writing their essay, then the false information about the placebo pill's side-effects should determine whether participants in the high-choice conditions exhibit more attitude change than participants in the low-choice conditions. When the pill is seen as the probable cause of their discomfort, people do not *need* to change their attitude to explain their behavior – they can misattribute it to the pill. Indeed, changing their attitude wouldn't be of much use, because they believe that the pill caused their arousal. In contrast, when the pill provides no explanation or even makes matters worse by making participants believe that they should be relaxed, then participants should think that their arousal arises because of their attitude-inconsistent behavior. To lower this arousal, they should change their attitude to match the behavior.

The results of this clever experiment are shown in Figure 7.3. As expected, the effect of choice salience was obtained only when participants were led to believe that the pill would have no effect or make them relaxed. In the arousal condition, participants had a ready-made explanation for their arousal. Thus, they did not need to change their attitude to reduce their arousal.

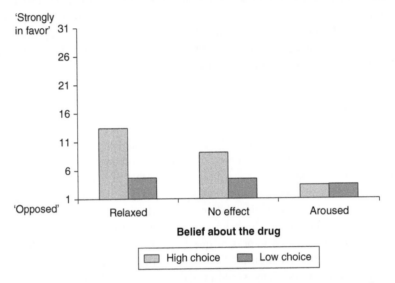

**Figure 7.3**    *Attitudes toward banning an inflammatory speaker after arguing in favor of a ban (Zanna & Cooper, 1974): effects of (a) prior choice in the counter-attitudinal advocacy and (b) the expected effect of a pill*

## The co-existence of self-perception and dissonance

Notwithstanding the above evidence, Fazio, Zanna, and Cooper (1977) suggested that self-perception and dissonance might both help to explain the effects of counter-attitudinal advocacy, but in different situations. These scientists suggested that a key consideration is whether people are being asked to express an attitude that is far from a position that they would accept or close to a position that they would accept. This idea fit prior research on Social Judgment Theory (Sherif, 1980; Sherif & Sherif, 1967), which we briefly mentioned in Chapter 5. This theory proposes that attitudes can include latitudes of acceptance, latitudes of rejection, and latitudes of non-commitment. The range of positions that a person accepts is labeled the *latitude of acceptance*; the range of attitudes that a person rejects is labeled the *latitude of rejection* and encompasses the range of positions that a person rejects; and the range or positions that a person neither accepts nor rejects is labeled the *latitude of non-commitment*.

Fazio et al. (1977) pointed out that some behaviors might be discrepant from a person's attitude *and* within their latitude of rejection, while others might be discrepant but within their latitude of acceptance. If so, dissonance processes should occur if an attitude-discrepant behavior is within one's latitude of rejection and therefore deviant enough to elicit dissonance. In contrast, self-perception processes might occur when an attitude-discrepant behavior is within one's latitude of acceptance, because the behavior is not deviant enough to elicit an arousal.

In a clever test of this prediction, Fazio et al. (1977) used the misattribution paradigm that Zanna and Cooper (1974) had devised for examining the effects of dissonance-based arousal on attitude change. In their adaptation of this paradigm, Fazio et al. asked participants to read statements about socio-political philosophy that were on an ideological continuum from "radicalism, extreme liberal" to "extreme conservative, reactionism." Participants indicated which statement was most acceptable and which other statements were acceptable and objectionable. Participants were then randomly assigned to write in support of a liberal philosophy that was most different from their attitude (see Figure 7.4). This essay supported a position that was either within the latitude of rejection or immediately beside this latitude, but actually in the latitude of acceptance. Thus, there was only one scale value difference between the two policies.

The experimenters then reminded some participants of their choice to write the essay and did not remind others. Then, prior to writing the essay, some of the participants were seated in a "new experimental booth," and they completed questions asking about feelings of discomfort sitting within the booths. These questions were used to encourage participants to misattribute any arousal that they were experiencing to the booth. Other participants received no special instruction about the booth.

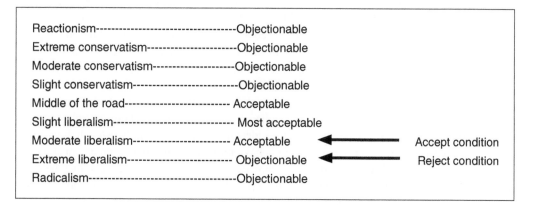

**Figure 7.4** *A participant's hypothetical responses to the latitudes measure used by Fazio et al. (1977)*

Next, participants rated the extent to which they perceived themselves as politically conservative or liberal. (Participants never wrote their essay, because all that's required to elicit dissonance is a *commitment* to writing the essay.) The researchers first looked at whether the participants who had received the reminder of choice to write the essay were subsequently more liberal than participants who had not received the reminder. This difference was found when participants agreed to write an essay in their latitude of rejection *and* when participants agreed to write an essay in their latitude of acceptance. Crucially, however, the misattribution of arousal reduced this difference when participants had agreed to write an essay that was in their latitude of rejection. When the essay position was within the latitude of acceptance, giving participants the opportunity to misattribute arousal to the booth did not eliminate the effect of choice on attitudes.

This pattern fit the researchers' prediction that dissonance explains our attitude change following a behavioral commitment we find objectionable, while self-perception explains our attitude change following a behavioral commitment we find at least somewhat acceptable. Overall, then, both theories may have some validity: cognitive dissonance processes may occur when people's actions contradict their initial attitude, whereas self-perception processes may occur when people's actions are at least somewhat pro-attitudinal.

## Hypocrisy: "Let's talk about sex again, baby . . ."

When people don't practice what they preach, they are normally labeled as *hypocrites*. Hypocrisy involves a discrepancy between a verbal behavior that promotes our attitude and a second behavior that contradicts our verbal statement. Hypocrisy involves its own type of inconsistency, but one that should not be any less discomforting than the type of counter-attitudinal advocacy we have described already. Indeed, research indicates that hypocrisy has powerful effects on attitude and behavior.

The best way to explain the effects of hypocrisy is by first describing its effects. In a great study, Stone, Aronson, Crain, Winslow, and Fried (1994) asked college students to make a videotaped speech arguing that condoms should be used every time people have sex. After making this speech, participants were asked to think about times when they had *not* used a condom. They were then given four U.S.$1 bills as payment and then offered a chance to buy condoms (for 10 cents each). Results indicated that participants who had made a public commitment about their positive attitude *and* then listed their hypocritical failures to use condoms subsequently purchased more condoms than participants in other, control conditions. (These control conditions included participants who had merely made the videotaped speech *or* simply listed their past failures to act.) In sum, participants changed their behavior after making a public statement about the importance of performing an action *and* then immediately thinking of a time when they behaved in the opposite way: their pro-attitudinal behavior (i.e., the attitude expression) contradicted their recalled behavior, eliciting behavior change.

There is evidence that the effects of hypocrisy occur because hypocrisy creates an aversive arousal. Subjective reports of guilt and discomfort following a hypocrisy induction predict the amount of behavior change (Son Hing, Li, & Zanna, 2002), and behavior change is reduced after people are given an opportunity to misattribute their arousal to another variable (Fried & Aronson, 1995). Hypocrisy effects have also been demonstrated for a variety of behaviors, including discrimination (Son Hing et al., 2002), recycling (Fried & Aronson, 1995), water conservation (Dickerson, Thibodeau, Aronson, & Miller, 1992), cigarette smoking (Peterson, Haynes, & Olson, 2008), and other health-related domains (see Stone & Focella, 2011).

Research has also considered variables that influence when hypocrisy effects are more or less likely to occur. At the person level, research has shown that the magnitude of hypocrisy effects differs as a function of variation across people in constructs such as self-esteem (Peterson et al., 2008) and self-concept complexity (McConnell & Brown, 2010). At the group level, research has shown that witnessing the hypocrisy of a member of one's group can affect a person's own attitudes and behavior, akin to vicarious self-perception (Gaffney, Hogg, Cooper, & Stone, 2012; see Research Highlight 7.2). At the same time, however, other experiments have found that people avoid seeing their own hypocrisy on topics that are moral (Batson, Thompson, & Chen, 2002; Batson, Thompson, Seuferling, Whitney, & Strongman, 1999). Perhaps hypocrisy inductions in experiments *make* people see their own inconsistency, increasing people's actual compliance with their own moral standards.

But what about the effects of hypocrisy on attitudes? These effects appear to come about when hypocrisy is made more public. Carrie Fried (1998) demonstrated this effect by making individuals aware of their hypocrisy, by having the experimenter read their listed failures to recycle aloud to them. In this case, subsequent behavior did not change, even though there was other evidence that participants did experience dissonance. How then did participants reduce their dissonance? Measures of attitude indicated that participants formed less positive attitudes about the importance of recycling.

Fried (1998) speculated that this effect on attitude occurred because the public visibility of the failures to recycle made this behavior relatively fixed. That is, participants couldn't easily change this behavior without looking bad, and it may have been easier to justify their hypocritical behavior by changing their attitude. This result raises many questions about when hypocrisy will cause attitude change rather than behavior change.

## KEY POINTS

- Cognitive Dissonance Theory suggests that behavior can cause discrepant cognitions, and people reduce the tension from these discrepant cognitions by changing their attitude.

- Dissonance may help to cause attitude change when people have expended high effort for little gain, choose between two items that are equally attractive, or are subtly made to choose to argue against their own attitude.

- The effects of counter-attitudinal advocacy on attitudes may be more likely to occur when freedom to choose is salient and people feel responsible for consequences that are threatening to their self-concept.

- Effects of counter-attitudinal advocacy occur partly because it elicits psychological discomfort.

- Contemplating our own hypocrisy can cause subsequent behavior or attitude change.

## RESEARCH HIGHLIGHT 7.2

### CAN WITNESSING OTHERS' HYPOCRISY MAKE YOU MORE PRO-ENVIRONMENTAL?

One of the fascinating aspects of the hypocrisy paradigm is its application to "real world" behaviors. As discussed in this chapter, seeing one's own hypocrisy can be an effective tool in eliciting behavior change. A recent study by Gaffney et al. (2012) explored whether witnessing the hypocrisy of another ingroup member can alter attitudes and behavioral intentions, and whether the level of change depends on whether the hypocrisy is viewed by a third party who was part of (or not part of) the same ingroup.

In their study, Gaffney and colleagues (2012) had university participants listen to a recorded interview made by an ingroup member (purportedly another student from their university) who stressed the importance of walking and cycling over car travel for making short journeys. After stressing the importance of pro-environmental behavior, the speaker then admitted having used a car for a short journey. The participants listened to the interview alongside a third party. For some participants, the third party claimed to be an ingroup member (i.e., a student from their own university); for other participants, this third party claimed to be an outgroup member (i.e., someone from a different city). The third party also either remarked on the hypocrisy or not, creating a 2 (group membership) x 2 (reaction) design. The study's dependent variable was participants' level of endorsement of pro-environmental attitudes and intentions.

The results of the study revealed that the greatest endorsement of pro-environmental views came from participants who heard an outgroup member comment on the hypocrisy, whereas there was least endorsement of pro-environmental views among participants in the condition where an outgroup member did not comment upon the hypocrisy. When the third party was an ingroup member, their response to the hypocrisy had no impact on participants' attitudes.

The authors explain their results by suggesting that having an outgroup member remark upon the hypocrisy of a fellow ingroup member leads a person to rally around and support the prevailing group norm. This result is important in several ways. While offering additional evidence regarding how hypocrisy can affect environmental attitudes, it also highlights how witnessing another's hypocrisy impacts our own attitudes, and how these effects are influenced by the characteristics and responses of other people who view the hypocrisy.

# CONCLUSION

The idea that behavior can shape attitudes (rather than merely the other way around) can be counter-intuitive to many new students of the psychology of attitudes. Yet this idea is supported by numerous experiments examining effects of behaviors ranging from role playing and initiations to decisions between close alternatives and arguing against one's own attitude. In this chapter, we have highlighted the scope of these effects and some of the primary explanations for understanding them. These explanations highlight that the effects of behavior involve emotional processes and cognitive guesswork within individuals.

# WHAT WE HAVE LEARNED

- Behavior can be caused by many subtle factors that we do not notice, other than our own attitudes.

- There are at least three important dimensions for classifying exploratory behavior, including distinctions between direct versus indirect experience, good versus bad outcomes, and approach versus avoidance behaviors.

- Self-Perception Theory indicates that we can use behavior to guess our attitudes when we don't know our attitudes well.

- People can experience uncomfortable tension (i.e., dissonance) after performing a behavior that is inconsistent with a strongly held prior attitude, and they may change their attitude to explain the behavior.

- Self-perception and dissonance may both occur, and they are based on cognitive and affective processes that follow behavior.

# WHAT DO YOU THINK?

- Could different mechanisms contribute to the results of different paradigms that have been used to test dissonance theory? For example, the mechanism underlying the post-decision spread may be different from the mechanism underlying counter-attitudinal advocacy. A series of experiments have shown that people become more favorable toward a chosen object in the post-decision paradigm partly because they come to associate *themselves* with the object. Because people see the self positively, this positive affect toward the self spills over onto evaluations of the object (Gawronski, Bodenhausen, & Becker, 2007). This evidence suggests that dissonance reduction may not be necessary to explain the effects of forced choice on attitude. Do you think that this mechanism or other mechanisms may explain attitude change in the induced compliance or effort justification paradigms?

- Research has demonstrated the utility of inducing hypocrisy to change attitudes and behavior. For example, a lab experiment by Stone and colleagues (1994) found that hypocrisy was successful in helping change students' perceptions about the risks of unprotected sex. Do you believe that this approach could be used to change behavior in the "real world?" Would a government campaign designed to highlight hypocrisy for something like recycling make people more likely to recycle?

# KEY TERMS

*Action-based model* – a model that explains post-decisional spreading of choice alternatives by proposing that it is partly driven by an action orientation.

*Biased scanning hypothesis* – the idea that, in role-playing situations, individuals search their memory for prior knowledge that supports their role.

*Cognitive Dissonance Theory* – a model predicting that people feel an aversive tension from having a set of two or more beliefs that do not seem to fit together.

*Counter-attitudinal advocacy* – presenting an attitude that opposes the person's initial attitude.

*Effort justification* – the idea that suffering hardship can influence attitudes.

*Foot-in-the-door technique* – a method that uses a slight act of compliance (leaving the door open to listen) to increase the likelihood of complying with a larger request (buying the product).

*Hypocrisy* – a discrepancy between a verbal behavior that promotes our attitude and a second behavior that contradicts our verbal statement.

*Latitude of acceptance* – the range of attitude positions that a person accepts.

*Latitude of rejection* – the range of attitude positions that a person rejects.

*Self-affirmation* – activity that helps to promote a subjective feeling of self-integrity, often by describing personal values.

*Self-Affirmation Theory* – the idea that individuals can reduce cognitive dissonance by restoring a sense of self-integrity.

*Self-Perception Theory* – the idea that individuals sometimes derive their own attitude by making inferences from their own behavior.

*Spreading of choice alternatives* – the difference between the post-decision appraisal of chosen and unchosen alternatives.

*Vicarious self-perception* – the idea that people might sometimes infer their own attributes by observing the actions of others.

*Weighting bias* – the idea that people differ in the weight they give negative and positive information in attitude processes.

# FURTHER READING

## BASIC

Gawronski, B. (2012) Back to the future of dissonance theory: Cognitive consistency as a core motive. *Social Cognition, 30*, 652–668.

Goldstein, N. J. and Cialdini, R. B. (2007) The spyglass self: A model of vicarious self-perception. *Journal of Personality and Social Psychology, 92*, 402–417.

Harmon-Jones, E. and Mills, J. (1999) An introduction to cognitive dissonance theory and an overview of current perspectives on the theory. In E. Harmon-Jones and J. Mills (eds), *Cognitive Dissonance: Progress on a Pivotal Theory in Social Psychology* (pp. 3–21). Washington, DC: American Psychological Association.

Martinie, M-A., Olive, T. and Milland, L. (2010) Cognitive dissonance induced by writing a counterattitudinal essay facilitates performance on a simple task but not on complex tasks that involve working memory. *Journal of Experimental Social Psychology, 46*, 587–594.

Olson, J. M. (1992) Self-perception of humor: Evidence for discounting and augmentation effects. *Journal of Personality and Social Psychology, 62*, 369–377.

## APPLIED

Albarracín, D., Cohen, J. B. and Kumkale, G. T. (2003) When communications collide with recipients' actions: Effects of the post-message behavior on intentions to follow the message recommendation. *Personality and Social Psychology Bulletin, 29*, 834–845.

Burger, J. M. and Guadagno, R. E. (2003) Self-concept clarity and the foot-in-the-door procedure. *Basic and Applied Social Psychology, 25*, 79–86.

Carrera, P., Muñoz, D., Callabero, A., Fernández, I. and Albaraccín, D. (2012) The present projects past behavior into the future while the past projects attitudes into the future: How verb tense moderates predictors of drinking intentions. *Journal of Experimental Social Psychology, 48*, 1196–1200.

Eisenstadt, D., Leippe, M. R., Stambush, M. A., Rauch, S. M. and Rivers, J. A. (2005) Dissonance and prejudice: Personal costs, choice, and change in attitudes and racial beliefs following counterattitudinal advocacy that benefits a minority. *Basic and Applied Social Psychology, 27*, 127–141.

Stone, J. and Focella, E. (2011) Hypocrisy, dissonance and the self-regulation processes that improve health. *Self and Identity, 10*, 295–303.

# 8

---

# BASIC PRINCIPLES IN HOW ATTITUDES ARE SHAPED

---

## QUESTIONS TO PONDER

1. Is your opinion ever influenced by things that seem irrelevant? If so, when do extraneous things have more or less of an effect on you?

2. If you don't like tofu because of how it tastes, would you be more persuaded by information that its taste has improved or by information about its high nutritional value?

3. How much are your opinions influenced by things that you do not notice?

4. How does the placement of beliefs in a logical sequence matter for persuasion?

## PREVIEW

The aim of this chapter is to provide a "big picture" perspective to help think about much of the evidence reviewed in the prior three chapters. To help integrate the extensive information on the cognitive, affective, and behavioral influences on attitudes, we summarize four simple, potential principles that appear to operate across these influences. First, attitudes can be influenced by information that has, at best, weak relevance to the attitude object. Second, the impact of weak information on attitudes can be reduced when people possess high motivation and ability to form a correct attitude. Third, attitude change partly depends on whether messages emphasize the content, structure, or functions that are the basis for the recipients' own attitudes. Fourth, attitude change can occur without conscious awareness of the persuasive factors. We then describe other factors relevant to these principles and potential additional principles.

# THE DIFFICULTY IN IDENTIFYING THE BASIC PRINCIPLES OF PERSUASION

Have you heard the saying "If it was easy, *anyone* could do it?" Our parents often said this when we were frustrated at difficulties learning a new skill, such as the hockey wrist shot or how to play the piano. The idea was that everyone would be a professional ice hockey star or concert pianist if these things were easy to master. Similarly, everyone would be rich and popular if they knew the art of persuasion so well that they could convince people of anything. But persuasion, like other skills, is not so easy. Much of this complexity was shown in the previous chapters describing how attitudes are shaped.

When things are complex, it can become difficult to see the forest and not the trees; we can get caught up in details and forget the big picture. Fortunately, there are several rules of thumb that might help to get a bigger view of how attitudes are shaped. We have previously speculated that four principles work best (Maio & Haddock, 2007). These principles are not "laws" of attitude formation and change; nor would we claim that they are entirely and completely correct. However, they can be considered as useful guides that can help us understand basic processes in attitude change. Like our three witches, they help to point out some interesting features as we explore the ideas and evidence.

# PRINCIPLE 1: INFLUENCE BY SILLY THINGS

The first principle we wish to highlight is that *attitudes can be influenced by information that has, at best, weak relevance to the attitude object*. For example, it is a bit bizarre that we are more likely to agree with people who are attractive, even though their attractiveness has absolutely no bearing on whether they are right or not. In these cases, our attitudes are clearly doing something other than help us be correct; they might make us incorrect as an indirect way of promoting our social relationships with others.

A surprising range of "silly" variables can influence attitudes and most people often appear to disbelieve that these variables actually influence *them* personally. Yet experiments have produced numerous examples of their effects. Some of the examples are relatively easy for people to accept. For instance, as discussed in Chapter 6, people can be more amenable to an argument when they are in a good mood than when they are in a bad mood. At one level, this is worrisome. If, for example, we agree to buy a new car partly because we are in a good mood, we wouldn't be giving enough weight to factors that are actually far more relevant and important, such as the car's cost and utility. The cost and utility will be with us long after the mood has passed. Thus, the effect of mood is at least somewhat worrying (and remarkable) even though this result probably confirms human intuition about persuasion.

The effects of other irrelevant variables are a bit more puzzling for our intuitions. We may have no trouble imagining that we would like to buy an attractive new coat after being told that it will come with a discount, but how would we feel after learning that the discount is no longer available? Experiments have found that people may remain favorable even after learning that the desirable consequence will *not* occur (Burger & Petty, 1981; Cialdini, 2008). Perhaps forming our initial attitude is like getting married: we become wedded and are unlikely to change our feelings even after learning that our partner may not be quite as we had imagined. By the time this discovery occurs, we have found new reasons to feel the way we do; the reasons for the earlier infatuation no longer matter.

Other somewhat unusual influences include effects of a communicator's rate of speech (Smith & Shaffer, 1995; Woodall & Burgoon, 1984) and accent (Gluszek & Dovidio, 2010), the use of humor (Conway & Dubé, 2002; Strick, Holland, van Baaren, & van Knippenberg, 2012), citations of consensus (Darke et al., 1998), the particular color cues contained within a persuasive appeal (Gerend & Sias, 2009), the communicator's name (Howard & Kerin, 2011), and the positive versus negative framing of the attributes (Blanton, Stuart, & VandenEijnden, 2001). The framing effects are particularly interesting because they merely involve showing the same attribute in two ways. For example, a message could state that brushing twice daily helps to *avoid tooth decay*, or it could say that brushing twice daily helps to *maintain healthy teeth*. These different statements essentially mean the same thing, but can differ in persuasiveness depending on one's current goals (Rothman & Salovey, 1997; Tykocinski, Higgins, & Chaiken, 1994).

There are also effects of likeable (Chaiken, 1980), attractive (Chaiken, 1979), powerful (French & Raven, 1959), certain (Karmarkar & Tormala, 2010), famous (Petty, Cacioppo, & Schumann, 1983), and ingroup sources (Whittler & Spira, 2002). These sources tend to cause more agreement with a message, although they can also occasionally cause disagreement (Petty, Fleming, & White, 1999; Roskos-Ewoldsen, Bichsel, & Hoffman, 2002).

All of these audience, source, and message factors can vary in the extent to which they seem irrelevant. Of course, they are not always completely irrelevant to the correctness of a message. There are occasions when it *is* reasonable for someone to be more persuaded by an attractive source than by an unattractive source. Would you be convinced by a shampoo that was being endorsed by someone with dull, lifeless hair (or, like both of the authors, very little hair)? If the shampoo was really effective, the person advocating it should have found it useful (Kahle & Homer, 1985).

There may also be individual differences and cultural differences in what we believe to be relevant information (Cialdini, Wosinska, Barrett, Butner, & Górnik-Durose, 1999; Livingston, 2001). People have their own theories of persuasion, enabling them to occasionally recognize the extraneous variables like mood and the nonextraneous ones (Friestad & Wright, 1999; Wilson & Brekke, 1994; Wilson, Houston, & Meyers, 1998). An important question for research is how these theories play their part in understanding attitude change (Sagarin, Cialdini, Rice, & Serna, 2002).

## KEY POINTS

- Attitudes are often influenced by variables that we would regard as being irrational.
- Variables that shape attitudes can seem more or less relevant to the attitude, falling on a continuum from high to low relevance.
- There may be individual differences and cultural differences in what we believe to be relevant information.

**RESEARCH HIGHLIGHT 8.1**

## WHAT'S IN A NAME? QUITE A LOT, IN THE CONTEXT OF PERSUASION!

Our name represents an important part of our self. We have a preference for letters that appear in our name compared to letters that don't appear in our name (see Koole, Dijksterhuis, & van Knippenberg, 2001), and the question "How much do you like your name, in total?" has been used as an implicit measure of self-esteem (Gebauer, Riketta, Broemer, & Maio, 2008). In the context of persuasion, research has explored whether we devote greater attention to information from another individual whose name is similar to our own. For example, would someone named Geoff be more likely to devote attention to a communicative appeal from Jeff compared to one from Stuart? This question was addressed by Howard and Kerin (2011), who tested the hypothesis that greater name similarity between a communicator and the message recipient would lead the recipient to devote greater attention to the information presented by the communicator.

To test this hypothesis, Howard and Kerin conducted a first study in which students evaluated a resumé. In one condition, the individual named on the resumé shared the same letter of the first and last name of the participant. In a second condition, there was no such match. The results revealed that participants in the similarity condition spent more time looking at the resumé (and remembered more of its contents) compared to participants in the dissimilarity condition.

In a subsequent study, Howard and Kerin explored whether this similarity–attention link would be found in the context of consumer product names. Here, participants saw a cogent advert for a brand of cranberry juice where part of the product name was similar to or different from the participant's name. Participants then had the chance to evaluate and sample the beverage. The results showed that participants in the similarity condition preferred and drank more of the brand compared to participants in the dissimilarity condition. Further, the link between attitudes and consumption behavior was stronger in the similarity condition compared to the dissimilarity condition.

These results shine a new light on factors that influence the degree to which individuals pay attention to information presented by others. In this case, an individual or product with a name similar to the message recipient was sufficient to elicit greater attention to relevant information.

# PRINCIPLE 2: INFLUENCE BY MOTIVATION AND ABILITY

It is fortunate that we are not entirely vulnerable to weak, irrelevant information. We tend to take for granted that people are usually influenced by rational, strong arguments, such as "this car uses less fuel and is therefore easier on your budget." Such information has a larger impact than weak information when people are motivated and able to think carefully about an issue. Thus, our second principle is that *the relative impact of weak information can be reduced when people possess high motivation and ability to form a correct attitude, except when the relevant information is difficult to interpret and the irrelevant information is difficult to identify.*

Here, we explicitly focus on the motivation and ability to form a *correct* attitude. As we saw in Chapter 5, high personal relevance of a topic and low distraction can increase this motivation and ability. High motivation and ability make people more likely to use information (e.g., the content of an argument) that is more directly relevant to the attitude object, rather than cues that are less relevant. For instance, according to the Elaboration Likelihood Model, people who are motivated and able can attempt to correct for the potential impact of extraneous information on their attitudes and beliefs (Wegener & Petty, 1997, 2001). The MODE Model (Fazio, 1990, 1995; Olson & Fazio, 2009) also highlights the importance of motivation and ability. Proponents of the Unimodel suggest that deeper consideration of information may cause the relevant information to override the impact of the irrelevant information, particularly when the irrelevant information is difficult to process (Pierro et al., 2004).

An important caveat is that the motivation to be correct can, by itself, also cause the use of irrelevant information on occasion. The Heuristic-Systematic Model predicts that people use less relevant persuasive information (e.g., source credibility) when they are highly motivated to form a correct attitude and all of the available relevant information is ambiguous or contradictory (Chaiken & Maheswaran, 1994; Chaiken et al., 1989). This effect may occur because the less relevant information becomes more relevant in the presence of contradictory information. Indeed, past research showing this effect has focused on a source characteristic – credibility or trustworthiness – that has potential relevance (Maheswaran & Chaiken, 1994). Another possibility is that people in this predicament simply need to base their views on some piece of information – whether it is a random toss of a coin or something with dubious validity.

**Function Witch:** *Another way to look at these effects is that ambiguous information might be causing people to be more influenced by whether the source of a message addresses the dominant attitude function for the message recipient (e.g., credibility helps to satisfy a need for knowledge).*

People in this situation may also expand their theories of the attitude object to include the information as a *plausible* guide. Information that would not normally seem relevant can become relevant after we imagine it differently. In other words, we might temporarily become a bit superstitious. We may not know if our country's finance minister is telling lies about the shape of our economy, but we decide that her winning smile must mean she is trustworthy. The result can be an *overinterpretation* of irrelevant evidence, at least when people are faced with difficulties identifying and correcting for this evidence (Pelham & Neter, 1995; Tetlock & Boettger, 1989; Tetlock, Lerner, & Boettger, 1996).

Notwithstanding these situations where use of "silly" information can persist, people's use of more relevant information might also be enhanced when they feel sufficiently confident about their own self-concept to be open-minded about ideas that challenge their views. In normal circumstances, people can be defensive when they receive information that challenges their views.

For example, Ziva Kunda (1987) found that caffeine consumption predicted women's negative reactions to a message linking caffeine to fibrocystic disease (a disease that affects women), but caffeine consumption did not predict message acceptance in men.

Claude Steele's (1988) Self-Affirmation Theory, which has had an important impact on our understanding of the effects of behavior on attitudes (see Chapter 7), may help to predict when this defensiveness can be reduced. According to this theory, self-affirmation may convey a sense of self-integrity, which enables people to be more open-minded about possible threats without feeling that their self-integrity would suffer from being wrong. This view was elegantly supported in research by David Sherman, Leif Nelson, and Claude Steele (2000). In one of their experiments, they asked women to read an article describing a link between caffeine consumption and fibrocystic disease. This message was of high relevance to women who drank high amounts of coffee and of low relevance to women who did not drink coffee. After reading the article, some of the women self-affirmed by completing a measure of their top ranked values (identified in a pre-test session). In contrast, women in a no-affirmation condition completed a measure of their fifth-ranked value. All participants then completed measures assessing their acceptance of the article and intentions to change their behavior.

Analyses of these measures revealed that, in the no-affirmation condition, the coffee-drinking women were more defensive and less accepting of the health information than the non-coffee-drinking women (see Figure 8.1). This result replicated the findings of Kunda (1987). More crucially, this tendency was reversed in the affirmation condition. In this condition, the coffee-drinking women were more accepting of the health information than the non-coffee drinkers. Futhermore, the coffee-drinking women were more willing to reduce their coffee intake than in the no-affirmation condition. Thus, the opportunity to self-affirm on an

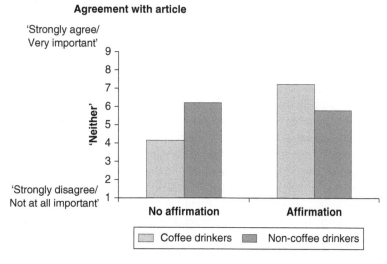

**Figure 8.1** *The effects of caffeine consumption and self-affirmation on persuasion (Sherman et al., 2000)*

important value reduced defensiveness among individuals most affected by the threatening content of the persuasive message.

A caveat about Sherman et al.'s (2000) study was its focus on a novel threat, rather than a threat that people already know a great deal about, such as smoking. This issue has been addressed in several experiments conducted by researchers in England (Harris & Napper, 2005). Participants in one experiment received vivid, high-threat, anti-smoking messages. Beforehand, participants were given an opportunity to self-affirm or were not. As expected, participants who did self-affirm were more accepting of the messages (see also Zhao & Nan, 2010). Harris and colleagues also found that self-affirmation increased people's pursuit of information promoting a healthy diet, after having received information that they had a poor diet (e.g., Epton & Harris, 2008). These effects appear to occur because self-affirmation encourages systematic processing of the threatening information (Correll, Spencer, & Zanna, 2004; Harris & Napper, 2005). Overall, a sense of integrity in the self may promote the use of relevant information in contexts that often elicit defensiveness, provided that people do not feel too vulnerable to the threat.

## KEY POINTS

- High motivation and ability make people more likely to use information that is more directly relevant to their attitude, rather than use information that is less relevant.

- Use of more relevant information may increase when people feel confident enough to be open-minded about ideas that challenge their views without experiencing a threat to their self-concept.

## PRINCIPLE 3: INFLUENCE BY A COMMON LANGUAGE

Our third potential principle is that attitude change partly depends on whether messages emphasize the content, structure, or functions that are the basis for the recipients' own attitude. Here's an example of what we mean. One of the authors has a friend who, a long time ago, did not like vegetarian hot dogs. He insisted that they tasted awful. The author insisted that veggie hot dogs are much better for you than the normal pork variety (of course, that's probably not saying much) and that there was one brand of veggie hot dog that was delicious and almost indistinguishable from the real thing. These arguments were utterly ineffective until one day when the author bought himself and his friend a "hot dog" from a sausage vendor in downtown Toronto. After his friend consumed the "hot dog" with glee, the author told him that the hot dog was actually a veggie dog. His friend reacted with disbelief and insisted on ordering a second one himself to detect the lie. It was the truth, of course, and the friend's attitude to veggie hot dogs (or at least that particular brand) changed forever. He hadn't been persuaded by "cold," cognitive information about the health benefits of veggie dogs, but he was persuaded by taste. According to our third principle, this persuasion may have occurred because his attitudes were based on taste to begin with. The chance to freely taste the veggie hot dog helped to address the primary basis for his attitude, and this match facilitated the attitude change.

Scientists examining persuasion have long been interested in whether the effectiveness of a persuasive appeal is enhanced by matching it to properties of the recipient's attitude. As described in Chapter 5, Carl Hovland, Irving Janis, and Harold Kelley's (1953) seminal theory of persuasion suggested that persuasive messages are more effective when they give an *incentive* for attitude change. Their model raised the possibility that this incentive is more likely to occur when people detect a match between the thrust of an appeal and the basis of their attitude.

Three types of matches can be considered, corresponding to our three witches. There can be matches to attitude content, attitude structure, and attitude function. Research has examined these three types of matches separately, with far more attention to content and function matches than to structure matches (so we do not cover structure matches here). What has research on matching found?

With regard to content matches, many scientists have considered how attitudes based on affective or cognitive information might be more or less susceptible to affective or cognitive appeals. An experiment by Kari Edwards (1990) provides an interesting illustration of matching effects. Her experiment involved two stages. In the first stage, she created new attitudes toward a fictitious beverage named "Power-Plus." Participants were exposed to positive information about the beverage that was affective (i.e., its taste or smell), *and* positive information that was cognitive (i.e., a description of its nutritional value). Edwards assumed that attitudes toward the beverage would be more strongly based on the type of information that they received first (like a primacy effect). In the second stage, participants were given negative affective and cognitive information about the beverage. As in the earlier attitude formation stage, Edwards assumed that the type of the appeal depended on the order of the affective or cognitive information, such that the type of information presented first would represent the major basis of the appeal.

Edwards found evidence of a relative matching effect: the affect-based appeal elicited significantly more change in attitudes that were affect-based, while the cognition-based appeal elicited somewhat (but not significantly) more change in cognition-based attitudes. Similar patterns have since been obtained using a variety of experimental materials, procedures, and attitude objects (Edwards & von Hippel, 1995; Fabrigar & Petty, 1999).

Other research has considered whether individual differences in attitude content elicit matching effects. People differ in the extent that their attitudes are generally based on affective and cognitive information: some people rely primarily on affective information, whereas others rely primarily on cognitive information (Huskinson & Haddock, 2004). It turns out that a strong affective intervention elicits more attitude change among individuals whose attitudes are affect-based, whereas a strong cognitive appeal elicits more attitude change among individuals whose attitudes are cognition-based (Huskinson & Haddock, 2004). The effectiveness of affect- and cognition-based interventions also depends on individual differences in the need for affect and need for cognition. The need for affect is the tendency to seek out and enjoy emotional experiences (Maio & Esses, 2001), whereas the need for cognition is the tendency to seek out and enjoy effortful cognitive tasks (Cacioppo & Petty, 1982). Research using self-report measures of these personality variables has found that affective messages are more persuasive among individuals who are higher in the need for affect (rather than low in this need), whereas cognitive messages are more persuasive among people who are higher in the need for cognition (Haddock, Maio, Arnold, & Huskinson, 2008).

In addition to considering how individual differences in personality influence content-based matching, research has considered how people's *meta-perceptions* of the bases of their attitudes influence the efficacy of affective and cognitive appeals. See, Petty, and Fabrigar (2008, 2013) have found that people who perceive their attitudes to be based primarily on affect have higher interest in processing affect-based appeals, whereas people who perceive their attitudes to be based primarily on cognition have higher interest in processing cognition-based appeals.

In early studies on content matching, the nature of the appeal was different so that it specifically targeted affective or cognitive information. For example, Huskinson and Haddock (2004) had participants taste a beverage (affect) or read about its attributes (cognition). An obvious question following from studies of this sort is whether similar matching effects can be found when differences in the affective and cognitive appeals are more subtle. This issue was addressed in a nice set of studies by Mayer and Tormala (2010). In one of their experiments, these researchers presented male and female participants with a poster for a fictitious film. In the affect condition, the poster contained quotes (offered by purported reviewers) saying things like "I feel this will be a winner," and "My feeling is that this movie trumps every movie of its kind." In the cognition condition, the words *feel* and *feeling* were simply replaced by the words *think* and *thought*. Based on research suggesting that women are affectively oriented compared to men, Mayer and Tormala hypothesized that women would rate the film more positively had they read the affect frame rather than the cognitive frame, whereas men would show the opposite effect. As can be seen in Figure 8.2, the findings were consistent with their predictions.

With regard to attitude function matches, many scientists have considered how attitudes serving different psychological needs might be more or less susceptible to persuasive interventions that emphasize different needs. Most of this research has used individual difference variables

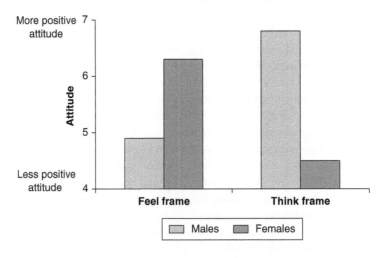

**Figure 8.2**   *The effects of affective versus cognitive frame and gender on attitudes (Mayer & Tormala, 2010)*

to deduce the functions of participants' attitudes before they receive a message. The most frequently studied individual difference in this context is self-monitoring (Snyder, 1974, 1986). As described in Chapter 2, high self-monitors are concerned with maintaining harmonious social relationships with others, and their attitudes are posited to primarily fulfill a social-adjustive function. In contrast, low self-monitors are concerned with fulfilling their own internal values and attitudes, and their attitudes are posited to primarily fulfill a value-expressive function. A number of experiments have demonstrated that high self-monitors are more persuaded by appeals targeting social-adjustive concerns, whereas low self-monitors are more persuaded by appeals targeting value-expressive concerns (DeBono, 2000; Prentice, 1987). This evidence supports the hypothesis that matches to attitude function are more persuasive than mismatches.

This function-based matching effect has been replicated and extended in other streams of research. In one particularly interesting line of work, Hirsh, Kang, and Bodenhausen (2012) explored whether personality-based matching effects would be found for the "Big Five" measures of personality (openness, conscientiousness, extraversion, agreeableness, and neuroticism; Costa & McCrae, 1992; Gosling, Rentfrow, & Swann, 2003). These researchers created five adverts for a fictitious brand of mobile phone, with one ad being targeted for each of the big five dimensions. Participants were asked to rate the effectiveness of each ad, as well as completing a big five personality questionnaire. For each of the five dimensions, there was a significant positive correlation between perceived advert efficacy and participants' scores on the matched traits. Further, there was no relation between efficacy and personality scores in mismatched cases. Because of well-documented links between the big five traits and individual differences in motivation (Ashton, Jackson, Helmes, & Paunonen, 1998), it is plausible that these matching effects are related to individual differences in the functions of participants' attitudes. Also, as noted by the authors, as websites collect more information about individual's personal preferences, they can create targeted adverts that match individuals' personality traits.

Additional evidence supporting the functional matching effect comes from research that has attempted to manipulate attitude function. In one experiment, participants were led to believe that their attitudes typically fulfilled either a social-adjustive or value-expressive function (Murray, Haddock, & Zanna, 1996). These participants were then more persuaded by a message that matched their perceived attitude function. Another experiment capitalized on evidence that some objects are more likely to serve an instrumental function (e.g., coffee), while others are more likely to serve a social-adjustive function (e.g., greeting cards). For example, Sharon Shavitt and colleagues (Shavitt, 1990; Shavitt & Nelson, 2000) found that attitudes toward objects that primarily fulfill an instrumental function were more likely to change in response to an instrumental appeal (e.g., emphasizing the product's flavor and freshness) than to a social-identity-based appeal (e.g., emphasizing the message recipient's personality and discernment). In contrast, attitudes toward objects that primarily fulfill a social-identity function were less likely to change in response to an instrumental-based appeal than to a social-identity-based appeal.

Despite these function-match effects, matching may not *always* enhance persuasion (Petty & Wegener, 1998b). Recall from Chapter 5 that the Elaboration Likelihood Model suggests three possible routes for an appeal to affect attitudes. In this context, matching may (1) act as a cue, (2) elicit more scrutiny or attention to matched appeals, or (3) bias thoughts about matched and mismatched appeals (Petty, Wheeler, & Bizer, 2000). Petty and colleagues have argued that matching could cause more *or* less persuasion when the enhanced scrutiny mechanism is operating, depending on the strength of the arguments contained within the matched message. If the arguments in an appeal are strong, enhanced scrutiny should cause more attitude change. However, if the arguments in an appeal are weak, enhanced scrutiny should cause less attitude change. In support of this prediction, Richard Petty and Duane Wegener (1998b) found that post-message attitudes were more strongly affected by argument strength when the message matched the functional basis of the recipient's attitude. Similarly, there is evidence that health promotion messages elicit more scrutiny when their content matches message recipients' motivational orientation to approach gains versus avoid losses (Updegraff, Sherman, Luyster, & Mann, 2007).

Enhanced scrutiny might be a mechanism that produces both content matching and function matching effects. This possibility fits past research because it has tended to use arguments that the researchers expected to be strong. In these instances, scrutiny of the messages should cause positive message-relevant thoughts and increase agreement with the message (Lavine & Snyder, 1996). Exceptions have occurred primarily in experiments where the appeals might have been counterargued with relative ease (Millar & Millar, 1990) or appeals have been highly discrepant to the recipient's attitude (See, Valenti, Ho, & Tan, 2013).

**Structure Witch:** *Would enhanced scrutiny occur if people perceived a structure match between their attitude and an appeal?*

If this mechanism is responsible for matching effects, then it would make sense to say that matching is an *enabler* of persuasion, but not an *elicitor* of persuasion. Through matching, people may be more accurate in their responses to a message, thereby detecting its strengths and weaknesses. The greater accuracy can arise because people are motivated to process messages that are relevant to their goals. In addition, people may find these messages easier to understand because the message is framed in a way that is compatible with their goals. In other words, matching is like phrasing a message in a language that best suits the recipient, making the message more interesting and easier to understand. When this is accompanied by strong arguments, the message may also become more compelling.

An additional factor that might help understand what underlies at least some types of matching effects comes from research on the amplification hypothesis (Clarkson, Tormala, & Rucker, 2008). Broadly stated, this hypothesis states that, as an attitude increases in certainty, it can become more open to change or more resistant to change, depending upon characteristics of the attitude. In research that applied the amplification hypothesis to content-based matching effects, Clarkson, Tormala, and Rucker (2011) speculated that increased attitude certainty would lead attitudes to become more open to matched information and more resistant to mismatched information. In a series of studies, Clarkson et al. (2011) found support for their hypothesis.

Yet another interesting issue in the context of matching is the role of matching to inner psychological conflicts. The emergence of implicit measures of attitudes makes it possible to examine discrepancies between self-reported, explicit personality traits and implicitly measured traits. A person might consciously think that he or she is shy, but show either high or low shyness on an implicit measure. A *large* discrepancy between the explicit and implicit measure would suggest an internal conflict on this trait dimension – an internal conflict that people may seek to resolve by paying more attention to information about the trait. By paying attention to information about the trait, they may discover something that helps to close the gap between their explicit and implicit self-assessments. A series of experiments have obtained support for this prediction (Briñol et al., 2006).

## KEY POINTS

- Affect-based messages may cause more change in attitudes that are affect-based, while cognition-based messages may cause more change in attitudes that are cognition-based.

- Messages that target the psychological functions fulfilled by an attitude may be more persuasive than messages that target different psychological functions, at least when the message arguments are strong.

- People may be influenced by matches *within* types of attitude content and function.

### RESEARCH HIGHLIGHT 8.2

### A DIFFERENT KIND OF MATCHING

In the examples of content matching we have described in this chapter, the research compares the relative effectiveness of affective appeals versus cognitive appeals. Is it also the case that matching can be effective *within* categories of attitude content? This question was addressed in elegant research conducted by DeSteno, Petty, Rucker, Wegener, & Braverman (2004). In one experiment, participants were made to feel sad or angry before reading an appeal highlighting the need to increase a state tax. For some participants, the tax increase was described as necessary to help alleviate events linked with sadness (e.g., suffering of special-needs infants). For the remaining participants, the tax increase was described as necessary to help alleviate events linked with feeling angry (e.g., without the tax, there will be increased traffic delays). After reading the sadness or anger appeal, participants indicated their attitude toward the tax increase.

The results of the experiment revealed that participants who were induced to feel sad were subsequently more persuaded by arguments that induce sadness than participants who were previously made to feel anger. In contrast, participants who were induced to feel anger were

*(Continued)*

(*Continued*)

more persuaded by arguments that induce anger than participants who had been made to experience sadness. These effects happened only among participants who were high in the need for cognition (Cacioppo et al., 1996), which is a personality trait that leads people to think carefully about messages. When the affect-matching occurred, participants thought that the arguments were more valid, and a statistical test indicated that this effect on perceptions of validity may have produced the increased persuasion.

# PRINCIPLE 4: INFLUENCE BY THE UNKNOWN

Our fourth principle is that attitude change can occur without conscious awareness of the persuasive factors. People may sometimes report attitudes without accurately knowing why they feel the way that they do (Nisbett & Wilson, 1977). For example, when we are presented with many consumer items that we like, we tend to choose items to our right, but people will never say "it was on the right" when explaining why they picked an item (see Casasanto, 2009, 2011, for a review of fascinating research on handedness and preferences). Instead, we focus on an assortment of inaccurate theories of the bases of the attitudes. As a result, introspection about why we feel the way we do can also cause people to change their attitudes (Wilson, Dunn et al., 1989). People also hold incorrect theories about the things that unreasonably bias their attitudes, and they may overcorrect or undercorrect for these factors as a result (Wegener & Petty, 1997; Wilson & Brekke, 1994). Introspection appears to be accurate only when we have very high knowledge about an attitude object (Wilson, Kraft, & Dunn, 1989). Presumably, high expertise of this sort gives us a better chance of remembering the true bases of our attitude when asked to describe them.

Part of the problem with introspection is that our attitudes may often be formed extremely quickly, with little awareness on our part. This speed is one reason why it is difficult to accept that persuasion always moves in a sequence of stages, as discussed by some of the models presented in Chapter 5. For example, several experiments have found that merely understanding a *false* statement is enough to cause instantaneous belief in its validity, and this belief is corrected only after further deliberate thinking (Gilbert, Tafarodi, & Malone, 1993). Similarly, abundant research by cognitive and social psychologists has made clear that people frequently take short-cuts to conclusions, rather than exhaustively considering evidence beforehand (Fiske & Taylor, 2008). For example, people might pay little attention to the content of a message and yield based on a source cue, like expertise (Chaiken, 1980; Petty et al., 1981). This evidence questions the necessity of thinking about attention and comprehension as conscious stages of processing.

More direct evidence for this principle was described in Chapter 6, where we saw that subliminal exposures to images of an attitude object elicited more positive attitudes without participants being aware of the exposures. For instance, experiments using classical conditioning paradigms revealed significant effects of subliminal emotional primes on diverse stimuli such as Chinese ideographs (Murphy & Zajonc, 1993), neutral words (De Houwer, Hendrickx, & Baeyens, 1997), and strangers (Krosnick et al., 1992). In addition, such effects can be obtained using both implicit and explicit measures of attitude (Olson & Fazio, 2001, 2002, 2006). Taken together, this research suggests that attitudes can be formed and changed without people's awareness of how the attitude was shaped.

Some of these results can be understood using the Value-Account Model proposed by Tillman Betsch and his colleagues (Betsch, Plessner, & Schallies, 2004; Betsch, Plessner, Schwieren, & Gütig, 2001). Their dual-process model suggests that attitudes can be produced by implicit processing (which occurs unintentionally and without awareness) and explicit processing (which occurs intentionally and with awareness). Implicit processing involves simply *adding* evaluative information into a hypothetical memory structure labeled the "value account." In contrast, explicit processing involves *averaging* new evaluative information with prior information.

Several studies by Betsch and colleagues have supported the model (see Betsch et al., 2004). One experiment asked participants to view television advertisements while at the same time reading aloud price information for stock market shares, which were shown scrolling at the bottom of the screen (Betsch et al., 2001). The results indicated that spontaneous attitude judgments toward individual shares correlated with the actual total yield of the shares, even though participants were unable to recall information about each share. In contrast, another experiment found direct evidence supporting the use of an averaging mechanism for explicit attitude formation (Betsch et al., 2001). All told, these results suggest that there is a different process for attitude formation that operates outside of our awareness than for attitude formation that operates at conscious levels.

Also, subliminal priming of motives can determine the effectiveness of subsequent persuasive messages. This effect occurs in specific conditions. The idea is that subliminal primes can activate goal-relevant cognitions (Fitzsimons & Bargh, 2003) and, when these thoughts are combined with a motivation to pursue the goal, the effectiveness of a relevant persuasive appeal is enhanced (Karremans, Stroebe, & Claus, 2006; Strahan, Spencer, & Zanna, 2002). Thus, both the prime and the pre-existing motivation must be present for a goal-relevant message to have greater success.

Erin Strahan, Steve Spencer, and Mark Zanna (2002) conducted an elegant set of experiments testing this hypothesis. After having avoided food and drink for three hours prior to one of these experiments, all participants completed a "taste test" on two types of cookies. Some of the participants were then offered water to quench their palate, while other participants were not offered water. These thirsty or satiated participants were then shown quick, subliminal flashes of either thirst-related or neutral words on a computer screen. Subsequently, all of the participants were given a chance to try different drinks. Analyses of participants' consumption indicated that thirsty participants who had also been primed with thirst-related words drank significantly more than all other participants. In essence, this research provides more support for the function matching principle that we describe above, but using a subliminal activator of attitude function.

Messages can also include subliminal visual cues or primes. These cues are shown so quickly that people cannot report having seen them, but the mind does register them to some degree nonetheless. Abundant evidence has documented that subliminal visual events do register in people's memory, and, more strikingly, they can affect people's attitudes and behavior.

A provocative example was obtained in two experiments conducted by Johan Karremans, Wolfgang Stroebe, and Jasper Claus (2006) in the Netherlands. These researchers used a computer to flash the phrase "Lipton Ice" for only 23 milliseconds on the computer screen. Before and after this quick flash, a string of Xs was shown (XXXXXXX). Next, participants took part in a study ostensibly gathering data about people's consumer choices. Participants were asked to indicate whether they would choose Lipton Ice or Spa Rood (a well-known mineral water in the Netherlands), if they were offered the drinks. The results of Karremans and colleagues' first experiment indicated that *thirsty* participants were more likely to choose Lipton Ice if this beverage had been subliminally primed before the choice than if a control word had been primed ("Npeic Tol"). Non-thirsty participants did not show this effect. Similarly, the results of their second experiment (see Figure 8.3) indicated that participants who had previously been given a salty snack (which made participants thirsty) were more likely to show the effect than participants who had not (see also Bermeitinger, Goelz, Johr, Neumann, & Ullrich, 2009). Thus, both experiments suggest that subliminal cues can affect attitudes and behavior when people are experiencing a need that is relevant to the cue (again pointing to a role for attitude function). That said, some recent research has argued that pre-existing needs are not necessary to elicit subliminal priming (see Loersch, Durso, & Petty, 2013).

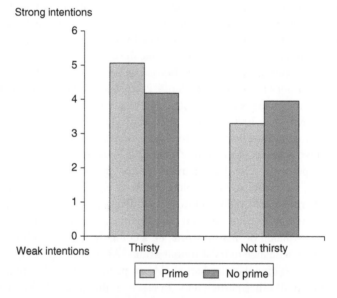

**Figure 8.3**   *The effects of thirst/non-thirst and prime on intentions to drink Lipton Ice (Karremans et al., 2006)*

Subliminal primes can influence persuasion processes in other ways. Rather than priming a brand name, Légal, Chappé, Coiffard, and Villard-Forest (2011) primed some participants with the phrase "to trust" before they read a persuasive appeal, whereas other participants did not receive this prime. To the extent that goals are important in eliciting subliminal persuasion effects, these researchers speculated that priming "to trust" would lead participants to become more trusting of the source of a persuasive appeal. After receiving (or not) the trust prime, participants were given 80 seconds to read a cogent persuasive message about the benefits of drinking tap water (as opposed to buying bottled water). After reading the message, participants rated aspects of the message as well as their intentions to drink tap water. As can be seen in Figure 8.4, the results revealed that primed participants were significantly more likely to agree with the content of the message, view the message source more favorably, and perhaps most importantly, indicate that they would be more likely to drink tap water and less likely to buy bottled water.

You might be reading about these effects and express a degree of concern and worry. Is it really that easy to persuade people without their knowledge? Are people helpless to the potential effects of subliminal persuasion? Addressing these concerns, research has considered the circumstances under which the effects of subliminal persuasion are minimized. One way this has been studied is by assessing the role of habits (see Chapter 4). Verwijmeren, Karremans, Stroebe, and Wigboldus (2011) tested whether pre-existing habits (e.g., a strong preference for a particular brand) regarding a subliminally primed brand would moderate the effects found by Karremans et al. (2006). Specifically, these authors argued that strong habits would constrain subliminal priming effects. To the extent that people have a strong habit for selecting (say) a certain beverage, this would limit the impact of subliminal information. In their study, Verwijmeren and colleagues found that, among people who had no strong habit or preference for a particular beverage, priming a particular brand had a significant effect on subsequent preferences only when people were thirsty (replicating Karremans et al., 2006). However, when participants had a strong habit

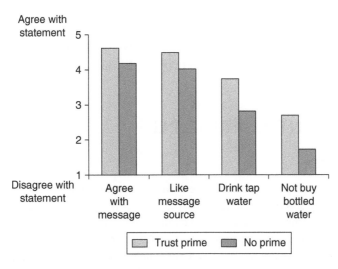

**Figure 8.4** *The effects of a trust prime on evaluations of a persuasive message (Légal et al., 2011)*

or preference for a particular beverage, priming them with their preferred brand led them to select that brand regardless of whether they were thirsty or not.

Verwijmeren, Karremans, Bernritter, Stroebe, and Wigboldus (2013) also assessed whether forewarning individuals about the presence of subliminal advertisements would minimize their effects on attitudes and behavior, in the same way that forewarning of a persuasive appeal can lead individuals to build up a defense. In one study, these researchers warned half of the participants that they would be receiving subliminal ads; other participants did not receive such a warning. Participants were then primed and asked to choose between the primed brand and another brand. Among non-warned participants, the subliminal primes influenced participants' attitudes, replicating previous findings. However, forewarning participants eliminated the effect. In a further study, they deftly varied the timing of the warning. Some participants were warned before they were primed, and others were warned after being primed but before they made their choice between products. Perhaps unsurprisingly, the warning eliminated the subliminal prime effect regardless of when the warning was provided. Being made aware of a sneaky influence attempt may automatically cause defensive reactions that protect us against unwanted change.

 *Content Witch: Most of the examples of nonconscious influence focus on cases where people formed attitudes based on emotional associations or primes. Does nonconscious influence also occur for cognitive and behavioral influences?*

## KEY POINTS

- We often lack accurate awareness of the real reasons why we hold particular attitudes.
- Attitudes may be produced by implicit processing (which occurs unintentionally and without awareness) and explicit processing (which occurs intentionally and with awareness).
- Subliminal cues may affect attitudes and behavior when people are experiencing a need that is relevant to the cue.

## OTHER POTENTIAL PRINCIPLES

## Logic matters

Have you ever skied or tried learning to ski? We are not sure that the cognitive approaches to persuasion do a good job of explaining how you get a person to try this activity. At first, a few friends say they are planning a ski trip and you think that sounds exciting, then you are standing part-way up a "beginner hill" that looks more like Mt. Everest, with little tykes zooming this way and that way. "This is nuts!" and "What am I doing here?" might cross your mind. Suddenly, you don't like skiing anymore, because it looks far more dangerous than you thought. The reasoning can go something like this:

1. If I go down that hill I will fall (eventually).
2. If I fall, I will break my leg or worse.
3. Therefore, I will break my leg.

For people in this situation, their attitude is not merely an average or sum of the beliefs that they will fall and break their leg; it is a logical chain that says they "will" break their leg. If you change the belief that they will fall, then breaking their leg is not a worry (even though they could break their leg for other reasons). Of course, ski instructors spend a great deal of time teaching people how to avoid falling, and not how to avoid breaking a limb – their teaching recognizes the logical sequence in most people's minds. Even though serious injury is what people *really* care about, making them believe that they won't fall is the solution to getting them to like skiing.

This example shows how logical connections between beliefs are also important for understanding persuasion. With this in mind, it is tempting to consider an additional principle in persuasion: *attitudes are influenced by people's views of the logical relations between beliefs that underpin the attitudes*. People think about logical connections among beliefs in complex ways that are different from merely adding up positives and negatives, and the importance of these logical connections is pointed out in so-called *probabilogical models of attitude change* (McGuire, 1960b; Wyer & Goldberg, 1970). These models predict how a person's belief in a conclusion may change when their belief in a related premise is altered. Experiments testing these models showed how a persuasive message could affect the belief it targeted *and* a belief logically related to it, despite not being explicitly targeted by the persuasive message.

William McGuire (1960a) supported the probabilogical model in a clever way, through a series of experiments demonstrating the *Socratic effect*: thinking about related beliefs causes people to make the beliefs more logically consistent with each other. This effect is one of our favorite pieces of attitude research, partly because it is so simple. It was detected by finding more consistency between beliefs about an issue or a person after a second questionnaire about the beliefs than after a prior questionnaire about them.

The Socratic effect has typically been shown by asking participants to make likelihood judgments about related beliefs. For example, participants have used scales from 0 "not at all likely" to 10 "extremely likely" in order to rate four beliefs about a hypothetical person (e.g., Henninger & Wyer, 1976). Participants would rate the chances that a person was part of a particular group; the extent to which the person has a particular attribute if he is part of the group; the extent to which the person has a particular attribute if he is *not* part of the group; and the extent to which the person had the attribute. The belief ratings would be more consistent with laws of logic in the second presentation of the questionnaire. This may occur partly because people try to reduce the discrepancies between their beliefs after they first become aware of them. In addition, it may occur because the first administration makes the connections between the beliefs more salient to people (Henninger & Wyer, 1976).

Models of persuasion have been rather limited in the role that they assign to these logical processes, despite their admirable job of considering the role of cognitive responses in persuasion. Cognitive models of persuasion need to explore these connections more fully if a more complete understanding of persuasion is to be gained. This exploration may yield basic principles beyond those described here and into the realm of studying the logic behind strong versus weak arguments (Hahn & Oaksford, 2007).

## Attitude strength

It is interesting to think about some specific principles that we have refrained from adding to our list. One additional principle of persuasion could be that *strong attitudes are more resistant to change and more predictive of behavior* (see Krosnick & Petty, 1995). The prior chapters have described consistent evidence that attitudes based on strong cognitions, affect, and/or behavior are more accessible from memory and are also more predictive of behavior (Chapter 4). In addition, attitudes are more resistant to change when they are based on extensive, consistent knowledge (Chapter 5), strong emotions (Chapter 6), and past behavioral experience (Chapter 7). These characteristics can all be viewed as indicators of attitude strength (Petty & Krosnick, 1995), and they are dependent on the three witches that we outlined earlier.

Despite these pieces of evidence, we resist proposing a principle based on attitude strength. Like other researchers (Krosnick, Boninger, Chuang, Berent, & Carnot 1993; Visser et al., 2006), we expect that there is more to be gained by examining the unique roles and interactions among different conceptualizations of attitude strength than by treating them solely as common indicators of a single underlying principle. Thus, although this potential principle merits consideration, it may be too broad to be useful.

## Information sequence

Another interesting potential principle would consider sequences in attitude formation and change: *information presented early in a persuasion sequence affects the construal of later information*. It is interesting that various models across the chapters have stressed the importance of sequence. Models focused on understanding stages in (a) the effects of attitudes on judgments and behavior (Chapter 4), (b) cognitive processes of attitude change (Chapter 5), and (c) effects of behavior on attitudes (Chapter 7). For example, the Cognition in Persuasion Model and the Elaboration Likelihood Model suggest that initial pre-message attitudes can bias later information processing, at least when the attitudes are strong. This principle also fits classic research on how we form impressions of others (Asch, 1946; Asch & Zukier, 1984; Hamilton & Zanna, 1974; Jones, Rock, Shaver, Goethals, & Ward, 1968) and may follow from basic principles of conversation (Rips, Brem, & Bailenson, 1999).

The Meta-Cognitive Model goes even further by predicting that timing affects meta-cognitive responses to a message. Specifically, a variable (e.g., source credibility, emotion) is more likely to affect meta-cognitions about the validity of reactions to a message when the variable follows the message than when it precedes the message (where the variable serves other roles). For instance, learning about source credibility after processing a message might make us more confident in positive *or* negative attitudes we have formed from the message itself, while learning about high source credibility beforehand tends to increase agreement with the message (e.g., by acting as a cue; Tormala, Briñol, & Petty, 2006). This evidence complements the earlier models and may eventually help to develop a general principle regarding information sequence.

## KEY POINTS

- Attitudes are influenced by people's views of the logical relations between beliefs that under-pin the attitudes.
- Strong attitudes are more resistant to change.
- Information presented early in a persuasion sequence affects the construal of later information.

## PRINCIPLES FROM ANOTHER POINT OF VIEW

In our view, four interesting principles are evident across this research: (1) attitude change can be elicited by extraneous features of a message or persuasion context; (2) motivation and ability to form a correct attitude increase the impact of relevant information; (3) persuasion is enabled by congruence between a persuasive message and accessible knowledge and goals; and (4) persuasion can occur without awareness. Together, these four principles help to summarize significant patterns across the literature, but it may also be possible to form additional principles based on the effects of logical relations between beliefs, attitude strength, and stages of processing.

Nonetheless, William McGuire (1983) wisely warned psychologists that the opposite of every principle in the field might also be true. We suspect that he is right. There may be circumstances in which the opposite of these principles is correct (e.g., cases where persuasion cannot occur with extraneous factors or without awareness). Although these principles help to summarize the remarkable achievements of persuasion research in the past 50 years, they should not be used blindly.

## WHAT WE HAVE LEARNED

- Attitudes can be influenced by information that has, at best, weak relevance to the attitude object.
- The impact of weak information on attitudes can be reduced when people possess high motivation and ability to form a correct attitude, except when the relevant information is difficult to interpret and the irrelevant information is difficult to identify.
- Attitude change partly depends on whether messages emphasize the content, structure, or functions that are the basis for the recipients' own attitudes.
- Attitude change can occur without conscious awareness of the persuasive factors.
- Future research might support additional principles of persuasion, including principles based on logical relations among beliefs, attitude strength, and information sequence.

# WHAT DO YOU THINK?

- There is evidence that the effect of appeal matching on message scrutiny goes beyond effects of matching to motives or motivational orientations. It turns out that the impact of vivid, concrete imagery to a message depends on its fit to the message argument. For example, a message against drinking before driving can state that alcohol slows reaction times, resulting in "bloody, bone-crushing accidents" *or* the slowing of reaction times "to a snail's pace" (Smith & Shaffer, 2000). Both statements lead to vivid images in the minds of participants, but the accident imagery is more relevant to a message arguing that alcohol is a danger to one's health. This difference is important because Smith and Shaffer found that argument scrutiny is higher when the content of the imagery fits the gist of the message than when the content of the imagery is irrelevant to the message. This evidence may fit the "common language" analogy that we used earlier in the chapter (Principle 3), but are there other "languages" that you might imagine?

- What makes a message strong? The models of persuasion do not provide a lot of help for figuring out which words should be put into a message. As described in this chapter, matching of content to the audience appears to be useful if the arguments are strong, but this is a rather general point. Marketers, advertisers, and campaigners can wonder about additional issues, such as the vividness of their arguments or the style with which they are framed. We have also highlighted the relevance of knowing about logical connections that people make between beliefs. These considerations remind us of the Scottish philosopher David Hume's (1985 [1739]) assertion that "it is not reason, which carries the prize, but eloquence." How are messages made eloquent and convincing?

- Advertisers often attempt to achieve eloquence by introducing tag questions into messages, such as "don't you think?" Blankenship and Craig (2007) proposed that tag questions have different effects when used by people with low versus high credibility. They predicted and found that tag questions increase message scrutiny when they come from a credible source, but decrease persuasion when they come from a less credible source. This evidence shows that determining the content of a successful message can be a complex affair.

# KEY TERMS

*Amplification hypothesis* – the idea that increases in attitude certainty can make the attitude more open or more resistant to change, depending upon other characteristics of the attitude.

*Big five* – an influential theory of personality including dimensions of openness, conscientiousness, extraversion, agreeableness, and neuroticism.

*Matching effects* – the finding that appeals that match aspects of the recipient are usually more likely to elicit attitude change.

*Meta-perceptions* – individuals' perceptions of whether their attitudes are based on affective information or cognitive information.

*MODE Model* – a model of attitudes and behavior that highlights the importance of motivation and opportunity as determinants of behavior.

*Probabilogical models* – models that predict how individuals' belief in a conclusion may change when their belief in a related premise is altered.

*Subliminal priming* – the presentation of information below a threshold on conscious recognition.

*Value-Account Model* – a dual-process model that suggests that attitudes can be produced by implicit processing and explicit processing.

# FURTHER READING

## BASIC

Cialdini, R. B. (2008) *Influence: Science and Practice* (5th edn). Boston, MA: Allyn & Bacon.

Shavitt, S. and Nelson, M. R. (2000) The social identity function in persuasion: Communicated meanings of product preferences. In G. R. Maio and J. M. Olson (eds), *Why We Evaluate: Functions of Attitudes* (pp. 37–57). Mahwah, NJ: Erlbaum.

Wegener, D. T. and Petty, R. E. (1997) The flexible correction model: The role of naive theories of bias in bias correction. *Advances in Experimental Social Psychology, 29*, 141–208.

## APPLIED

Corner, A. and Hahn, U. (2009) Evaluating science arguments: Evidence, uncertainty, and argument strength. *Journal of Experimental Psychology: Applied, 15*, 199–212.

Handley, I. M. and Runnion, B. M. (2011) Evidence that unconscious thinking influences persuasion based on argument quality. *Social Cognition, 29*, 668–682.

Hirsh, J. B., Kang, S. K. and Bodenhausen, G. V. (2012) Personalized persuasion: Tailoring persuasive appeals to recipient personality traits. *Psychological Science, 23*, 578–581.

Loersch, C., Durso, G. R. O. and Petty, R. E. (2013) Vicissitudes of desire: A matching mechanism for subliminal persuasion. *Social Psychological and Personality Science, 4*, 624–631.

# SECTION 4

## INTRODUCTION: WHAT MORE IS THERE TO LEARN?

So far, we have learned what attitudes are, what they do, and how they are shaped. Hopefully, you have learned a lot through reading these sections of the book. That said, there are still a number of issues that we have yet to cover, and there are lots of questions that attitude researchers have not yet addressed. In this final section of the book, we introduce you to many of these issues.

Chapter 9, entitled "The internal world," examines how factors *within* individuals influence their attitudes. For instance, it examines effects of body movements (e.g., moving our head up and down), ingested substances (e.g., alcohol and caffeine), and aging. We will also consider the ability of implicit measures and neuroanatomical techniques to look deeper into attitudes.

Given the title of Chapter 9, you can probably guess the title of Chapter 10 (with no peeking ahead!). This chapter turns to how factors *outside* the individual influence their attitudes. We presume that you, like us, don't live in a social vacuum. Chapter 10 will consider how time, relationships, groups, and culture all influence our attitudes. For example, we will see how our relationships with others can affect the way we process information relevant to our attitudes. Further, we will see that there can be powerful cultural effects on attitudes.

In the final chapter, we turn to the future. We highlight future issues in the study of attitudes by first returning to the three witches of attitude content, structure, and function. We will point out how research can be advanced by a more thorough consideration of relations among attitude content, structure, and function. After summarizing these issues, we will describe directions in which attitudes research in general is growing, and ways in which it can still be expanded.

# 9

---

# THE INTERNAL WORLD

---

## QUESTIONS TO PONDER

1. Do implicit measures assess our "true" attitudes?

2. Are implicit measures better than explicit measures?

3. Does nodding or shaking your head influence your attitudes?

4. How do alcohol and caffeine consumption influence our attitudes?

5. Are some attitudes heritable?

6. Which regions of the brain are most strongly associated with attitude responses?

7. Does our age affect our susceptibility to attitude change?

## PREVIEW

We have called this chapter "The internal world," because we wish to emphasize how, broadly speaking, factors *within* the individual influence their attitudes. "Internal" has a variety of meanings in our context – be it something in our brain, an action we perform with our body, or something we consume in our body. In this chapter, we want to highlight some of these factors and describe how they can influence our attitudes. To start, we consider whether implicit measures assess our "true and unconscious" attitudes and whether implicit measures might be "better" than explicit measures. From there, we discuss how bodily movements can affect attitudes, as well as how consuming alcohol or caffeine can influence our attitudes. We also want to introduce you to research that uses neuropsychological techniques to address questions such as where attitude judgments are likely to be represented in the brain and when they occur. Finally, we also describe how lifespan changes, in particular aging, influence our susceptibility to attitude change.

# IMPLICIT WINDOWS INTO ATTITUDES

Why did attitude researchers become interested in developing implicit measures of attitude? While there are a number of answers to this question (see Fazio & Olson, 2003; Greenwald & Banaji, 1995; Petty, Fazio, & Briñol, 2009), one of the primary motivations was the knowledge that in many circumstances, an individual's responses on an explicit measure of attitude may not provide an accurate depiction of their opinion. For example, in many cultures it is not appropriate to admit disliking another racial, religious, or ethnic group. This concern led some attitude researchers to question whether self-report measures of prejudice provided a valid indication of an individual's underlying attitude. To account for these concerns, attitude researchers sought to develop psychometrically sound measures that did not ask people to make an active and deliberative consideration of their attitude. Some of these measures were introduced in Chapter 1. In this section of the chapter, we briefly highlight some of the novel questions and areas of research that have resulted from the development of implicit measures of attitude.

As originally conceptualized, one perceived advantage of implicit measures of attitude was the belief that they are less likely to be influenced by social desirability concerns and other unwanted influences. However, is that the case? To date, it seems that people may be capable of influencing their responses on implicit measures. For example, an individual's responses on implicit measures can differ as a function of whether the measure is completed in a public versus private setting. In one experiment, Boysen, Vogel, and Madon (2006) asked American college students to complete an implicit measure of attitudes (the IAT; Greenwald et al., 1998) toward homosexuality. Participants randomly assigned to a private setting condition were led to believe that the experimenter would not examine their responses. In contrast, participants in a public setting condition were led to believe that the experimenter would examine their responses. The authors hypothesized that completing the task in a public setting would cause respondents to report more favorable attitudes. The results of the experiment supported the researchers' hypothesis. Similarly, research has demonstrated that responses on a race IAT can be affected by whether participants had previously been briefly exposed to a film clip showing African Americans in a gang environment as opposed to a family barbeque (Wittenbrink, Judd, & Park, 2001; see also Blair, 2002; Gawronski & Bodenhausen, 2006; Rydell & Gawronski, 2009, for additional evidence). Because individuals' responses on implicit measures can be affected by the social context in which the measures are completed, the responses are not necessarily providing an indication of an individual's "true" attitude.

More generally, research regarding the merits of implicit measures has generated substantial discussion. In particular, there has been much debate about the merits of the IAT (see, e.g., Blanton & Jaccard, 2006; Blanton, Jaccard, Christie, & Gonzales, 2007; Blanton, Jaccard, Gonzales, & Christie, 2006; De Houwer, Teige-Mocigemba, Spruyt, & Moors, 2009; Karpinski & Hilton, 2001; Meissner & Rothermund, 2013; Olson & Fazio, 2003, 2004a; Wentura & Rothermund, 2007). The emphasis on the qualities of the IAT is likely due to the overwhelming popularity of this measure. While there is strong evidence supporting the predictive validity of the IAT (e.g., Greenwald et al., 2009), research has also demonstrated that there are many variables that can have an unwanted influence on responses to it. For example, responses can be influenced by factors such as the dominance of a particular category during judgment (Sargent, Kahan, & Mitchell, 2007), various non-decision processes (Klauer, Voss, Schmitz, & Teige-Mocigemba, 2007), the degree to which the measure assesses attitudes toward target concepts versus exemplars of concepts (De Houwer, 2001a), and associations with an object that are not personally endorsed (Karpinski & Hilton, 2001; Olson & Fazio, 2004; see De Houwer et al., 2009, for a general discussion). Researchers have also developed multinomial processing tree models to help account for sources of variation within the IAT (Meissner & Rothermund, 2013). Further, the IAT is not immune to faking. There is evidence that people can fake attitudes toward new topics on this measure (see De Houwer, Beckers, & Moors, 2007; Steffens, 2004). In light of such evidence, researchers have developed paradigms that are designed to partially detect and correct for faked IAT responses (Cvencek, Greenwald, Brown, Gray, & Snowden, 2010). There is also evidence that response latencies to incongruent trials can be reduced by having individuals form implementation intentions on how to respond to such trials (Webb, Sheeran, & Pepper, 2012). While these types of studies highlight some concerns about the IAT, it is nonetheless a very useful measure. Further, it is important to note that no measure is perfect by itself, and there are limitations in other alternative implicit measures of attitude (De Houwer, 2001a; De Houwer & De Bruycker, 2007; De Houwer et al., 2009; Fazio & Olson, 2003; Klauer & Mierke, 2005).

The development of implicit measures of attitude has led researchers to re-think how they conceptualize important social psychological concepts. While implicit and explicit measures tend to show moderate correlations (Nosek, 2007), the magnitude of the relation suggests that they do not necessarily measure the same thing. This means that sometimes an individual might have a high score on an explicit measure of a construct, while at the same time having a low score on an implicit measure of the same construct (or vice versa). These types of dissociations have led researchers to develop and test new ways of thinking about concepts such as self-esteem and prejudice (to name just two). For example, within the study of self-esteem, researchers have considered the implications of reporting a positive attitude toward the self on an explicit measure of self-esteem (e.g., strongly agreeing with the item "I have high self-esteem"; Robins, Hendin, & Trzesniewski, 2001), while reporting a negative attitude toward the self on an implicit measure of self-esteem (e.g., a negative score on a self-esteem IAT; Greenwald & Farnham, 2000). These individuals, who have been described as possessing defensive self-esteem, have been documented as showing more in-group favoritism and reporting stronger attitudes (Haddock & Gebauer, 2011; Jordan, Logel, Spencer, Zanna, & Whitfield, 2009).

Further, given the extent to which responses on implicit measures of attitude can predict behavior (Greenwald et al., 2009; Perugini et al., 2010), research has also considered ways through which the spontaneous evaluations assessed by implicit measures can be changed. Different streams of research have used important social psychological concepts in an effort to reduce implicit prejudice (for a thorough review of changing implicitly measured attitudes, see Sritharan & Gawronski, 2010). In one study, Shook and Fazio (2008; see Research Highlight 9.1) found that White first-year university students randomly assigned to an interracial dormitory room subsequently expressed more positive implicit racial attitudes compared to White students who had been allocated a room with another White student. In a different line of research, Devine, Forscher, Austin, and Cox (2012) tested the efficacy of an intervention designed to reduce implicit racial biases. The intervention included increased contact, instructions about individuating outgroup members, and imagining counter-stereotypic outgroup members. The researchers gave the intervention to one group of students, whereas another group of students served as a control. Implicit racial attitudes, as measured by the IAT, were administered at the start of the study, as well as four and eight weeks after the manipulation. As can be seen in Figure 9.1, the results of the study revealed that the manipulation had a positive effect. At both four and eight weeks after the manipulation, participants in the intervention condition exhibited more positive IAT scores than participants in the control condition.

From our perspective, it is interesting that recent evidence also flags the potential for using implicit measures to tap attitude content, structure, and function. At the level of content, our own research has sought to develop an approach for implicitly assessing the extent to which an attitude is based on cognitive, affective, and behavioral information (Maio, Haddock, Valle, Bernard, & Huskinson, 2014). At the level of structure, implicit measures have been adapted to measure the positive and negative evaluations separately, consistent with the bidimensional approach to attitude structure (de Liver, van der Pligt, & Wigboldus, 2007). Finally, at the level of function, researchers have shown that implicit measures can be used to assess the motives that are associated with particular groups (Johnson et al., 2006), which suggests that we can use the same technique to assess the functions of attitudes toward different groups and other attitude objects.

These developments show that implicit measures provide a useful window for viewing attitude content, structure, and function. The measures are useful for better circumventing people's conscious efforts at controlling their responses. As a result, they are better at showing how attitudes look "upstream" before they filter through conscious processing (Fazio & Olson, 2003). This early glimpse does not necessarily mean that implicit measures are superior to explicit ones; it simply means that they provide a view of an earlier stage in the activation and use of attitudes.

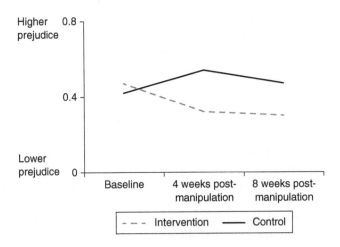

**Figure 9.1**   *The effects of a prejudice intervention on IAT D-scores (Devine et al., 2012)*

## RESEARCH HIGHLIGHT 9.1

### HOW YOUR FIRST-YEAR UNIVERSITY ROOMMATE CAN INFLUENCE YOUR ATTITUDES

Starting university represents a substantial lifestyle change. For many students, going to university means moving away from home and living in university halls of residence. In many cases students share rooms, with universities often allocating students to rooms on a random basis. This allocation process has important consequences – in many cases, a first-year roommate becomes a close confidant and life-long friend. What other influences might result?

In a fascinating study, Natalie Shook and Russell Fazio (2008) examined whether university residence room assignments influence implicitly measured racial attitudes. Based on the notion that increased contact can positively influence intergroup attitudes (Pettigrew & Tropp, 2006), Shook and Fazio tested whether White students who had been randomly allocated to a shared room with a Black student would later report more positive implicitly measured racial attitudes compared to White students who had been allocated a shared room with another White student. The study involved two sessions, with the first at the beginning of an academic term and the second at the end of the term. At each session, the researchers assessed levels of satisfaction with the roommate, as well as an implicit measure of prejudice (the evaluative priming measure; see Chapter 1). At both the start and end of the study, lower roommate satisfaction scores were reported by participants with a Black roommate. Despite greater dissatisfaction with the roommate, Shook and Fazio found that participants in interracial rooms expressed significantly more positive racial attitudes over time (compared to no change in attitudes among participants with a same-race roommate). The results suggest that increased contact led to more positive implicitly measured attitudes, despite less satisfaction.

This work has important basic and applied implications and has been followed up in interesting ways. For example, subsequent research by Shook and Clay (2012) found that both Black and White students randomly assigned to an interracial roommate relationship rated themselves as more attached to their university compared to students not assigned to an interracial residence room. Further, Black students paired with White students received higher grades in their first term compared to Black students who were paired with another Black student.

# KEY POINTS

- While implicit measures of attitude are less susceptible to social desirability concerns, they are not immune to these types of effects.

- Implicit measures of attitude can be adapted to examine attitude content, structure, and function.

- Evidence suggests that implicitly measured racial attitudes can be changed through increased contact and interventions intended to break the "habit" of prejudice.

# LET'S GET PHYSICAL: THE EFFECTS OF BODY MOVEMENTS ON ATTITUDES

Chapter 7 described the effects of complex actions on our attitudes. These actions involved a high degree of thinking and feeling. For instance, the actions included undergoing severe initiations, choosing between attractive objects, and writing counter-attitudinal essays. Our attitudes might also be influenced by actions that are much simpler and more mechanical in nature. Our bodies can do many such actions. We can run at considerable speed (or, in our cases, inconsiderable speed), sit calmly, smile, frown, push things away, pick them up, and so on. A fascinating possibility is that specific motor actions are deeply tied to different levels of approval or disapproval. As a result, different types of motor actions (e.g., pushing versus pulling) may affect attitudes in different ways. If so, we would have to conclude that there is a concrete, physical component of attitudes that goes beyond what we have described so far. Below we describe evidence showing that there are many ways in which such physical effects on attitudes can arise.

## Motor actions and emotion

To understand the potential effects of motor actions on attitudes, it makes sense to first consider relevant evidence that facial expressions influence emotion. A creative demonstration of this effect was provided by Fritz Strack, Leonard Martin, and Sabine Stepper (1988). These researchers asked participants to look at different cartoon drawings from Gary Larson's *The Far Side* series, while holding a pen in their mouth. Participants were asked to hold the pen by gripping it with their teeth *or* by gripping it with their lips. Try this yourself (it's best to do it in front of a mirror). You'll see that holding a pen with your teeth forces the muscles around your mouth to simulate a smile. In contrast, you'll see that holding a pen with your lips forces your mouth to simulate a frown. It turns out that participants who held the pen in their teeth (inducing a smile) were significantly more amused by the cartoons than participants who held the pen in their lips (inducing a frown). The powerful aspect of this finding is that participants had *no idea* that they were simulating a smile or frown. There was something quite direct about the way in which the facial expressions influenced emotion. Given this subtle influence on emotion, might attitudes (which are partly based on emotion) also be shaped by motor actions?

## Motor actions and attitude

A clever study by Gary Wells and Richard Petty (1980) illustrates the effects of motor action on attitude. These scientists asked participants to nod their heads up and down *or* shake them from side to side while listening over headphones to an editorial. Participants believed they were in a study looking at the quality of a new type of headphone. They were told that nodding would simulate the effect of jogging on earphone quality, whereas shaking would simulate the effect of cycling on earphone quality. In reality, the experimenters were interested in these behaviors because nodding (up and down) is typically seen as a gesture of agreement. In contrast, shaking (from side to side) is typically seen as a gesture of disagreement.

The authors were interested in seeing whether nodding and shaking would influence a participant's level of agreement with the content of the editorial message. The results of the study demonstrated that nodders agreed with the message more than shakers (see also Briñol & Petty, 2003). Thus, bodily actions associated with a particular evaluative tendency can influence how we process information.

Another important type of body movement involves the flexion (contraction) of limbs versus their extension. When you grasp food in your hand and pull it toward your mouth, the action involves contracting or shortening numerous muscles in the hand to pull the fingers together and contracting muscles in your arm to bend it at the elbow. In contrast, if you press something away from you, you extend your fingers outward and extend the arm to a straight position. Philosophers and psychologists have long believed that the grasping reflex has special significance for showing something vital about the way we think (Givler, 1921). Even our language includes phrases like "grasping an idea" versus "grasping at straws."

John Cacioppo, Joseph Priester, and Gary Berntson (1993) conducted several ingenious experiments demonstrating the effects of arm muscle flexion and extension on attitudes. In one experiment, participants were seated at a desk and asked to say whether they liked or disliked 24 different Chinese ideographs. In the flexion condition, participants were asked to indicate their attitudes while gently lifting their palms up against the bottom of the table. In the extension condition, participants gave their attitudes while gently pressing their palms down against the top of the table. Try these actions yourself. You will notice that the pulling motion involves contracting the arm, while the pressing motion involves extending the arm.

After indicating their attitudes in this way, participants then sorted the ideographs from the least likeable to the most likeable. Remarkably, analyses of these rankings indicated that the ideographs viewed during arm flexion were subsequently liked significantly more than the ideographs viewed during arm extension. At the same time, participants did not rate the arm flexion and extension task as being different in enjoyment, difficulty, or effort. Together with the results of several other experiments, these findings fit the conclusion that arm contraction and extension are automatically linked to different motivational orientations to either approach (grasp) things or avoid them.

Additional lines of research have considered other ways in which physical actions, attributes, and body states can influence evaluative judgments. In one neat line of work, Daniel Casasanto and colleagues (Casasanto, 2009, 2011; Casasanto & Chrysikou, 2011) considered how handedness influences how individuals represent concepts in positive or negative ways – such that left-handers and right-handers might perceive things differently. In one study testing this possibility, Casasanto (2009) asked participants to draw two animals, one in each of two boxes that were placed side-by-side on a page. Individuals were asked to draw a "good" animal in one box and a "bad" animal in the other box. The results revealed that left-handed participants were more likely to draw their good animal in the left-hand box, whereas right-handed participants were more likely to draw their good animal in the right-hand box. It was argued that left-handed individuals are more likely to associate left with good, whereas right-handed individuals are more likely to associate right with good. Amazingly, these types of body specificity effects have been documented with children as young as five years old (Casasanto & Henetz, 2012).

In a similar vein, research has also found that orienting individuals to their left or right influences political evaluations in a corresponding manner. In one particularly clever demonstration of this effect, Oppenheimer and Trail (2010) randomly assigned American participants to sit in a chair that leaned either to the left or the right (this was done by removing a set of wheels from either side of the chair's base). While sitting in the chair, participants rated their liking for the Democratic (more left-oriented) and Republican (more right-oriented) parties. As shown in Figure 9.2, Oppenheimer and Trail found that participants leaning to the left expressed greater support for the Democratic party compared to participants leaning to the right (a trend in the opposite direction was found in support for the Republican party). In both of these examples, left/right physical/spatial orientation influenced individuals' perceptions and evaluations.

Finally, research has also demonstrated interesting ways in which body states can influence evaluative judgments. In one set of studies, Risen and Critcher (2011) explored the *visceral fit* hypothesis – the notion that individuals perceive experiences and outcomes integrated with their current visceral state as more likely to occur. These researchers offered numerous interesting demonstrations of this effect. In one study, participants were taken outside and asked to complete a survey regarding their attitude toward different issues, one of which was global warming. While participants completed the questionnaire, the experimenter recorded the outside temperature. The results revealed that participants expressed greater belief in global warming on warm days rather than cold days. Subsequent work by these scientists suggested that the visceral fit effect occurs because the experience of a visceral state (such as being warm) makes it easier (and more likely) for people to simulate matching world states.

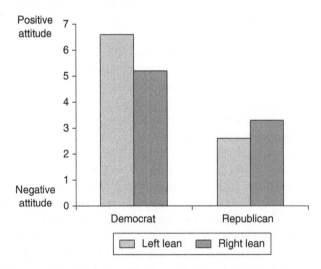

**Figure 9.2**   *The effects of leaning left or right on attitudes toward the American Democrat and Republican parties (Oppenheimer & Trail, 2010)*

## RESEARCH HIGHLIGHT 9.2

### IS SWAYING FROM SIDE-TO-SIDE ASSOCIATED WITH GREATER ATTITUDE AMBIVALENCE?

In this chapter, we have highlighted a few ways in which performing a certain physical action influences the favorability of attitudes. Building upon these findings, research has also considered the relation between physical actions and an important property of an attitude. Elsewhere in the book, we have highlighted the concept of attitude ambivalence. Recently, one set of Dutch researchers considered whether there is a bidirectional relationship between ambivalence and physical movements, such that greater attitude ambivalence is associated with more exaggerated side-to-side physical movements. To test this possibility, Schneider and colleagues (2013) conducted a study in which participants were first asked to stand on a Nintendo Wii Balance Board (which can be used to assess body movements). Some participants were then made to feel ambivalent, whereas other participants were not, and the researchers assessed the degree to which participants swayed from one side to the other. The results showed that ambivalent participants showed greater side-to-side body movements (swaying back and forth) compared to non-ambivalent participants. In a subsequent study, the researchers tested the opposite causal path. Here, it was found that participants who were asked to move from side-to-side expressed greater subjective ambivalence compared to participants who were asked to move up and down.

These studies by Schneider and colleagues are noteworthy for demonstrating that the effects of physical movements go beyond mere evaluations, as well as highlighting the bidirectional influence of physical movements and attitudinal properties.

## How do motor actions affect attitude?

Drawing on the Elaboration Likelihood Model of Persuasion (Chapter 5), Pablo Briñol and Richard Petty (2008) have provided an interesting perspective on the effects of smiling, grasping, and other behaviors on how attitudes are shaped in a persuasion context. Consistent with the model's third proposition (see Chapter 5), they propose that bodily actions can function as a cue, an argument, or a factor affecting the amount of issue-relevant thinking and the amount of bias in these thoughts. In addition, congruent with the Meta-Cognitive Model (see Chapter 5), they propose that bodily actions can affect confidence in these thoughts.

The role of bodily actions as a cue should occur when there is a lack of motivation and ability to think about a persuasive message. For example, imagine that we have no interest in buying a car, but we are asked to grip a pen in our teeth while hearing a message in favor of a new hybrid-fuel vehicle. This subtle method to induce smiling might cause us to like the vehicle more, irrespective of whether the ad gives weak or strong arguments in favor of the vehicle's environmental efficiency and utility. Presumably, the effects of arm flexion and extension obtained by

Cacioppo et al. (1993) reflect this kind of process, because participants' evaluations of Chinese ideographs were not of high personal importance to them (see also Priester, Cacioppo, & Petty, 1996; Tom, Pettersen, Lau, Burton, & Cook, 1991).

In other circumstances, we might have at least some potential interest in buying the hybrid-fuel automobile. In this case, the act of smiling might determine how much we think about the information about the car, causing strong arguments to be more impactful than weak ones. This type of effect has been obtained for a different behavior: reclining (laying down) versus standing. Imagine talking to a car salesperson while reclining on an easy chair in her office, rather than standing up. Which behavior do you think would cause you to think more deeply about the information she is presenting?

Rich Petty, Gary Wells, Martin Heesacker, Tim Brock, and John Cacioppo (1983) conducted an elegant experiment examining this issue. As in the experiment by Wells and Petty (1980), undergraduate students were asked to try a new headphone to rate its qualities. Some participants were then told to lie down while testing the headphone, whereas others were told to stand up. Participants then listened to a message containing either strong or weak arguments in favor of having undergraduates complete oral comprehensive examinations as a prerequisite to graduation (something most students would not want!). After hearing the strong or weak arguments advocating the exams, participants subsequently rated their attitude toward this topic. Amazingly, the reclining participants were differentially persuaded by the strong and weak arguments, but the standing participants were not. It looks as though the reclining participants thought enough about the message to detect its strengths or weaknesses, while these attributes and flaws were completely missed by the standing participants.

Why did this effect occur? A compelling answer can't be given yet. It could be the case that the reclining position is one that we subconsciously associate with deep thinking. Indeed, most people's image of psychotherapy involves someone lying on a couch to deeply examine personal issues. Although this may be true, a skeptic might also wonder why people don't just get sleepy on the couch. It's not just personal experience that causes us to mention this: people sleep lying down and are alert standing up, so there is a natural association between reclining and rest. It would be interesting to discover the extent to which these different associations with reclining are influential.

## Additional mechanisms

There is another effect that can occur when people are especially motivated to think about a topic. Briñol and Petty (2008) suggested that variables can also affect our confidence in the thoughts that we have after reading a message. They posit that this process can occur when people enact a behavior *after* receiving information and forming cognitive responses to it (i.e., in situations that involve high personal relevance and ability). In this context, the behaviors may affect *confidence* in the cognitive responses that emerged. Head nodding, for example, should cause higher confidence in any positive responses to strong arguments and in any negative responses to weak arguments. In contrast, head shaking might cause people to doubt their positive responses to the strong arguments and their negative responses to the weak arguments. As a result, nodding after receipt of the message should result in attitudes that are more influenced by message strength than head shaking after receipt of the message. This is exactly what Briñol and Petty (2003) found in a clever study. They also found that participants reported more confidence in their thoughts about the message after head nodding than after head shaking, consistent with their proposal that the behaviors were affecting confidence in thoughts (Briñol & Petty, 2004). Across numerous experiments, this pattern has been revealed for a variety of other behaviors that might cause people to doubt themselves or have confidence in themselves, such as head nodding or shaking and writing cognitive responses with their writing hand or non-writing hand.

Other researchers have offered different perspectives on the potential processes underlying the effects of physical movements on attitudes. First, Daniel Wegner and colleagues (e.g., Wegner, Fuller, & Sparrow, 2003; Wegner, Sparrow, & Winerman, 2004) demonstrated that individuals do not possess foolproof knowledge of whether they or someone else caused or performed an action. Building on this research, Taylor, Lord, and Bond (2009) designed a series of clever studies designed to assess whether inferential cues can moderate the effects of physical actions on attitudes. Across their work, these researchers found that merely believing that one has performed a movement, even in the absence of any actual movement, was sufficient to elicit embodiment effects. Further, they found that if an individual does not perceive causal agency when performing an action (e.g., they perceived someone else was responsible for performing the act), they are unlikely to show attitude change. The findings of Taylor and colleagues are quite provocative, and are important in helping to build our understanding of the complex processes involved in how our bodies can influence our attitudes.

## KEY POINTS

- Smiling may elicit more positive emotion than frowning.
- Actions associated with approval or approach (e.g., head shaking, pulling) may cause more positive attitudes than actions associated with disapproval or avoidance.
- Motor actions may influence attitudes by acting as cues, influencing deliberation, biasing attitude-relevant elaboration, or affecting thought confidence.

## REVEALING THE BIOLOGICAL UNDERPINNINGS OF ATTITUDES

The evidence for effects of physical actions on attitudes raises questions about deeper, biological influences. Biological processes in attitudes are now receiving more attention than in the past. Relevant biological factors include physiological associates of attitudes and the impact of drugs such as alcohol and caffeine, as well as possible genetic influences.

# The influence of alcohol and caffeine on attitudes

Anyone who has "enjoyed" the after-effects of having consumed too much alcohol knows that alcohol impairs our ability to think. From a social psychological perspective, research on *alcohol myopia* (Steele & Josephs, 1990) has addressed how alcohol intoxication influences information processing. According to the alcohol myopia perspective, individuals under the influence of alcohol have a reduced capacity to process information, and tend to react primarily to salient and impelling cues in their environment. As part of this cognitive impairment, Steele and Josephs (1990) noted that intoxicated individuals develop exaggerated perceptions of their own abilities. For example, Banaji and Steele (1989) asked students to rate the importance of a series of personality attributes, as well as their own actual and ideal standing on each attribute. Participants completed this task twice – before and after they were either intoxicated or had consumed a placebo drink. Banaji and Steele found that intoxicated participants reported an inflated sense of self for attributes that were both personally important to the participant and for which their pre-intoxication ratings suggested that their actual standing on the attribute was lower than what they wanted it to be.

What are the effects of alcohol myopia on an individual's attitudes? In a fascinating set of experiments, Tara MacDonald, Mark Zanna, and Geoff Fong (1995) assessed how the consumption of alcohol influences individuals' attitudes toward drinking and driving. While attitudes toward drinking and driving tend to be very negative (thanks largely to campaigns about the negative consequences of this behavior), is it possible that being intoxicated affects these attitudes? Specifically, can intoxication lead to *less negative* attitudes about drinking and driving? In MacDonald and colleagues' first experiment addressing this question, male Canadian university students arrived at the lab and were randomly assigned to a sober or drunk condition. Participants in the sober condition simply completed a set of questions about their attitude toward drinking and driving. While participants in the drunk condition completed the same attitude questions, they completed these measures *after* having consumed an amount of alcohol that gave them a blood alcohol level that approximated the legal driving limit in Ontario (the Canadian province in which the study took place).

Does being intoxicated make people less negative about drinking and driving? The answer to this question is not as simple as you might expect. In designing their dependent measures, the researchers developed different sets of questions. One set of questions included items such as "If I drink and drive the next time that I am out at a party or a bar, I would find it acceptable." The second set of questions included items such as "If I only had a short distance to drive home the next time that I am at a party or a bar, I would drive while intoxicated." Read these statements again. Do you notice an important difference between them? As intended by the authors, the second question includes a contingency, or impelling cue, that, consistent with the alcohol myopia hypothesis, might elicit less disagreement among intoxicated individuals. The authors expected sober and intoxicated participants to be equally negative in their reported attitude toward the non-contingent items. However, they predicted that intoxicated participants would show less disagreement with the statements that included an impelling cue. The results supported the researchers' hypothesis: intoxicated participants had less negative attitudes toward drinking and driving, but only for the contingent items.

Of course, you might be saying to yourself "Wow, that's interesting, but how many people do the majority of their drinking in a psychology lab?" (As far as we're aware, that group of people is small.)

You are correct in thinking that this is a domain where the lab environment does not really match the "real world" environment in which people typically consume alcohol. To account for these concerns, MacDonald and colleagues (1995) conducted a field experiment at a location where students are often known to have a drink (or perhaps even two) – a campus pub. In this study, the participants were students who drove their car to the pub. Consenting participants were randomly assigned to an early or late condition. That is, they completed the attitude measure either when they first arrived at the pub (around 8.30 p.m. – the "early" group) or when they were ready to leave the pub at the end of the night (around 12.30 a.m. – the "late" group). Further, all participants agreed to take a breathalyzer (blood alcohol) test before they left the pub. For the purpose of the analysis, the key participants were those individuals who were intoxicated at the end of the evening – they represent the individuals who would need to make a decision about whether to drive after having consumed alcohol. Because these individuals were randomly assigned to the early or late condition, approximately half completed the attitude measures when they were sober (early in the evening), whereas the rest completed the attitude measures when they were intoxicated (at the end of the evening). The results of this field study matched those of the lab study – participants who were intoxicated expressed less negative attitudes toward drinking and driving, but only when a contingency was embedded in the question. (We should point out that the experimenters informed the pub management of any intoxicated participant; the management was legally responsible for ensuring that intoxicated participants did not drink and drive.)

This pattern of findings has been replicated with other risky behaviors, such as deciding whether or not to use a condom when having sexual intercourse with a new partner (see MacDonald, MacDonald, Zanna, & Fong, 2000). Taken together, these results have a number of important implications. First, they demonstrate how alcohol can impact an individual's attitudes and decisions. Second, given that intoxicated individuals report less negative attitudes to behaviors such as drinking and driving and having unprotected sex, it suggests that campaigns to further reduce the incidence of these behaviors should attempt to target individuals when they are likely to be intoxicated. To our knowledge, no evidence has tested whether, for instance, placing anti-drinking and driving posters in a pub is more successful in reducing drinking and driving than placing the same posters in a bus shelter.

A quite different line of research has assessed the effect of alcohol consumption on individuals' evaluations of attractiveness – of both other people and their own self-perceptions. The popular axiom of "beer goggles" suggests that when intoxicated, we see potential romantic partners as more physically attractive. This axiom was tested by Lyvers, Cholakians, Puorro, and Sundram (2011), who conducted a study in an Australian campus pub where they assessed participants' blood alcohol levels and asked participants to rate the attractiveness of opposite sex individuals. These researchers found empirical support for the "beer goggles" effect, though the mechanism underlying the effect was unclear. As to whether the effect generalizes to self-perceived attractiveness, field and experimental studies by Bègue, Bushman, Zerhouni, Subra, and Ourabah (2013) found that drunk individuals perceived themselves as more attractive, bright, and funny. Unfortunately, independent judges did not agree with these boosted self-perceptions.

Another popular drug among students (and professors alike) is caffeine. Like millions of others, both of us start the day with a large cup of coffee. We hope that the caffeine will help kick start our brain in preparation for another exciting day at work. Consistent with this lay belief, research has revealed that caffeine increases cognitive processes such as memory recall and logical reasoning

(Smit & Rogers, 2000; Smith, Maben, & Brockman, 1994). How might caffeine influence attitudinal processes? This question was addressed in a nice set of experiments by Martin, Laing, Martin, and Mitchell (2005). In one study, participants were given approximately 200 mg of caffeine (the equivalent of two cups of espresso) or a placebo before reading a persuasive appeal that contained either strong or weak arguments against voluntary euthanasia. (This message was counter-attitudinal for the participants.) As we're sure you remember, argument quality manipulations help to assess the degree to which individuals systematically process information designed to change their attitude (see Chapter 5). If caffeine increases cognitive processing, participants who have consumed caffeine should show a greater argument quality effect compared to participants in a control condition. This is exactly what was found by Martin and colleagues. While both groups of participants reported greater attitude change after reading the strong compared to weak arguments, this effect was significantly stronger among participants in the caffeine group (see Figure 9.3). Furthermore, participants in the caffeine group showed greater recall of the message, and the positivity of individuals' thoughts about the message accounted for their degree of attitude change.

***Function Witch:*** *Does being intoxicated lead individuals to believe that their attitudes fulfill a particular need or function?*

***Structure Witch:*** *To the degree that caffeine increases thoughfulness, consuming a triple-shot of espresso might lead someone to devote an extraordinary amount of attention to resolving any perceived inconsistencies among their attitudes.*

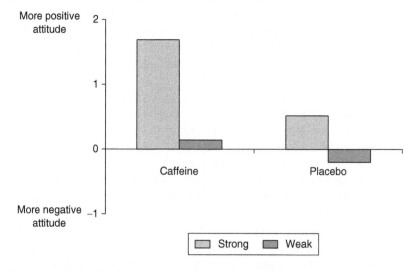

**Figure 9.3**  *Amount of attitude change as a function of caffeine consumption and argument quality (P. Y. Martin et al., 2005)*

# Is there a genetic component to attitudes?

Another emerging and provocative biological perspective on attitudes examines genetic factors. The underlying assumption in this research is that genes could establish general predispositions that shape environmental experiences in ways that increase the likelihood of developing specific attitudes. For example, children might pick on other children who are naturally small for their age more than their larger peers, with the result that the smaller children might develop anxieties about social interaction. These anxieties, in turn, may shape their attitudes toward social events, such as dances and parties, or even their attitudes toward technologies that enable social interaction with less anxiety (i.e., virtual internet communities). This example shows how the genetic path is indirect and mediated by its effects on body, brain, and personality. It is extremely unlikely that there are direct, one-to-one connections between genes and attitudes, such as a gene for attitudes toward internet communities.

There is now a body of research revealing associations between genes and attitudes. This research has focused on the attitudes of twins raised in separate or shared environments. Twin studies help to isolate a genetic component because we know that twins share at least 50% of their genetic make-up. In research testing a sample of identical twins who were raised apart, Arvey, Bouchard, Segal, and Abraham (1989) found that approximately 30% of the variance in participants' self-reported job satisfaction was attributable to genetic factors. These findings suggest that respondents' attitudes toward their jobs appeared to be partly due to heritability. In addition, Eaves, Eysenck, and Martin (1989) reported the results of two surveys involving almost 4,000 pairs of same-sex twins. A variety of social attitudes were assessed, including crime, religion, race, and lifestyle. Heritability estimates for individual items ranged from 1% to 62%, with a median of 39%, further suggesting that heritability has a role in understanding attitudes. In the domain of political attitudes, Settle, Dawes and Fowler (2009) estimated that heritability accounted for approximately half of the variation in political partisan preferences.

Abraham Tesser (1993) hypothesized that attitudes that are highly heritable might have a biological basis that makes attitude change difficult, which could lead individuals to develop psychological defenses to protect these attitudes. In other words, individuals may seek out environments that are compatible with their highly heritable attitudes. Tesser (1993; Tesser & Crelia, 1994) tested this idea in several ways. In all of his studies, attitudes that had been shown by Eaves et al. (1989) to have either high or low heritability coefficients were studied. In one study, individuals were found to provide answers more quickly for high than low heritability attitudes. In another study, individuals were found to be less affected by conformity pressure when reporting high than low heritability attitudes. Finally, individuals found agreement feedback more reinforcing when the agreement occurred for highly heritable attitudes than when it occurred for less heritable attitudes. These findings imply that attitude strength is positively correlated with attitude heritability (see also Olson, Vernon, Harris, & Jang, 2001). This line of research converges with findings demonstrating that attitudes perceived to be more heritable are also considered as being more strongly based on moral grounds (Brandt & Wetherell, 2012).

But is there evidence for the indirect pathways mentioned above? That is, are there some specific, genetically influenced characteristics that systematically bias experience so as to induce particular attitudes? Tesser (1993) identified several possibilities, including intelligence and temperament. In another set of studies, James Olson and colleagues (2001) measured some potential mediators of attitude heritability in a study of more than 300 pairs of same-sex twins, including physical characteristics and personality traits. Most of these characteristics and traits were highly heritable in the sample of twins, and they were correlated with attitudes that were heritable. For example, the personality trait of sociability yielded a significant heritability coefficient (i.e., genetic correlation) and significant correlations with measures of heritable attitudes. These data suggest that the heritability of sociability might account, in part, for at least some heritable attitudes (see also Jost, 2006).

*Function Witch:* Are attitude objects that usually fulfill different functions more likely to be influenced by heritability? In particular, are attitude objects that fulfill a social adjustive function (i.e., attitudes we may hold that are partially based on views of others) especially likely to possess a heritable component?

## KEY POINTS

- Alcohol can affect our attitudes as a result of intoxication, leading individuals to pay more attention to salient features of the environment.
- Caffeine influences the attention individuals devote to persuasive messages.
- Some studies suggest that there is an indirect link between genes and attitudes.

## NEUROLOGICAL PROCESSES UNDERLYING ATTITUDES

In the last two decades, research in experimental psychology has been greatly influenced by advances in our capabilities of "looking inside" the human brain. For example, advances in brain-imaging technology have led psychologists to become more interested in the neuroanatomical processes underlying human thought and action. These advances have also had a substantial impact on social psychology. This millennium has seen growth in the field of social cognitive neuroscience (SCN). As described by Kevin Ochsner and Matthew Lieberman (2001; see also Blakemore, Winston, & Frith, 2004), the field of SCN can be defined as studying the *social* behavior of motivated individuals (S), examining the *cognitive* mechanisms that give rise to behavioral processes (C), and investigating the *neurological* systems that instantiate these processes (N). SCN has provided many novel insights across social psychology, including the field of attitudes. In this section of the chapter, we highlight some of the areas in which SCN research has expanded our understanding of attitudes.

## Tools of the trade

A grandfather of one of the authors used to love working on his car. Unfortunately, this skill was not passed on to his grandson, who was surprised to learn that a "piston" was not only a member of Detroit's professional basketball team, but also an integral part of a car's engine. This lack of interest in cars didn't stop the grandfather from buying his grandson a comprehensive tool set. When the gift was given, the grandfather explained that "every good mechanic needs a good set of tools" (or, in this case, a set of tools that has remained largely untouched for over 25 years). Just as a mechanic needs tools when working on a car, a neuroscientist needs tools to understand the functions of the human brain. Therefore, before we start describing SCN research on attitudes, we want to provide a brief introduction into some of the tools that researchers use.

One of the most common tools used in SCN research is *functional Magnetic Resonance Imaging* (fMRI). An fMRI scanner uses an incredibly strong magnet that allows measurement of changes in levels of blood oxygenation within different areas of the brain. Blood oxygenation levels indicate how active a brain region is, so to test whether a particular area of the brain might be involved in performing a task (such as reporting an attitude), a researcher would compare blood oxygen levels in an area (or areas) of the brain during a control task and an experimental task (see Cunningham et al., 2009). If there is a significant difference in blood oxygen levels in a particular region of the brain in response to the experimental task compared to the control task, it suggests that this region of the brain is involved in the process of interest.

It is possible to ask similar questions using a technique called *Positron Emission Tomography* (PET). This technique relies on detecting levels of radioactive decay. Prior to being scanned, participants are injected with small amounts of radioactive isotopes. These are transported in blood, and higher concentrations of the isotopes will congregate in those areas of the brain that are more active. A PET scanner is able to detect how much radioactivity is coming from a given region, and this gives an indication of how active that region is (Happe et al., 1996).

*Electroencephalography* (EEG) and *Magnetoencephalography* (MEG) are other important tools of the cognitive neuroscientist's trade. When large numbers of neurons communicate, electrical and magnetic fields are generated. EEG and MEG provide measures of the electrical and magnetic fields, respectively, and because of this they offer a way to measure the time course of brain activity. Both of these techniques can provide measurements of changes in brain activity on a millisecond by millisecond basis. It is not possible to attain this kind of temporal resolution with fMRI or with PET (Cunningham et al., 2009; Dale et al., 2000). It is also possible to estimate which parts of the brain are responsible for the activity that is measured on the surface of the head with EEG and MEG. The magnetic measure is better suited to this, but EEG has the advantage of having greater sensitivity to brain activity, so the two techniques have different strengths and weaknesses.

Sometimes you need a number of tools in order to correctly perform a job. Just as you need a number of tools to fix your car, researchers will often use a number of tools in their attempts to understand the neural bases of human behavior. As many of these tools have complimentary strengths, they are often used in combination. For example, if a researcher is interested in determining the location *and* time course of neural activity, they might take advantage of the complimentary strengths offered by fMRI and MEG.

Of course, there is a completely different type of tool available to the neuroscientist. Unlike the techniques described above, this tool does not cost a large amount of money to purchase and operate. This tool is people. Not just people who volunteer to participate in studies using the technologies we have introduced, but also people who differ in psychologically meaningful ways. Often, we can gain valuable insights regarding the neural processes underlying behavior by comparing participants who have unique skills or deficits. For example, if a researcher hypothesizes that intact episodic and semantic memory systems are necessary to perform a particular task, a study comparing individuals with or without these impairments would allow the researcher to test their hypothesis.

# The "wheres" of attitude judgments

Integrative research between social psychologists and cognitive neuroscientists has addressed questions regarding the "wheres" of attitude judgments. In particular, this research has focused on brain structures relevant to evaluative judgments, focusing on activity in the amygdala and the prefrontal cortex (PFC).

## The amygdala

The amygdala is a small, almond shaped structure in the medial temporal lobe of the brain. Neuroscientific research has demonstrated the association between the amygdala and affective processing of information (e.g., Herbert et al., 2009; Phelps, 2006; Zald, 2003). This research has shown that the amygdala is involved in assessing the emotional significance of stimuli, that is, both positive and negative stimuli that are relevant to a person's current goal or situation (e.g., Arana et al., 2003; Baxter & Murray, 2002).

Given the importance of the amygdala in affective processing, it is perhaps not surprising that researchers have explored how amygdala activation relates to the favorability of an individual's attitudes. One particularly fascinating area of investigation has used fMRI to explore the role of the amygdala in individuals' responses to social groups. In a seminal piece of research, Elizabeth Phelps and colleagues (2000) examined how participants' responses on implicit and explicit measures of prejudice toward Blacks were associated with levels of activity in the amygdala in response to the independent presentation of Black and White faces.

In a first study, Phelps and colleagues (2000) explored amygdala activity in response to unfamiliar Black and White faces. They showed White participants Black and White faces while the participants' brains were being scanned by fMRI. After the imaging was completed, participants completed implicit and explicit measures of racial prejudice toward Blacks. The implicit measure of the attitude was the IAT (Greenwald et al., 1998), while the explicit measure of prejudice was the Modern Racism Scale. This scale includes direct questions such as "Over the past few years the government and news media have shown more respect to African Americans than they deserve."

Phelps and colleagues tested whether individuals' scores on the implicit and explicit measures of prejudice were correlated with amygdala activity in response to the unfamiliar Black faces (relative to the unfamiliar White faces). The results revealed that amygdala activity was related to scores on the implicit, but not explicit, measure of prejudice. Specifically, greater amygdala activity in response to the Black faces was associated with more anti-Black prejudice as measured by the IAT. These results were interpreted by suggesting that there is a general learned negative evaluation of unfamiliar Black faces. To test this explanation, Phelps and colleagues' (2000) second study tested whether their observed effect would disappear if participants were presented with familiar and well-liked Black and White individuals. In this second study, the faces viewed by participants during the fMRI scan included popular and respected figures such as Michael Jordan, Will Smith, Larry Bird, and Tom Cruise. Here, Phelps and colleagues found no relation between amygdala activation and direct and indirect attitudes for familiar and well-liked stimuli.

This research is interesting in a number of ways. First, the divergence between responses on implicit and explicit attitude measures is consistent with what we have seen elsewhere in this book. Second, the results converge with past research highlighting that spontaneous actions tend to be more highly associated with implicit measures of attitude compared to explicit measures of attitude. Future research should continue to explore how social factors influence activity in the amygdala in response to different stimuli.

Other strands of research have considered the role of the amygdala in evaluative-based judgments. Within this line of work, one area we find particularly interesting is that of political attitudes and behavior. Research has explored how political views are associated with amygdala size and activation in response to political stimuli. Regarding amygdala volume, Kanai, Feilden, Firth, and Rees (2011) assessed whether there are differences in brain structure among individuals who possess liberal versus conservative political beliefs. These researchers found that conservatism was associated with increased size of the amygdala, whereas liberalism was associated with increased gray matter volume in the anterior cingulate cortex (an area associated with empathy and decision-making processes; Decety & Jackson, 2004).

Regarding the role of the amygdala and its activation in response to political stimuli, Knutson, Wood, Spampinato, and Grafman (2006) found that when individuals were presented with images of politicians they supported and opposed, there was greater amygdala activation in response to images of politicians supported by the participant. More recently, Nicholas Rule and colleagues (2010) asked participants to perform simulated voting judgments of political candidates. Convergent with the findings indicated above, Rule and colleagues found greater amygdala activation for candidates who participants chose to support. Taken together, these (and other) studies offer some fascinating insights into the role of the amygdala in understanding political preferences.

## The prefrontal cortex

A number of studies have explored the role of the prefrontal cortex (PFC) in emotional processing. The prefrontal cortex is an area of the brain that is important in planning complex decisions and behavior. The role of the PFC has been considered with respect to the study of attitudes. In one set of studies, William Cunningham and colleagues (2003, 2004) found greater PFC activation for evaluative judgments (e.g., good versus bad) to non-evaluative judgments (e.g., present versus past). The PFC, therefore, appears to be relevant to evaluative responding.

Another area of the PFC, the ventrolateral (vl) PFC, has also been shown to be involved in evaluative processing relevant to our attitude content witch. In particular, activity in this region was found in association with evaluative judgments (versus non-evaluative judgments). Moreover, Cunningham et al. (2004) found that ratings of ambivalence were significantly correlated with activity in this area of the vlPFC. The more that respondents felt ambivalent about an attitude object, the greater the brain activity. We hope that future research will consider whether different forms of ambivalence might be associated with different patterns of brain activity.

One area of the frontal region, the anterior cingulate cortex (ACC), has been implicated with regard to the action-based Model of Cognitive Dissonance (Harmon-Jones, Harmon-Jones, Serra, & Gable, 2011). As you might recall (see Chapter 7), the action-based model suggests that after making a decision (e.g., choosing a toaster over an equally liked kettle), we engage in actions to support that decision, in order to alleviate dissonance. Harmon-Jones, Harmon-Jones et al. (2011) tested whether such actions would correspond with greater activity in the ACC, as the ACC has been found to be involved in neural processing related to cognitive conflict. Consistent with their expectations, these researchers found that commitment to behavioral action was indeed associated with greater ACC activity.

## The "whens" of attitude judgments

In addition to fMRI research on the neural basis of evaluation, experiments have employed event-related potential (ERP) methodology to help understand the time course involved in attitude judgments. For example, John Cacioppo and colleagues (1996) found a strong late positive activation over posterior parietal areas of the brain during affective judgments, about 500–600 milliseconds following the presentation of an attitude object. Subsequent research by Cunningham et al. (2005) found an earlier activation – at about 475 milliseconds after the presentation of an attitude object; this was most prominent over anterior sites and was associated with evaluative judgments of socially relevant concepts. Cunningham et al. (2005) also found that the activation was greater on the right side of the brain for negatively rated objects and greater on the left side of the brain for positively rated objects. More recently, another fascinating study using ERPs found that, compared to political moderates, anarchists showed different patterns of neural markers in response to political stimuli, but not apolitical stimuli (Dhont, Van Hiel, Pattyn, Onraet, & Severens, 2012). The use of ERPs allowed the authors to make novel conclusions regarding how anarchists differ from moderates in how they think about political information.

Taken together, these studies provide revealing insights into the time course through which we make evaluative judgments. From our perspective, the most important observation may be that positively and negatively valenced stimuli are linked to dissociable processes; thus, it is likely that ambivalence will arise when there is a response in both the positive and negative systems.

## On people, paper, and pens

As mentioned earlier, not all SCN research requires the use of expensive equipment. Sometimes, ideas can be tested using people, paper, and pens. As an example, one issue of interest to attitude researchers concerns how attitudes are represented in memory. Expanding upon this idea, you can ask whether individuals with memory problems (e.g., Alzheimer's dementia) have access to their attitudes. In a recent study, one of the authors and colleagues compared how

16 individuals in the early stages of Alzheimer's dementia compared to control participants in their ability to remember their opinions (Haddock, Newson, & Haworth, 2011). In this study, participants were presented with photos of various objects and asked to name each attitude object and then to indicate the degree to which they liked the object (and were confident of their attitude). Participants responded to the attitude questions on two occasions, separated by one week.

The results of the study showed that memory-impaired individuals retained a high level of insight into their attitudes. Other analyses suggested that memory-impaired individuals tended to show less attitude change toward disliked objects (e.g., rats) compared to liked objects (e.g., chocolate chip cookies). In other words, memory-impaired individuals seem to have greater insight into what they do not like, suggesting that they might be less inclined to shift their negative attitudes across time than their positive attitudes. These results might reflect an example of the "negativity effect," a phenomenon in which negative information elicits more attention and influences evaluations more strongly than positive information (Baumeister, Bratslavsky, Finkenauer, & Vohs, 2001; Ito, Larsen, Smith, & Cacioppo, 1998). Within the current context, this bias might be an expression of a strategy in which memory-impaired individuals attempt to manage their environment by concentrating on what they know they do not like. At the same time, future research is warranted to better understand this effect and to consider its implications for everyday functioning among individuals with Alzheimer's dementia.

SCN paradigms have also been used to test predictions regarding attitude-relevant processing. In a fascinating study, Lieberman, Ochsner, Gilbert, and Schacter (2001) explored whether behavior-induced attitude change can occur even when people don't remember performing the relevant behavior. As you will recall from Chapter 7, Brehm (1956) conducted a famous study in which participants had to choose one of two household items that, earlier in the experiment, they had equally liked. Brehm found that participants grew to like the chosen item much more than the unchosen item (which became liked much less). That is, the difference in preference grew larger after one item had been selected over the other. The mechanism assumed to be behind this effect is the presumed dissonance between behavior and prior attitude, which is reduced by changing the attitude. The principle is that memory is important in eliciting this effect, as the initial behavior itself (in this case, rating the appliances as equally favorable) must be remembered in order for dissonance to occur.

Lieberman and colleagues wondered whether explicit memory is indeed necessary to elicit the Brehm effect. Explicit memory refers to conscious recollection of past events. To test whether explicit memory of performing a behavior is necessary for the behavior-induced recall effect, Lieberman et al. (2001) needed to create a situation where a person performs a behavior (in this case, selecting one object over another) that is then forgotten. To do this, they used patients with anterograde amnesia. If explicit memory is needed to show behavior-induced attitude change, individuals with anterograde amnesia shouldn't exhibit the effect. To test their hypothesis, the researchers had 12 amnesic individuals and matched controls rank a series of art prints. Participants were then asked to select between two prints that had been rated equally liked. After a short delay, they were asked to re-rank the complete series of prints. The results of the study were very interesting. First, Lieberman and colleagues found that the amnesiacs and controls differed in memory for which prints were selected in the initial phase of the experiment. Control participants had almost perfect memory of what they had done, whereas the amnesic participants were, as you'd expect, responding at chance level. This suggests that the amnesic patients had no memory for the key behavior – which print they had selected. However, despite this important difference, both groups showed equal levels of attitude change in the second ranking of the prints. This suggests that explicit memory is not required to elicit behavior-induced attitude change. In this study, comparing individuals with and without a particular impairment led the researchers to test an important question in an innovative way.

## KEY POINTS

- Social cognitive neuroscience has made important contributions to understanding where and when attitudinal responses are represented.
- Studies using clinical samples can contribute to understanding how attitudes are represented in memory.

## ATTITUDES OVER THE LIFESPAN

As we have seen elsewhere in the book, most research on attitude change has examined how attitudes change after an intervention, such as the presentation of a persuasive message. A different approach examines how attitudes change naturally over time. This research uses developmental-lifespan models of psychology, which provide an interesting perspective on attitudes. These models emphasize cognitive, motivational, and social changes over the lifespan and attempt to show how they might influence attitudes.

A number of studies have considered the relation between age and susceptibility to attitude change (Alwin, Cohen, & Newcomb, 1991; Sears, 1981, 1983; see Briñol & Petty, 2005, for a review). In perhaps the strongest evidence to date, Penny Visser and Jon Krosnick (1998) found convincing evidence supporting what is referred to as the *life-stages hypothesis* (see Figure 9.4). This hypothesis proposes that there is a curvilinear relation between age and susceptibility to attitude change, with greater susceptibility among young adults and the elderly. In studies involving large national American surveys that addressed attitudes toward topics such as global warming and preferential university admission policies for racial minorities, Visser and Krosnick found that susceptibility to attitude change was greatest in early adulthood (e.g., among individuals less than 30 years old) and late adulthood (e.g., among individuals more than 80 years old).

What might account for this curvilinear relation between age and susceptibility to attitude change? Visser and Krosnick speculated that the personal importance of social issues (and an individual's knowledge about such issues) may differ across the lifespan. When people are young, they might not attach much importance to issues such as capital punishment, gun control, and defence spending. In late adulthood, elderly people might become disengaged with social policy issues. To test this idea, Visser and Krosnick assessed lifespan changes in attitude importance, attitude certainty, and perceived knowledge about a range of social policy issues. Consistent with expectations, the findings revealed that perceptions of attitude importance, attitude certainty, and knowledge about issues were higher in middle adulthood compared to early and late adulthood.

Taking it one step further, what is it that makes attitudes stronger (and thus less likely to change) across certain phases of the lifespan? One possible explanation, developed by Eaton, Visser, Krosnick, and Anand (2009), is that these changes in strength are linked to the different social roles we carry out during different phases of our life. For example, if, during adulthood, individuals carry out social roles that are associated with high status, prestige, and power, this could lead them to possess attitudes that are more resistant to change, because there is a norm that having a powerful status is linked with being resolute in one's views (Eaton et al., 2009). These researchers tested this proposal using large national surveys in the United States. Across a series of studies, Eaton and colleagues found that middle-aged individuals are more likely to be in positions of power, and that these status effects play a role in mediating the effect of age on attitude change. While provocative, Eaton et al. acknowledge that other mechanisms (such as changes in social networks, age differences in cognitive abilities) could also account for the curvilinear relation between age and susceptibility to attitude change. Further, as noted by Visser and Krosnick (1998), even individuals' interpretation of terms such as "welfare" might differ across the lifespan, which could contribute to the curvilinear pattern. Another consideration is that aging affects people's perspective on time: as they get older, people feel that the time in front of them is less

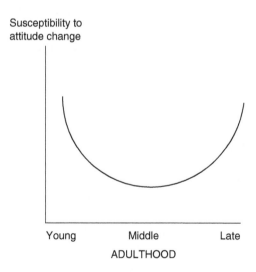

**Figure 9.4**  *A depiction of the life-stages hypothesis on the relation between age and susceptibility to attitude change*

expansive (Carstensen, 2006). This is important because of evidence that, when people are made to feel that time is short, they show more openness to attitude change than when they feel that time is expansive (DeWall, Visser, & Levitan, 2006).

## KEY POINTS

- There may be a curvilinear relation between age and susceptibility to attitude change, with greater susceptibility among young adults and the elderly.
- There are several plausible explanations for the relation between age and attitude change, including effects on social networks, attitude strength, message interpretation, and time perspective.

## WHAT WE HAVE LEARNED

- While implicit measures of attitude are less susceptible to social desirability concerns, they are not immune to these types of effects.
- Behaviors associated with approval or approach (e.g., head shaking, pulling) may cause more positive attitudes than actions associated with disapproval or avoidance.
- Motor actions may influence attitudes by acting as cues, influencing deliberation, biasing attitude-relevant elaboration, or affecting thought confidence.
- The consumption of alcohol and caffeine can influence the favorability of our attitudes and our susceptibility to attitude change.
- Some studies suggest that there is an indirect link between genes and attitudes.
- Social cognitive neuroscience has made important contributions to understanding where and when attitudinal responses are represented.

## WHAT DO YOU THINK?

- The evidence for effects of bodily actions on attitudes is intriguing, and the perspective offered by Briñol and Petty (2008) helps to account for results thus far. Nonetheless, the experiments described in this chapter have examined behaviors that possess very clear meanings for most people. For example, we tend to spontaneously associate nodding with agreement. If the meaning of these behaviors varies between people and situations, will the effect of the behavior change?

- We have reviewed evidence suggesting that our susceptibility to attitude change alters across the lifespan. What do you think is the most likely explanation for this effect?

# KEY TERMS

*Alcohol myopia* – the idea that individuals under the influence of alcohol have a reduced capa-city to process information, and tend to react primarily to salient and impelling cues in their environment.

*Amygdala* – a structure in the medial temporal lobe of the brain that is linked with affective processing of information.

*Anterior cingulate cortex* – a region of the brain associated with decision-making processes.

*Attitude embodiment* – the idea that performing a physical act can influence the favorability of an individual's attitude.

*Body-specificity hypothesis* – a framework describing how concepts of handedness influence how individuals represent concepts in positive or negative ways.

*EEG – Electroencephalography* – a technique that offers a way to measure the time course of brain activity.

*Heritability* – in the context of attitudes, this is the idea that genes could establish general predispositions that shape environmental experiences in ways that increase the likelihood of developing specific attitudes.

*Life stages hypothesis* – the idea that there is a curvilinear relation between age and suscepti-bility to attitude change, with greater susceptibility among young adults and the elderly.

*MEG – Magnetoencephalography* – a technique that offers a way to measure the time course of brain activity.

*PET – Positron emission tomography* – a technique that gives an indication of the activity level of a particular brain region.

*PFC – Prefrontal cortex* – a region in the brain that is important in planning complex decisions and behavior.

*SCN – Social cognitive neuroscience* – a discipline that studies the *social* behavior of motivated individuals (S), examining the *cognitive* mechanisms that give rise to behavioral processes (C), and investigating the *neurological* systems that instantiate these processes (N).

*Social desirability* – the tendency to respond to questions in a manner that makes one's self look good.

*Visceral fit hypothesis* – the notion that individuals perceive experiences and outcomes integrated with their current visceral state as more likely to occur.

# FURTHER READING

## BASIC

Briñol, P. and Petty, R. E. (2003) Overt head movements and persuasion: A self-validation analysis. *Journal of Personality and Social Psychology, 84,* 1123–1139.

Cacioppo, J. T., Priester, J. R. and Berntson, G. G. (1993) Rudimentary determinants of attitudes: II. Arm flexion and extension have differential effects on attitudes. *Journal of Personality and Social Psychology, 65,* 5–17.

Casasanto, D. (2009) Embodiment of abstract concepts: Good and bad in right- and left-handers. *Journal of Experimental Psychology: General, 138,* 351–367.

Cunningham, W. A., Haas, I. J. and Jahn, A. (2011) Attitudes. In J. Decety & J. T. Cacioppo (eds), *The Oxford Handbook of Social Neuroscience* (pp. 212–226). New York: Oxford University Press.

Fazio, R. H. and Olson, M. A. (2003) Implicit measures in social cognition research: Their meaning and use. *Annual Review of Psychology, 54,* 297–327.

## APPLIED

Devine, P. G. Forscher, P. S., Austin, A. J. and Cox, W. T. L. (2012) Long-term reduction in implicit race bias: A prejudice habit-breaking intervention. *Journal of Experimental Social Psychology, 48,* 1267–1278.

MacDonald, T. K., Zanna, M. P. and Fong, G. T. (1995) Decision-making in altered states: The effects of alcohol on attitudes toward drinking and driving. *Journal of Personality and Social Psychology, 68,* 973–985.

Shook, N. J. and Fazio, R. H. (2008) Interracial roommate relationships: An experimental test of the contact hypothesis. *Psychological Science, 19,* 717–723.

# 10

---

## THE EXTERNAL WORLD

---

## QUESTIONS TO PONDER

1. How does message repetition influence attitudes?

2. Do sets of messages have to be on the same topic to influence agreement with each message?

3. How do people maintain "balance" between their attitudes and those of other people?

4. How can relationships affect attitudes?

5. Do minorities influence attitudes in the same way as majorities?

6. How do people respond to messages promoting values from Western and Eastern cultures?

## PREVIEW

Research is often about snapshots. We take pictures of processes that are occurring and attempt to draw conclusions from the patterns that we see. Pictures taken from different angles reveal different information, and psychological research takes snapshots of processes inside people. Psychological research on attitudes is no exception. All of the research described in the prior chapters – and particularly the chapter before this one – has focused on processes happening inside people's heads.

The present chapter attempts to widen the focus and include more of the external world. We start by describing how issues pertaining to time influence our attitudes. For example, what happens when we hear a persuasive message (e.g., a particular television advert) over and over? From there, we discuss how interpersonal factors can influence attitudes. How do our close personal relationships and group memberships affect our attitudes? We conclude by assessing cultural influences on attitude processes. For instance, are people from individualist and collectivist cultures more likely to be persuaded by different types of messages? These types of factors have received attention, but not as much as they could receive. This chapter will identify research relevant to these issues and explain why they are important.

## TIME

Most research on attitude change looks at the effect of receiving *one* cognitive, affective, or behavioral intervention on attitudes, over a limited period of time. For instance, participants may receive a single message arguing in favor of a brand of detergent. In contrast, we live in a world where millions of messages are presented more than once. One presentation of a message in favor of a particular product will be interpreted in light of past messages we received for the same brand, and numerous messages about other brands. For example, television advertisements often occur in lengthy sequences, and advertisers may even present two different advertisements for the same product in the same commercial segment. Interesting cognitive processes are created by the presence of more than one persuasive message over time. This section highlights different examples of these processes.

## Repeated messages

The simplest example of a multi-message environment occurs when the same message is presented repeatedly. John Cacioppo and Richard Petty (1979b) conducted two experiments that examined this message environment. In these experiments, university students heard a message containing many strong arguments in favor of an increase in university spending. Participants received the message either once, three times, or five times. Afterward, they rated their attitudes toward the recommendation and wrote about their thoughts while hearing the message.

Cacioppo and Petty (1979b) found that participants' attitudes and issue-relevant thoughts were more consistent with the message when it was presented three times than when it was only presented once. In contrast, participants were significantly less persuaded when the message was presented five times than when it was presented three times. In short, message repetition increased persuasion only to a point (three exposures), after which it decreased persuasion.

Cacioppo and Petty (1979b) interpreted this result using their Elaboration Likelihood Model of persuasion. Specifically, they suggested that repetition increased the ability to comprehend the strong arguments to a point, after which the message became tedious. This tedium may have led recipients to counter-argue the message. Nonetheless, it is also possible that people experience a feeling that their freedom of opinion is being threatened when messages repeatedly try to sway their views (Miller, 1976), and this is important because people tend to react negatively when they feel that their freedom is being threatened (Brehm & Brehm, 1981). Notwithstanding this possibility, it is clear that increased comprehension is useful for explaining the increased agreement with fewer repetition stages, because subsequent research found that three exposures to *weak* arguments *decreases* persuasion relative to one exposure (Cacioppo & Petty, 1985). This decrease should happen if repeated exposure makes it easier for people to see the flaws in the messages (as well as the strengths).

## Supporting and contradictory messages

Persuasive messages can be seen as "good" or "bad," depending on the quality of the argument and whether we agree with the point they are trying to make. Nonetheless, they often seem sinister because they try to get us to do or feel something, and this gets our defenses up. They can also be seen as containing ideas that might spread if unchecked, like viruses. It is this last metaphor that inspired William McGuire (1964) to conduct classic studies examining the effects of giving people a sequence of messages that say very different things about the same attitude object.

His research studied people's ability to resist attacks against well-known *truisms*: beliefs that are so widely accepted that people rarely question them and, consequently, fail to ever develop arguments to support them. Examples of truisms vary from medical beliefs such as "It is good to brush your teeth frequently" to social values such as "It is important to be helpful" (Maio & Olson, 1998b). McGuire showed that people dramatically reduce their acceptance of medical health truisms after they are given arguments attacking them. For instance, people believe much less in the importance of brushing their teeth or helping others as a result of a mere couple of paragraphs summarizing some new arguments against the ideas (Bernard, Maio, & Olson, 2003a; McGuire, 1964).

McGuire (1964) suggested that people can be exposed to prior messages that provide one of two types of defenses against such attacks. *Supportive defenses* provide people with information supporting the belief that is about to be attacked, while *refutational defenses* provide people with arguments against the belief and rebuttals of the arguments. McGuire compared supportive defenses to vitamin supplements, which strengthen resistance by providing ammunition for fighting a threat. In contrast, McGuire compared refutational defenses to medical inoculations against disease. Medical inoculations give people a small dose of a weakened virus so that the immune system can learn to recognize and defend against a stronger version of the virus. Similarly, refutational defenses expose people to a small sample of arguments against the truisms, giving people the chance to form counter-arguments. In essence, the refutational "inoculation" gives people the same supporting information as in the supportive defense, with an added glimpse of what attacks can look like.

It turns out that this inoculation approach is particularly effective at increasing resistance to subsequent attacks, although supportive defenses can be effective as well (McGuire, 1964). At the same time, the defenses work better when they help people to form arguments that are directly relevant to the subsequent attacks than when they help to form arguments that defend the truism, but are *not* directly threatened by the subsequent attacks (see McGuire, 1964). As an example, an inoculation stating that "studies show that tooth-brushing enhances tooth enamel" can better defend against the subsequent argument that "tooth-brushing damages teeth" than an inoculation stating that "studies show that tooth-brushing freshens breath."

The Meta-Cognitive Model of attitude (Petty et al., 2007) provides a framework for helping to understand these effects, with an interesting twist. Recall the Meta-Cognitive Model's assumption that people form beliefs about the validity of their own thoughts (Chapter 5). This model is relevant because people might not always see their resistance of a prior message, such as an inoculation message, as being *completely* legitimate or completely correct.

For example, people might doubt their own attitudes after receiving a persuasive message if they discover that they were influenced by the minority status of the source of the message (Tormala et al., 2007). Alternatively, they might be led to suspect that they had generated weak counterarguments against an earlier attack (even when they were not actually weak). Zackary Tormala and colleagues have found that, when people suspect that they have resisted a message in an illegitimate way (e.g., because of the source or weak counterarguments), they can become less certain about their attitude (Tormala, Clarkson, & Petty, 2006; Tormala et al., 2007). Consequently, this lower certainty makes them *more* susceptible to a subsequent persuasive message.

In other circumstances, resistance against an initial persuasive message in a sequence can induce higher certainty. For instance, people might believe that they resisted arguments from a source that was very credible or that they resisted very strong arguments. Resistance in both cases would seem impressive, because the resistance occurred in the face of a strong challenge. Consequently, resistance in both cases leads to attitudes that are held with more certainty than if weaker threats had been posed, causing *lower* subsequent attitude change (Tormala et al., 2006).

## Spillover to different messages

In both of the previous examples of a multi-message environment, the messages focused on the same topic. This focus makes sense to most people. After all, messages on completely different topics shouldn't affect each other, . . . should they?

It turns out that this intuition would be wrong. There are reasons to expect that the impact of a message can be shaped by a message on a different topic before it. Imagine that we hear a commercial about a new hybrid-fuel car, and the commercial gives *lots* of information about it. By the time the advertisement is over, we know everything about the car - from its fuel consumption to its speed from 0 to 60. Immediately following this message, we hear a commercial for a new store opening nearby, and this commercial contains a moderate amount of information about the store, but much less information than was in the prior message. Wouldn't we be disappointed by the comparative lack of information in the second message? The contrast between them would make it seem that the second message lacked information, compared to the first message. Conversely, wouldn't we be impressed by the information in the commercial about the store if we had just received extremely little information about the hybrid-fuel car? The contrast between them would make it seem that the second message had a lot of information, compared to the first message. As a result, we would be much less persuaded by the commercial in favor of the store after hearing the car commercial with a lot of information than after hearing the one with little information.

This reasoning was tested by Zackary Tormala and Richard Petty (2007). In a series of experiments, these researchers exposed participants to a persuasive message promoting a department store. In each experiment, participants first received another message containing much more or much less information about something else (e.g., a car). Participants then rated the extent to which the advertisement promoting the department store contained a lot of information and rated their attitude toward the store. As expected, participants thought that they received more information about the store when the first message contained little information than when it contained a lot of information. Moreover, those who thought they had received a lot of knowledge from the message about the store agreed more highly with that message, reporting a more favorable attitude. Thus, participants were affected by the amount of information in the prior, irrelevant message.

Tormala and Clarkson (2007) have since shown that perceptions of the source of a message can change in a similar way. The scientists found that a prior low-credibility source can enhance the persuasiveness of a subsequent moderately credible source speaking on a different topic, whereas a prior high-credibility source can decrease the persuasiveness of a subsequent moderately credible source speaking on a different topic. This interesting pattern shows that participants were affected by source credibility for a prior, irrelevant message.

Overall, then, messages on completely different topics do affect each other. Our interpretations of the content and source of a message depend on previous messages we have received.

## Messages through time that have a point

One of the great things about most novels is that they take time to finish. If you could read one in just 90 minutes, it might have been as good to see a film. If either of us picks up a good book, however, we can guarantee we will be moving slowly through the story for a few weeks or even months! Moreover, a fun aspect of most novels is that the novel moves forward in time with you: characters move through events in a timeline, evolving, adapting, and changing.

This capacity of a single story to unfold over time is important because many stories also convey subtle or not-so-subtle messages. These messages may be in the dominant "moral of the story" or in events that happen to characters. Any narrative, including brief essays, films, and some forms of commercial advertisement, is capable of conveying a message in this way. So an important question is whether these types of messages, which weave events across time, affect attitudes. As shown in Research Highlight 10.1, research has indicated that narratives can shape attitudes (Green & Brock, 2000; Marsh, Mead, & Roediger, 2003; Prentice, Gerrig, & Bailis, 1997).

### RESEARCH HIGHLIGHT 10.1

### AN INUIT BOY AND HIS DOG

Melanie Green and Timothy Brock (2000) found that readers who became involved in a story subsequently reported attitudes more congruent with the narrative's theme. In one experiment, participants read a short story about an Inuit boy and his dog. These characters become stranded on an ice floe without food or supplies. During the night, both characters consider killing the other for food, and, in the morning, both are rescued. Green and Brock (2000) found that readers who became involved in the story subsequently attributed greater importance to the values of friendship and loyalty, which were promoted by the story.

Green and Brock suggest that *transportation* causes this type of attitude change. Transportation is a process by which people become deeply immersed into a narrative world (Gerrig, 1993). Green and Brock (2000) suggested that narratives may be particularly persuasive because transportation causes people to temporarily lose access to some of their real-world

*(Continued)*

(*Continued*)

knowledge and makes them less able to counter-argue persuasive arguments that they encounter within the story. Several studies have found evidence supporting this role of transportation (Dal Cin, Zanna, & Fong, 2004; Marsh & Fazio, 2006). In addition, several experiments have found that people experience more transportation when their personality and features of the narrative (e.g., first-person perspective, ingroup members) promote lower self-consciousness (Kaufman & Libby, 2012). In combination, the research in the past decade has helped to reveal more information about when and how transportation influences attitudes.

## KEY POINTS

- We live in a "message-dense environment" that makes it important to consider exposure to information over time.

- Moderate repetition may increase message comprehension and more persuasion for strong messages, but less persuasion for weak ones.

- Our resistance to a message can increase resistance to subsequent messages on the same topic, as long we see our initial resistance as being legitimate.

- The effect of a message can depend on the nature of a prior message on a completely different topic.

## RELATIONSHIPS

The bulk of the research described in this text has focused on the attitudes of individuals. That is, the experiments have helped to gain knowledge about how any given person, on average, holds, maintains, and uses their attitudes. However, people don't live in isolation; we have many relationships with others, including parents, spouses, siblings, children, friends, neighbors, colleagues, acquaintances, and even people we may know only remotely (e.g., over the Internet). Research could focus on trying to understand the effects of these relationships, instead of ignoring them in the analyses. Social psychologists like to stress that we do not live in a social vacuum. People influence us in a truly enormous number of ways, through their real and imagined presence (Allport, 1985). This section highlights examples of how the consideration of relationships offers important insights into attitudes.

## Social balance: my enemy's enemy is my friend

One of the earliest and best-known examples of a theory to tackle social influences on attitude was Fritz Heider's (1946, 1958) Balance Theory. This theory is often regarded as an early forerunner to Cognitive Dissonance Theory. Like Dissonance Theory, Balance Theory asserts that people seek harmony among their thoughts about an attitude object. Tests of Dissonance Theory focused on how people manage inconsistency between their attitudes and thoughts about their own behavior, while tests of Balance Theory focused on how people manage inconsistency between their attitude and their thoughts about another person's attitude.

Balance Theory's emphasis on thoughts about another person's attitude proved to be vitally important. This theory suggested that people can mentally represent *attitude triads*, which contain (a) the individual's own attitude toward an object, (b) another person's attitude toward the object, and (c) the individual's own attitude toward the other person. (The theory also suggested that we can represent other types of connections with objects and people, such as shared identities or ownership, but connections in attitude have received the most attention.) In Figure 10.1, the person's attitude toward an object is represented by the line from P (*Person*) to AO (*Attitude Object*), the other person's attitude toward the object is shown by the line from OP (*Other Person*) to AO, and the person's attitude toward the other person is shown by the line from P to OP. Heider proposed that people seek balance in these connections and that imbalance is uncomfortable or aversive to people.

Phrased simply, balance occurs when people agree with someone they like or disagree with someone they dislike. For example, you might like the England football (soccer) team, but have a close friend who cannot stand it. Presumably, England's football successes and failures then make it difficult to sustain your positive attitude toward your friend, putting the friendship in jeopardy! Ending the friendship is one way to restore balance, but balance can also be restored by deciding you don't like the England football team, or by deciding (perceiving) that your friend does like it.

Many experiments have supported this reasoning by asking people to rate their level of comfort with different hypothetical situations representing different combinations of attitudes in this model. These

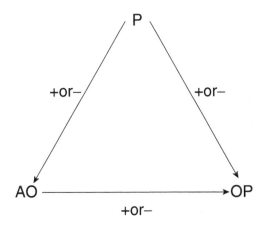

**Figure 10.1** *Diagram of an attitude triad involving a person (P), an attitude object (AO), and another person (OP)*

experiments have found an *attraction* effect and an *agreement* effect (Insko, 1984; Zajonc, 1968). The attraction effect is that we prefer situations where we like another person compared to situations where we dislike another person, regardless of attitudes toward the object. For example, we might meet a new person, Jill, and learn that she likes or dislikes our favorite rock band. On average we would prefer to like Jill than to dislike her, even though this effect is somewhat reversed when she dislikes our favorite band. The agreement effect is that we like situations where we agree with another person (i.e., share the same attitude toward the object) better than situations where we disagree with that person (regardless of attitudes toward the person). For example, on average we would prefer to agree with Jill about the band, even though this preference is somewhat reversed when we do not like her.

Analyses of people's ratings of hypothetical scenarios can separate attraction and agreement effects from the preference for balance, which always involves attraction and agreement at the same time *or* unattraction and disagreement at the same time. When John Cacioppo and Richard Petty (1981) did this, they found that balance and agreement effects increased when people were given more time or motivation to contemplate the situations; in contrast, attraction effects were unaffected by manipulations of time and motivation. These results are consistent with evidence that balanced connections are distinctly represented in memory (von Hecker, 1993).

Together, the results suggest that relationships between people possess a unique character, which must be considered for a full understanding of attitudes. The importance of this idea is reinforced by evidence of balance-like effects in research that has gone beyond the hypothetical scenarios studied in typical tests of Balance Theory. For instance, we like people who punish our enemies but reward our friends (Aronson & Cope, 1968). In addition, people appear to assume that their political views are shared by political candidates whom they like and not by those whom they dislike (Granberg & Brent, 1974; Ottati, Fishbein, & Middlestadt, 1988). Of interest, recent analyses of data from a large-scale survey distributed on Facebook indicate that we also overestimate our level of agreement with friends on political attitudes, even when we think we discuss these issues with them (Goel, Mason, & Watts, 2010). Furthermore, we tend to modify our attitudes to fit those of our partners in close relationships (Davis & Rusbult, 2001). When this evidence is considered with recent extensions to marketing (Basil & Herr, 2006) and advertising (Russell & Stern, 2006), it is clear that Balance Theory's identification of the role of relationships in attitudes is very important.

## Relationships and ambivalence

Relationships have an interesting effect on people's feelings of ambivalence toward an attitude object. Recall from Chapter 3 that research can assess two types of ambivalence: potential ambivalence and felt ambivalence. Social relationships appear to be vital for understanding the sources of felt ambivalence (Kaufman & Uhlenberg, 1998; Luescher & Pillemer, 1998). A compelling demonstration of the importance of relationships was provided by Joseph Priester and Richard Petty (2001). In one of their studies, students rated their attitudes and their parents' attitudes toward 12 attitude objects, such as exercising, donating blood, and watching television. These measures enabled the researchers to calculate the differences between each participant's attitudes and the participant's perceptions of their parents' attitudes.

The researchers also measured participants' potential and felt ambivalence toward each attitude object. Then, they looked at the extent to which felt ambivalence was linked to both (a) the participant-parent attitude differences and (b) potential ambivalence. The results indicated that the participant-parent attitude differences predicted feelings of ambivalence even after potential ambivalence was statistically controlled for (and vice-versa). This role of attitude discrepancies was then replicated for other types of role relationships (e.g., fellow students), attitude objects, and using procedures that manipulated participants' perceptions of interpersonal attitude discrepancy. Thus, interpersonal discrepancies in attitude were important predictors of feelings of ambivalence.

## Shared dissonance with another person

Chapter 7 focused on what happens if we perform a behavior that contradicts our own attitude or is difficult to explain in some way. We could also ask what would happen if someone we know or like performed a behavior that contradicts our own attitude. What if a family member lied about his or her attitude toward a sensitive topic and we were a silent witness? Would our close bond to the person cause us to change our attitudes in the same way as the person does?

A provocative experiment by Sakai (1999) explored this issue. This scientist used a paradigm similar to that used by Festinger and Carlsmith (1959), except that two people, including a confederate, completed the boring tasks. The confederate was asked to lie and say that the tasks were interesting. The confederate then asked the participant to accompany him during this lie, while the confederate did all of the speaking (i.e., lying). In a control condition, the participant remained in a corner of the room while the confederate lied about the tasks. Analyses of attitudes after the lie revealed that participants who had been asked to directly accompany the confederate grew to like the tasks more than participants who were allowed to remain less directly involved. Thus, despite the absence of any overt, spoken behavior by the participant, there was something about being together that made the participant share the same psychological fate (see also Zanna & Sande, 1987). The pattern is consistent with the notion of *vicarious dissonance*; that is, participants may have experienced cognitive dissonance as a result of the behavior of the other individual.

Like the Festinger and Carlsmith experiment, Sakai's experiment was highly intriguing but not definitive by itself. There are several potential explanations for the effect. For example, was the participants' inactive accompaniment actually an action in its own right, because it signaled agreement with the lie? Does the role of choice (a key variable in dissonance theory) change when the behavior is performed by another? That is, does the person's choice or the partner's choice affect this type of behavior-induced attitude change? It will take some time to discover the mechanisms in this interesting effect.

---

*Structure Witch: Combining this evidence with the evidence described in the prior section, would observation of a romantic partner's counter-attitudinal behavior increase our ambivalence on the attitude topic?*

---

From this point of view, it is encouraging that other researchers have started to investigate the idea that we can vicariously experience dissonance. This progress was noted in Chapter 7, where Research Highlight 7.2 described how we can be influenced by hypocritical acts by an ingroup member.

## Nature of the relationship

If relationships affect attitudes, then it is important to consider that relationships vary in many ways. For instance, we may be more satisfied with some relationships than with others. We may also be more committed to some relationships, and we may have more or less power in them. In theory, any relationship characteristic could affect the attitudes an individual forms and maintains.

Power is an interesting example of a relationship variable that can influence the manner in which people form and maintain attitudes. Classic research indicates that messages delivered by powerful individuals produce more attitude change than messages delivered by powerless sources (French & Raven, 1959). More recently, Pablo Briñol, Richard Petty, Carmen Valle, Derek Rucker, and Alberto Becerra (2007) predicted that making people feel powerful *before* receiving a persuasive message would validate their existing attitudes and thus reduce their need to pay attention to the subsequent appeal. In contrast, these researchers predicted that a feeling of power *after* a message has been processed would validate the thoughts they had generated in response to the message, consequently increasing reliance on their thoughts about the message in shaping their attitudes. If this hypothesis is correct, then people who feel less powerful in relationships might process persuasive communications differently from people who feel more powerful, depending on when the person does or does not feel powerful.

 *Content Witch:* Do these hypotheses mean that power increases reliance on the cognitive component of attitudes?

In one experiment testing this hypothesis, undergraduate psychology students at the Universidad Autónoma de Madrid were asked to assume the role of manager (high power) or employee (low power) in a role-play of a meeting at work. (The manager was even given a taller and better-looking chair to enhance the feeling of power!) Then, as part of another study, participants received an advertisement for a new mobile phone and rated their attitude toward the phone.

To test whether participants had scrutinized the persuasive message carefully (see Chapter 5), the advertisement contained either strong arguments (e.g., the battery could be recharged in five minutes) or weak arguments (e.g., the PIN code was just two digits long). As expected, Briñol and colleagues (2007) found that participants were significantly more persuaded by the strong than the weak arguments only when participants had previously enacted the role of someone relatively low in power (see Figure 10.2). In contrast, in a similar experiment that manipulated power *after* the message had been presented, participants were significantly more persuaded by the strong than the weak arguments only when participants enacted the role of someone relatively high in power. This

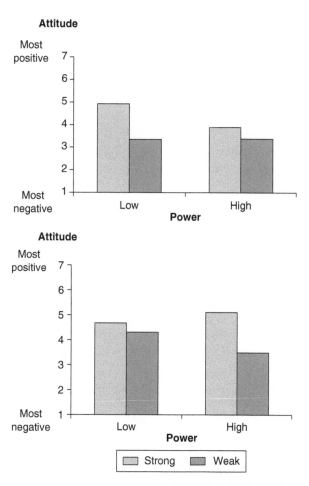

**Figure 10.2** *Effects of experienced power and message strength on post-message attitudes when power is manipulated before (top panel) and after (bottom panel) the message (Briñol et al., 2007)*

result (among others) fits the hypothesis that participants who were higher in power were more influenced by the positive thoughts elicited by the strong message and the negative thoughts elicited by the weak message, due to their greater confidence in the validity of these thoughts.

There is a need for more research on power and other relationship variables, as their potential effects on attitudes are numerous. For instance, there is evidence that merely reminding people of past experiences of power over others increases their tendency to think abstractly (Smith & Trope, 2006). Perhaps, then, the experience of high personal power increases people's focus on more abstract arguments in a message and reduces their focus on more concrete arguments. To us, this is an interesting possibility for future research, among many others.

## KEY POINTS

- Consistent with Balance Theory, there is evidence that people seek harmony between their attitudes and those of others.

- Inconsistency between personal attitudes and the attitudes of our important others (e.g., our parents) may lead to feelings of ambivalence.

- Our attitudes may be influenced by the behavior of other individuals with whom we interact.

- Personal power may decrease our openness to subsequent new arguments and increase reliance on prior beliefs and feelings.

# GROUPS

Our discussion of relationships considered the role of attitudes in the context of another person, but attitudes also emerge in groups of people. Groups can shape our views, and we can influence the views of groups. For example, have you ever noticed a change in your own attitudes as you moved from one group of friends to another? Perhaps this change occurred as you moved from one workplace to another or from junior school to high school? The effects of groups on attitudes (and vice versa) are diverse and powerful, and many effects described earlier in this chapter and others (e.g., effects of the social adjustment function, norms in the Theory of Planned Behavior) reflect the importance of group processes. We highlight several additional examples in this chapter. Effects like these have led some researchers to suggest that attitude theory and research should consider more deeply the roles of groups and social identity processes in attitudes (Hogg & Smith, 2007) and attitude strength (Eaton, Majka, & Visser, 2008).

## Vicarious dissonance again

In the prior section on relationships, we considered evidence that briefly accompanying another person may lead to effects of that person's subsequent behavior on our own attitudes, through socially shared dissonance processes. In theory, we might also experience dissonance vicariously as a result of behavior from any individual who is seen as part of our own group. Provocative research by Michael Norton, Benoît Monin, Joel Cooper, and Mike Hogg (2003) demonstrates this process. These researchers conducted experiments with participants who were university students opposed to a tuition fee increase. In one experiment, participants arrived at the lab separately, but took part in the study with another person (who was not known to them). The experimenter asked each participant to listen to a tape recording of the other participant. The recording actually featured the voices of two actors. In the recording, the "other participant" was asked to make a speech favoring an increase in tuition fees, so that the Dean of the university could use the arguments to press for a fee increase. The "other participant" was heard to object to this position, after which the experimenter either reminded the participant of his or her choice to make this speech or did not remind the participant of his or her choice. The tape then played a bland speech from the "other participant," stating that higher tuition fees were necessary to hire good faculty and maintain modern facilities for students. Participants were then asked to rate their attitudes toward the speech.

Norton and colleagues (2003) examined the extent to which the "other participant's" level of choice (in making the speech) influenced participants' attitudes toward the tuition fee increases. At the same time, these scientists examined participants' degree of identification with their college. Identification was examined because the researchers believed that dissonance should be felt more strongly when there is a strong bond between the person who committed the dissonant act and the individual who learned about the act. As expected, attitudes were more likely to change in the (counter-attitudinal) direction advocated by the "other participant" when participants heard the experimenter giving the "other participant" a choice than when the recording did not make choice salient, but only for people who identified more strongly with their college.

# Majority influence

If you were in a group of six people trapped on a small rowboat far from land, with few supplies, it would be pretty important to get along with your shipmates. If you start to become alienated from the others, there is a chance they might cut you off from supplies or even throw you overboard. Perhaps this is why the cliché "Don't rock the boat" is often used to tell people to go along with others, despite any personal objections. Groups are important to us, so we need to adapt our actions and attitudes to them.

The effects of groups on attitudes have been obtained in powerful, controlled experiments. These experiments were inspired by Solomon Asch's (1956) famous experiments demonstrating a strong influence of groups on beliefs. In his experiments, participants in groups of five were asked to pick a figure that was the same size as a test figure. For example, they would be shown three lines of different lengths (e.g., 7, 9, and 11 inches) and asked to identify the line that was the same length as a fourth line (e.g., 9 inches). The task was easy, and everyone got it right when tested on their own. However, this wasn't the case when each participant was placed in a group of five people, four of whom were actually confederates of the experimenter. The experimenter had planned for all four confederates to indicate an answer that was patently and obviously incorrect for some of the judgments performed in this group. Despite the obvious nature of majority's mistake, one-third of the participants agreed with their wrong answer in more than half of the 12 trials where the majority made their "error." Only 23% of participants never agreed with the incorrect majority; most participants (77%) agreed with the majority's error in at least one trial where an obvious mistake was made!

The tendency for people to agree with group consensus has vitally important implications for opinion shifts within group discussions. There is a strong tendency for a *group polarization* effect: individuals' attitudes become more extreme than the group's average view after group discussion (Isenberg, 1986). If the individuals' initial tendency is favorable, the individuals become even more favorable after group discussion; if the individuals' initial tendency is unfavorable, the individuals become even more unfavorable after group discussion. For example, a group of people who are somewhat against genetic cloning will become more strongly against cloning after they chat with each other about the issue, whereas a group of people who are somewhat for genetic cloning will become more strongly for cloning after their own discussion.

*Structure Witch: By creating more extreme attitudes, does group discussion cause attitudes to adopt a unidimensional structure?*

The dominant explanation for this effect is that a desire to fit with the group is important. This explanation is supported by abundant evidence that group polarization occurs because (1) group members give each other new reasons to hold the attitude they share (e.g., Burnstein & Vinokur, 1977), and (2) people in a group like to make themselves look good by making themselves appear more committed than average to the group's position (e.g., Goethals & Zanna, 1979). Thus, while the effect statistically is a move against conformity with an initial view, it actually represents a process of a group coming together more strongly, while perhaps balancing an individual need for uniqueness.

## RESEARCH HIGHLIGHT 10.2

### IMAGINE IF YOUR FATHER KNEW

The group polarization studies are powerful examples of how the *actual* presence of others shapes attitudes. However, most people are particularly surprised to learn that other people affect our attitudes and behavior even when their presence is merely imagined (Baldwin & Holmes, 1987; Garcia, Weaver, Moscowitz, & Darley, 2002). A provocative study by Mark Baldwin and John Holmes (1987) demonstrated this effect by asking female university students to think about two of their campus peers or two of their older relatives. The women were later asked to help another experimenter with an additional (ostensibly unrelated) study. This study involved reading and evaluating a fictional passage from a popular women's magazine, depicting a woman having a sexual dream about a man she found attractive. Subsequent analyses of attitudes toward the erotic passage indicated that the women who had previously imagined their campus peers liked the passage more than those who had previously imagined their older relatives. It seems that merely *imagining* their peers brought to mind more liberal moral standards than imagining their (staid?) older relatives!

There are hundreds of demonstrations of the influence of groups on individuals' judgment and attitudes, and a lot of research has examined reasons for this influence. One classic theory proposed that people adapt their opinions to their social groups because of *normative influence*, which is a desire to be liked, and because of *informational influence*, which is a desire to be accurate. In other words, agreement helps people get along with their groups and we may feel more confident about the truth of our opinions when everyone agrees (Deutsch & Gerard, 1955). There is evidence to support these explanations (Prislin & Wood, 2005) and evidence to suggest that conformity helps us to avoid a state of cognitive dissonance that occurs when our views don't match those of our group (Matz & Wood, 2005). In addition, it seems clear that these motives compete with a motive to express one's own values and beliefs (Chen, Schechter, & Chaiken, 1996; Johnson & Eagly, 1989; Lundgren & Prislin, 1998), which may partly reduce conformity and contribute to the way in which people make themselves somewhat better-than-average in the group polarization effect. Together, these processes may help to explain interesting evidence that attitudes are stronger among people who think their attitudes match the consensus of their groups, but only when people seek to belong to the group; when people desire uniqueness, attitudes are stronger to the extent that they differ from the group (Clarkson, Tormala, Rucker, & Dugan, 2013).

## Norms: "Do as I say and not as I do"

Robert Cialdini and colleagues have pointed to two additional ways in which the real or imagined influence of others might occur: groups show what other people do *and* what they think you should do (Cialdini, Kallgren, & Reno, 1991). In other words, groups convey norms that describe others' actions, which can be labeled as *descriptive norms*, and norms that prescribe or proscribe actions, which can be labeled as *injunctive norms*. These descriptive and injunctive norms can then determine behaviors in different ways.

This hypothesis has been supported by important research that looked at methods for promoting environmentally conscious behavior (Cialdini, 2003). Cialdini noticed an important problem with an award winning, anti-littering campaign – one that had been praised by the advertising industry and public alike. The ad showed a Native American canoeing up a river, from a clean forest along progressively littered riverbanks in a metropolitan area, shedding a tear for emphasis at the end of the journey. Cialdini suggested that this ad made it appear as though *everyone* was littering, even though it showed terrible consequences of littering and suggested that littering should stop. Cialdini suggested that the descriptive norm might have overpowered the effect of the injunctive norm, potentially explaining why *more* littering occurred after the ad.

To test this hypothesis, Cialdini and his colleagues devised field experiments that exposed people to messages that used descriptive or injunctive norms to promote an environmental conservation behavior. One imaginative experiment revealed the importance of this distinction by placing signs on pathways through Arizona's Petrified Forest National Park. During five consecutive weekends, these signs asked visitors not to take petrified wood from the park. One type of sign emphasized a descriptive norm by stating "Many past visitors have removed petrified wood from the Park, changing the natural state of the Petrified Forest." The other type of sign emphasized an injunctive norm by stating "Please don't remove the petrified wood from the Park, in order to preserve the natural state of the Petrified Forest."

As predicted, the injunctive norm placard resulted in significantly less theft of wood than the descriptive norm message. Additional field studies revealed a remarkable level of success for pro-recycling television and radio commercials that were designed using the same principles, namely by describing descriptive norms and injunctive norms that both support the sought-after behavior (by suggesting that most people recycle and that people should recycle). These messages achieved a 25% increase in recycling tonnage in four Arizona communities. Thus, these experiments demonstrate the importance of descriptive and injunctive norms.

The experiments also make a larger point. Specifically, messages aimed at attitude and behavior change can be effective, if they are based on relevant psychological theory and evidence. In contrast, approaches based merely on the designers' intuition may backfire (Maio et al., 2009).

Despite this important evidence, we must remember that norms don't affect everyone to the same extent. People's personality affects the role of norms. Earlier in the book, we noted one relevant personality variable: high self-monitors are individuals who are more likely to follow social norms than low self-monitors, who tend to rely more strongly on internal attitudes and beliefs to guide their behaviors (Snyder, 1986).

The role of norms also depends on situational factors. For instance, people's behaviors are more influenced by norms when they highly identify with the group that is the source of the norms. In one fascinating test of this idea, farmers were more influenced by their group norms for a particular sustainable agricultural practice when they identified highly with their group (Fielding, Terry, Masser, & Hogg, 2008). Other research has found that the role of norms may be amplified when people are experiencing feelings of uncertainty (Smith, Hogg, Martin, & Terry, 2007).

The role of personality differences and the role of situations are also important in light of recent evidence that descriptive and injunctive norms work in different ways. Using a task that presented an injunctive or descriptive norm and then measured the speed of responding to words related to different goals, Ryan Jacobsen, Chad Mortensen, and Robert Cialdini (2011) found that injunctive norms have a stronger connection to goals related to interpersonal harmony, while descriptive norms are more closely connected to accuracy goals. This difference may cause people who are high in personality traits related to social-adjustment goals or accuracy goals to respond differently to these norms. Related to this idea, these scientists found that completion of an effortful attention control task decreased subsequent effort to conform with injunctive norms (which presumably conflicted with personal goals), but not descriptive norms (which presumably help the self by promoting accuracy).

Such findings have important implications for real-world efforts to change behavior by reminding people of what they should do or of what others tend to do. For this reason, we expect this to be an area of research that will continue to flourish.

## Minority influence

Our examples of group influence so far have focused on the effect of majority pressure in a group. If opinions always revolved around the majority, the scenario would be very depressing for advocates of social change, and many of the radical changes in the past centuries wouldn't have been achieved by the minorities that pressed for them. A renowned French social psychologist, Serge Moscovici (1980), argued that minorities can also influence majorities, and he provided provocative evidence to support this view.

For instance, Moscovici, Lage, and Naffrechoux (1969) conducted a clever inversion of the Asch (1956) line-judging experiment. In their experiment, the confederates became the minority instead of the majority. Four participants were placed in groups with two confederates and asked to judge a series of six blue slides that varied in brightness. Participants were asked to indicate the color and brightness of the slides. When participants indicated the color of the slides in groups *without* the confederates, they were judged correctly nearly 100% of the time. However, when the minorities insisted that they saw green slides on all of the trials, the participants shifted to agree with the minority's response on over 8% of the trials. This number is smaller than the shift induced in Asch's research (wherein 32% agreed with more than half of the errant trials), but still significant considering that the stimuli were *unambiguous* in nature (because they elicited 100% agreement about color without confederates). Interestingly, only 1.25% gave the minority's response when the minority stated "green" only two-thirds of the time. This finding and later evidence suggest that minorities must appear to be consistent in order to influence others (Wood, Lundgren, Ouellette, Busceme, & Blackstone, 1994).

You might expect that the effects of minorities on ambiguous subjective judgments, such as attitudes, should be even more powerful. Supporting this view, studies since Moscovici's experiments have found that minorities can influence diverse attitudes. In studies presenting persuasive messages from minorities, there have been significant effects on attitudes toward university policies (Crano & Chen, 1998), community service (Baker & Petty, 1994), and a ban on guns (Alvaro & Crano, 1997), among many other issues. These findings suggest that minority influence may be an important part of attitude formation and change.

# Modes of minority and majority influence

Considerable debate has occurred over whether minorities and majorities affect attitudes in different ways. A thorough review of research on this topic is beyond the scope of this chapter, but it is now clear that majorities and minorities can both elicit persuasion and that each source can trigger the same or different methods of message processing (Baker & Petty, 1994; Kruglanski & Mackie, 1991; Martin, 1998). Robin Martin and colleagues (Martin, Hewstone, & Martin, 2007) conducted experiments that provided an interesting demonstration of this potential for majorities and minorities to trigger different methods of message processing. These scientists told students that their university had assembled a focus group to discuss the implementation of new oral comprehensive exams. Some participants were told that 9 of the 11 participants in the focus group agreed with the exams (majority condition), while other participants were told that 2 of the 11 were in favor of the exams (minority message). The experimenters then manipulated the extent to which students were motivated (Experiment 1) or able (Experiment 2) to think carefully about a message on the topic. Participants then read a series of strong or weak arguments in favor of the exams and then rated their attitudes toward the exams.

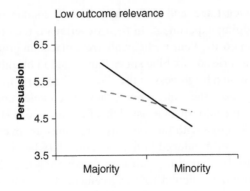

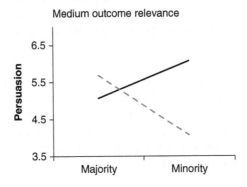

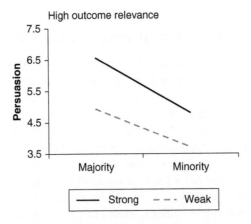

**Figure 10.3**   *Effects of outcome relevance, majority versus minority source, and argument strength on persuasion (Martin, Hewstone, & Martin, 2007)*

The principal results of the research are shown in Figure 10.3. Results indicated that participants were more persuaded by the majority than the minority view when they had little motivation or ability to elaborate on the arguments. In contrast, when motivation or ability was moderate, the presence of a minority source (but not a majority source) caused participants to base their attitudes on the strength of the arguments. When motivation or ability was high, the participants were influenced by the strength of the arguments, regardless of whether the position was advocated by the majority or minority.

These results provide an interesting integration of research on majority influence with research on persuasion (see Martin, Martin, Smith, & Hewstone, 2007). Several theories suggest that majority information acts somewhat like a simple cue – "If everyone says so, it must be true" (Darke et al., 1998) – whereas minorities stimulate more thought (Moscovici, 1980). Martin et al.'s evidence suggest that these roles depend on the extent to which majority and minority positions receive a lot of scrutiny, which is consistent with models described in Chapter 5, and with the Elaboration Likelihood Model in particular (Petty & Cacioppo, 1986). Also, more recent experiments indicate that majority sources of a message also make people more confident in their thoughts about the message arguments if they learn about the source after the message, or increase confidence in the message position if they learn about the source before the message (Horcajo, Petty, & Briñol, 2010). When confident about their thoughts on the arguments, message recipients' attitudes become stronger when the arguments are strong than when they are weak. In contrast, when confident about the message position, argument quality has less of an effect.

Minority sources may themselves have complex effects. An important review found that studies comparing minority and majority influence did not reliably obtain evidence consistent with the idea that minorities elicit more issue-relevant thought than majorities (Wood et al., 1994). Majorities and minorities both stimulate extra thinking about the issue when their views are surprising to the message recipient (Baker & Petty, 1994). Minority influence also appears to depend on other factors, such as whether the group is seen as being similar or dissimilar to the self in some other respect or as being particularly innovative. For instance, when the minority is disliked, the minority may actually cause less agreement (De Dreu, 2007; De Vries & De Dreu, 2001). Minorities may also have a smaller effect on the key attitude that is being debated than on other attitudes and beliefs that are relevant, but not the focus (Crano & Alvaro, 1998). It may turn out that this effect on diverse attitudes has some connection to intriguing evidence that minorities can stimulate more creative thinking (Peterson & Nemeth, 1996).

Regardless of exactly how minorities and majorities influence attitudes, it is clear that both can be effective. This impact has far-reaching implications for groups. Through attitude change, majorities can gradually become minorities and vice versa. People might witness these changes as they happen, and these perceptions of change may have their own effects. They might heighten fear of the change or lead to more thinking about reasons to change. It turns out that perceptions of change do matter (e.g., Gordijn, De Vries, & De Dreu, 2002), and research has begun to explore the dynamic implications of change for persuasion (Prislin & Christiensen, 2005).

## KEY POINTS

- Individuals' attitudes tend to become more extreme in the direction of the group's average view after group discussion.

- Even the imagined presence of others may shape attitudes.

- Knowing what people do (descriptive norms) has a different effect on attitudes and behavior than knowing what people think we should do (injunctive norms).

- Consistent minorities can influence majority opinion significantly.

- Minority and majority status may evoke different types of information processing, depending on other motivational and cognitive factors.

# CULTURE

Just as relationships between two people can occur in larger groups, groups exist within broader cultures. It could be argued that the role of culture has been underestimated in the study of attitudes. In real-life contexts, people tend to develop cultures containing shared attitudes (Cullum & Harton, 2007), but we know relatively little about this process. Part of the problem is that most of the influential research on attitudes has emerged either from relatively wealthy nations in Europe (e.g., Britain, Germany, Netherlands) or from wealthy nations that have strong historical and cultural connections to Europe (e.g., United States, Canada, Australia). This means that the ideas being tested were drawn from a somewhat narrow cultural perspective – when you consider that perspectives from Africa, South and Central America, and Asia have not had a large voice. So it is quite important to wonder whether the evidence we have described throughout the book would hold in these other parts of the world. Thus, social psychologists have recently become particularly interested in broad differences between so-called Eastern cultures, such as Japan, China, and India, and Western cultures, such as the United States, Canada, and Europe.

## Collectivism and individualism

Culture is a complex construct. Triandis (1989) suggested that diverse variables, like complexity of social organization and population density, influence the prevalence of different social contexts, and these contexts may motivate people to focus on collective action or individual striving. This perspective is applicable to a variety of cultures, but research has focused on suggestions that Eastern cultural practices more strongly emphasize collective social roles than Western cultural practices, which more strongly emphasize individual autonomy (Markus & Kitayama, 1991). *Collectivistic cultures* foster a view of the self that emphasizes interdependence with others, whereas *individualistic cultures* foster a view of the self that emphasizes independence from others (Singelis, 1994). Although there have been criticisms of this view and the research testing it (Oyserman, Coon, & Kemmelmeier, 2002), it has generated a number of interesting ideas and evidence that help to understand the factors that shape attitudes and what attitudes do.

Foremost in this list of research is evidence that culture influences conformity. It turns out that there is stronger evidence of conformity in Asch's (1956) line-judging paradigm in collectivist cultures than in individualist cultures (Bond & Smith, 1996). In addition, there is a stronger influence of social consensus information in collectivist cultures than in individualist cultures (Cialdini, Wosinka, Barrett, Butner, & Górnik-Durose, 2001). That is, exposure to information about social consensus causes people to shift their attitudes to fit in with the common view, but this influence is more prevalent in collectivist cultures than in individualistic cultures. Thus, cultural setting helps to predict the extent to which we adapt our judgments and attitudes to group norms.

*Function Witch: Does the greater effect of conformity in collectivist cultures indicate that attitudes in these cultures are more likely to reflect a social-adjustment function?*

# Persuasion and culture

One important implication for attitudes is that people may be more influenced by persuasive messages that match their dominant cultural orientation than by messages that mismatch their dominant cultural orientation. This idea is consistent with the matching effects we discussed in Chapter 8. If people from Western cultures are more individualistic, then they should be more favorable to products that are paired with cogent messages stressing independence and autonomy than to products paired with messages stressing interdependence and togetherness. In contrast, people from Eastern cultures should be more favorable to products paired with cogent messages stressing interdependence than to products paired with messages stressing independence. In a comparison of responses to advertisements among American and Chinese consumers, Wang, Bristol, Mowen, and Chakraborty (2000) obtained evidence supporting this hypothesis. Furthermore, there is evidence that people with backgrounds in both Western and Eastern cultures respond favorably toward messages emphasizing both cultural perspectives, but only if they tend to mentally interconnect (rather than segregate) their experiences of both cultures (Lau-Gesk, 2003).

These results fit the broader view that attitude functions, and not just attitudes per se, adapt to culture. If people live in a culture that stresses independence or interdependence, then it should be adaptive to form attitudes that help to fulfill these aims. As a result, attitudes should be more influenced by appeals that fit these goals than by appeals that do not. Thus, effects of culture are important for understanding attitude function and its role.

The effects of culture are also relevant to attitude structure. There is evidence that North Americans prefer messages with less information than do East Asians (Wang, Masuda, Ito, & Rashid, 2012). Further, when information in a message is conflicting, individuals in a North American culture tend to weight one side of the conflict more highly, whereas individuals in East Asian cultures tend to attempt to use both sets of information (Aaker & Sengupta, 2000). This difference suggests that there is a potential for higher ambivalence in East Asian cultures. This is an intriguing possibility that, to our knowledge, remains to be explored.

# Dissonance and culture

Another important perspective is that attitudinal processes are much the same across cultures, but the content of them and their functions vary. This idea is exemplified by Festinger's (1957) description of Cognitive Dissonance Theory. He explicitly indicated that cultural norms help to dictate when two cognitions might be viewed as consistent or inconsistent, and that cultures might vary in how they deal with dissonance. Eating with one's hands is a violation of politeness and hygiene beliefs in some countries, but not in others. In addition, some cultural traditions might lead people to trivialize behavioral and attitudinal inconsistencies that do arise, while others seek to harmonize the inconsistencies through change. These cultural differences would cause the "classic" dissonance effects to vary across cultures.

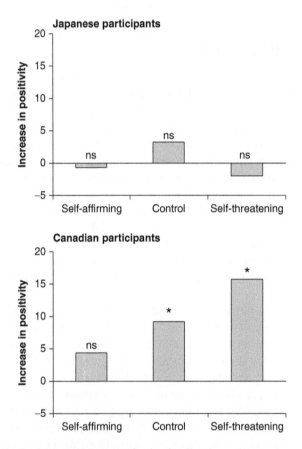

**Figure 10.4**   *Effects of culture and nature of prior feedback on change to a more favorable evaluation of chosen CDs (Heine & Lehman, 1997)*

*Note*: ns = nonsigificant, * = significant

Studies have shown that classic dissonance effects are different among people from collectivist cultures than among people from individualist cultures. A seminal example was provided by two social psychologists in Canada, Steven Heine and Darrin Lehman (1997). They asked Canadian participants and Japanese visitors to Canada to choose as research payment one of two music CDs that they had rated positively on a prior questionnaire. As described in Chapter 8, people are uncomfortable making choices between two highly attractive items, and people reduce this discomfort by becoming much more positive toward the chosen item.

As shown in Figure 10.4, Heine and Lehman found that Japanese participants were less likely to show evidence of this dissonance-based attitude change following a free-choice task than were Canadian participants. Moreover, the Japanese participants were unaffected by receiving personality test feedback that was positive or negative. The positive feedback should have affirmed participants' self-integrity, while the negative feedback threatened it. Yet this manipulation of self-affirmation versus threat only influenced dissonance-based attitude change among the Canadian participants, consistent with previous research (see Chapter 8).

Does this result mean that people in collectivist cultures are *not* affected by dissonance? This conclusion is probably wrong. One problem with this conclusion is that there are many ways to elicit dissonance (e.g., insufficient behavioral justification, enduring hardship for trivial gains) and several ways to resolve it (e.g., trivialization, adding consonant cognitions). It will take some time to explore all of these possibilities, but already there is some evidence of dissonance in Japanese samples (Sakai, 1999). A second problem is evidence that the causes of dissonance may be different in collectivist and individualist cultures. These experiments have found that people who identify strongly with Asian culture show stronger justification of decisions that will affect a close friend than of decisions that will affect themselves, whereas the reverse occurs for people who identify with this culture to a lesser extent (Hoshino-Browne, Zanna, Spencer, & Zanna, 2004). Similarly, Japanese people experience dissonance effects when they consider a counter-attitudinal act from the perspective of others (Kitayama, Snibbe, Markus, & Suzuki, 2004). Thus, people from collectivist cultures may experience dissonance when their acts or cognitions are dissonant with the collectivist, other-oriented perspective created by their culture.

## KEY POINTS

- There is stronger evidence of conformity to majority views in collectivist cultures than in individualist cultures.
- People may be more influenced by cogent persuasive messages that match their cultural orientation than by messages that mismatch their cultural orientation.
- The causes and effects of dissonance-based attitude change may be different in collectivist and individualist cultures.

# THE EXTERNAL WORLD: AN AERIAL VIEW

This chapter addressed the fact that the world bombards people with a variety of persuasive appeals and that we form our attitudes in the middle of diverse personal relationships and connections to broader social groups. We seek balance between our attitudes and those of others, and groups create a tremendous pressure to conform and avoid "rocking the boat." At the same time, minorities within a group can cause attitude change, and they may do so in different ways from majorities. At the same time, most of the past research on attitudes is Western-centric; direct studies of cultural differences have shown that effects of behavior and persuasive messages on attitudes can depend on the culture in which a person lives. Together, the time, relationship, group, and culture variables demonstrate the importance of considering the world outside of the person when looking at attitudes.

## WHAT WE HAVE LEARNED

- The effects of any particular message can depend on whether we have seen it in the past, other messages we have just encountered, and the way in which it unfolds events over time.

- People's attitudes are sensitive to their relationships with other people and knowledge about these other people's attitudes.

- Attitudes can be shaped by majority group pressures and minority views, but the ways in which majorities and minorities influence attitudes can depend on motivational and cognitive factors.

- Cultural differences in collectivism and individualism can have a significant impact on how attitudes respond to new information (e.g., others' behaviors, persuasive messages) and to cognitive dissonance.

## WHAT DO YOU THINK?

- Narratives seem to have great potential to change attitudes, but research on this topic is still in its relative infancy. Can you think of instances of famous films or novels that you think had a large influence on the public's attitudes? Alternatively, is there a genre of fiction that is most provocative and influential (e.g., science fiction, historical drama, fantasy)?

- Research on romantic relationships has revealed that they vary in numerous ways. For instance, some relationships are characterized by high levels of commitment and satisfaction and others are characterized by lower levels of commitment and satisfaction. How might these variables affect the way in which couples respond to the same persuasive messages?

- Although effects of culture on attitudes are important, there are complexities in identifying the exact cultural differences to study. What are some other important differences between cultures, beyond the very simple distinction between Eastern collectivist ideology and Western individualist ideology?

- As globalization continues, people may increasingly possess multiple identities encompassing their past and present cultures. They may even possess multiple identities stemming from their heritage. For example, one of the authors is a Canadian of English-Italian descent who has lived in Wales for 20 years. Try to guess who he cheers for in the FIFA World Cup (Answer: It depends on whether Canada qualifies). How do multiple identities affect attitudes and attitude change?

# KEY TERMS

*Agreement effect* – in attitude triads, we like situations where we agree with another person (i.e., share the same attitude toward the object) better than situations where we disagree with that person (regardless of attitudes toward the person).

*Attitude triads* – mental representations containing (a) the individual's own attitudes toward an object, (b) another person's attitudes toward the object, and (c) the individual's own attitude toward the other person.

*Attraction effect* – in attitude triads, this is the tendency to prefer situations where we like another person compared to situations where we dislike another person, regardless of their attitudes toward an object.

*Collectivistic cultures* – cultures that emphasize interdependence with others.

*Descriptive norms* – norms that describe others' actions.

*Group polarization* – individuals' attitudes tendency to become more extreme than the group's average view after group discussion.

*Individualistic cultures* – cultures that emphasize independence from others.

*Informational influence* – conformity to a group out of a desire to be accurate.

*Injunctive norms* – norms that prescribe or proscribe actions.

*Normative influence* – conformity to a group out of a desire to be liked.

*Refutational defenses* – interventions that provide people with arguments against a belief and rebuttals of the arguments.

*Supportive defenses* – interventions that provide people with information supporting a belief that is about to be attacked.

*Transportation in a narrative* – a process by which people become deeply immersed in the world depicted in the narrative.

*Truisms* – beliefs that are so widely accepted that people rarely question them and fail to develop arguments to support them.

*Vicarious dissonance* – aversive cognitive discrepancies elicited by the behavior of another individual.

# FURTHER READING

## BASIC

Cialdini, R. B., Wosinska, W., Barrett, D. W., Butner, J. and Górnik-Durose, M. (1999) Compliance with a request in two cultures: The differential impact of social proof and commitment/consistency on collectivists and individualists. *Personality and Social Psychology Bulletin, 25,* 1242–1253.

Kaufman, G. F. and Libby, L. K. (2012) Changing beliefs and behavior through experience-taking. *Journal of Personality and Social Psychology, 103,* 1–19.

Prislin, R. and Wood, W. (2005) Social influence in attitudes and attitude change. In D. Albarracín, B. T. Johnson and M. P. Zanna (eds), *The Handbook of Attitudes* (pp. 671–705). Mahwah, NJ: Erlbaum.

## APPLIED

Cialdini, R. B. (2003) Crafting normative messages to protect the environment. *Current Directions in Psychological Science, 12,* 105–109.

Garner, R. (2005) Post-it Note persuasion: A sticky influence. *Journal of Consumer Psychology, 15,* 230–237.

Thompson, R. and Haddock, G. (2012) Sometimes stories sell: When are narrative appeals most likely to work? *European Journal of Social Psychology, 42,* 92–102.

Wang, C. L., Bristol, T., Mowen, J. C. and Chakraborty, G. (2000) Alternative modes of self-construal: Dimensions of connectedness-separateness and advertising appeals to the cultural and gender-specific self. *Journal of Consumer Psychology, 9,* 107–115.

# 11

---

## AN EYE TO THE FUTURE

---

### QUESTIONS TO PONDER

1. Why is synergism in attitude components important?
2. Are there only two dimensions in attitude structure?
3. How many attitude functions are there?
4. Do attitudes persist over time?
5. Do our theories help us understand attitude change for topics of social importance?

---

### PREVIEW

This chapter completes our tour of research on attitudes by highlighting some basic issues that cut across topics described throughout the book. There are fascinating questions that have yet to be addressed in research on attitudes. We begin to outline some of these questions by revisiting the three broad properties of attitude that have been highlighted throughout the volume: attitude content, structure, and function. For each one, we describe some puzzles that remain unsolved. After highlighting these questions, we describe ways in which attitudes research in general should be expanded. There are a number of exciting avenues for future research.

---

## CONTENT, STRUCTURE, AND FUNCTION REVISITED

Many years ago, one of the authors met his father-in-law for lunch in downtown Toronto, at a hotel that happened to be hosting a nationwide conference for the global retailer, Wal-Mart.

Wal-Mart had occupied the entire hotel for the meeting of its employees, and it had used a large space on the ground floor to display a variety of items, ranging from coffee mugs and T-shirts to pens. The striking thing about the items was that they were all labeled with the same motto – "*Attitude is everything*." It was like being in a wonderland of attitude. Presumably, the purpose was to reinforce Wal-Mart's emphasis on positive employee attitudes toward work and customers. Not only did the company expect employees to learn this attitude, they actually expected the employees to *buy* the memorabilia – these weren't freebees. Feeling invigorated by the conference, employees were supposed to come away with a sincere appreciation of their motto and want to purchase a memento of its value. The importance of this was not lost on the author as he happily walked to the cash desk with his arms full of items to purchase (as exhibits for his lectures on attitudes, of course).

Of course, the importance of attitudes goes beyond the retail sector. It also strikes us whenever we act as consultants on projects related to important societal issues, such as discrimination, unhealthy eating, binge drinking, organ donation, and environmental degradation. We always find ourselves amazed by the level of interest in evidence that has come from attitudes research. Perhaps the most striking thing is how studies on very basic, theoretical questions lead to insights that eventually capture a lot of attention in applied areas, even when the original aim did not necessarily involve an applied problem.

For this reason, it is worth taking some time to think about the basic, theoretical issues that we have covered. Each chapter in this text has raised important theoretical topics and questions. By now, you might be somewhat dazed by all of the evidence and ideas we have covered. So how can we summarize the exciting issues that remain and integrate the evidence? We can solve this problem by using the three broad properties of attitude that we've described throughout this book: attitude content, structure, and function. As we describe next, each one raises key issues that cut across the text.

## Attitude content: "Where is this CAB going?"

In Chapter 2, we introduced the taxi CAB of attitudes – the idea that attitudes have *cognitive*, *affective*, and *behavioral* components. Most research has examined the effects of cognition, affect, *or* behavior on attitudes. That is, the emphasis in individual studies has often been on *one* of these types of information. Yet we know that these three types of information are usually interdependent. Alice Eagly and Shelley Chaiken (1993) refer to this interdependence as *synergism* within attitudes. The cognitive, affective, and behavioral information in an attitude influence each other. Over time, beliefs can influence feelings, feelings can guide behaviors, behaviors can shape thoughts, and so on. More recently, research by David Trafimow and colleagues (2012) has revealed that valenced beliefs can bring into line evaluations of logically *irrelevant* beliefs about an attitude object; that is, logical connections are not needed for attitudes to elicit a synergistic influence within beliefs. Within and between attitude components, all that may be needed is a psychological connection, rather than a logical one.

Is there a particular sequence in which influences between components tend to occur, or do they happen in parallel? One influential suggestion was that emotion tends to precede cognition (Zajonc,

1980), but this proposal is contentious (Gordon & Holyoak, 1983; Lazarus, 1982). Nonetheless, some affective processes in memory do appear to occur faster than some cognitive processes (Smith & DeCoster, 2000), and attitudes research has not yet explored these differences fully.

Another intriguing issue is whether the effects of each type of content change when the other types of content are strong as opposed to weak. For example, it could be the case that beliefs and feelings are less important in understanding a person's attitude when the effect of past behavior on attitudes is very strong. This should be the case when people have strong habits linked with their attitude. Of course, as we learned in Chapter 4, habits are notoriously hard to break. More relevant to our point, habits can predict behavior independently of relevant attitudes and the thoughts and emotions they subsume (Ajzen, 2002; Wood, Quinn, & Kashy, 2002). Once a habit is in place, it can take on a life of its own, often with little thought and emotion. Thus, there might be something quite unique about the role of behavior in attitudes.

We cannot be certain about this conclusion, however, until we also examine the processes that occur when cognitions or emotions are quite strong. The role of affect, in particular, may also be quite unique. Some research demonstrates that feelings contribute to our assessments of moral rights and wrongs more than any relevant beliefs we bring to bear. Some acts are judged as immoral because they evoke feelings of disgust, and this is easily seen in people's feelings about acts that produce a strong repulsion, in the absence of any real negative consequences. For example, people tend to feel repugnance and moral derision at the thought of a man having sex with a dead chicken and then eating it, independently of their assessments of the harmfulness of this action (Haidt, Koller, & Dias, 1993). A strong emotional response is also thought to guide people's reactions to challenges against cherished social values, such as freedom and equality (Bernard, Maio, & Olson, 2003a, 2003b; Maio & Olson, 1998b), so it is interesting and important to ask about the role of strong emotion in attitudes more generally. Because a role of strong emotion appears for moral judgments and values that are widely shared, the role of emotion may also be particularly important for attitudes that are widely shared.

In addition, the impact of all three types of attitude content may depend on *when* they are processed. Each type of information can be processed as it is encountered (i.e., "on-line processing") or after (i.e., "memory-based processing"). Attitudes are stronger when they are derived from on-line processing of information than when they are derived from memory-based processing (Bizer, Tormala, Rucker, & Petty, 2006). So, for example, people should form stronger attitudes toward a new brand of ice cream if they are prompted to form their opinion of it while hearing information about its taste, nutritional value, and cost. In contrast, people should form weaker attitudes toward the brand if they form their opinion of it only well after hearing this information (based on their memory of the information). This effect of on-line versus memory-based processing is important partly because some information might be especially likely to lead to instant attitudes. For instance, it is hard to imagine a person not forming an attitude toward an ice cream that tastes awful or great, immediately after tasting it.

Each type of information may also vary in its relevance to the attitude and to relevant behavior. Attitudes predict behavior better when attitudes are based on knowledge that has high relevance to the behavior than when attitudes are based on knowledge that has low relevance for the behavior, especially when people have time to think about their behavior (Fabrigar, Petty, Smith, & Crites, 2006). This result shows that, although attitudes encapsulate cognitive beliefs, the effects of the beliefs on attitudes can depend on the amount of match between the beliefs and relevant behavior.

## Attitude structure: effects of the conflicts within

The United Kingdom has a government department called Foresight. It has the fascinating task of predicting and understanding the future course of major societal issues over a period of several decades. For several years in the mid-2000s, this department worked with experts from many major fields (e.g., medicine, psychology, sociology) to help model potential long-term trajectories in obesity. One of their first major tasks was to develop a model of the problem. In the end, they emerged with a complex systems map involving more than 50 different variables, with four key variables that play a central role. After reading this text, it shouldn't surprise you to learn that one of the key variables had to do with attitudes. After months of discussion of data from different scientific disciplines, attitudinal ambivalence emerged as one of the four factors vital to understanding problems with weight regulation, because of inherent conflict between people's taste for unhealthy foods and activities and their dislike for the negative outcomes of these foods and activities.

Although we certainly agree with the Foresight group's conclusion about the importance of attitude ambivalence, we also know that ambivalence is complicated and that research on this variable still needs to come to grips with some basic issues. For instance, a lot of researchers have wondered about the lack of correspondence between measures assessing potential ambivalence and measures assessing feelings of ambivalence (Conner & Armitage, 2009; DeMarree, Wheeler, Briñol, & Petty, 2014). As described earlier in the book, people often report feelings of ambivalence that don't quite match the high or low number of conflicting evaluations that they can bring to mind about an object (i.e., potential ambivalence). Among other reasons, this lack of correspondence can occur because people's feelings of ambivalence are affected by whether they (a) mind inconsistency in their attitude and are aware of it (Newby-Clark, McGregor, & Zanna, 2002), (b) are aware of other people's attitudes being different from their own (Priester & Petty, 2001), or (c) have some reason to doubt the validity of the information supporting their attitudes (Tormala & DeSensi, 2008). Feelings of ambivalence will be much higher when people are aware of inner conflict, don't like to experience such conflict, are aware of divergent opinions with other people, and doubt the basis for their attitudes. Moreover, people can even feel ambivalent when all their beliefs have the same valence, but the meanings of the beliefs are subjectively incongruent; for example, it may seem strange that a person can be both highly assertive and humble, causing feelings of ambivalence toward a person described as having these positive traits, even though no negative information is present (Gebauer, Maio, & Pakizeh, 2013). All of these factors influence feelings of ambivalence, but are not incorporated into calculations of potential ambivalence.

These findings help to solve an interesting puzzle, but it is important to also figure out whether potential and felt ambivalence predict different outcomes. Given that felt ambivalence involves more conscious experience of the ambivalence than potential ambivalence, it may be the case that measures of felt ambivalence are subject to the same limitations as other self-report, explicit scales.

In contrast, measures of potential ambivalence might be more like implicit measures, because they don't require that people report on their self-perceived levels of ambivalence; ambivalence is assessed on their behalf. If this is true, potential ambivalence might be a better predictor of relevant judgments and behaviors (Bassili, 1996), or it might just be a better predictor of judgments and behaviors that are relatively nonconscious themselves (similar to evidence described in Chapter 9). Alternatively, feelings of ambivalence may simply tap into a broader array of information than potential ambivalence, making the subjective measure frequently a better predictor of relevant outcomes. Future research can help discern which of these ideas works best.

Another important step involves discovering more about how potential ambivalence is related to measures of conflict between components of attitudes. Many studies have assessed the amount of inconsistency between people's overall attitude and the evaluations implied by their beliefs about the attitude object. This consistency is labeled as *evaluative-cognitive inconsistency*, and studies measuring it have found that it is an indicator of attitude strength: attitudes are less resistant to persuasion and worse predictors of behavior when evaluative-cognitive inconsistency is high than when it is low. At first glance, evaluative-cognitive inconsistency is similar to potential ambivalence, because both reflect the amount of difference between evaluations and both are reflective of attitude strength. But is this the whole story?

Not really. We can also measure inconsistency between an attitude and any one of its components. That is, there can be evaluative-cognitive, evaluative-affective, and evaluative-behavioral inconsistency. In addition, potential ambivalence can occur within each component (i.e., cognition, affect, or behavior) or between them. That is, there can be intra-cognitive, intra-affective, intra-behavioral, cognitive-affective, cognitive-behavioral, and affective-behavioral ambivalence. What are the relations among these different types of consistency? It turns out that there can actually be little association between measures of evaluative inconsistency and potential ambivalence, even when both measures focus on the same attitude components (Maio, Esses, & Bell, 2000). This difference is important because we know that both measures moderate the impact of attitudes on judgments and behavior. Yet, at present, the relation between these two important variables has not been fully addressed and requires attention.

Perhaps part of the solution will be evident by looking at the extent to which both variables relate to another type of conflict, mentioned in Chapter 9. Specifically, recent research has begun to take note of attitudes that differ on explicit and implicit measures. An obvious explanation for these differences is that people are not reporting their attitudes accurately on the explicit measures (Fazio & Olson, 2003); however, another possibility is that they hold attitudes that differ (Wilson et al., 2000). In either event, explicit/implicit discrepancies are interesting because they predict higher scrutiny of new information, similar to the effects of ambivalence described in Chapter 2 (Briñol et al., 2006; Rydell, McConnell, & Mackie, 2008; see also Chapter 9).

Finally, our discussion of attitude structure throughout this text has focused on the possibility that attitudes might subsume two dimensions, rather than one. Instead of merely evaluating objects on a continuum from negative to positive, as is traditionally assumed, we may evaluate them on a continuum from neutral to negative *and* on a continuum from neutral to positive. But what if this division into two does not go far enough? Perhaps three or more dimensions are needed to capture attitudes effectively.

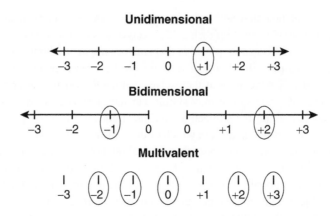

**Figure 11.1**   *Three different views of attitude representations (Breckler, 2004)*

One intriguing discussion of this view has been provided by Steven Breckler (2004), a researcher who also provided some of the pivotal evidence on the separability of the cognitive, affective, and behavioral content in attitudes. According to his *multivalence* perspective, attitudes can subsume many evaluations, which can cluster in different ways. Ambivalence is merely one special case of multivalence that allows only two evaluations, each of which must be on different sides of neutral.

As shown in Figure 11.1, multivalence allows for varying positive positions and varying negative positions, and it includes differences in evaluation that do not necessarily cross the boundary between positive and negative evaluation. Thus, it can be indirectly assessed partly by looking at the simple range or variance across a person's responses to different attitude items (which could all be positive or all negative), rather than looking strictly at the amount of conflict between the amount of positive attitude and the amount of negative attitude. It turns out that assessments of attitude variability reflect the presence of value-conflict on an issue (Breckler, 2004). In addition, attitudes with lower multivalence (assessed with a somewhat different technique than Breckler developed) may be better predictors of behavior (Armitage, 2003). An interesting challenge for future research is to tease apart the distinctions between ambivalence and multivalence.

## Attitude function: a need for more information about motivations

Attitude function has received less research attention than attitude content and structure. This relative neglect has occurred even though most theories of attitudes and attitude change stress the goals that attitudes serve (e.g., accuracy, value-expression). Although the research to date has yielded some important insights, such as the evidence for a primary role of the object-appraisal function (see Chapter 2), many mysteries remain.

Perhaps the most important issue is the need for greater clarification regarding the link between attitude function and attitude content. It could be argued that attitude function is closely related to attitude content (see Eagly & Chaiken, 1993, pp. 479–490). For example, if attitudes toward cycling to work are based on a need to save money on transport, then these attitudes should be based on beliefs about the extent to which cycling saves money. Similarly, if attitudes toward wearing a leather jacket are based on a psychological need to enhance social relations, then these attitudes should be based on beliefs about the extent to which the leather jacket will make you look good and therefore popular among people you like. In other words, one could say that attitudes serving different functions should differ in the content of the beliefs that support the attitudes.

If attitude functions really are about motivations and not just attitude content, however, then there should be some important unique features of attitude function that reflect basic properties of motivational processes more generally (Kruglanski et al., 2002; McClelland, 1985). First, satisfaction of the motives should cause pursuit or avoidance of the attitude object (depending on whether it is liked or disliked) to decrease. Second, the motives should get stronger the more they are unfulfilled, in the same way that people get hungry when their physiological need to eat is unfulfilled. Third, people should pursue a motive in whichever means is not blocked to them. In this framework, motives are rarely eliminated completely; they simply ebb and flow depending on the circumstances.

It should be possible to explore such differences in attitude function when people have the same attitude content. This can be achieved by giving people identical information about an attitude object, while arousing or threatening different motives or functions that are pertinent to the attitude object (Maio & Olson, 2000c). For instance, a new car can be described as being economical, sporty, and environmentally friendly. Soon thereafter, a person might be given a message that makes it seem that times are tight and people need to save money or that it is important to follow through on personal values. If the messages are effective, people should weight the information they received in a way that reflects the motivations that have become more important for them. In other words, they should form attitudes from the same information, but with different goals in mind. Research has begun to incorporate this type of approach (Maio & Olson, 1995a; Marsh & Julka, 2000; McGregor, Zanna, Holmes, & Spencer, 2001; Murray et al., 1996), especially in studies of the roles of values in attitude change (e.g., Blankenship & Wegener, 2012; Blankenship, Wegener, & Murray, 2012). This framework provides a promising avenue for disentangling effects of attitude function from effects of attitude content.

Another vital issue involves re-examining the number and types of attitude functions. Theories of attitude function have not relied on actual data to determine empirically the precise number of relevant motivations. There are no direct tests of the assumption that the ego-defensive, knowledge, social-adjustive, utilitarian, and value-expressive functions represent all possible motivational bases of attitudes.

Additional attitude functions could be suggested. For example, as described earlier in the text, research on Festinger's (1964) Cognitive Dissonance Theory has supported the hypothesis that people seek consistency in their beliefs. There is also evidence that there are individual differences in need for consistency (Cialdini, Trost, & Newsom, 1995), such that the effects of dissonance are larger among individuals who more strongly desire consistency. In fact, people who are high in the need for consistency also avoid attitudinal ambivalence more generally (Newby-Clark et al., 2002). Thus, need for consistency could be another basic attitude function.

To form a comprehensive list of attitude functions, other areas of psychology should be considered as well. Personality psychology is one area of study that has attempted to identify basic dimensions of human motivation. Drawing on prior research in personality and clinical psychology, Henry Murray's clinical psychology research group (1938) formed a highly influential theory, which outlined 27 basic human needs. Although they also alluded to the potential for several additional needs (e.g., a need to be different from others, a need to preserve and repair), their research focused on 20 motivations shown in Table 11.1. This list included some motives that are easily recognizable in theories of attitude function, such as the need for understanding (similar to the knowledge function) and the need for defendance (similar to the ego-defensive function). The list also included needs that are not in any theories of attitude function, such as a need to dominate

**Table 11.1**  *Murray's (1938) 20 psychological needs*

Abasement – to surrender

Achievement – to overcome obstacles and exercise power

Affiliation – to form friendships and affiliations

Aggression – to assault or injure

Autonomy – to resist influence

Counteraction – to regain honor through action

Defendance – to defend oneself against belittlement

Deference – to willingly follow superiors

Dominance – to influence or control

Exhibition – to attract attention to oneself

Inviolacy – to avoid loss of self-respect and failure

Nurturance – to nourish and aid

Order – to arrange and keep tidy

Play – to relax and amuse oneself

Rejection/Seclusion – to snub, ignore, exclude, and be apart form others

Sentience – to obtain sensual and tactile gratification

Sex – to seek sexual pleasure

Succorance – to seek aid and protection

Superiority – to gain achievement and recognition

Understanding – to comprehend events and relations.

others and to nurture others. Yet Murray speculated that many of the motives are important to understanding attitudes. If future research finds evidence of persuasive matching effects for these or other motives (see Chapter 8), there will be more support for including them in a list of the psychological needs that attitudes serve. Our main point is that an integrative approach assisted functional theorists when attitude function research first began (Katz, 1960; Smith et al., 1956), and it may be time for some further reintegration.

This reintegration would also need to consider how functions change at different levels of analysis. Gregory Herek (1986) suggested that some functions can be served by the expression of attitudes (social-adjustment, value-expression), whereas other functions are served by the possession of attitudes. For example, if you think that a particular political candidate will help prevent child poverty, and this is important to you, then you can express your values by praising the candidate to others. That is, talking about your attitude is a way of serving a key function for the attitude (i.e., value-expression). In contrast, other attitude functions do not become fulfilled by communication about them. For example, if a person possesses a negative attitude toward violent films, this attitude can enable him or her to avoid the films every time they are advertised – the person never has to talk about this attitude to others in order for the attitude to serve this (utilitarian, object-appraisal) function, and voicing the attitude to others would not necessarily help to avoid the films.

We could also distinguish between motives that are fulfilled by particular attitude positions and by attitudes per se (Maio et al., 2004 ). All attitudes simplify interaction with the environment (i.e., the object-appraisal function), regardless of whether the attitudes are negative or positive. For example, people who have no prior attitude toward iPhones should have more difficulty deciding whether or not to purchase one of these devices than people who definitely like or dislike them. Both the positive attitude and the negative attitude would serve the knowledge function. Other attitude functions are more specific, because they explain *why* people hold their particular neutral, negative, positive, or ambivalent attitude. For instance, the social-adjustive function explains why people might like iPhones if the phones are popular among their friends, but dislike iPhones if the phones are unpopular among their friends. This function expresses the idea that the negativity or positivity of attitudes toward iPhones depends on whether they help our social relations or not. Here, it may be critical that we are looking at the function of an object per se, and not simply the function of the attitude toward the object (Kruglanski & Stroebe, 2005).

Building on their analysis of attitude content (as described above), Leandre Fabrigar and colleagues (2006) suggested that attitude function might exert different effects depending on the relevance of the functions to subsequent behavior. These researchers suggest that attitudes may predict behavior better when they are based on goals that have high relevance to the behavior than when attitudes are based on goals that have low relevance for the behavior. To our knowledge, this provocative hypothesis has not yet been tested. Nonetheless, it may be most applicable when applied to the valence-specific attitude functions (e.g., social-adjustment, ego-defense). In these cases, different functions can imply different attitude valence and different behaviors, creating occasional mismatches between the attitude and the subsequent behavior when different motives are relevant to the attitude and the behavior.

## KEY POINTS

- Reciprocal influences among cognitive, affective, and behavioral information raise questions about the way in which each type of information is processed.

- Behavioral and affective content may have particularly strong influences on attitude, but the effects of each type of content may depend on when they are processed and the behavior they are predicting.

- Attitude structure could subsume conflict between conscious and nonconscious levels and between different types of attitude content, with more dimensions in conflict than simply a negative dimension and a positive dimension.

- The links between attitude function and attitude content make it important to isolate the unique effects of attitude function, while attaining greater clarity about the number of functions and the relations among them.

## INTEGRATING CONTENT, STRUCTURE, AND FUNCTION

This text has shown that attitudes are diverse. They are not merely judgments of favorability and unfavorability. They include cognitive, affective, and behavioral information, varying attitude structure, and diverse motivational functions. Attitudes also vary in more specific ways, including their accessibility from memory, self-perceived importance, and the certainty with which they are held. These diverse properties are worth considering together.

## Relations among content, structure, and function

Chapter 2 noted that attitude content, structure, and function are not independent. We have structured much of this textbook by focusing on attitude content and noting the relevance of attitude structure and function as we went along. Now that the bulk of the evidence has been covered, it is worth revisiting connections between these three properties of attitude.

As noted in Chapter 2, attitude function and content may be closely connected in many everyday attitudes. For example, value-expressive attitudes toward an automobile might be more strongly based on feelings than are utilitarian attitudes (Ennis & Zanna, 2000). In general, value-expressive attitudes may be more emotional, because of the strong emotional response thought to underlie cherished social values (Bernard et al., 2003a, 2003b; Maio & Olson, 1998b). Attitudes serving an ego-defensive function may possess a similarly strong foundation in emotion, consistent with classic psychoanalytic theory about the emergence of neurotic emotional behavior (Freud, 1966). It would be intriguing to see more tests of these ideas.

In addition, it would be interesting to learn more about the role of attitude function in attitude structure. Ambivalent attitude structures should be aversive to individuals because they subsume dissonance between cognitions (Maio et al., 1996; Newby-Clark et al., 2002; Nordgren, van

Harreveld, & van der Pligt, 2006). At the same time, these attitudes may be less useful for guiding behavior (Armitage & Conner, 2000). Because they fail to provide a single, useful summary of current knowledge, ambivalent attitudes might be less likely to serve a knowledge function.

Megan Thompson and Mark Zanna (1995) indirectly studied this issue by testing whether there are specific personality characteristics that are held by individuals who frequently possess ambivalent attitudes. The results were somewhat surprising. Specifically, these scientists found that participants who possessed ambivalent attitudes across many attitude issues were lower in need for cognition and higher in fear of invalidity. Put simply, people who are low in the desire to exert mental effort on complex problems (i.e., low in need for cognition) or high in the fear of being wrong (i.e., high fear of invalidity) are more likely to possess ambivalent attitudes. The ambivalence may help them to save time and energy in reaching a decisive opinion and help them "sit on the fence" enough to avoid being completely wrong. This evidence implies that there can be a tactical laziness to ambivalence, and it contradicts the idea that ambivalent attitudes are less likely to serve a knowledge function. To the contrary, the people who should be most motivated to adopt attitudes serving this function (e.g., people high in fear of invalidity) are more likely to adopt ambivalent attitudes.

Perhaps, however, there is a vital distinction between having attitudes that accurately summarize information and having attitudes that are useful guides for behavior, even though both roles are often seen as characteristic of the knowledge function. Ambivalence may be useful for summarizing information, but less useful for behavior (van Harreveld et al., 2009). If this is true, then we may need to think of the knowledge function as involving separate information and action functions, which are not distinguished in current theories of attitude function. This issue is further highlighted by evidence that "wanting" and "liking" are different. For instance, people who fail to get a prize want it more and are more likely to choose it later (Litt, Khan, & Shiv, 2010). At the same time, they evaluate it more negatively after they fail to get it, and discard it relatively quickly after receiving it. Our appetites for action and our attitudes can be different, although they may harmonize in the long run.

Another interesting question is whether the positive and negative dimensions of attitudes fulfill different content and functions. Most measures of attitude allow for different content to influence the positive and negative dimensions of evaluation. For example, we might like ice cream because it is tasty, but dislike it because it is fattening. In contrast, the Individual Association Questionnaire is a new technique (Sedek, Piber-Dabrowksa, Maio, & von Hecker, 2011) that measures positivity and negativity in a manner that keeps the content describing an attitude object (e.g., Germans) the same, by using synonyms of the same characteristic, but which vary in their valence (e.g., hardworking vs. workaholic). Such an approach can be used to examine attitude valence in a way that is at least somewhat separable from effects of content and function.

Related to this possibility, the bidimensional view indicates that positive and negative affective responses to attitude objects have distinct properties (Cacioppo et al., 1997), and we previously described neurological and behavioral evidence for this point of view (Chapters 2 and 9). This evidence makes us wonder whether the needs fulfilled by positive and negative dimensions of attitudes tend to differ. For example, positivity might be more strongly connected to needs for belongingness with others and creativity, while negativity is more strongly connected with needs for security and self-protection. At the same time, we might wonder whether the functions of each dimension simply add together, or does one dimension's functions tend to override the other dimension's functions? Negative reactions tend to be stronger than positive ones (Cacioppo et al., 1997), so it is plausible that the functions underlying negative responses might dominate attitudes.

The potential for one dimension's functions to dominate the other is just one example of many issues that arise if we take seriously the view that attitudes subsume different positive and negative dimensions. However, there is interesting overlap between this idea and recent evidence that people have dispositional attitudes; that is, people vary in the extent to which they like things in general and dislike things in general (Hepler & Albarracín, 2013). This interesting personality difference presumably reflects differences in tendencies to utilize positive versus negative content, perhaps helping to address psychological needs to see the world more or less positively or more or less negatively. For some people, the functions served by the positive dimensions of their attitudes may be more important than those served by the negative dimensions of their attitudes. In contrast, for other people, the functions served by the negative dimensions of their attitude may dominate. These are fascinating questions worthy of answers.

## What shapes content, structure, and function?

In works of fiction, we hardly ever read anything about how witches come to be who they are. Were they troubled as children? Like *The Joker* from the *Batman* comic books and movies, did they fall in a vat of toxic waste? The focus is always on the events the characters shape. Similarly, we have focused on understanding the effects of our three 'witches' and not so much on the factors that influence them.

The major exception to this was our discussion of how cognitive, affective, and behavioral processes shape attitudes in Chapters 5, 6, and 7. Attitudes should come to take on content that reflects the way they were formed. For instance, attitudes shaped by mere exposure should be based initially on affective information, with little accompanying cognitive and behavioral content. Similarly, attitudes shaped by self-perception of behavior should be based initially on the behavioral information, with little accompanying affective and cognitive content. Thus, these chapters potentially reveal important ways in which attitude content is shaped.

We have not said as much about the way in which the structure and function witches themselves are shaped because there is much less evidence regarding them. Yet their development raises many interesting issues. One interesting issue is that research has not systematically tested whether attitude structure changes after persuasive interventions. We learned in Chapter 9 that messages might cause discrepancies to emerge between explicit measures of attitude and implicit measures of attitude and that this evidence fits the idea that ambivalence emerges between the positive and negative dimensions of attitude. However, little evidence directly examines whether ambivalence is affected by messages and whether there are differences in the way different types of ambivalence emerge (e.g., potential ambivalence, felt ambivalence, cognitive-affective ambivalence). There may also be important ramifications for attitude strength. For instance, messages that influence ambivalence may also affect attitude certainty, importance, and accessibility.

A similar issue exists for attitude function. How do persuasive messages shape the functions of attitudes? Chapter 8 described evidence that messages are more likely to change attitudes when the messages match the function of recipients' attitude than when the messages mismatch the function of recipients' attitude. But what happens to the function of the attitude itself? Perhaps a mismatching message causes the attitude to partly change the function that it serves, leads to an attitude that has a different function, or produces an attitude that serves multiple functions. If multiple functions do arise, the attitude might become stronger because of its ability to serve diverse motives (see also Cialdini, 2008, for his discussion of "consistency").

These speculations illustrate just some of the reasons why it is important to no longer treat attitude valence as though it is the *only* aspect of attitudes that can change after exposure to a persuasive intervention. Most research on persuasion has simply used explicit, self-report questions of attitude to assess effects of messages. Although research on persuasion has begun to include implicit measures of attitude (Petty et al., 2006; Smith, De Houwer, & Nosek, 2013), it is worth considering that the content, structure, and function of attitudes can vary as well. These properties of attitude are too important to neglect as dependent variables in their own right, and we anticipate that future research will help us to better understand their development.

## KEY POINTS

- Attitudes that serve different value-expressive or ego-defensive functions may be more likely to contain emotional content than attitudes serving other functions.
- Ambivalent attitudes may serve unique attitude functions and not simply less of a knowledge function.
- The positive and negative dimensions of attitudes may serve different functions.
- Interventions that change attitudes might also shape the content, structure, and function of the attitudes.

## GENERAL ISSUES

There are a number of broad issues that confront future attitudes research. Four issues are particularly important: relations to processes in non-human animals, diverse effects of interventions, attitude persistence, and attitude topics.

## Humans are animals

Attitudes research has almost exclusively focused on humans, even though there is nothing about the concept that binds it exclusively to humans. It is clear that we are not the only animal to form evaluations of objects, and there are many parallels between how we form and change attitudes and how animals appear to do so. The difficulty in making these comparisons is that we cannot use verbal self-report measures easily with most animals. Sign language can be used with other primates, but, for other animals, we have to rely on overt behaviors that are less varied in their semantic content. This is not an unsolvable problem, however, as a lot of research with humans also uses overt behaviors to reveal a great deal about attitudes.

This use of behaviors to record attitudes in humans is most evident in implicit measures of attitudes. As described in Chapter 1, these measures often use response times or error rates, and an implicit measure has been developed for use with rhesus macaques (Macaca mulatta; Mahajan et al., 2011). An interesting feature of our responses to these measures is how they change in different contexts. It has been pointed out that this variability is similar to ways in which context affects evaluative behavior in animals (Gawronski & Cesario, 2013). For instance, echoing dissonance research described in Chapter 7, there is evidence for dissonant-related processes in monkeys and young children (Egan, Bloom, & Santos, 2010; Egan, Santos, & Bloom, 2007). Research Highlight 11.1 shows similar evidence for dissonance processes in rats (Lydall, Gilmour, & Dwyer, 2010).

Future research may help to give further insight into how attitudinal processes are similar and different across species. For many attitudinal processes that are automatic and functional in nature, there is reason to suspect that they should be discernible in non-human species as well (see Lydall et al., 2010). An interesting issue is whether the more deliberative, thoughtful processes (e.g., for elaboration in attitude change) also have parallels across species.

Such research would undoubtedly benefit from evolutionary perspectives on human social behavior. We have noted how evolutionary perspectives can be relevant to attitude formation and to neurological processes in attitudes, but there is scope for much more investigation. Like other animals, humans' likelihood of reproductive success depends on individuals' characteristics and their fit to the situation. Attitudes and behavior may at times reflect inherited biases that were adaptive in prior contexts and may or may not continue to be adaptive now. This may be evident in how we form and change attitudes. For instance, Kathleen Vohs, Jaideep Sengupta, and Darren Dahl (2014) found that women respond more negatively to sexual imagery in ads than men, but only when the imagery is used to promote cheap products. These scientists argued that, from an evolutionary point of view, sex is more risky and costly for women because of their greater parental investment, and pairing sex with cheap products may go against ingrained views on the preciousness of sex. Future research may benefit from an evolutionary viewpoint on other factors that affect the ways in which we form and change attitudes (e.g., physical attractiveness, power).

## RESEARCH HIGHLIGHT 11.1

### DO RATS EXPERIENCE COGNITIVE DISSONANCE?

In Chapter 9, we noted Lieberman et al.'s (2001) evidence that dissonance-based attitude change may occur unconsciously, as it occurs even in amnesiacs who are unable to consciously recall their past behavior. Emma Lydall, Gary Gilmour, and Dominic Dwyer (2010) noted this interesting finding and observations that dissonance-based attitude change can occur in monkeys and children. They suggested that this evidence is consistent with an automatic effect of dissonance that could occur even in rats. This provocative hypothesis was suggested half a century earlier by Lawrence and Festinger (1962), but was not conclusively evaluated by them.

To address this issue, Lydall et al. (2010) conducted an experiment that aimed to discover effort justification in rats. Recall from Chapter 7 that according to Cognitive Dissonance Theory, high effort to obtain a reward should lead to more positive evaluations of the reward. To examine this process in rats, the experimenters trained 16 male rats to press a lever in order to gain one minute of access to a 10% sugar solution. Then the rats were exposed to one of four experimental conditions. Two of these conditions dispensed sugar solution as a reward for the rats' effort at pressing the lever. In a low effort condition, the rats had to press the lever 10 times to obtain access to the sugar solution. In a high effort condition, the rats had to press the lever 50 times to obtain access to the sugar solution. In the other two conditions, the sugar solution was dispensed at the same rate as in either the low effort or high effort condition, but without the rat having to work to obtain this reward. The reward in these two "yoked" conditions was determined by other rats that were pressing a lever in other chambers. Each rat received all four experimental conditions, and the order of exposure to the conditions was counterbalanced across the rats.

The key dependent variable was the average number of times that the rats licked the sugar solution dispenser in each cluster of licks, because many prior studies have established that the number of licks per cluster is a reliable indicator of the extent to which rats like a solution. Results indicated that the rats licked more times when they were in the high effort condition than when they were in the low effort condition. This suggests that the solution that they had worked harder to obtain became more pleasant to them. Crucially, the rats that received the solution in a manner that was yoked to these two conditions did not exhibit this difference. Thus, the difference in evaluation was due to effort expended and not simply to the difference in rate of presentation of the sugar solution.

## Diverse effects

The chapters that examined how attitudes are shaped focused on how cognitive, affective, and behavioral interventions change the valence of attitudes, but, as we noted earlier in this chapter, a much broader range of attitude properties could have been examined. By now, we hope that you appreciate that attitude valence is not the only important property of attitudes, but a few more examples might help to illustrate why it is important to examine other attitude properties when looking at the effects of interventions on attitude.

One useful example is provided by past research on the effects of counter-attitudinal behavior. Festinger (1964) outlined several alternative ways to resolve dissonance following counter-attitudinal behavior. Two alternative methods involve trivializing the importance of the action and denying responsibility for the action. These methods are likely to be used when they are made salient through a questionnaire presented before the assessment of attitude (Gosling, Denizeau, & Oberlé, 2006; Simon, Greenberg, & Brehm, 1995). Attitude change, then, is not the only consequence of dissonance. Past research found evidence for attitude change partly because it did not make salient the other options. This does not diminish the importance of attitude change; it merely shows that attitude change must be considered in a broader framework.

Indeed, dissonance may also affect various aspects of attitude strength, such as attitude accessibility, attitude certainty, or attitude importance. Such effects might happen when the factors that lead to attitude change are not present. For example, when there is low choice to lie about an attitude or the attitude is held strongly, then dissonance-related attitude change should not occur (see Chapter 7). Nonetheless, lying in these circumstances can cause the attitude to become more accessible from memory, which causes it to have a greater impact on subsequent judgments (Johar & Sengupta, 2002; Maio & Olson, 1995b, 1998a).

Research on other topics reinforces this point. For example, some clever experiments have found that the mere act of resisting persuasion affects attitude certainty, which determines whether people subsequently change their attitudes (Tormala & Petty, 2002; Tormala, Clarkson, & Petty, 2006). In addition, research has shown that contact with people from another ethnic, religious, or social group provides one particular form of behavioral experience that increases attitude strength. An example of this effect was revealed in an interesting study of the effects of friendship with gay men on anxiety about gay men and attitudes toward them. As shown in Figure 11.2, Christiana Vonofakou, Miles Hewstone, and Alberto Voci (2007) found that heterosexual individuals who report more friendship with gay men experience lower anxiety about the group, which is associated with higher attitude accessibility and stronger self-reports of attitude strength. These findings are interesting because most past research on contact with people from another group has supported the hypothesis that contact with an outgroup decreases prejudice, at least when the members of the outgroup are seen as prototypical members of the group (Brown, Eller, Leeds, & Stace, 2007). Vonofakou et al. replicated this effect of outgroup contact on attitude (i.e., friendship predicted more favorable attitudes) and, even after controlling for this impact, found that contact resulted in greater self-report

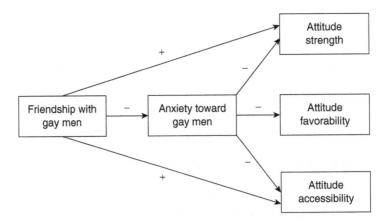

**Figure 11.2**  *Effects of friendship with gay men on anxiety toward gay men, attitudes toward them, and the accessibility and strength of these attitudes (Vonofakou et al., 2007)*

*Note*: A + (plus) sign indicates that higher levels of the variable to the left of the arrow predict higher levels of the variable to the right of the arrow. Conversely, a − (minus) sign indicates that higher levels of the variable to the left of the arrow predict lower levels of the variable to the right of the arrow.

attitude strength and accessibility. In other words, behavioral experience with another social group reduces prejudice *and* makes the newfound attitude stronger. By including measures of attitude strength together with the measures of attitude, these scientists were able to find that the effects of outgroup contact are even more practically important than previously revealed.

## Attitude persistence

Most experiments on attitude change have examined the effects of a persuasive appeal immediately after message presentation. We need to expand our knowledge about what happens to attitudes over a longer period. On average, how long does attitude change last? Do repeated messages cause longer attitude change than single presentations? Do some types of message (e.g., emotional ones) cause longer attitude change than others (e.g., cognitive messages)?

To date, there are no strong answers to these questions. By and large, the effects of interventions on attitudes decrease over time (Cook & Flay, 1978). Yet some experiments from the 1930s to 1950s found that attitudes measured immediately after a message of some kind (e.g., a film) could show less change than attitudes measured later. The tendency for messages to elicit more change over time was named the *sleeper effect* (Hovland et al., 1949).

Researchers suggested that the sleeper effect occurs when the messages contain a fatal flaw (e.g., a speaker who lacked credibility), which people forget after a while (Hovland et al., 1953). To be more precise, the idea was that people do not spontaneously associate the flaw with the topic when they think of the topic at a later time, although they could recall the flaw if asked (Kelman & Hovland, 1953). Ironically, however, some researchers argued that the evidence supporting the sleeper effect itself contained a fatal flaw: the effect was often not statistically reliable (Gillig & Greenwald, 1974; Pratkanis, Greenwald, Leippe, & Baumgardner, 1988). This criticism undermined researchers' confidence in this effect.

Subsequent experiments showed that the sleeper effect can occur, but only when a long list of pre-conditions are met (Cook, Gruder, Hennigan, & Flay, 1979; Gruder, Cook, Hennigan, Flay, & Halamaj, 1978). Enough time should pass to allow the strength of the mental association between the flaw and the message to decrease, but the passage of time should not be so big as to cause the message's impact to decay too greatly; the message itself must be persuasive, the fatal flaw must be noticeable enough to reduce attitude change in the first exposure to the message, and the flaw should be evident after the message has been processed. Obviously, this is a complex set of circumstances! The major connection among them is that they may cause people to "forget" the flaw faster than the message (Pratkanis et al., 1988).

More recent evidence has supported these conclusions, while adding additional conditions (Kumkale & Albarracín, 2004). In particular, the sleeper effect is more likely when people are more motivated and able to think about the persuasive message (Priester, Wegener, Petty, & Fabrigar, 1999). This result fits assumptions from the contemporary dual- and single-route models of persuasion described in Chapter 5.

Overall, the evidence regarding the sleeper effect suggests that the content of persuasive information and the context in which it is shown are important for understanding the impact of a message over time. In Chapter 9, we noted that the effects of attitudinal interventions over time may also depend on whether an implicit or an explicit measure of attitude is used. It would be great if future research integrates these sets of evidence to yield a simple, elegant theory of attitudinal persistence.

# Attitude topics

Much of the research on how attitudes are shaped has examined attitude change in a somewhat indirect way, by examining the effects of diverse variables on the attitudes that people form about novel issues (e.g., comprehensive exams) or objects (a certain type of telephone answering machine). This focus on novel attitude objects leaves a lot of research on "attitude change" open to the criticism that it is actually examining "attitude formation," or, at best, "attitude change" for weakly held attitudes.

This limitation is one reason why it is important to consider a more diverse set of attitude topics in persuasion research. Another reason is the aforementioned evidence that people have dispositional tendencies to like or dislike things (Hepler & Albarracín, 2013); if topic-specific knowledge plays an important role, then it may be important to show this through contrasts between different topics.

You might think that the set of attitude topics is already diverse. Indeed, we have covered research that examined attitudes toward social groups (e.g., racial attitudes), policies (e.g., university tuition fees), health-relevant behaviors (e.g., smoking), religious behavior (e.g., attending church or synagogue), environmental behaviors (e.g., recycling), food items (e.g., jams), household utensils (e.g., razors), simple tasks (e.g., choices between objects), and even humorous stimuli (e.g., cartoons). We would not want to deny this diversity, which is of fundamental importance for seeing the power of the attitude concept. Nonetheless, there are important ways in which the diversity can still be better.

A lot of research that has focused on basic processes in attitude change has tended to focus on a narrow range of topics, including educational policies (e.g., tuition fees, comprehensive exams) and commercial products (telephone answering machines, mobile phones). In the related fields of marketing and advertising, they say it is a lot easier to sell commercial products (e.g., shoes) than to sell social ideas, such as recycling and equal opportunities (Rothschild, 1979; Wiebe, 1951). Indeed, as noted in Chapter 10, research has found that common approaches to advocating environmentally friendly behavior in advertising actually encourage less of the behavior, by making the environmentally unfriendly behavior appear to be common and something that everyone does (Cialdini, 2003). Similarly, studies of anti-racism advertising in the United Kingdom and Canada found that a widely distributed set of these advertisements may backfire among those who are ambivalent toward ethnic minorities (Maio et al., 2009) and when the messages focus on external, social reasons not to be prejudiced (Legault, Gutsell, & Inzlicht, 2011).

Resistance to social marketing may occur because the issues are much more relevant to personal values and the self-concept, and people are resistant to being persuaded about self-relevant issues (Cohen, Aronson, & Steele, 2000; Correll et al., 2004). The challenge is for persuasion researchers to collect more data on applications to social issues and to understand factors that predict resistance to persuasion in these applied contexts. This step has already begun in the field of marketing, which has tackled these issues through a distinct sub-discipline, labeled *social marketing*.

Similarly, there are subfields of psychology that look at changing particular types of attitude with social importance. This activity is reflected in a lot of the research that has examined methods for reducing prejudice, as described earlier in this chapter and in other portions of the text. The fields of health, consumer, and environmental psychology have also seen input from attitudes theory. Over time, this input will grow. Researchers will become increasingly confident about testing basic theories of attitude in diverse topic domains, bringing us full-circle back to many of the practical questions that inspired attitudes research in the first place.

## KEY POINTS

- Attitude change interventions can shape properties of attitude other than attitude valence.
- Attitude change interventions can decay over time or increase over time, depending on personal and situational factors.
- Effects of interventions on attitudes toward novel issues may be different than effects of interventions on attitudes toward topics that are long-standing issues with applied significance.

## NEXT STEPS

Our tour of social psychological research on attitudes is now over. We have seen a vast amount of information about what attitudes are, why they matter, how they are shaped, and their place in our internal and external worlds. At the same time, this chapter extended our critical thinking about the borders of this vast expanse of information. This chapter has shown that the three properties of attitude – content, structure, and function – make the concept of attitude a powerful but complex construct. We need a great deal of further research to help address limitations in our understanding of attitude content, structure, and function. The limitations include a need to better reflect the synergy between attitude components, a consideration of different potential attitude structures beyond ambivalence, and the potential existence of diverse additional attitude functions. Furthermore, interesting issues include the potentially diverse effects of interventions on properties other than attitude valence, persistence of attitudes across time, and the applicability of current models across diverse applied topics.

At this point, it's also fair to ask whether new theoretical frameworks can be generated to help address these issues simultaneously, in a parsimonious way, without simply adding greater levels of detail. Given the huge strides that have been made in research to this point, we are hopeful for the future. We optimistically expect that future progress will continue to expand the empirical evidence for understanding attitudes, while modifying current theory and adding new perspectives in ways that elegantly put it all together, even better than before.

## WHAT WE HAVE LEARNED

- There are reciprocal influences among cognitive, affective, and behavioral information.
- Cognitive, affective, and behavioral content may have different levels of influence on attitude.

- Attitude structure may vary in multiple ways other than reflecting two evaluative (negative *and* positive) dimensions or one (negative-positive).
- Attitude content, structure, and function may be interrelated in interesting ways.
- Interventions that change attitude valence might also shape other properties of attitudes, including their strength, content, structure, and function.
- It is important to discover ways to predict whether attitude change interventions will decay over time or increase over time.
- More research should attempt to examine the effects of interventions on attitudes toward topics that are familiar and of worldly relevance.

# WHAT DO YOU THINK?

We think it is fitting to close this text with deep-thinking, "big-picture" questions that challenge the most basic assumptions throughout the book. The text provides most of the information you need to start thinking about these questions. Otherwise, you might want to read the text again.

- Is there really such a thing as attitude?
- Do attitudes really *change*, rather than simply expand to include more cognitions, emotions, and behaviors?
- What has attitudes research taught us that our grandparents could not already say?
- Is Wal-Mart right? Are they right to claim "Attitude is Everything"?

# KEY TERMS

*Multivalence* – the idea that attitudes can subsume many evaluations, which can cluster in different ways.

*Sleeper effect* – the tendency for messages to elicit more change over time.

*Synergism within attitudes* – the influences of cognitive, affective, and behavioral information in an attitude on each other.

## FURTHER READING

Now that you have read this book, you are ready to enjoy some deep articles that make people really think about what attitudes are and what they do. A special issue of the journal *Social Cognition* (2007, Vol. 25, Issue 5) is very handy for this purpose. Although this special issue was published more than seven years ago, it gives a comprehensive picture of complex challenges that still confront current research on attitudes.

# GLOSSARY

*Acceptance-Yielding Impact Model*   a framework stating that messages should cause attitude change when they change the beliefs underlying people's attitudes, their evaluations of these beliefs, or both.

*Action-Based Model*   a model that explains post-decisional spreading of choice alternatives by proposing that it is partly driven by an action orientation.

*Affective component of attitudes*   feelings or emotions linked to an attitude object.

*Agreement effect*   in attitude triads, we like situations where we agree with another person (i.e., share the same attitude toward the object) better than situations where we disagree with that person (regardless of attitudes toward the person).

*Alcohol myopia*   the idea that individuals under the influence of alcohol have a reduced capacity to process information, and tend to react primarily to salient and impelling cues in their environment.

*AMP*   affect misattribution paradigm, an implicit measure assessing attitudes through effects of primes on evaluations of stimuli.

*Amplification hypothesis*   the idea that increases in attitude certainty can make the attitude more open or more resistant to change, depending upon other characteristics of the attitude.

*Amygdala*   a structure in the medial temporal lobe of the brain that is linked with affective processing of information.

*Anterior cingulate cortex*   a region of the brain associated with decision-making processes.

*Attitude*   an overall evaluation of an object that is based on cognitive, affective, and behavioral information.

*Attitude accessibility*   the ease of retrieval of the attitude from memory.

*Attitude ambivalence*   the existence of many positive *and* many negative elements in an attitude.

*Attitude certainty*   individuals' degree of certainty and confidence in their attitude.

*Attitude content*   the types of information that influence attitudes.

*Attitude embodiment*   the idea that performing a physical act can influence the favorability of an individual's attitude.

*Attitude extremity*   an attitude's deviation from neutrality.

*Attitude functions*   the reasons why people hold attitudes, including the psychological needs served by attitudes.

*Attitude importance*   individuals' judgments about the significance of their attitude to them personally.

*Attitude objects*   anything that is evaluated along a dimension of favorability.

*Attitude strength*   their stability, ability to withstand attack, capacity to influence how we process information, and ability to guide behavior.

*Attitude triads*   mental representations containing (a) the individual's own attitudes toward an object, (b) another person's attitudes toward the object, and (c) the individual's own attitude toward the other person.

*Attitude valence*   the positive versus negative direction of evaluation.

*Attitude–behavior measurement correspondence*   the extent to which measures of attitude and behavior refer to the same actions, targets, context, and time.

*Attraction effect*   in attitude triads, this is the tendency to prefer situations where we like another person compared to situations where we dislike another person, regardless of the person's attitudes toward an object.

*Behavior conditioning*   pairing an emotion with a behavior that has been performed.

*Behavioral component of attitudes*   past behaviors or experiences regarding an attitude object.

*Behavioral intentions*   a pre-behavior decision to perform or not perform the action.

*Beliefs*   thoughts or attributes associated with an attitude object.

*Biased scanning hypothesis* the idea that, in role-playing situations, individuals search their memory for prior knowledge that supports their role.

*Big 5* An influential theory of personality including dimensions of openness, conscientiousness, extraversion, agreeableness, and neuroticism.

*Body-specificity hypothesis* a framework describing how concepts of handedness influence how individuals represent concepts in positive or negative ways.

*Central route* attitude change that occurs through its impact on cognitive responses to the message content, according to the Elaboration Likelihood Model of persuasion.

*Classical conditioning* learning that occurs based on the repeated pairing of a conditioned stimulus and an unconditioned stimulus.

*Cognition-in-Persuasion Model* a stage model stating that interpretation of a message cues the recall of relevant knowledge, which is used to determine our evaluation.

*Cognitive component of attitudes* the beliefs, thoughts, and attributes we associate with an object.

*Cognitive dissonance* a state of imbalance among beliefs, including the beliefs that support a person's attitudes.

*Cognitive Dissonance Theory* a model predicting that people feel an aversive tension from having a set of two or more beliefs that do not seem to fit together.

*Collective self-cognitions* how the individual feels judged by others.

*Collectivistic cultures* cultures that emphasize interdependence with others.

*Congeniality effect* the purported tendency to better remember information that is congruent with our attitudes than information incongruent with our attitudes.

*Content-specific measures of attitude components* a methodology using semantic differential scales that refer to cognition, affect, or behavior.

*Counter-attitudinal advocacy* presenting an attitude that opposes the person's initial attitude.

*Deliberative behavior* actions that are relatively thoughtful.

*Descriptive norms* norms that describe others' actions.

*EAI scales* equal appearing interval scales, a technique that classifies self-report items according to degree of valence, prior to asking respondents to indicate their agreement or disagreement with each item.

*EEG – Electroencephalography*   a technique that offers a way to measure the time course of brain activity.

*Effort justification*   the idea that suffering hardship can influence attitudes.

*Ego-defensive function*   the ability of attitudes to protect an individual's self-esteem.

*Elaboration Likelihood Model*   a dual-process model that distinguishes between central and peripheral routes to attitude change.

*Emotion learning*   exposure to an attitude object that is accompanied by events that have emotional consequences.

*Emotional beliefs*   those that refer to the consequences of an action for feelings and well-being.

*EP*   evaluative priming, a technique for implicitly measuring attitudes by examining the speed with which we classify evaluative stimuli after seeing evaluatively congruent or incongruent primes.

*ERPs*   event-related potentials, measure electrical activity in the cerebral cortex.

*Evaluative-affective consistency*   the amount of congruence between an individual's attitude and the person's feelings and emotions.

*Evaluative-behavioral consistency*   the amount of congruence between an individual's attitude and the person's past behaviors.

*Evaluative-cognitive consistency*   the amount of congruence between an individual's attitude and the person's beliefs.

*Expectancy*   belief that a behavior will produce a desired consequence.

*Explicit measures*   techniques that measure attitudes by directly asking respondents.

*Exposure (evaluative) conditioning*   the repeated presentation of an attitude object paired with an affective sensation.

*Externalization function*   the ability of attitudes to defend the self against internal conflict.

*Extrapersonal associations*   knowledge about what others think or feel about the attitude object.

*facial EMG*   facial electromyography, assesses electrical activity in facial muscles that control smiling, frowning, and other emotional expressions.

*fMRI*   functional magnetic resonance imaging, measures oxygen utilization in areas of the brain.

*Foot-in-the-door technique*   a method that uses a slight act of compliance to increase the likelihood of complying with a larger request.

*Group polarization*   individuals' attitudes tendency to become more extreme than the group's average view after group discussion.

*GSR*   galvanic skin response, assessing activity in the sweat glands along surfaces of the hand.

*Habits*   automatic behaviors that occur as a response to cues and are capable of being enacted without conscious monitoring, while being difficult to control.

*Habituation*   after repeated exposure, individuals get used to a new stimulus and see it as less threatening.

*Hedonic Contingency Model*   a model arguing that message recipients in a good mood are likely to devote substantive attention to persuasive appeals that help them maintain their positive affect.

*Heritability*   in the context of attitudes, this is the idea that genes could establish general predispositions that shape environmental experiences in ways that increase the likelihood of developing specific attitudes.

*Heuristic processing*   the use of simple judgmental rules.

*Heuristic-Systematic Model*   a dual-process model that distinguishes between heuristic and systematic routes to attitude change.

*Hypocrisy*   a discrepancy between a verbal behavior that promotes our attitude and a second behavior that contradicts our verbal statement.

*IAT*   Implicit Association Test, an implicit measure assessing attitudes by examining effects of pairing attitude object targets with positive or negative targets in a task that categorizes the identity or valence (e.g., good or bad) of the targets.

*Implementation intentions*   "if-then" plans specifying behaviors that a person will need to perform in order to achieve a goal.

*Implicit measures*   techniques for assessing attitudes without individuals' awareness or control over how their attitude is being measured.

*Impulsive system*   according to the Reflective-Impulsive Model, this system guides and elicits behavior through automatic associative links.

*Incidental affect*   an affective state that influences judgment of an attitude object, but is not linked to the object (e.g., mood).

*Individualistic cultures*   cultures that emphasize independence from others.

*Information Processing Paradigm*   a model proposing that a message must navigate a series of stages to elicit attitude change.

*Informational influence*   conformity to a group out of a desire to be accurate.

*Injunctive norms*   norms that prescribe or proscribe actions.

*Instrumental beliefs*   those that refer to the personal, material costs and benefits of an action.

*Integral affect*   feelings associated with an attitude object.

*Knowledge function*   the ability of attitudes to organize information about attitude objects.

*Latitude of acceptance*   the range of attitude positions that a person accepts.

*Latitude of rejection*   the range of attitudes that a person rejects.

*Life stages hypothesis*   the idea that there is a curvilinear relation between age and susceptibility to attitude change, with greater susceptibility among young adults and the elderly.

*Likert scales*   self-report measures of attitude that ask respondents to rate their extent of agreement versus disagreement with items.

*Matching effects*   the finding that appeals that match aspects of the recipient are usually more likely to elicit attitude change.

*Measurement reliability*   the degree to which test scores are free from errors in measurement.

*Measurement validity*   the extent that test scores assess the construct it is designed to measure.

*MEG – Magnetoencephalography*   a technique that offers a way to measure the time course of brain activity.

*Mere exposure effect*   the notion that the more we are exposed to an attitude object, the more we tend to like it.

*Meta-Cognitive Model*   a model that considers how "thoughts about thoughts" influence persuasion.

*Meta-perceptions*   individuals' perceptions of whether their attitudes are based on affective information or cognitive information.

*MODE Model*   a model of attitudes and behavior that highlights the importance of motivation and opportunity as determinants of behavior.

*Mood-as-information* a perspective stating that mood may be a source of data that people use when figuring out how they feel about objects.

*Mood-congruence effect* the tendency for people to express attitudes that match their current mood.

*Mood-Congruent Expectancies Approach* a model arguing that people in a good mood or a bad mood are more likely to engage in enhanced processing of a message when mood-congruent expectancies are disconfirmed.

*Multicomponent Model* attitudes are evaluations of an object that summarize cognitive, affective, and behavioral information.

*Multivalence* the idea that attitudes can subsume many evaluations, which can cluster in different ways.

*Need for affect* the tendency to seek out and enjoy emotional experiences.

*Need for cognition* stable differences in the desire to engage in and enjoy effortful cognitive activity.

*Normative beliefs* beliefs about how people who are important to us expect us to act.

*Normative influence* conformity to a group out of a desire to be liked.

*Normative outcomes* approval and disapproval from others that might occur from performing a behavior.

*Object-appraisal function* the ability of attitudes to summarize the positive and negative attributes of objects in our social world.

*Observational learning* learning that occurs through watching others.

*Open-ended measures of attitude components* a technique that asks participants to freely list beliefs, feelings, or behaviors linked to their attitude.

*Overjustification effect* when rewards decrease the intrinsic attractiveness of an activity or object.

*Perceived behavioral control* individuals' perceptions about whether they possess the resources and opportunities required to perform a behavior.

*Perceptual fluency* the ease with which information is processed. Greater ease represents greater fluency.

*Peripheral route* attitude change that occurs by considering simple characteristics of a message.

*Personalized IAT*  personalized Implicit Association Test, an implicit measure assessing attitudes by examining effects of pairing attitude object targets with positive or negative targets in a task that categorizes the identity of the targets and their personal attitude valence (e.g., *I* like or *I* dislike).

*PET – Positron emission tomography*  a technique that gives an indication of the activity level of a particular brain region.

*Prefrontal cortex*  a region in the brain that is important in planning complex decisions and behavior.

*Private self-consciousness*  awareness of personal and internal characteristics.

*Probabilogical models*  models that predict how individuals' belief in a conclusion may change when their belief in a related premise is altered.

*Public self-consciousness*  awareness of public image.

*Reflective system*  according to the Reflective-Impulsive Model, this system guides and elicits behavior via a reasoned consideration of available information.

*Reflective-Impulsive Model*  proposes that behavior is controlled by a reflective system and an impulsive system.

*Refutational defenses*  interventions that provide people with arguments against a belief and rebuttals of the arguments.

*Reverse correlation data reduction*  in studies of facial perception, this technique builds a picture of participants' mental image of a face by asking them to choose the most accurate among digitally scrambled images of the face.

*Salient beliefs*  those that are easy to recall and link to the behavior.

*Selective attention*  the tendency to notice and focus on attitude-congruent and attitude-incongruent information to different degrees.

*Selective exposure*  the tendency to seek out different amounts of attitude-congruent and attitude-incongruent information.

*Selective interpretation*  the tendency to be biased in our judgments of the meaning and significance of attitude-relevant information.

*Selective memory*  the effect of attitudes on the types of attitude-relevant information we remember (e.g., attitude incongruent).

*Self-affirmation*  activity that helps to promote a subjective feeling of self-integrity, often by describing personal values.

*Self-efficacy*   individuals' belief that they can successfully execute a behavior.

*Self-identity outcomes*   effects of a behavior on the self-concept.

*Self-Affirmation Theory*   the idea that individuals can reduce cognitive dissonance by restoring a sense of self-integrity.

*Self-monitoring orientation*   individual differences in how people vary their behavior to suit the situation.

*Self-Perception Theory*   the idea that individuals sometimes derive their own attitude by making inferences from their own behavior.

*Semantic differential scales*   a self-report measure of attitude that uses responses to bipolar scales anchored by oppositely valenced adjectives at the ends (e.g., very good to very bad).

*Sleeper effect*   the tendency for some messages to elicit more change over time.

*Social adjustment function*   the ability of attitudes to help us identify with people whom we like and to dissociate from people whom we dislike.

*Social cognition*   how individuals elaborate upon and process socially relevant information.

*Social cognitive neuroscience* (SCN)   a discipline that studies the *social* behavior of motivated individuals (S), examining the *cognitive* mechanisms that give rise to behavioral processes (C), and investigating the *neurological* systems that instantiate these processes (N).

*Social desirability*   the tendency to respond to questions in a manner that make one's self look good.

*Social Judgment Model*   a model in which individuals weigh new information and compare it to their attitude.

*Spontaneous behavior*   actions that are relatively automatic.

*Spreading of choice alternatives*   the difference between the post-decision appraisal of chosen and unchosen alternatives.

*Subjective norms*   perceived social pressure to perform or not perform a behavior.

*Subliminal priming*   the presentation of information below a threshold on conscious recognition.

*Supportive defenses*   interventions that provide people with information supporting a belief that is about to be attacked.

*Synergism within attitudes*   the influences of cognitive, affective, and behavioral information in an attitude on each other.

*Systematic processing*   analytic and thorough examination of attitude-relevant information.

*Tolerance for ambiguity*   individual differences in being accepting of things that are unknown or unclear.

*Transportation in a narrative*   a process by which people become deeply immersed in the world depicted in the narrative.

*Truisms*   beliefs that are so widely accepted that people rarely question them and fail to develop arguments to support them.

*Unimodel*   a single-process model of persuasion.

*Utilitarian function*   the ability of attitudes to maximize rewards and minimize punishments obtained from attitude objects.

*Utilitarian outcomes*   rewards and punishments associated with performing a behavior.

*Value*   the perceived importance of a consequence of a behavior.

*Value-Account Model*   a dual-process model that suggests that attitudes can be produced by implicit processing and explicit processing.

*Value-expressive function*   the ability of an attitude to express an individual's self-concept and central values.

*Vicarious dissonance*   aversive cognitive discrepancies elicited by the behavior of another individual.

*Vicarious self-perception*   the idea that people might sometimes infer their own attributes by observing the actions of others.

*Visceral fit hypothesis*   the notion that individuals perceive experiences and outcomes integrated with their current visceral state as more likely to occur.

*Weighting bias*   the idea that people differ in the weight they give negative and positive information in attitude processes.

*Yale Model of Persuasion*   a program of research that examined the factors that determine when persuasive messages cause attitudes to change.

# REFERENCES

Aaker, J. L. and Sengupta, J. (2000) Additivity versus attenuation: The role of culture in the resolution of information incongruity. *Journal of Consumer Psychology*, *9*, 67–82.

Abelson, R. P., Kinder, D. R., Peters, M. D. and Fiske, S. T. (1982) Affective and semantic components of political person perception. *Journal of Personality and Social Psychology*, *42*, 619–630.

Adorno, T. W., Frenkel-Brunswik, E., Levinson, D. J. and Sanford, R. N. (1950) *The Authoritarian Personality*. New York: Harper and Row.

Ajzen, I. (1991) The theory of planned behavior. *Organizational Behavior and Human Decision Processes*, *50*, 179–211.

Ajzen, I. (2002) Residual effects of past on later behavior: Habituation and reasoned action perspectives. *Personality and Social Psychology Review*, *6*, 107–122.

Ajzen, I. and Fishbein, M. (1977) Attitude–behavior relations: A theoretical analysis and review of empirical research. *Psychological Bulletin*, *84*, 888–918.

Ajzen, I. and Fishbein, M. (1980) *Understanding attitudes and predicting social behavior*. Englewood Cliffs, NJ: Prentice Hall.

Ajzen, I. and Madden, T. J. (1986) Prediction of goal-directed behavior: Attitudes, intentions and perceived behavioral control. *Journal of Experimental Social Psychology*, *22*, 453–474.

Ajzen, I., Brown, T. C. and Carvajal, F. (2004) Explaining the discrepancy between intentions and actions: The case of hypothetical bias in contingent valuation. *Personality and Social Psychology Bulletin*, *30*, 1108–1121.

Albarracín, D. (2002) Cognition in persuasion: An analysis of information processing in response to persuasive communications. In M. P. Zanna (ed.), *Advances in Experimental Social Psychology* (Vol. 34, pp. 61–130). San Diego, CA: Academic Press.

Albarracín, D. and Kumkale, G. T. (2003) Affect as information in persuasion: A model of affect identification and discounting. *Journal of Personality and Social Psychology*, *84*, 453–469.

Albarracín, D. and Wyer, R. S., Jr. (2000) Cognitive impact of past behavior: Influences on beliefs, attitudes and future behavioral decisions. *Journal of Personality and Social Psychology*, *79*, 5–22.

Albarracín, D., Cohen, J. B., and Kumkale, G. T. (2003) When communications collide with recipients' actions: Effects of the post-message behavior on intentions to follow the message recommendation. *Personality and Social Psychology Bulletin, 29*, 834–845.

Albarracín, D., Gillette, J. C., Earl, A. N., Glasman, L. R., Durantini, M. R. and Ho, M. H. (2005) A test of major assumptions about behavior change: A comprehensive look at the effects of passive and active HIV-prevention interventions since the beginning of the epidemic. *Psychological Bulletin, 131*, 856–897.

Albarracín, D., Johnson, B. T., Fishbein, M. and Mullerleile, P. A. (2001) Theories of reasoned action and planned behavior as models of condom use: A meta-analysis. *Psychological Bulletin, 127*, 144–161.

Albarracín, D., Johnson, B. T. and Zanna, M. P. (eds) (2005) *The Handbook of Attitudes*. Mahwah, NJ: Erlbaum.

Albert, M. (1975) Feelings. On *Feelings* [LP]. New York: RCA.

Allport, G. W. (1935) Attitudes. In C. Murchison (ed.), *Handbook of Social Psychology* (pp. 798–844). Worcester, MA: Clark University Press.

Allport, G. W. (1985) The historical background of social psychology. In G. Lindzey and E. Aronson (eds), *The Handbook of Social Psychology* (3rd edn, Vol. 1). New York: Random House.

Altemeyer, B. (1996) *The Authoritarian Spectre*. Cambridge, MA: Harvard University Press.

Alvaro, E. M. and Crano, W. D. (1997) Indirect minority influence: Evidence for leniency in source evaluation and counterargumentation. *Journal of Personality and Social Psychology, 72*, 949–964.

Alwin, D. F., Cohen, R. L. and Newcomb, T. M. (1991) *Political Attitudes Over the Life Span: The Bennington Women After Fifty Years*. Madison, WI: University of Wisconsin Press.

American Psychological Association (1985) *Standards for Educational and Psychological Testing*. Washington, DC: American Psychological Association.

Arana, F. S., Parkinson, J. A., Hinton, E., Holland, A. J., Owen, A. M. and Roberts, A. C. (2003) Dissociable contributions of the human amygdala and orbitofrontal cortex to incentive motivation and goal selection. *Journal of Neuroscience, 23*, 9632–9638.

Armitage, C. J. (2003) Beyond attitudinal ambivalence: Effects of belief homogeneity on attitude-intention-behavior relations. *European Journal of Social Psychology, 33*, 551–563.

Armitage, C. J. and Conner, M. (2000) Attitudinal ambivalence: A test of three key hypotheses. *Personality and Social Psychology Bulletin, 26*, 1421–1432.

Armitage, C. J. and Conner, M. (2001) Efficacy of the theory of planned behaviour: A meta-analytic review. *British Journal of Social Psychology, 40*, 471–499.

Aronson, E. (1969) The theory of cognitive dissonance: A current perspective. *Advances in Experimental Social Psychology, 4*, 1–34.

Aronson, E. and Cope, V. (1968) My enemy's enemy is my friend. *Journal of Personality and Social Psychology, 8*, 8–12.

Aronson, E. and Mills, J. (1959) The effect of severity of initiation on liking for a group. *Journal of Abnormal and Social Psychology, 59*, 177–181.

Arvey, R. D., Bouchard, T. J., Segal, N. L. and Abraham, N. L. (1989) Job satisfaction: Environmental and genetic components. *Journal of Applied Psychology, 74*, 187–192.

Asch, S. E. (1946) Forming impressions of personality. *Journal of Abnormal and Social Psychology*, *41*, 258–290.

Asch, S. E. (1952) *Social Psychology*. Englewood Cliffs, NJ: Prentice Hall.

Asch, S. E. (1956) Studies of independence and conformity: I. A minority of one against a unanimous majority. *Psychological Monographs*, *70*(9), 1–70.

Asch, S. E. and Zukier, H. (1984) Thinking about persons. *Journal of Personality and Social Psychology*, *46*, 1230–1240.

Ashton, M. C., Jackson, D. N., Helmes, E. and Paunonen, S. V. (1998) Joint factor analysis of the Personality Research Form and the Jackson Personality Inventory: Comparisons with the Big Five. *Journal of Research in Personality*, *32*, 243–250.

Aubrey, J. S. (2006) Exposure to sexually objectifying media and body self-perceptions among college women: An examination of the selective exposure hypothesis and the role of moderating variables. *Sex Roles*, *55*, 159–172.

Axsom, D. and Cooper, J. (1985) Cognitive dissonance and psychotherapy: The role of effort justification in inducing weight loss. *Journal of Experimental Social Psychology*, *21*, 149–160.

Baeyens, F., Eelen, P., Crombez, G. and De Houwer, J. (2001) On the role of beliefs in observational flavor conditioning. *Current Psychology: Developmental, Learning, Personality, Social*, *20*, 183–203.

Baker, S. M. and Petty, R. E. (1994) Majority and minority influence: Source-position imbalance as a determinant of message scrutiny. *Journal of Personality and Social Psychology*, *67*, 5–19.

Balcetis, E. and Dunning, D. (2006) See what you want to see: Motivational influences on visual perception. *Journal of Personality and Social Psychology*, *91*, 612–625.

Baldwin, M. W. and Holmes, J. (1987) Salient private audiences and awareness of the self. *Journal of Personality and Social Psychology*, *52*, 1087–1098.

Banaji, M. R. and Steele, C. M. (1989) Alcohol and self-evaluation: Is a social cognition approach beneficial? *Social Cognition*, *7*, 137–151.

Bandura, A. (1977) Self-efficacy: Toward a unifying theory of behavior change. *Psychological Review*, *84*, 191–215.

Bandura, A. and Rosenthal, T. L. (1967) Vicarious classical conditioning as a function of arousal level. *Journal of Personality and Social Psychology*, *7*, 111–116.

Bandura, A., Blanchard, E. B. and Ritter, B. (1969) Relative efficacy of desensitization and modeling approaches for inducing behavioral, affective and attitudinal changes. *Journal of Personality and Social Psychology*, *13*, 173–199.

Bargh, J. A., Chaiken, S., Govender, R. and Pratto, F. (1992) The generality of the automatic attitude activation effect. *Journal of Personality and Social Psychology*, *62*, 893–912.

Baron, A. S. and Banaji, M. R. (2006) The development of implicit attitudes: Evidence of race evaluations from ages 6, 10, and adulthood. *Psychological Science*, *17*, 53–58.

Basil, D. Z. and Herr, P. M. (2006) Attitudinal balance and cause-related marketing: An empirical application of balance theory. *Journal of Consumer Psychology*, *16*, 391–403.

Bassili, J. N. (1996) Meta-judgmental versus operative indexes of psychological attributes: The case of measures of attitude strength. *Journal of Personality and Social Psychology, 71*, 637–653.

Bastardi, A., Uhlmann, E. L. and Ross, L. (2011) Wishful thinking: Belief, desire, and the motivated evaluation of scientific evidence. *Psychological Science, 22*, 731–732.

Batson, C. D., Thompson, E. R. and Chen, H. (2002) Moral hypocrisy: Addressing some alternatives. *Journal of Personality and Social Psychology, 83*, 330–339.

Batson, C. D., Thompson, E. R., Seuferling, G., Whitney, H. and Strongman, J. A. (1999) Moral hypocrisy: Appearing moral to oneself without being so. *Journal of Personality and Social Psychology, 77*, 525–537.

Baumeister, R. F., Bratslavsky, E., Finkenauer, C. and Vohs, K. D. (2001) Bad is stronger than good. *Review of General Psychology, 5*, 323–370.

Baxter, M. G. and Murray, E. A. (2002) The amygdala and reward. *Nature Reviews Neuroscience, 3*, 563–573.

Bègue, L., Bushman, B.J., Zerhouni, O., Subra, B. and Ourabah, M. (2013) Beauty is in the eye of the beer holder: People who think they are drunk also think they are attractive. *British Journal of Psychology, 104*, 225–234.

Bell, D. W. and Esses, V. M. (2002) Ambivalence and response amplification: A motivational perspective. *Personality and Social Psychology Bulletin, 28*, 1143–1152.

Bell, D. W., Esses, V. M. and Maio, G. R. (1996) The utility of open-ended measures to assess intergroup ambivalence. *Canadian Journal of Behavioral Science, 28*, 12–18.

Bem, D. J. (1965) An experimental analysis of self-persuasion. *Journal of Experimental Social Psychology, 1*, 199–218.

Bem, D. J. (1972) Self-perception theory. In L. Berkowitz (ed.), *Advances in Experimental Social Psychology* (Vol. 6, pp. 1–62). San Diego, CA: Academic Press.

Berger, S. M. (1962) Conditioning through vicarious instigation. *Psychological Review, 69*, 450–466.

Berlyne, D. E. (1966) Curiosity and exploration. *Science, 153*, 25–33.

Berlyne, D. E. (1970) Novelty, complexity and hedonic value. *Perception and Psychophysics, 8*, 279–286.

Bermeitinger, C., Goelz, R., Johr, N., Neumann, M. and Ullrich K. H. (2009) The hidden persuaders break into the tired brain. *Journal of Experimental Social Psychology, 45*, 320–326.

Bernard, M. M., Maio, G. R. and Olson, J. M. (2003a) Effects of introspection about reasons for values: Extending research on values-as-truisms. *Social Cognition, 21*, 1–25.

Bernard, M. M., Maio, G. R. and Olson, J. M. (2003b) The vulnerability of values to attack: Inoculation of values and value-relevant attitudes. *Personality and Social Psychology Bulletin, 29*, 63–75.

Betsch, T., Plessner, H. and Schallies, E. (2004) The value-account model of attitude formation. In G. Haddock and G. R. Maio (eds), *Contemporary Perspectives on the Psychology of Attitudes* (pp. 251–274). New York: Psychology Press.

Betsch, T., Plessner, H., Schwieren, C. and Gütig, R. (2001) I like it but I don't know why: A value-account approach to implicit attitude formation. *Personality and Social Psychology Bulletin, 27*, 242–253.

Bizer, G. Y., Tormala, Z. L., Rucker, D. D. and Petty, R. E. (2006) Memory-based versus on-line processing: Implications for attitude strength. *Journal of Experimental Social Psychology, 42*, 646–653.

Blair, I. V. (2002) The malleability of automatic stereotypes and prejudice. *Personality and Social Psychology Review, 6*, 242–261.

Blair, I. V., Ma, J. E. and Lenton, A. P. (2001) Imagining stereotypes away: The moderation of implicit stereotypes through mental imagery. *Journal of Personality and Social Psychology, 81*, 828–841.

Blakemore, S. J., Winston, J. and Frith, U. (2004) Social cognitive neuroscience: Where are we heading? *Trends in Cognitive Science, 8*, 216–222.

Blankenship, K. L. and Craig, T. Y. (2007) Language and persuasion: Tag questions as powerless speech or as interpreted in context. *Journal of Experimental Social Psychology, 43*, 112–118.

Blankenship, K. L. and Wegener, D. T. (2008) Opening the mind to close it: Considering a message in light of important values increases message processing and later resistance to change. *Journal of Personality and Social Psychology, 94*, 196–213.

Blankenship, K. L. and Wegener, D. T. (2012) Value activation and processing of persuasive messages. *Social Psychological and Personality Science, 3*, 391–397.

Blankenship, K. L., Wegener, D. T. and Murray, R. A. (2012) Circumventing resistance: Using values to indirectly change attitudes. *Journal of Personality and Social Psychology, 103*, 606–621.

Blanton, H. and Jaccard, J. (2006) Tests of multiplicative models in psychology: A case study using the unified theory of implicit attitudes, stereotypes, self-esteem and the self-concept. *Psychological Review, 113*, 155–169.

Blanton, H., Jaccard, J., Christie, C. and Gonzales, P. (2007) Plausible assumptions, questionable assumptions and post hoc rationalizations: Will the real IAT, please stand up? *Journal of Experimental Social Psychology, 43*, 399–409.

Blanton, H., Jaccard, J., Gonzales, P. and Christie, C. (2006) Decoding the Implicit Association Test: Perspectives on criterion prediction. *Journal of Experimental Social Psychology, 42*, 192–212.

Blanton, H., Stuart, A. E. and VandenEijnden, R. J. J. M. (2001) An introduction to deviance-regulation theory: The effect of behavioral norms on message framing. *Personality and Social Psychology Bulletin, 27*, 848–858.

Bless, H., Mackie, D. M. and Schwarz, N. (1992) Mood effects on encoding and judgmental processes in persuasion. *Journal of Personality and Social Psychology, 63*, 585–595.

Bluemke, M. and Friese, M. (2008) Reliability and validity of the Single-Target IAT (ST-IAT): Assessing automatic affect towards multiple attitude objects. *European Journal of Social Psychology, 38*, 977–997.

Bodenhausen, G. V. (1993) Emotions, arousal and stereotypic judgments: A heuristic model of affect and stereotyping. In D. M. Mackie and D. L. Hamilton (eds), *Affect, Cognition and Stereotyping: Interactive Processes in Group Perception* (pp. 13–37). San Diego, CA: Academic Press.

Bohner, G. and Wänke, M. (2002) *Attitudes and Attitude Change*. New York: Psychology Press.

Bond, R. and Smith, P. B. (1996) Culture and conformity: A meta-analysis of studies using Asch's (1952, 1956) line-judging task. *Psychological Bulletin, 119*, 111–137.

Bornstein, R. F. (1989) Exposure and affect: Overview and meta-analysis of research, 1968–1987. *Psychological Bulletin, 106*, 265–289.

Bornstein, R. F. (1993) Mere exposure effects with outgroup stimuli. In D. M. Mackie and D. L. Hamilton (eds), *Affect, Cognition and Stereotyping: Interactive Processes in Group Perception* (pp. 195–211). San Diego, CA: Academic Press.

Bornstein, R. F. and D'Agostino, P. (1992) Stimulus recognition and the mere exposure effect. *Journal of Personality and Social Psychology, 63*, 545–552.

Bornstein, R. F. and D'Agostino, P. (1994) The attribution and discounting of perceptual fluency: Preliminary tests of a perceptual fluency/attributional model of the mere exposure effect. *Social Cognition, 12*, 103–128.

Bornstein, R. F., Kale, A. R. and Cornell, K. R. (1990) Boredom as a limiting condition on the mere exposure effect. *Journal of Personality and Social Psychology, 58*, 791–800.

Bornstein, R. F., Leone, D. R. and Galley, D. J. (1987) The generalizability of subliminal mere exposure effects: Influence of stimuli perceived without awareness on social behavior. *Journal of Personality and Social Psychology, 53*, 1070–1079.

Bossard, J. (1932) Residential propinquity as a factor in marriage selection. *American Journal of Sociology, 38*, 219–224.

Bower, G. H. (1991) Mood congruity of social judgments. In J. P. Forgas (ed.), *Emotion and Social Judgment* (pp. 31–53). Oxford: Pergamon.

Boysen, G. A., Vogel, D. L. and Madon, S. (2006) A public versus private administration of the Implicit Association Test. *European Journal of Social Psychology, 36*, 845–856.

Bradley, S. D., III and Meeds, R. (2004) The effects of sentence-level context, prior word knowledge, and need for cognition on information processing of technical language in print ads. *Journal of Consumer Psychology, 14*, 291–302.

Brandt, M. J. and Wetherell, G. (2012) What attitudes are moral attitudes? The case for heritability. *Social Psychological and Personality Science, 3*, 172–179.

Brannon, L. A., Tagler, M. J. and Eagly, A. H. (2007) The moderating role of attitude strength in selective exposure to information. *Journal of Experimental Social Psychology, 43*, 611–617.

Breckler, S. J. (1984) Empirical validation of affect, behavior and cognition as distinct components of attitude. *Journal of Personality and Social Psychology, 47*, 1191–1205.

Breckler, S. J. (2004) Hold still while I measure your attitude: Assessment in the throes of ambivalence. In G. Haddock and G. R. Maio (eds), *Contemporary Perspectives on the Psychology of Attitudes* (pp. 77–92). Hove: Psychology Press.

Breckler, S. J. and Berman, J. S. (1991) Affective responses to attitude objects: Measurement and validation. *Journal of Social Behavior and Personality, 6*, 529–544.

Breckler, S. J. and Wiggins, E. C. (1989) Affect versus evaluation in the structure of attitudes. *Journal of Experimental Social Psychology, 25*, 253–271.

Breckler, S. J. and Wiggins, E. C. (1991) Cognitive responses in persuasion: Affective and evaluative determinants. *Journal of Experimental Social Psychology, 27*, 180–200.

Brehm, J. (1956) Postdecision changes in the desirability of alternatives. *Journal of Abnormal and Social Psychology*, *52*, 384–389.

Brehm, S. and Brehm, J. (1981) *Psychological Reactance: A Theory of Freedom and Control.* New York: Academic Press.

Breslin, C. W. and Safer, M. A. (2011) Effects of event valence on long-term memory for two baseball championship games. *Psychological Science*, *22*, 1408–1412.

Brickman, P., Redfield, J., Harrison, A. A. and Crandall, R. (1972) Drive and predisposition as factors in the attitudinal effects of mere exposure. *Journal of Experimental Social Psychology*, *8*, 31–44.

Briñol, P. and Petty, R. E. (2003) Overt head movements and persuasion: A self-validation analysis. *Journal of Personality and Social Psychology*, *84*, 1123–1139.

Briñol, P. and Petty, R. E. (2004) Self-validation processes: The role of thought confidence in persuasion. In G. Haddock and G. R. Maio (eds), *Contemporary Perspectives on the Psychology of Attitudes* (pp. 205–226). Philadelphia, PA: Psychology Press.

Briñol, P. and Petty, R. E. (2005) Individual differences in attitude change. In D. Albarracín, B. T. Johnson and M. P. Zanna (eds), *The Handbook of Attitudes and Attitude Change* (pp. 575–615) Mahwah, NJ: Erlbaum.

Briñol, P. and Petty, R. E. (2008) Embodied persuasion: Fundamental processes by which bodily responses can impact attitudes. In G. R. Semin and E. R. Smith (eds), *Embodiment Grounding: Social, Cognitive, Affective and Neuroscientific Approaches* (pp. 184–207). Cambridge, UK: Cambridge University Press.

Briñol, P. and Petty, R. E. (2009) Persuasion: Insights from the self-validation hypothesis. In M. P. Zanna (ed.), *Advances in Experimental Social Psychology*. New York: Academic Press.

Briñol, P., Petty, R. E., Valle, C., Rucker, D. D. and Becerra, A. (2007) The effects of message recipients' power before and after persuasion: A self-validation analysis. *Journal of Personality and Social Psychology*, *93*, 1040–1053.

Briñol, P., Petty, R. E. and Wheeler, S. C. (2006) Discrepancies between explicit and implicit self-concepts: Consequences for information processing. *Journal of Personality and Social Psychology*, *91*, 154–170.

Brock, T. C. (1967) Communication discrepancy and intent to persuade as determinants of counterargument production. *Journal of Experimental Social Psychology*, *3*, 269–309.

Brown, R., Eller, A., Leeds, S. and Stace, K. (2007) Interrgroup contact and intergroup attitudes: A longitudinal study. *European Journal of Social Psychology*, *37*, 692–703.

Buhrmester, M. D., Blanton, H. and Swann, W. B. (2011) Implicit self-esteem: Nature, measurement and a new way forward. *Journal of Personality and Social Psychology*, *100*, 365–385.

Bullens, L., van Harreveld, F., Förster, J. and van der Pligt, J. (2013) Reversible decisions: The grass isn't merely greener on the other side, it's also very brown over here. *Journal of Experimental Social Psychology*, *49*, 1093–1099.

Burger, J. M. (1999) The foot-in-the-door compliance procedure: A multiple-process analysis and review. *Personality and Social Psychology Bulletin*, *3*, 303–325.

Burger, J. M. and Guadagno, R. E. (2003) Self-concept clarity and the foot-in-the-door procedure. *Basic and Applied Social Psychology*, *25*, 79–86.

Burger, J. M. and Petty, R. E. (1981) The low-ball compliance technique: Task or person commitment? *Journal of Personality and Social Psychology*, *49*, 492–500.

Burnstein, E. and Vinokur, A. (1977) Interpersonal comparison versus persuasive argumentation: A more direct test of alternative explanations for group-induced shifts in individual choice. *Journal of Experimental Social Psychology*, *9*, 236–245.

Cacioppo, J. T. and Petty, R. E. (1979a) Attitudes and cognitive response: An electrophysiological approach. *Journal of Personality and Social Psychology*, *37*, 2181–2199.

Cacioppo, J. T. and Petty, R. E. (1979b) Effects of message repetition and position on cognitive response, recall and persuasion. *Journal of Personality and Social Psychology*, *37*, 97–109.

Cacioppo, J. T. and Petty, R. E. (1981) Effects of extent of thought on the pleasantness ratings of P-O-X triads: Evidence for three judgmental tendencies in evaluating social situations. *Journal of Personality and Social Psychology*, *40*, 1000–1009.

Cacioppo, J. T. and Petty, R. E. (1982) The need for cognition. *Journal of Personality and Social Psychology*, *42*, 116–131.

Cacioppo, J. T. and Petty, R. E. (1985) Central and peripheral routes to persuasion: The role of message repetition. In L. F. Alwitt and A. A. Mitchell (eds), *Psychological Processes and Advertising Effects* (pp. 91–111). Maywah, NJ: Erlbaum.

Cacioppo, J. T., Crites, S. L., Jr. and Gardner, W. L. (1996) Attitudes to the right: Evaluative processing is associated with lateralized late positive event-related brain potentials. *Personality and Social Psychology Bulletin*, *22*, 1205–1219.

Cacioppo, J. T., Gardner, W. L. and Berntson, G. G. (1997) Beyond bipolar conceptualizations and measures: The case of attitudes and evaluative space. *Personality and Social Psychology Review*, *1*, 3–25.

Cacioppo, J. T., Marshall-Goodell, B. S., Tassinary, L. G. and Petty, R. E. (1992) Rudimentary determinants of attitudes: Classical conditioning is more effective when prior knowledge about the attitude stimulus is low than high. *Journal of Experimental Social Psychology*, *28*, 207–233.

Cacioppo, J. T., Petty, R. E., Feinstein, J. A. and Jarvis, W. B. G. (1996) Dispositional differences in cognitive motivation: The life and times of individuals varying in need for cognition. *Psychological Bulletin*, *119*, 197–253.

Cacioppo, J. T., Petty, R. E., Kao, C. F. and Rodriguez, R. (1986) Central and peripheral routes to persuasion: An individual difference perspective. *Journal of Personality and Social Psychology*, *51*, 1032–1043.

Cacioppo, J. T., Priester, J. R. and Berntson, G. G. (1993) Rudimentary determinants of attitudes: II. Arm flexion and extension have differential effects on attitudes. *Journal of Personality and Social Psychology*, *65*, 5–17.

Calanchini, J., Gonsalkorale, K., Sherman, J. W. and Klauer, K. C. (2013) Counter-prejudicial training reduces activation of biased associations and enhances response monitoring. *European Journal of Social Psychology*, *43*, 321–325.

Cameron, C. D., Brown-Iannuzzi, J. L. and Payne, B. K. (2012) Sequential priming measures of implicit social cognition: A meta-analysis of associations with behavior and explicit attitudes. *Personality and Social Psychology Review*, *16*, 330–350.

Carrera, P., Muñoz, D., Callabero, A., Fernández, I. and Albaraccín, D. (2012) The present projects past behavior into the future while the past projects attitudes into the future: How verb tense moderates predictors of drinking intentions. *Journal of Experimental Social Psychology*, *48*, 1196–1200.

Carstensen, L. L. (2006) The influence of a sense of time on human development. *Science*, *312*, 1913–1915.

Casasanto, D. (2009) Embodiment of abstract concepts: Good and bad in right- and left-handers. *Journal of Experimental Psychology: General*, *138*, 351–367.

Casasanto, D. (2011) Different bodies, different minds: The body-specificity of language and thought. *Current Directions in Psychological Science*, *20*, 378–383.

Casasanto, D. and Chrysikou, E. G. (2011) When left is 'right': Motor fluency shapes abstract concepts. *Psychological Science*, *22*, 419–422.

Casasanto, D. and Henetz, T. (2012) Handedness shapes children's abstract concepts. *Cognitive Science*, *36*, 359–372.

Celuch, K., Lust, J. and Showers, L. (1998) A test of a model of consumers' responses to product manual safety information. *Journal of Applied Social Psychology*, *28*, 377–394.

Chaiken, S. (1979) Communicator physical attractiveness and persuasion. *Journal of Personality and Social Psychology*, *37*, 1387–1397.

Chaiken, S. (1980) Heuristic versus systematic information processing and the use of source versus message cues in persuasion. *Journal of Personality and Social Psychology*, *39*, 752–766.

Chaiken, S. (1987) The heuristic model of persuasion. In M. P. Zanna, J. M. Olson and C. P. Herman (eds), *Social Influence: The Ontario Symposium* (Vol. 5, pp. 3–39). Mahwah, NJ: Erlbaum.

Chaiken, S. and Baldwin, M. W. (1981) Affective-cognitive consistency and the effect of salient behavioral information on the self-perception of attitudes. *Journal of Personality and Social Psychology*, *41*, 1–12.

Chaiken, S. and Maheswaran, D. (1994) Heuristic processing can bias systematic processing: Effects of source credibility, argument ambiguity and task importance on attitude judgment. *Journal of Personality and Social Psychology*, *66*, 460–473.

Chaiken, S., Duckworth, K. L. and Darke, P. (1999) When parsimony fails. . . . *Psychological Inquiry*, *10*, 118–123.

Chaiken, S., Liberman, A. and Eagly, A. H. (1989) Heuristic and systematic processing within and beyond the persuasion context. In J. S. Uleman and J. A. Bargh (eds), *Unintended Thought* (pp. 212–252). New York: Guilford Press.

Chaiken, S., Pomerantz, E. M. and Giner-Sorolla, R. (1995) Structural consistency and attitude strength. In R. E. Petty and J. A. Krosnick (eds), *Attitude Strength: Antecedents and Consequences* (pp. 387–412). Mahwah, NJ: Erlbaum.

Charng, H-W., Piliavin, J. A. and Callero, P. C. (1988) Role identity and reasoned action in the prediction of repeated behavior. *Social Psychology Quarterly*, *51*, 303–317.

Chartrand, T. L., van Baaren, R. B. and Bargh, J. A. (2006) Linking automatic evaluation to mood and information processing style: Consequences for experienced affect, impression formation and stereotyping. *Journal of Experimental Psychology: General*, *135*, 70–77.

Chen, S. and Chaiken, S. (1999) The heuristic-systematic model in its broader context. In S. Chaiken and Y. Trope (eds), *Dual-process Theories in Social Psychology* (pp. 73–96). New York: Guilford Press.

Chen, S., Schechter, D. and Chaiken, S. (1996) Getting at the truth or getting along: Accuracy-versus impression-motivated heuristic and systematic processing. *Journal of Personality and Social Psychology*, *71*, 262–275.

Cialdini, R. B. (2003) Crafting normative messages to protect the environment. *Current Directions in Psychological Science*, *12*, 105–109.

Cialdini, R. B. (2008) *Influence: Science and Practice* (5th edn). Boston, MA: Allyn & Bacon.

Cialdini, R. B., Kallgren, C. A. and Reno, R. R. (1991) A focus theory of normative conduct: A theoretical refinement and reevaluation of the role of norms in human behavior. *Advances in Experimental Social Psychology*, *21*, 201–234.

Cialdini, R. B., Trost, M. R. and Newsom, J. T. (1995) Preference for consistency: The development of a valid measure and the discovery of surprising behavioral implications. *Journal of Personality and Social Psychology*, *69*, 318–328.

Cialdini, R. B., Wosinska, W., Barrett, D. W., Butner, J. and Górnik-Durose, M. (2001) The differential impact of two social influence principles on individualists and collectivists in Poland and the United States. In W. Wosinska and R. B. Cialdini (eds), *The Practice of Social Influence in Multiple Cultures: Applied Social Research* (pp. 33–50). Mahwah, NJ: Erlbaum.

Cialdini, R. B., Wosinska, W., Barrett, D. W., Butner, J. and Górnik-Durose, M. (1999) Compliance with a request in two cultures: The differential impact of social proof and commitment/consistency on collectivists and individualists. *Personality and Social Psychology Bulletin*, *25*, 1242–1253.

Clark, J. K., Wegener, D. T. and Fabrigar, L. R. (2008) Attitude ambivalence and message-based persuasion: Motivated processing of proattitudinal information and avoidance of counterattitudinal information. *Personality and Social Psychology Bulletin*, *34*, 565–577.

Clark, J. K., Wegener, D. T., Habashi, M. M. and Evans, A. T. (2012) Source expertise and persuasion: The effects of perceived opposition or support on message scrutiny. *Personality and Social Psychology Bulletin*, *38*, 90–100.

Clarkson, J. J., Tormala, Z. L. and Rucker, D. D. (2008) A new look at the consequences of attitude certainty: The amplification hypothesis. *Journal of Personality and Social Psychology*, *95*, 810–825.

Clarkson, J. J., Tormala, Z. L. and Rucker, D. D. (2011) Cognitive and affective matching effects in persuasion: An amplification perspective. *Personality and Social Psychology Bulletin*, *37*, 1415–1427.

Clarkson, J. J., Tormala, Z. L., Rucker, D. D. and Dugan, R. G. (2013) The malleable influence of social consensus on attitude certainty. *Journal of Experimental Social Psychology*, *49*, 1019–1022.

Clore, G. L. and Schnall, S. (2005) The influence of affect on attitude. In D. Albarracín, B. T. Johnson and M. P. Zanna (eds), *The Handbook of Attitudes* (pp. 437–489). Mahwah, NJ: Erlbaum.

Cohen, G. L., Aronson, J. and Steele, C. M. (2000) When beliefs yield to evidence: Reducing biased evaluation by affirming the self. *Personality and Social Psychology Bulletin*, *26*, 1151–1164.

Conner, M. and Armitage, C. J. (2009) Attitudinal ambivalence. In W. Crano and R. Prislin (eds), *Attitudes and Persuasion* (pp. 261–286). New York: Psychology Press.

Conner, M. and Norman, P. (2005) *Predicting Health Behaviour: Research and Practice with Social Cognition Models* (2nd edn). Maidenhead: Open University Press.

Conner, M. and Sparks, P. (2002) Ambivalence and attitudes. *European Review of Social Psychology*, *12*, 37–70.

Conner, M., Lawton, R., Parker, D., Chorlton, K., Manstead, A. S. R. and Stradling, S. (2007) Application of the Theory of Planned Behaviour to the prediction of objectively assessed breaking of posted speed limits. *British Journal of Psychology*, *98*, 429–453.

Conway, M. and Dubé, L. (2002) Humor in persuasion on threatening topics: Effectiveness is a function of audience sex role orientation. *Personality and Social Psychology Bulletin*, *28*, 863–873.

Cook, T. D. and Flay, B. R. (1978) The persistence of experimentally induced attitude change. In L. Berkowitz (ed.), *Advances in Experimental Social Psychology* (Vol. 11, pp. 1–57). San Diego, CA: Academic Press.

Cook, T. D., Gruder, C. L., Hennigan, K. M. and Flay, B. R. (1979) History of the sleeper effect: Some logical pitfalls in accepting the null hypothesis. *Psychological Bulletin*, *86*, 662–679.

Cooke, L. J., Chambers, L. C., Añez, E. V. and Wardle, J. (2011) Facilitating or undermining? The effect of reward on food acceptance: A narrative review. *Appetite*, *57*, 493–497.

Cooke, R. and Sheeran, P. (2004) Moderation of cognition-intention and cognition-behaviour relations: A meta-analysis of properties of variables from the theory of planned behaviour. *British Journal of Social Psychology 43*, 159–186.

Cooper, J. and Fazio, R. H. (1984) A new look at dissonance theory. In L. Berkowitz (ed.), *Advances in Experimental Social Psychology* (Vol. 17, pp. 229–266). San Diego, CA: Academic Press.

Corner, A. and Hahn, U. (2009) Evaluating science arguments: Evidence, uncertainty, and argument strength. *Journal of Experimental Psychology: Applied*, *15*, 199–212.

Corr, P. J. (2008) Reinforcement sensitivity theory (RST): Introduction. In P. J. Corr (ed.), *The Reinforcement Sensitivity Theory of Personality* (pp. 1–43). Cambridge: Cambridge University Press.

Correll, J., Park, B., Judd, C. M. and Wittenbrink, B. (2002) The police officer's dilemma: Using ethnicity to disambiguate potentially threatening individuals. *Journal of Personality and Social Psychology*, *83*, 1314–1329.

Correll, J., Park, B., Judd, C. M., Wittenbrink, B., Sadler, M. S. and Keesee, T. (2007) Across the thin blue line: Police officers and racial bias in the decision to shoot. *Journal of Personality and Social Psychology*, *92*, 1006–1023.

Correll, J., Spencer, S. J. and Zanna, M. P. (2004) An affirmed self and an open mind: Self-affirmation and sensitivity to argument strength. *Journal of Experimental Social Psychology*, *40*, 350–356.

Costa, P. T. and McCrae, R. R. (1992) *Revised NEO Personality Inventory (NEO-PI-R) and NEO Five-Factor Inventory (NEO-FFI) Professional Manual*. Odessa, FL: Psychological Assessment Resources.

Craik, F. I. M. (2002) Levels of processing: Past, present and future. *Memory, 10*, 305–318.

Craik, F. I. M. and Lockhart, R. S. (1972) Levels of processing: A framework for memory research. *Journal of Verbal Learning and Verbal Behavior, 11*, 671–684.

Crandall, J. E. (1968) Effects of need for approval and intolerance of ambiguity upon stimulus preference. *Journal of Personality, 36*, 67–83.

Crano, W. D. and Alvaro, E. M. (1998) The context/comparison model of social influence: Mechanisms, structure and linkages that underlie indirect attitude change. *European Review of Social Psychology, 8*, 175–202.

Crano, W. D. and Chen, X. (1998) The leniency contract and persistence of majority and minority influence. *Journal of Personality and Social Psychology, 74*, 1437–1450.

Crano, W. D. and Sivacek, J. (1984) The influence of incentive-aroused ambivalence on overjustification effects in attitude change. *Journal of Experimental Social Psychology, 20*, 137–158.

Critcher, C. and Gilovich, T. (2010) Inferring attitudes from mental behavior. *Personality and Social Psychology Bulletin, 36*, 1255–1266.

Crites, S. L., Fabrigar, L. R. and Petty, R. E. (1994) Measuring the affective and cognitive properties of attitudes: Conceptual and methodological issues. *Personality and Social Psychology Bulletin, 20*, 619–634.

Cryder, C. E., Lerner, J. S., Gross, J. J. and Dahl, R. E. (2008) Misery is not miserly. *Psychological Science, 19*, 525–530.

Cullum, J. and Harton, H. C. (2007) Cultural evolution: Interpersonal influence, issue importance and the development of shared attitudes in college residence halls. *Personality and Social Psychology Bulletin, 33*, 1327–1339.

Cunningham, W. A., Espinet, S. D., DeYoung, C. G. and Zelazo, P. D. (2005) Attitudes to the right – and left: Frontal ERP asymmetries associated with stimulus valence and processing goals. *NeuroImage, 28*, 827–834.

Cunningham, W. A., Haas, I. J. and Jahn, A. (2011) Attitudes. In J. Decety & J. T. Cacioppo (eds), *The Oxford Handbook of Social Neuroscience* (pp. 212–226). New York: Oxford University Press.

Cunningham, W. A., Johnson, M. K., Gatenby, J. C., Gore, J. C. and Banaji, M. R. (2003) Neural components of social evaluation. *Journal of Personality and Social Psychology, 85*, 639–649.

Cunningham, W. A., Packer, D. J., Kesek, A. and Van Bavel, J. J. (2009) Implicit measurement of attitudes: A physiological approach. In R. E. Petty, R. H. Fazio and P. Briñol (eds), *Attitudes: Insights from a New Wave of Implicit Measures* (pp. 485–512). New York: Psychology Press.

Cunningham, W. A., Preacher, K. J. and Banaji, M. R. (2001) Implicit attitude measures: Consistency, stability and convergent validity. *Psychological Science, 12*, 163–170.

Cunningham, W. A., Raye, C. L. and Johnson, M. K. (2004) Implicit and explicit evaluation: fMRI correlates of valence, emotional intensity and control in the processing of attitudes. *Journal of Cognitive Neuroscience, 16*, 1717–1729.

Cunningham, W. A., Van Bavel, J. J. and Johnsen, I. R. (2008) Affective flexibility: Evaluative processing goals shape amygdala activity. *Psychological Science, 19*, 152–160

Cvencek, D., Greenwald, A. G., Brown, A., Gray, N. and Snowden, R. (2010) Faking of the Implicit Association Test is statistically detectable and partly correctable. *Basic and Applied Social Psychology, 32*, 302–314.

Dal Cin, S., Zanna, M. P. and Fong, G. T. (2004) Narrative persuasion and overcoming resistance. In E. Knowles and J. Linn (eds), *Resistance to persuasion* (pp. 175–191). Mahwah, NJ: Erlbaum.

Dale, A. M., Liu, A. K., Fischl, B. R., Buckner, R. L., Belliveau, J. W., Lewine, J. D. and Halgren, E. (2000) Dynamic statistical parametric mapping: Combining fMRI and MEG for high-resolution imaging of cortical activity. *Neuron, 25*, 55–67.

Darke, P. R., Chaiken, S., Bohner, G., Einwiller, S., Erb, H. P. and Hazlewood, J. D. (1998) Accuracy motivation, consensus information and the law of large numbers: Effects on attitude judgment in the absence of argumentation. *Personality and Social Psychology Bulletin, 24,* 1205–1215.

Das, E. E. J., DeWit, J. B. F. and Stroebe, W. (2003) Fear appeals motivate acceptance of action recommendations: Evidence for a positive bias in the processing of persuasive messages. *Personality and Social Psychology Bulletin, 29,* 650–664.

Dasgupta, A. G. and Greenwald, A. G. (2001) Exposure to admired group members reduces automatic intergroup bias. *Journal of Personality and Social Psychology, 81,* 800–814.

Davidson, A. R. and Jaccard, J. J. (1979) Variables that moderate the attitude–behavior relation: Results of a longitudinal survey. *Journal of Personality and Social Psychology, 37,* 1364–1376.

Davis, V. L. and Rusbult, C. E. (2001) Attitude alignment in close relationships. *Journal of Personality and Social Psychology, 81,* 65–84.

De Dreu, C. K. W. (2007) Minority dissent, attitude change and group performance. In A. R. Pratkanis (ed.), *The Science of Social Influence: Advances and Future Progress* (pp. 247–270). New York: Psychology Press.

De Houwer, J. (2001a) A structural and process analysis of the Implicit Association Test. *Journal of Experimental Social Psychology, 37,* 443–451.

De Houwer, J. (2001b) Contingency awareness and evaluative conditioning: When will it be enough? *Consciousness and Cognition, 10,* 550–558.

De Houwer, J. and De Bruycker, E. (2007) The Implicit Association Test outperforms the Extrinsic Affective Simon Task as a measure of interindividual differences in attitudes. *British Journal of Social Psychology, 46,* 401–421.

De Houwer, J., Baeyens, F. and Field, A. P. (2005) Associative learning of likes and dislikes: Some current controversies and possible ways forward. *Cognition & Emotion, 19,* 161–174.

De Houwer, J., Beckers, T. and Moors, A. (2007) Novel attitudes can be faked on the Implicit Association Test. *Journal of Experimental Social Psychology, 43,* 972–978.

De Houwer, J., Hendrickx, H. and Baeyens, F. (1997) Evaluative learning with 'subliminally' presented stimuli. *Consciousness and Cognition, 6,* 87–107.

De Houwer, J., Teige-Mocigemba, S., Spruyt, A. and Moors, A. (2009) Implicit measures: A normative analysis and review. *Psychological Bulletin, 135,* 347–368.

De Houwer, J., Thomas, S. and Baeyens, F. (2001) Associative learning of likes and dislikes: A review of 25 years of research on human evaluative conditioning. *Psychological Bulletin, 127,* 853–869.

de Liver, Y., van der Pligt, J. and Wigboldus, D. (2007) Positive and negative associations underlying ambivalent attitudes. *Journal of Experimental Social Psychology, 43,* 319–326.

De Vries, N. K. and De Dreu, C. K. W. (2001) Group consensus and minority influence: Introduction and overview. In C. K. W. De Dreu and N. K. De Vries (eds), *Group Consensus and Minority Influence: Implications for Innovation* (pp. 1–14). Malden, MA: Blackwell.

de Zilva, D., Mitchell, C. J. and Newell, B. R. (2013) Eliminating the mere exposure effect through changes in context between exposure and test. *Cognition & Emotion, 27*, 1345–1358.

DeBono, K. G. (1987) Investigating the social adjustive and value expressive functions of attitudes: Implications for persuasion processes. *Journal of Personality and Social Psychology, 52*, 279–287.

DeBono, K. G. (2000) Attitude functions and consumer psychology: Understanding perceptions of product quality. In G. R. Maio and J. M. Olson (eds), *Why We Evaluate: Functions of Attitudes* (pp. 195–222). Mahwah, NJ: Erlbaum.

Decety, J. and Jackson, P. L. (2004) The functional architecture of human empathy. *Behavioral and Cognitive Neuroscience Reviews, 3*, 71–100.

Dechêne, A., Stahl, C., Hansen, J. and Wänke, M. (2009) Mix me a list: Context moderates the truth effect and the mere exposure effect. *Journal of Experimental Social Psychology, 45*, 1117–1122.

DeMarree, K. G., Wheeler, C. S., Briñol, P. and Petty, R. E. (2014). Wanting other attitudes: Actual-desired attitude discrepancies predict feelings of ambivalence and ambivalence consequences. *Journal of Experimental Social Psychology, 53*, 5–18.

DeSteno, D., Petty, R. E., Rucker, D. D., Wegener, D. T. and Braverman, J. (2004) Discrete emotions and persuasion: The role of emotion-induced expectancies. *Journal of Personality and Social Psychology, 86*, 43–56.

Deutsch, M. and Gerard, H. B. (1955) A study of normative and informational influences upon individual judgment. *Journal of Abnormal and Social Psychology, 51*, 629–636.

Devine, P. G. Forscher, P. S., Austin, A. J. and Cox, W. T. L. (2012) Long-term reduction in implicit race bias: A prejudice habit-breaking intervention. *Journal of Experimental Social Psychology, 48*, 1267–1278.

DeWall, C. N., Visser, P. S. and Levitan, L. C. (2006) Openness to attitude change as a function of temporal perspective. *Personality and Social Psychology Bulletin, 32*, 1010–1023.

Dhont, K., Van Hiel, A., Pattyn, S., Onraet, E. and Severens, E. (2012) A step into the anarchist's mind: Examining political attitudes and ideology through event-related brain potentials. *Social Cognitive and Affective Neuroscience, 7*, 296–303.

Dickerson, C., Thibodeau, R., Aronson, E. and Miller, D. (1992) Using cognitive dissonance to encourage water conservation. *Journal of Applied Social Psychology, 22*, 841–854.

Ditto, P. H., Munro, G. D., Apanovitch, A. M., Scepansky, J. A. and Lockhart, L. K. (2003) Spontaneous skepticism: The interplay of motivation and expectation in responses to favorable and unfavorable medical diagnoses. *Personality and Social Psychology Bulletin, 29*, 1120–1132.

Dotsch, R., Wigboldus, D. H. J. and van Knippenberg, A. (2011) Biased allocation of faces to social categories. *Journal of Personality and Social Psychology, 100*, 999–1014.

Dovidio, J. F., Kawakami, K., Johnson, C., Johnson, B. and Howard, A. (1997) On the nature of prejudice: Automatic and controlled processes. *Journal of Experimental Social Psychology, 33*, 510–540.

Dulany, D. E. (1961) Hypotheses and habits in verbal operant conditioning. *Journal of Abnormal and Social Psychology*, *63*, 251–263.

Eagly, A. H. (1992) Uneven progress: Social psychology and the study of attitudes. *Journal of Personality and Social Psychology*, *63*, 693–710.

Eagly, A. H. and Chaiken, S. (1993) *The Psychology of Attitudes*. Fort Worth, TX: Harcourt Brace Jovanovich.

Eagly, A. H. and Chaiken, S. (1998) Attitude structure and function. In D. T. Gilbert, S. T. Fiske and G. Lindzey (eds), *The Handbook of Social Psychology* (4th edn, Vol. 1, pp. 269–322). New York: McGraw-Hill.

Eagly, A. H. and Chaiken, S. (2007) The advantages of an inclusive definition of attitude. *Social Cognition*, *25*, 582–602.

Eagly, A. H., Chen, S., Chaiken, S. and Shaw-Barnes, K. (1999) The impact of attitudes on memory: An affair to remember. *Psychological Bulletin*, *125*, 64–89.

Eagly, A. H., Mladinic, A. and Otto, S. (1994) Cognitive and affective bases of attitudes toward social groups and social policies. *Journal of Experimental Social Psychology*, *30*, 113–137.

Eastwick, P. W., Eagly, A. H., Finkel, E. J. and Johnson, S. E. (2011) Implicit and explicit preferences for physical attractiveness in a romantic partner: A double dissociation in predictive validity. *Journal of Personality and Social Psychology*, *101*, 993–1011.

Eaton, A. A., Majka, E. A. and Visser, P. S. (2008) Emerging perspectives on the structure and function of attitude strength. *European Review of Social Psychology*, *19*, 165–201.

Eaton, A. A., Visser, P. S., Krosnick, J. A. and Anand, S. (2009) Social power and attitude strength over the life course. *Personality and Social Psychology Bulletin*, *35*, 1646–1660.

Eaves, L. J., Eysenck, H. J. and Martin, N. G. (1989) *Genes, Culture and Personality*. London: Academic Press.

Edwards, K. (1990) The interplay of affect and cognition in attitude formation and change. *Journal of Personality and Social Psychology*, *59*, 202–216.

Edwards, K. and von Hippel, W. (1995) Hearts and minds: The priority of affective and cognitive factors in person perception. *Personality and Social Psychology Bulletin*, *21*, 996–1011.

Effron, D. A. and Miller, D. T. (2012) How the moralization of issues grants social legitimacy to act on one's attitudes. *Personality and Social Psychology Bulletin*, *38*, 690–701.

Egan, L. C., Bloom, P. and Santos, L. R. (2010) The origins of cognitive dissonance evidence from children and monkeys. *Journal of Experimental Social Psychology*, *46*, 204–207.

Egan, L. C., Santos, L. R. and Bloom, P. (2007) Choice induced preferences in the absence of choice. *Psychological Science*, *18*, 978–983.

Eisenstadt, D., Leippe, M. R., Stambush, M. A., Rauch, S. M. and Rivers, J. A. (2005) Dissonance and prejudice: Personal costs, choice, and change in attitudes and racial beliefs following counterattitudinal advocacy that benefits a minority. *Basic and Applied Social Psychology*, *27*, 127–141.

Eiser, J. R. (1994) *Attitudes, Chaos, and the Connectionist Mind*. Oxford: Blackwell.

Eiser, J. R., Shook, N. J. and Fazio, R. H. (2007) Attitude learning through exploration: Advice and strategy appraisals. *European Journal of Social Psychology*, *37*, 1046–1056.

Ekman, P. and Friesen, W. V. (1986) A new pan-cultural expression of emotion. *Motivation and Emotion*, *10*, 159–168.

Ekman, P., Levenson, R. W. and Friesen, W. V. (1983) Autonomic nervous system activity distinguishes between emotions. *Science*, *221*, 1208–1210.

Elms, A. C. (1975) The crisis of confidence in social psychology. *American Psychologist*, *30*, 967–976.

Ennis, R. and Zanna, M. P. (2000) Attitude function and the automobile. In G. R. Maio and J. M. Olson (eds), *Why We Evaluate: Functions of Attitude* (pp. 395–415). Mahwah, NJ: Erlbaum.

Epton, T. and Harris, P. R. (2008) Self-affirmation promotes health behavior change. *Health Psychology*, *74*, 746–752.

Esses, V. M. and Maio, G. R. (2002) Expanding the assessment of attitude components and structure: The benefits of open-ended measures. In W. Stroebe and M. Hewstone (eds), *European Review of Social Psychology* (Vol. 12, pp. 71–102). Chichester: Wiley.

Esses, V. M., Haddock, G. and Zanna, M. P. (1993) Values, stereotypes and emotions as determinants of intergroup attitudes. In D. M. Mackie and D. L. Hamilton (eds), *Affect, Cognition and Stereotyping: Interactive Processes in Group Perception* (pp. 137–166). New York: Academic Press.

Fabrigar, L. R. and Petty, R. E. (1999) The role of affective and cognitive bases of attitudes in susceptibility to affectively and cognitively based persuasion. *Personality and Social Psychology Bulletin*, *25*, 363–381.

Fabrigar, L. R., Petty, R. E., Smith, S. M. and Crites, S. L. (2006) Understanding knowledge effects on attitude-behavior consistency: The role of relevance, complexity and amount of knowledge. *Journal of Personality and Social Psychology*, *90*, 556–577.

Fazio, R. H. (1990) Multiple processes by which attitudes guide behavior: The MODE model as an integrative framework. In M. P. Zanna (ed.), *Advances in Experimental Social Psychology* (Vol. 23, pp. 75–109), San Diego, CA: Academic Press.

Fazio, R. H. (1995) Attitudes as object-evaluation associations: Determinants, consequences and correlates of attitude accessibility. In R. E. Petty and J. A. Krosnick (eds), *Attitude Strength: Antecedents and Consequences* (pp. 247–282). Hillsdale, NJ: Erlbaum.

Fazio, R. H. (2000) Accessible attitudes as tools for object appraisal: Their costs and benefits. In G. R. Maio and J. M. Olson (eds), *Why We Evaluate: Functions of Attitudes* (pp. 1–36). Mahwah, NJ: Erlbaum.

Fazio, R. H. (2007) Attitudes as object-evaluation associations of varying strength. *Social Cognition*, *25*, 603–637.

Fazio, R. H. and Olson, M. A. (2003) Implicit measures in social cognition research: Their meaning and use. *Annual Review of Psychology*, *54*, 297–327.

Fazio, R. H. and Williams, C. J. (1986) Attitude accessibility as a moderator of the attitude-perception and attitude-behavior relations: An investigation of the 1984 presidential election. *Journal of Personality and Social Psychology*, *51*, 505–514.

Fazio, R. H., Effrein, E. A. and Falender, V. J. (1981) Self-perceptions following social interaction. *Journal of Personality and Social Psychology*, *41*, 232–242.

Fazio, R. H., Eiser, J. R. and Shook, N. J. (2004) Attitude formation through exploration: Valence asymmetries. *Journal of Personality and Social Psychology*, *87*, 293–311.

Fazio, R. H., Jackson, J. R., Dunton, B. C. and Williams, C. J. (1995) Variability in automatic activation as an unobtrusive measure of racial attitudes: A bona fide pipeline? *Journal of Personality and Social Psychology*, *69*, 1013–1027.

Fazio, R. H., Sanbonmatsu, D. M., Powell, M. C. and Kardes, F. R. (1986) On the automatic activation of attitudes. *Journal of Personality and Social Psychology*, 50, 229–238.

Fazio, R. H., Zanna, M. P. and Cooper, J. (1977) Dissonance and self-perception: An integrative view of each theory's proper domain of application. *Journal of Experimental Social Psychology*, *13*, 464–479.

Festinger, L. (1951) Architecture and group membership. *Journal of Social Issues*, *7*, 152–163.

Festinger, L. (1957) *A Theory of Cognitive Dissonance*. Evanston, IL: Row, Peterson.

Festinger, L. (1964) *Conflict, Decision and Dissonance*. Stanford, CA: Stanford University Press.

Festinger, L. and Carlsmith, J. M. (1959) Cognitive consequences of forced compliance. *Journal of Abnormal and Social Psychology*, *58*, 203–210.

Festinger, L., Schachter, S. and Back, K. W. (1950) *Social Pressures in Informal Groups: A Study of Human Factors in Housing*. New York: Harper.

Fiedler, K. (1991) On the task, the measures and the mood in research on affect and social cognition. In J. P. Forgas (ed.), *Emotion and Social Judgements* (pp. 83–104). New York: Pergamon.

Fielding, K. S., Terry, D. J., Masser, B. M. and Hogg, M. A. (2008) Integrating social identity theory and the theory of planned behaviour to explain decisions to engage in sustainable agricultural practices. *British Journal of Social Psychology*, *47*, 23–48.

Finlay, K. A., Trafimow, D. and Villareal, A. (2002) Predicting exercise and health behavioral intentions: Attitudes, subjective norms, and other behavioral determinants. *Journal of Applied Social Psychology*, *32*, 342–358.

Fischer, P. (2011) Selective exposure, decision uncertainty and cognitive economy: A new theoretical perspective on confirmatory information search. *Social and Personality Psychology Compass*, *5*, 751–762.

Fishbein, M. and Ajzen, I. (1975) *Belief, Attitude, Intention and Behavior: An Introduction to Theory and Research*. Reading, MA: Addison-Wesley.

Fishbein, M. and Ajzen, I. (1981) Acceptance, yielding and impact: Cognitive responses to message content. In R. E. Petty, T. M. Ostrom and T. C. Brock (eds), *Cognitive Responses in Persuasion*. Hillsdale, NJ: Erlbaum.

Fiske, S. T. and Taylor, S. E. (2008) *Social Cognition: From Brains to Culture*. New York: McGraw-Hill.

Fitzsimons, G. M. and Bargh, J. A. (2003) Thinking of you: Nonconscious pursuit of interpersonal goals associated with relationship partners. *Journal of Personality and Social Psychology*, *84*, 148–164.

Forgas, J. P. (1992) On bad mood and peculiar people: Affect and person typicality in impression formation. *Journal of Personality and Social Psychology*, *62*, 863–875.

Forgas, J. P. (1995) Mood and judgement: The affect infusion model (AIM). *Psychological Bulletin*, *117*, 39–66.

Forgas, J. P. and Bower, G. H. (1987) Mood effects on person perception judgements. *Journal of Personality and Social Psychology*, *53*, 53–60.

Forgas, J. P. and Moylan, S. J. (1987) After the movies: Transient mood and social judgments. *Personality and Social Psychology Bulletin, 13*, 467–477.

Freedman, J. L. (1965) Long-term behavioral effects of cognitive dissonance. *Journal of Experimental Social Psychology, 1*, 145–155.

Freedman, J. L. and Fraser, S. (1966) Compliance without pressure: The foot-in-the-door technique. *Journal of Personality and Social Psychology, 4*, 195–202.

Freedman, J. L. and Sears, D. O. (1965) Selective exposure. In L. Berkowitz (ed.), *Advances in Experimental Social Psychology* (Vol. 2, pp. 57–97). New York: Academic Press.

Freedman, J. L., Cunningham, J. A. and Krismer, K. (1992) Inferred values and the reverse-incentive effect in induced compliance. *Journal of Personality and Social Psychology 62*, 357–368.

French, J. R. P. J. and Raven, B. H. (1959) The bases of social power. In D. Cartwright (ed.), *Studies in Social Power* (pp. 150–167). Ann Arbor, MI: University of Michigan Press.

Freud, A. (1966) *The Ego and the Mechanisms of Defense* (revised edn). New York: International Universities Press.

Frey, D. (1986) Recent research on selective exposure to information. In L. Berkowitz (ed.), *Advances in Experimental Social Psychology* (Vol. 19, pp. 41–80). San Diego, CA: Academic Press.

Fried, C. B. (1998) Hypocrisy and identification with transgressions: A case of undetected dissonance. *Basic and Applied Social Psychology, 20*, 145–154.

Fried, C. B. and Aronson, E. (1995) Hypocrisy, misattribution and dissonance reduction. *Personality and Social Psychology Bulletin, 21*, 925–933.

Friestad, M. and Wright, P. (1999) Everyday persuasion knowledge. *Psychology and Marketing, 16*, 185–194.

Froming, W. J., Walker, G. R. and Lopyan, K. J. (1982) Public and private self-awareness: When personal attitudes conflict with societal expectations. *Journal of Experimental Social Psychology, 18*, 476–487.

Gaes, G. G., Kalle, R. J. and Tedeschi, J. T. (1978) Impression management in the forced compliance situation. *Journal of Experimental Social Psychology, 14*, 493–510.

Gaffney, A. M., Hogg, M. A., Cooper, J. and Stone, J. (2012) Witness to hypocrisy: Reacting to ingroup hypocrites in the presence of others. *Social Influence, 7*, 98–112.

Galdi, S., Gawronski, B., Arcuri, L. and Friese, M. (2012) Selective exposure in decided and undecided individuals: Differential relations to automatic associations and conscious beliefs. *Personality and Social Psychology Bulletin, 38*, 559–569.

Garcia, S. M., Weaver, K., Moscowitz, G. B. and Darley, J. M. (2002) Crowded minds: The implicit bystander effect. *Journal of Personality and Social Psychology, 83*, 843–853.

Garner, R. (2005) Post-it Note persuasion: A sticky influence. *Journal of Consumer Psychology, 15*, 230–237.

Gawronski, B. (2012) Back to the future of dissonance theory: Cognitive consistency as a core motive. *Social Cognition, 30*, 652–668.

Gawronski, B. and Bodenhausen, G. V. (2006) Associative and propositional processes in evaluation: An integrative review of implicit and explicit attitude change. *Psychological Bulletin, 132*, 692–731.

Gawronski, B. and Cesario, J. (2013) Of mice and men: What animal research can tell us about context effects on automatic responses in humans. *Personality and Social Psychology Review*, *17*, 187–215.

Gawronski, B. and Walther, E. (2012) What do memory data tell us about the role of contingency awareness in evaluative conditioning? *Journal of Experimental Social Psychology*, *48*, 617–623.

Gawronski, B. and Ye, Y. (2014) What drives priming effects in the affect misattribution procedure? *Personality and Social Psychology Bulletin*, *40*, 3–15.

Gawronski, B., Bodenhausen, G. V. and Becker, A. P. (2007) I like it, because I like myself: Associative self-anchoring and post-decisional change of implicit evaluations. *Journal of Experimental Social Psychology*, *43*, 221–232.

Gebauer, J. E., Maio, G. R. and Pakizeh, A. (2013) Feeling torn when everything feels right: Semantic incongruence causes felt ambivalence. *Personality and Social Psychology Bulletin*, *39*, 777–791.

Gebauer, J. E., Riketta, M., Broemer, P. and Maio, G. R. (2008) "How much do you like your name?" An implicit measure of global self-esteem. *Journal of Experimental Social Psychology*, *44*, 1346–1354.

Gerend, M. A. and Sias, T. (2009) Message framing and color priming: How subtle threat cues affect persuasion. *Journal of Experimental Social Psychology*, *45*, 999–1002.

Gerrig, R. J. (1993) *Experiencing Narrative Worlds: On the Psychological Activities of Reading*. New Haven, CT: Yale University Press.

Gerull, F. C. and Rapee, R. M. (2002) Mother knows best: Effects of maternal modeling on the acquisition of fear and avoidance behaviour in toddlers. *Behavior Research and Therapy*, *40*, 279–287.

Gilbert, D. T. and Ebert, J. E. J. (2002) Decisions and revisions: The affective forecasting of changeable outcomes. *Journal of Personality and Social Psychology*, *82*, 503–514.

Gilbert, D. T., Tafarodi, R. W. and Malone, P. S. (1993) You can't not believe everything you read. *Journal of Personality and Social Psychology*, *65*, 221–233.

Gillig, P. and Greenwald, A. G. (1974) Is it time to lay the sleeper effect to rest? *Journal of Personality and Social Psychology*, *29*, 132–139.

Giner-Sorolla, R. (1999) Affect in attitude: Immediate and deliberative perspectives. In S. Chaiken and Y. Trope (eds), *Dual Process Theories in Social Psychology* (pp. 441–461). New York: Guilford.

Giner-Sorolla, R. (2001) Guilty pleasures and grim necessities: Affective attitudes in dilemmas of self-control. *Journal of Personality and Social Psychology*, *80*, 206–221.

Givler, R. C. (1921) The intellectual significance of the grasping reflex. *Journal of Philosophy*, *18*, 617–629.

Glasman, L. R. and Albarracín, D. (2006) Forming attitudes that predict future behavior: A meta-analysis of the attitude–behavior relation. *Psychological Bulletin*, *132*, 778–822.

Gluszek, A. and Dovidio, J. F. (2010) Speaking with a non-native accent: Perceptions of bias, communication difficulties and belonging in the US. *Journal of Language and Social Psychology*, *29*, 224–234.

Godin, G., Conner, M. and Sheeran, P. (2005) Bridging the intention-behavior 'gap': The role of moral norm. *British Journal of Social Psychology*, *44*, 497–512.

Goel, S., Mason, W. and Watts, D. J. (2010) Real and perceived attitude agreement in social networks. *Journal of Personality and Social Psychology*, *99*, 611–621.

Goethals, G. R. and Zanna, M. P. (1979) The role of social comparison in choice shifts. *Journal of Personality and Social Psychology*, *37*, 1469–1476.

Goldstein, N. J. and Cialdini, R. B. (2007) The spyglass self: A model of vicarious self-perception. *Journal of Personality and Social Psychology*, *92*, 402–417.

Gollwitzer, P. M. (1999) Implementation intentions: Strong effects of simple plans. *American Psychologist*, *54*, 493–503.

Gollwitzer, P. M. and Brandstätter, V. (1997) Implementation intentions and effective goal pursuit. *Journal of Personality and Social Psychology*, *73*, 186–199.

Gollwitzer, P. M. and Sheeran, P. (2006) Implementation intentions and goal achievement: A meta-analysis of effects and processes. In M. P. Zanna (ed.), *Advances in Experimental Social Psychology* (Vol. 38, pp. 249–268). San Diego, CA: Academic Press.

Gorassini, D. R. and Olson, J. M. (1995) Does self-perception change explain the foot-in-the-door effect? *Journal of Personality and Social Psychology*, *69*, 91–105.

Gordijn, E. H., De Vries, N. K. and De Dreu, C. K. W. (2002) Minority influence on focal and related attitudes: Change in size, attributions and information processing. *Personality and Social Psychology Bulletin*, *28*, 1315–1326.

Gordon, P. C. and Holyoak, K. J. (1983) Implicit learning and generalization of the 'mere exposure' effect. *Journal of Personality and Social Psychology*, *45*, 492–500.

Gosling, P., Denizeau, M. and Oberlé, D. (2006) Denial of responsibility: A new mode of dissonance reduction. *Journal of Personality and Social Psychology*, *90*, 722–733.

Gosling, S. D., Rentfrow, P. J. and Swann, W. B. (2003) A very brief measure of the Big-Five personality domains. *Journal of Research in Personality*, *37*, 504–528.

Granberg, D. and Brent, E. E. (1974) Dove-hawk placements in the 1968 election: Application of social judgment and balance theories. *Journal of Personality and Social Psychology*, *29*, 687–695.

Green, M. C. and Brock, T. C. (2000) The role of transportation in the persuasiveness of public narratives. *Journal of Personality and Social Psychology*, *79*, 701–721.

Greenwald, A. G. (1968) Cognitive learning, cognitive response to persuasion and attitude change. In A. G. Greenwald, T. C. Brock and T. A. Ostrom (eds), *Psychological Foundations of Attitudes* (pp. 147–170). New York: Academic Press.

Greenwald, A. G. (1969) The open-mindedness of the counterattitudinal role player *Journal of Experimental Social Psychology*, *5*, 375–388.

Greenwald, A. G. and Banaji, M. R. (1995) Implicit social cognition: Attitudes, self-esteem, and stereotypes. *Psychological Review*, *102*, 4–27.

Greenwald, A. G. and Farnham, S. D. (2000) Using the Implicit Association Test to measure self-esteem and self-concept. *Journal of Personality and Social Psychology*, *79*, 1022–1038.

Greenwald, A. G., McGhee, D. and Schwartz, J. (1998) Measuring individual differences in implicit cognition: The Implicit Association Test. *Journal of Personality and Social Psychology*, *74*, 1464–1480.

Greenwald, A. G., Nosek, B. A. and Banaji, M. R. (2003) Understanding and using the Implicit Association Test: I. An improved scoring algorithm. *Journal of Personality and Social Psychology, 85,* 197–216.

Greenwald, A. G., Poehlman, T. A., Uhlmann, E. and Banaji, M. R. (2009) Understanding and using the Implicit Association Test: III. Meta-analysis of predictive validity. *Journal of Personality and Social Psychology, 97,* 17–41.

Gruder, C. L., Cook, T. D., Hennigan, K. M., Flay, B. R. and Halamaj, J. (1978) Empirical tests of the absolute sleeper effect predicted from the discounting cue hypothesis. *Journal of Personality and Social Psychology, 36,* 1061–1074.

Haddock, G. and Gebauer, J. E. (2011) Defensive self-esteem impacts attention, attitude strength, and self-affirmation processes. *Journal of Experimental Social Psychology, 47,* 1276–1284.

Haddock, G. and Huskinson, T. L. H. (2004) Individual differences in attitude structure. In G. Haddock and G. R. Maio (eds), *Contemporary Perspectives on the Psychology of Attitudes* (pp. 35–56). Hove: Psychology Press.

Haddock, G., & Maio, G. R. (eds) (2012) *Psychology of Attitudes: Key Readings.* London: SAGE.

Haddock, G. and Zanna, M. P. (1997) Impact of negative advertising on evaluations of political leaders: The 1993 Canadian federal election. *Basic and Applied Social Psychology, 19,* 205–223.

Haddock, G. and Zanna, M. P. (1998) On the use of open-ended measures to assess attitudinal components. *British Journal of Social Psychology, 37,* 129–149.

Haddock, G., Maio, G. R., Arnold, K. and Huskinson, T. (2008) Should persuasion be affective or cognitive? The moderating effects of need for affect and need for cognition. *Personality and Social Psychology Bulletin, 34,* 769–778.

Haddock, G., Newson, M. and Haworth, J. (2011) Do memory-impaired individuals report stable attitudes? *British Journal of Social Psychology, 50,* 234–245.

Haddock, G., Rothman, A. J., Reber, R. and Schwarz, N. (1999) Forming judgments of attitude certainty, intensity and importance: The role of subjective experiences. *Personality and Social Psychology Bulletin, 25,* 770–781.

Haddock, G., Zanna, M. P. and Esses, V. M. (1993) Assessing the structure of prejudicial attitudes: The case of attitudes toward homosexuals. *Journal of Personality and Social Psychology, 65,* 1105–1118.

Haddock, G., Zanna, M. P. and Esses, V. M. (1994a) Mood and the expression of intergroup attitudes: The moderating role of affect intensity. *European Journal of Social Psychology, 24,* 189–205.

Haddock, G., Zanna, M. P. and Esses, V. M. (1994b) The (limited) role of trait-based stereotypes in predicting attitudes toward Native Peoples. *British Journal of Social Psychology, 33,* 83–106.

Haemmerlie, F. M. and Montgomery, R. L. (1982) Self-perception theory and unobtrusively biased interactions: A treatment for heterosexual anxiety. *Journal of Counseling Psychology, 29,* 362–370.

Hafer, C. L., Reynolds, K. L. and Obertynski, M. A. (1996) Message comprehensibility and persuasion: Effects of complex language in counterattitudinal appeals to laypeople. *Social Cognition, 14,* 317–337.

Hagger, M. S., Chatzisarantis, N. L. D. and Harris, J. (2006) From psychological need satisfaction to intentional behavior: Testing a motivational sequence in two behavioral contexts. *Personality and Social Psychology Bulletin*, *32*, 131–148.

Hahn, U. and Oaksford, M. (2007) The rationality of informal argumentation: A Bayesian approach to reasoning fallacies. *Psychological Review*, *114*, 704–732.

Haidt, J., Koller, S. H. and Dias, M. G. (1993) Affect, culture and morality, or is it wrong to eat your dog? *Journal of Personality and Social Psychology*, *65*, 613–628.

Hamilton, D. L. and Zanna, M. P. (1974) Context effects in impression formation: Changes in connotative meaning. *Journal of Personality and Social Psychology*, *29*, 649–654.

Han, H. A., Czellar, S., Olson, M. A. and Fazio, R. H. (2010) Malleability of attitudes or malleability of the IAT? *Journal of Experimental Social Psychology*, *46*, 286–298.

Han, H. A., Olson, M. A. and Fazio, R. H. (2006) The influence of experimentally-created extrapersonal associations on the Implicit Association Test. *Journal of Experimental Social Psychology*, 42, 259–272.

Handley, I. M. and Runnion, B. M. (2011) Evidence that unconscious thinking influences persuasion based on argument quality. *Social Cognition*, *29*, 668–682.

Hansen, J. and Wänke, M. (2009) Liking what is familiar: The importance of unconscious processes. *Social Cognition*, *27*, 161–182.

Happe, F., Ehlers, S., Fletcher, P., Frith, U., Johansson, M., Gillberg, C., Dolan, R., Frackowiak, R. and Frith, C. (1996) "Theory of mind" in the brain: Evidence from a PET scan study of Asperger syndrome. *NeuroReport*, *8*, 197–201.

Harmon-Jones, C., Schmeichel, B. J., Inzlicht, M. and Harmon-Jones, E. (2011) Trait approach motivation relates to dissonance reduction. *Social Psychological and Personality Science*, *2*, 21–28.

Harmon-Jones, E. and Allen, J. J. B. (2001) The role of affect in the mere exposure effect: Evidence from psychophysiological and individual differences approaches. *Personality and Social Psychology Bulletin*, *27*, 889–898.

Harmon-Jones, E. and Harmon-Jones, C. (2002) Testing the action-based model of cognitive dissonance: The effect of action orientation on post-decisional attitudes. *Personality and Social Psychology Bulletin*, *28*, 711–723.

Harmon-Jones, E. and Mills, J. (1999) An introduction to cognitive dissonance theory and an overview of current perspectives on the theory. In E. Harmon-Jones and J. Mills (eds), *Cognitive Dissonance: Progress on a Pivotal Theory in Social Psychology* (pp. 3–21). Washington, DC: American Psychological Association.

Harmon-Jones, E., Amodio, D. M. and Harmon-Jones, C. (2009) Action-based model of dissonance. *Advances in Experimental Social Psychology*, *41*, 119–166.

Harmon-Jones, E., Brehm, J. W., Greenberg, J., Simon, L. and Nelson, D. E. (1996) Evidence that the production of aversive consequences is not necessary to create cognitive dissonance. *Journal of Personality and Social Psychology*, *70*, 5–16.

Harmon-Jones, E., Harmon-Jones, C., Fearn, M., Sigelman, J. D. and Johnson, P. (2008) Left frontal cortical activation and spreading of alternatives: Tests of the action-based model of dissonance. *Journal of Personality and Social Psychology*, *94*, 1–15.

Harmon-Jones, E., Harmon-Jones, C., Serra, R. and Gable, P. A. (2011) The effect of commitment on relative left frontal cortical activity: Tests of the action-based model of dissonance. *Personality and Social Psychology Bulletin*, *37*, 395–408.

Harris, P. R. and Napper, L. (2005) Self-affirmation and the biased processing of threatening health-risk information. *Personality and Social Psychology Bulletin*, *31*, 1250–1263.

Hart, W., Albarracín, D., Eagly, A. H., Brechan, I., Lindberg, M. J. and Merrill, L. (2009) Feeling validated versus being correct: A meta-analysis of selective exposure to information. *Psychological Bulletin*, *135*, 555–588.

Hastorf, A. H. and Cantril, H. (1954) They saw a game: A case study. *Journal of Abnormal and Social Psychology*, *49*, 129–134.

Heesacker, M. H., Petty, R. E. and Cacioppo, J. T. (1983) Field dependence and attitude change: Source credibility can alter persuasion by affecting message-relevant thinking. *Journal of Personality*, *51*, 653–666.

Heider, F. (1946) Attitudes and cognitive organization. *Journal of Psychology*, *21*, 107–112.

Heider, F. (1958) *The Psychology of Interpersonal Relations*. New York: Wiley.

Heine, S. J. and Lehman, D. R. (1997) Culture, dissonance and self-affirmation. *Personality and Social Psychology Bulletin*, *23*, 389–400.

Henninger, M. and Wyer, R. S. (1976) The recognition and elimination of inconsistencies among syllogistically related beliefs: Some new light on the 'Socratic effect.' *Journal of Personality and Social Psychology*, *34*, 680–693.

Hepler, J. and Albarraćin, D. (2013) Attitudes without objects: Evidence for a dispositional attitude, its measurement and its consequences. *Journal of Personality and Social Psychology*, *104*, 1060–1076.

Herbert, C., Ethofer, T., Anders, S., Junghöfer, M., Wildgruber, D., Grodd, W. and Kissler, J. (2009) Amygdala activation during reading of emotional adjectives: An advantage for pleasant content. *Social Cognitive and Affective Neuroscience*, *4*, 35–49.

Herek, G. M. (1986) The instrumentality of attitudes: Toward a neofunctional theory. *Journal of Social Issues*, *42*, 99–114.

Herek, G. M. (1987) Can functions be measured? A new perspective on the functional approach to attitudes. *Social Psychology Quarterly*, *50*, 285–303.

Herek, G. M. (2000) The social construction of attitudes: Functional consensus and divergence in the US public's reactions to AIDS. In G. Maio and J. Olson (eds), *Why We Evaluate: Functions of Attitudes* (pp. 325–364). Mahwah, NJ: Erlbaum.

Heyman, J. and Ariely, D. (2004) Effort for payment: A tale of two markets. *Psychological Science*, *15*, 787–793.

Himmelfarb, S. (1993) The measurement of attitudes. In A. H. Eagly and S. Chaiken, *The Psychology of Attitudes*. Fort Worth, TX: Harcourt Brace Jovanovich.

Hirsh, J. B., Kang, S. K. and Bodenhausen, G. V. (2012) Personalized persuasion: Tailoring persuasive appeals to recipient personality traits. *Psychological Science*, *23*, 578–581.

Hogg, M. A. and Smith, J. R. (2007) Attitudes in social context: A social identity perspective. *European Journal of Social Psychology*, *18*, 89–131.

Holbrook, A. L. and Krosnick, J. A. (2005) Meta-psychological vs. operative measures of ambivalence: Differentiating the consequences of perceived intra-psychic conflict and real intra-psychic conflict. In S. C. Craig and M. D. Martinez (eds), *Ambivalence and the Structure of Public Opinion*. New York: Palgrave Macmillan.

Holbrook, A. L., Berent, M. K., Krosnick, J. A., Visser, P. S. and Boninger, D. S. (2005) Attitude importance and the accumulation of attitude-relevant knowledge in memory. *Journal of Personality and Social Psychology*, *88*, 749–769.

Holland, R., Aarts, H. and Langendam, D. (2006) Breaking and creating habits on the working floor: A field-experiment on the power of implementation intentions. *Journal of Experimental Social Psychology*, *42*, 776–783.

Holland, R., Verplanken, B. and van Knippenberg, A. (2002) On the nature of attitude-behavior relations: The strong guide, the weak follow. *European Journal of Social Psychology*, *32*, 869–876.

Horcajo, J., Petty, R. E. and Briñol, P. (2010) The effects of majority versus minority source status on persuasion: A self-validation analysis. *Journal of Personality and Social Psychology*, *99*, 498–512.

Hoshino-Browne, E., Zanna, A. S., Spencer, S. J. and Zanna, M. P. (2004) Investigating attitudes cross-culturally: A case of cognitive dissonance among East Asians and North Americans. In G. Haddock and G. R. Maio (eds), *Contemporary Perspectives on the Psychology of Attitudes*. London: Psychology Press.

Houston, D. A. and Fazio, R. H. (1989) Biased processing as a function of attitude accessibility: Making objective judgments subjectively. *Social Cognition*, *7*, 51–66.

Hovland, C. I. and Weiss, W. (1951) The influence of source credibility on communication effectiveness. *Public Opinion Quarterly*, *15*, 487–518.

Hovland, C. I., Janis, I. L. and Kelley, H. H. (1953) *Communication and Persuasion: Psychological Studies of Opinion Change*. New Haven, CT: Yale University Press.

Hovland, C. I., Lumsdaine, A. A. and Sheffield, F. D. (1949) *Experiments on Mass Communication*. Princeton, NJ: Princeton University Press.

Howard, D. J. and Kerin, R. A. (2011) The effects of name similarity on message processing and persuasion. *Journal of Experimental Social Psychology*, *47*, 63–71.

Huberman, G. (2001) Familiarity breeds investment. *The Review of Financial Studies*, *14*, 659–680.

Hume, D. (1985[1739]) *Treatise of Human Nature*. London: Penguin.

Huntsinger, J. R. (2013) Narrowing down to the automatically activated attitude: A narrowed conceptual scope improves correspondence between implicitly and explicitly measured attitudes. *Journal of Experimental Social Psychology*, *49*, 132–137.

Huskinson, T. L. and Haddock, G. (2004) Individual differences in attitude structure: Variance in the chronic reliance on affective and cognitive information. *Journal of Experimental Social Psychology*, *40*, 83–90.

Hynie, M., MacDonald, T. K. and Marques, S. (2006) Self-conscious emotions and self-regulation in the promotion of condom use. *Personality and Social Psychology Bulletin*, *32*, 1072–1084.

Insko, C. A. (1965) Verbal reinforcement of attitude. *Journal of Personality and Social Psychology*, *2*, 621–623.

Insko, C. A. (1984) Balance theory, the Jordan paradigm and the Wiest tetrahedron. In L. Berkowitz (ed.), *Advances in Experimental Social Psychology* (Vol. 18, pp. 89–140). San Diego, CA: Academic Press.

Insko, C. A. and Butzine, K. W. (1967) Rapport, awareness and verbal reinforcement of attitude. *Journal of Personality and Social Psychology*, *6*, 225–228.

Insko, C. A. and Cialdini, R. B. (1969) A test of three interpretations of attitudinal verbal reinforcement. *Journal of Personality and Social Psychology*, *12*, 333–341.

Isen, A. M., Shalker, T. E., Clark, M. and Karp, L. (1978) Affect, accessibility of material in memory and behavior: A cognitive loop? *Journal of Personality and Social Psychology*, *36*, 1–12.

Isenberg, D. J. (1986) Group polarization: A critical review and meta-analysis. *Journal of Personality and Social Psychology*, *50*, 1141–1151.

Ito, T. A., Larsen, J. T., Smith, N. K. and Cacioppo, J. T. (1998) Negative information weighs more heavily on the brain: The negativity bias in evaluative categorizations. *Journal of Personality and Social Psychology*, *75*, 887–900.

Jacobson, R. P., Mortensen, C. R. and Cialdini, R. B. (2011) Bodies obliged and unbound: Differentiated response tendencies for injunctive and descriptive social norms. *Journal of Personality and Social Psychology*, *100*, 433–448.

Jamieson, D. W. and Zanna, M. P. (1989) Need for structure in attitude formation and expression. In A. G. Greenwald, A. R. Pratkanis and S. J. Breckler (eds), *Attitude Structure and Function* (pp. 383–406). Hillsdale, NJ: Erlbaum.

Janis, I. L. and Feshbach, S. (1953) Effects of fear-arousing communications. *Journal of Abnormal Social Psychology*, *48*, 78–92.

Janis, I. L. and Gilmore, J. B. (1965) The influence of incentive conditions on the success of role-playing in modifying attitudes. *Journal of Personality and Social Psychology*, *1*, 17–27.

Janis, I. L. and King, B. T. (1954) The influence of role playing on opinion change. *Journal of Abnormal and Social Psychology*, *49*, 211–218.

Janis, I. L. and Mann, L. (1965) Effectiveness of emotional role-playing in modifying smoking habits and attitudes. *Journal of Experimental Research in Personality*, *1*, 84–90.

Johar, G. V. and Sengupta, J. (2002) The effects of dissimulation on the accessibility and predictive power of weakly held attitudes. *Social Cognition*, *20*, 257–293.

Johnson, A. L., Crawford, M. T., Sherman, S. J., Rutchick, A. M., Hamilton, D. L., Ferreira, M. B. and Petrocelli, J. V. (2006) A functional perspective on group memberships: Differential need fulfillment in a group typology. *Journal of Experimental Social Psychology*, *42*, 707–719.

Johnson, B. T. and Eagly, A. H. (1989) Effects of involvement on persuasion: A meta-analysis. *Psychological Bulletin*, *106*, 290–314.

Johnson, B. T. and Eagly, A. H. (1990) Involvement and persuasion: Types, traditions and the evidence. *Psychological Bulletin*, *107*, 375–384.

Johnson, B. T., Lin, H., Symons, C. S., Campbell, L. A. and Ekstein, G. (1995) Initial beliefs and attitudinal latitudes as factors in persuasion. *Personality and Social Psychology Bulletin*, *21*, 502–511.

Johnson, R. W., Kelly, R. J. and LeBlanc, B. W. (1995) Motivational basis of dissonance: Aversive consequences or inconsistency. *Personality and Social Psychology Bulletin, 21*, 850–855.

Jonas, E., Schulz-Hardt, S., Frey, D. and Thelen, N. (2001) Confirmation bias in sequential information search after preliminary decisions: An expansion of dissonance theoretical research on selective exposure to information. *Journal of Personality and Social Psychology, 80*, 557–571.

Jonas, K., Diehl, M. and Broemer, P. (1997) Effects of attitudinal ambivalence on information processing and attitude-intention consistency. *Journal of Experimental Social Psychology, 33*, 190–210.

Jones, C. R., Fazio, R. H. and Olson, M. A. (2009) Implicit misattribution as a mechanism underlying evaluative conditioning. *Journal of Personality and Social Psychology, 96*, 933–948.

Jones, C. R., Olson, M. A. and Fazio, R. H. (2010) Evaluative conditioning: The 'How' question. In M. P. Zanna and J. M. Olson (eds), *Advances in Experimental Social Psychology* (Vol. 43, pp. 205–255). San Diego, CA: Academic Press.

Jones, E. E., Rock, L., Shaver, K. G., Goethals, G. E. and Ward, L. M. (1968) Pattern of performance and ability attribution: An unexpected primacy effect. *Journal of Personality and Social Psychology, 10*, 317–340.

Jordan, C. H. and Zanna, M. P. (1999) How to read a journal article in social psychology. In R. F. Baumeister (ed.), *The Self in Social Psychology* (pp. 461–470). Philadelphia, PA: Psychology Press. Available at http://arts.uwaterloo.ca/~sspencer/psych253/readart.html (accessed May 20, 2014).

Jordan, C. H., Logel, C., Spencer, S. J., Zanna, M. P. and Whitfield, M. L. (2009) The heterogeneity of self-esteem: Exploring the interplay between implicit and explicit self-esteem. In R. E. Petty, R. H. Fazio and P. Briñol (eds), *Attitudes: Insights from the New Implicit Measures* (pp. 251–281). New York: Psychology Press.

Jost, J. T. (2006) The end of the end of ideology. *American Psychologist, 61*, 651–670.

Judd, C. M. and Kulik, J. A. (1980) Schematic effects of social attitudes on information processing and recall. *Journal of Personality and Social Psychology, 38*, 569–578.

Kahle, L. R. and Homer, P. M. (1985) Physical attractiveness of the celebrity endorser: A social adaptation perspective. *Journal of Consumer Research, 11*, 954–961.

Kanai, R., Feilden, T., Firth, C. and Rees, G. (2011) Political orientations are correlated with brain structure in young adults. *Current Biology, 21*, 677–680.

Kaplan, K. J. (1972) On the ambivalence-indifference problem in attitude theory and measurement: A suggested modification of the semantic differential technique. *Psychological Bulletin, 77*, 361–372.

Karmarkar, U. R. and Tormala, Z. L. (2010) Believe me, I have no idea what I'm talking about: The effects of source certainty on consumer involvement and persuasion. *Journal of Consumer Research, 46*, 1033–1049.

Karpinski, A. and Hilton, J. L. (2001) Attitudes and the implicit association test. *Journal of Personality and Social Psychology, 81*, 774–788.

Karpinski, A. and Steinman, R. B. (2006) The single category implicit association test as a measure of implicit social cognition. *Journal of Personality and Social Psychology, 91*, 16–32.

Karremans, J. C., Stroebe, W. and Claus, J. (2006) Beyond Vicary's fantasies: The impact of subliminal priming and brand choice. *Journal of Experimental Social Psychology*, *42*, 792–798.

Katz, D. (1960) The functional approach to the study of attitudes. *Public Opinion Quarterly*, *24*, 163–204.

Katz, D. and Stotland, E. (1959) A preliminary statement to a theory of attitude structure and change. In S. Koch (ed.), *Psychology: A Study of a Science* (Vol. 3, pp. 423–475). New York: McGraw-Hill.

Kaufman, G. and Uhlenberg, P. (1998) Effects of life course transitions on the quality of relationships between adult children and their parents. *Journal of Marriage and the Family*, *60*, 924–938.

Kaufman, G. F. and Libby, L. K. (2012) Changing beliefs and behavior through experience-taking. *Journal of Personality and Social Psychology*, *103*, 1–19.

Kelman, H. C. and Hovland, C. I. (1953) 'Reinstatement' of the communicator in delayed measurement of opinion change. *Journal of Abnormal and Social Psychology*, *48*, 327–335.

Keltner, D. and Lerner, J. S. (2010) Emotion. In D. T. Gilbert, S. T. Fiske and G. Lindsay (eds), *The Handbook of Social Psychology* (5th edn, pp. 312–347). New York: McGraw-Hill.

Kempf, D. S. (1999) Attitude formation from product trial: Distinct roles of cognition and affect for hedonic and functional products. *Psychology and Marketing*, *16*, 35–50.

Killeya, L. A. and Johnson, B. T. (1998) Experimental induction of biased systematic processing: The directed thought technique. *Personality and Social Psychology Bulletin*, *24*, 17–33.

Kitayama, S., Snibbe, A. C., Markus, H. R. and Suzuki, T. (2004) Is there any 'free' choice? Self and dissonance in two cultures. *Psychological Science*, *15*, 527–533.

Klauer, K. C. and Mierke, J. (2005) Task-set inertia, attitude accessibility and compatibility-order effects: New evidence for a task-set switching account of the IAT effect. *Personality and Social Psychology Bulletin*, *31*, 208–217.

Klauer, K. C., Voss, A., Schmitz, F. and Teige-Mocigemba, S. (2007) Process components of the Implicit Association Test: A diffusion-model analysis. *Journal of Personality and Social Psychology*, *93*, 353–368.

Knobloch-Westerwick, S. and Meng, J. (2009) Looking the other way: Selective exposure to attitude-consistent and counterattitudinal political information. *Communication Research*, *36*, 426–448.

Knowles, E. D., Lowery, B. S. and Schaumberg, R. L. (2010) Racial prejudice predicts opposition to Obama and his health care reform plan. *Journal of Experimental Social Psychology*, *46*, 420–423.

Knutson, K. M., Wood, J. N., Spampinato, M. V. and Grafman, J. (2006) Politics on the brain: An fMRI investigation. *Social Cognitive and Affective Neuroscience*, *1*, 25–40.

Koole, S. L., Dijksterhuis, A. and van Knippenberg, A. (2001). What's in a name: Implicit self-esteem and the automatic self. *Journal of Personality and Social Psychology*, *80*, 1–17.

Kraus, S. J. (1995) Attitudes and the prediction of behavior: A meta-analysis of the empirical literature. *Personality and Social Psychology Bulletin*, *21*, 58–75.

Krizan, Z., Miller, J. C. and Johar, O. (2010) Wishful thinking in the 2008 U.S. presidential election. *Psychological Science*, *21*, 140–146.

Krosnick, J. A. and Petty, R. E. (1995) Attitude strength: An overview. In R. E. Petty and J. A. Krosnick (eds), *Attitude Strength: Antecedents and Consequences* (pp. 1–24). Hillsdale, NJ: Erlbaum.

Krosnick, J. A., Betz, A. L., Jussim, L. J. and Lynn, A. R. (1992) Subliminal conditioning of attitudes. *Personality and Social Psychology Bulletin, 18*, 152–162.

Krosnick, J. A., Boninger, D. S., Chuang, Y. C., Berent, M. K. and Carnot, C. G. (1993) Attitude strength: One construct or many related constructs? *Journal of Personality and Social Psychology, 65*, 1132–1151.

Krosnick, J. A, Judd, C. M. and Wittenbrink, B. (2005) Attitude measurement. In D. Albarracín, B. T. Johnson and M. P. Zanna (eds), *Handbook of Attitudes and Attitude Change*. Mahwah, NJ: Erlbaum.

Kruglanski, A. W. (2013) Only one? The default interventionist perspective as a unimodel: Commentary on Evans and Stanovich. *Perspectives on Psychological Science, 8*, 242–247.

Kruglanski, A. W. and Gigerenzer, G. (2011) Intuitive and deliberative judgments are based on common principles. *Psychological Review, 118*, 97–109.

Kruglanski, A. W. and Mackie, D. M. (1991) Majority and minority influence: A judgmental process analysis. *European Review of Social Psychology, 1*, 229–261.

Kruglanski, A. W. and Stroebe, W. (2005) The influence of beliefs and goals on attitudes: Issues of structure, function and dynamics. In D. Albarracín, B. T. Johnson and M. P. Zanna (eds), *The Handbook of Attitudes* (pp. 323–368). Mahwah, NJ: Erlbaum.

Kruglanski, A. W. and Thompson, E. P. (1999) Persuasion by a single route: A view from the unimodel. *Psychological Inquiry, 10*, 83–109.

Kruglanski, A. W., Fishbach, A., Erb, H., Pierro, A. and Mannetti, L. (2004) The parametric unimodel as a theory of persuasion. In G. Haddock and G. R. Maio (eds), *Contemporary Perspectives on the Psychology of Attitudes* (pp. 399–422). New York: Psychology Press.

Kruglanski, A. W., Shah, J. Y., Fishbach, A., Friedman, R., Chun, W. Y. and Sleeth-Keppler, D. (2002) A theory of goal systems. In M. P. Zanna (ed.), *Advances in Experimental Social Psychology* (Vol. 34, pp. 331–378). San Diego, CA: Academic Press.

Kumkale, G. T. and Albarracín, D. (2004) The sleeper effect in persuasion: A meta-analytic review. *Psychological Bulletin, 130*, 143–172.

Kumkale, G. T., Albarracín, D. and Seignourel, P. J. (2010) The effects of source credibility in the presence or absence of prior attitudes: Implications for the design of persuasive communication campaigns. *Journal of Applied Social Psychology, 40*, 1325–1356.

Kunda, Z. (1987) Motivated inference: Self-serving generation and evaluation of causal theories. *Journal of Personality and Social Psychology, 53*, 636–647.

Kunda, Z. (1990) The case for motivated reasoning. *Psychological Bulletin, 108*, 480–498.

Kunst-Wilson, W. R. and Zajonc, R. B. (1980) Affective discrimination of stimuli that cannot be recognized. *Science, 207*, 557–558.

LaPiere, R. (1934) Attitudes versus actions. *Social Forces, 13*, 230–237.

Larsen, R. J. and Diener, E. (1987) Affect intensity as an individual difference characteristic: A review. *Journal of Research in Personality, 21*, 1–39.

Lasswell, H. D. (1948) The structure and function of communication in society. In L. Bryson (ed.), *The Communication of Ideas: Religion and Civilization Series* (pp. 37–51). New York: Harper and Row.

LaTour, M. S. and Ford, J. (2006) Retrospective and prospective views of 'fear arousal' in 'fear appeals'. *International Journal of Advertising, 25*, 409–413.

LaTour, M. S. and Rotfeld, H. J. (1997) There are threats and (maybe) fear-caused arousal: Theory and confusions of appeals to fear and fear arousal itself. *Journal of Advertising, 26*, 45–59.

Lau-Gesk, L. G. (2003) Activating culture through persuasion appeals: An examination of the bicultural consumer. *Journal of Consumer Psychology, 13*, 301–315.

Lavine, H. and Snyder, M. (1996) Cognitive processing and the functional matching effect in persuasion: The mediating role of subjective perceptions of message quality. *Journal of Experimental Social Psychology, 32*, 580–604.

Lavine, H., Thomsen, C. J., Zanna, M. P. and Borgida, E. (1998) On the primacy of affect in the determination of attitudes and behavior: The moderating role of affective-cognitive ambivalence. *Journal of Experimental Social Psychology, 34*, 398–421.

Lawrence, D. H. and Festinger, L. (1962) *Deterrents and Reinforcement: The Psychology of Insufficient Reward*. Stanford, CA: Stanford University Press.

Lawton, R., Conner, M. and Parker, D. (2007) Beyond cognition: Predicting health risk behaviors from instrumental and affective beliefs. *Health Psychology, 26*, 259–267.

Lazarus, R. S. (1982) Thoughts on the relations between emotions and cognition. *American Psychologist, 37*, 1019–1024.

Lee, A. Y. (2001) The mere exposure effect: An uncertainty reduction explanation revisited. *Personality and Social Psychology Bulletin, 27*, 1255–1266.

Légal, J., Chappé, J., Coiffard, V. and Villard-Forest, A. (2011) Don't you know that you want to trust me? Subliminal goal priming and persuasion. *Journal of Experimental Social Psychology, 48*, 358–360.

Legault, L., Gutsell, J. N. and Inzlicht, M. (2011) Ironic effects of antiprejudice messages: How motivational interventions can reduce (but also increase) prejudice. *Psychological Science, 22*, 1472–1477.

Lepper, M. R., Greene, D. and Nisbett, R. E. (1973) Undermining children's intrinsic interest with extrinsic reward: A test of the 'overjustification' hypothesis. *Journal of Personality and Social Psychology, 28*, 129–137.

Lerner, J. S., Small, D. A. and Loewenstein, G. (2004). Heart strings and purse strings. Carryover effects of emotions on economic decisions. *Psychological Science, 15*(5), 337–341.

Lieberman, M. D., Ochsner, K. N., Gilbert, D. T. and Schacter, D. L. (2001) Do amnesics exhibit cognitive dissonance reduction? The role of explicit memory and attention in attitude change. *Psychological Science, 12*, 135–140.

Likert, R. (1932) A technique for the measurement of attitudes. *Archives of Psychology, 140*, 5–53.

Lipkus, I. M., Green, J. D., Feaganes, J. R. and Sedikides, C. (2001) The relationship between attitudinal ambivalence and desire to quit smoking among college smokers. *Journal of Applied Social Psychology, 31*, 113–133.

Litt, A., Khan, U. and Shiv, B. (2010) Lusting while loathing: Parallel counterdriving of wanting and liking. *Psychological Science, 21*, 118–125.

Litvak, S. B. (1969) Attitude change by stimulus exposures. *Psychological Reports, 25*, 391–396.

Livingston, R. W. (2001) What you see is what you get: Systematic variability in perceptual-based social judgment. *Personality and Social Psychology Bulletin, 27*, 1086–1096.

Loersch, C., Durso, G. R. O. and Petty, R. E. (2013) Vicissitudes of desire: A matching mechanism for subliminal persuasion. *Social Psychological and Personality Science, 4*, 624–631.

Loersch, C., McCaslin, M. J. and Petty, R. E. (2011) Exploring the impact of social judgeability concerns on the interplay of associative and deliberative attitude processes. *Journal of Experimental Social Psychology, 47*, 1029–1032.

Loewenstein, G. F., Weber, E., Hsee, C. K. and Welch, N. (2001) Risk as feelings. *Psychological Bulletin, 127*, 267–286.

Lord, C. G., Ross, L. and Lepper, M. R. (1979) Biased assimilation and attitude polarization: The effects of prior theories on subsequently recalled evidence. *Journal of Personality and Social Psychology, 37*, 2098–2109.

Lowery, B. S., Hardin, C. D. and Sinclair, S. (2001) Social influence on automatic racial prejudice. *Journal of Personality and Social Psychology, 81*, 842–855.

Luescher, K. and Pillemar, K. (1998) Intergenerational ambivalence: A new approach to the study of parent–child relations in later life. *Journal of Marriage and Family, 60*, 413–445.

Lundgren, S. and Prislin, R. (1998) Motivated cognitive processing and attitude change. *Personality and Social Psychology Bulletin, 24*, 715–726.

Luttrell, A., Briñol, P., Petty, R. E., Cunningham, W. and Diaz, D. (2013) Metacognitive confidence: A neuroscience approach. *Revista de Psicología Social, 28*, 317–332.

Lydall, E. S., Gilmour, G. and Dwyer, D. M. (2010) Rats place greater value on rewards produced by high effort: An animal analogue of the 'effort justification' effect. *Journal of Experimental Social Psychology, 46*, 1134–1137.

Lyvers, M. F., Cholakians, E., Puorro, M. and Sundram, S. (2011) Alcohol intoxication and self-reported risky sexual behaviour intentions with highly attractive strangers in naturalistic settings. *Journal of Substance Use, 16*, 99–108.

Ma, Y., Yang, S. and Han, S. (2011) Attitudes influence implicit racial face categorization in a perceptual task. *Group Processes & Intergroup Relations, 14*, 887–899.

MacDonald, T. K. and Zanna, M. P. (1998) Cross-dimension ambivalence toward social groups: Can ambivalence affect intentions to hire feminists? *Personality and Social Psychology Bulletin, 24*, 427–441.

MacDonald, T. K., MacDonald, G., Zanna, M. P. and Fong, G. T. (2000) Alcohol, sexual arousal and intentions to use condoms in young men: Applying alcohol myopia theory to risky sexual behavior. *Health Psychology, 19*, 290–298.

MacDonald, T. K., Zanna, M. P. and Fong, G. T. (1995) Decision-making in altered states: The effects of alcohol on attitudes toward drinking and driving. *Journal of Personality and Social Psychology, 68*, 973–985.

Maddux, J. E. and Rogers, R. W. (1983) Protection motivation and self-efficacy: A revised theory of fear appeals and attitude change. *Journal of Experimental Social Psychology, 19*, 469–479.

Mahajan, N., Martinez, M. A., Gutierrez, N. L., Diesendruck, G., Banaji, M. R. and Santos, L. R. (2011) The evolution of intergroup bias: Perceptions and attitudes in rhesus macaques. *Journal of Personality and Social Psychology*, *100*, 387–405.

Maio, G. R. and Esses, V. M. (2001) The need for affect: Individual differences in the motivation to approach or avoid emotions. *Journal of Personality*, *69*, 583–616.

Maio, G. R. and Haddock, G. (2004) Theories of attitude: Creating a witches' brew. In G. Haddock and G. R. Maio (eds), *Contemporary Perspectives on the Psychology of Attitudes* (pp. 425–453). Hove: Psychology Press.

Maio, G. R. and Haddock, G. (2007) Attitude change. In A. W. Kruglanski and E. T. Higgins (eds), *Social Psychology: Handbook of Basic Principles* (2nd edn, pp. 565–586). New York: Guilford Press.

Maio, G. R. and Olson, J. M. (1995a) Relations between values, attitudes and behavioral intentions: The moderating role of attitude function. *Journal of Experimental Social Psychology*, *31*, 266–285.

Maio, G. R. and Olson, J. M. (1995b) The effect of attitude dissimulation on attitude accessibility. *Social Cognition*, *13*, 127–144.

Maio, G. R. and Olson, J. M. (1998a) Attitude dissimulation and persuasion. *Journal of Experimental Social Psychology*, *34*, 182–201.

Maio, G. R. and Olson, J. M. (1998b) Values as truisms: Evidence and implications. *Journal of Personality and Social Psychology*, *74*, 294–311.

Maio, G. R. and Olson, J. M. (2000a) Emergent themes and potential approaches to attitude function: The function-structure model of attitudes. In G. R. Maio and J. M. Olson (eds), *Why We Evaluate: Functions of Attitudes* (pp. 417–442). Mahwah, NJ: Erlbaum.

Maio, G. R. and Olson, J. M. (2000b) What is a 'value-expressive' attitude? In G. R. Maio and J. M. Olson (eds), *Why We Evaluate: Functions of Attitudes* (pp. 249–269). Mahwah, NJ: Erlbaum.

Maio, G. R. and Olson, J. M. (eds) (2000c) *Why We Evaluate: Functions of Attitudes*. Mahwah, NJ: Erlbaum.

Maio, G. R., Bell, D. W. and Esses, V. M. (1996) Ambivalence and persuasion: The processing of messages about immigrant groups. *Journal of Experimental Social Psychology*, *32*, 513–536.

Maio, G. R., Esses, V. M., Arnold, K. and Olson, J. M. (2004) The function-structure model of attitudes: Incorporating the need for affect. In G. Haddock and G. R. Maio (eds), *Contemporary Perspectives on the Psychology of Attitudes* (pp. 7–34). New York: Psychology Press.

Maio, G. R., Esses, V. M. and Bell, D. W. (2000) Examining conflict between components of attitudes: Ambivalence and inconsistency are distinct constructs. *Canadian Journal of Behavioural Science*, *32*, 58–70.

Maio, G. R., Haddock, G., Valle, C., Huskinson, T. and Bernard, M. M. (2014). *Using the Component Facilitation Test to examine the psychological components of social values*. Unpublished manuscript.

Maio, G. R., Haddock, G., Watt, S. E., Hewstone, M. and Rees, K. J. (2009) Implicit measures and applied contexts: An illustrative examination of anti-racism advertising. In R. E. Petty, R. H. Fazio and P. Brinol (eds), *Attitudes: Insights from the New Wave of Implicit Measures*. Mahwah, NJ: Psychology Press.

Maio, G. R., Verplanken, B., Manstead, A. S. R., Stroebe, W., Abraham, C. S., Sheeran, P. and Conner, M. (2007). Social psychological factors in lifestyle change and their relevance to policy. *Journal of Social Issues and Policy Review*, *1*, 99–137.

Manstead, A. S. R. and van Eekelen, S. A. M. (1998) Distinguishing between perceived behavioral control and self-efficacy in the domain of academic achievement intentions and behaviors. *Journal of Applied Social Psychology*, *28*, 1375–1392.

Markus, H. R. and Kitayama, S. (1991) Culture and self: Implications for cognition, emotion and motivation. *Psychological Review*, *98*, 224–253.

Marsh, E. J. and Fazio, L. K. (2006) Learning errors from fiction: Difficulties in reducing reliance on fictional stories. *Memory and Cognition*, *34*, 1140–1149.

Marsh, E. J., Mead, L. M. and Roediger, H. L. III (2003) Learning facts from fiction. *Journal of Memory and Language*, *49*, 519–536.

Marsh, K. L. and Julka, D. L. (2000) A motivational approach to experimental tests of attitude functions theory. In G. R. Maio and J. M. Olson (eds), *Why We Evaluate: Functions of Attitudes* (pp. 271–294). Mahwah, NJ: Erlbaum.

Martin, P. Y., Hamilton, V. E., McKimmie, B. M., Terry, D. J. and Martin, R. (2007) Effects of caffeine on persuasion and attitude change: The role of secondary tasks in manipulating systematic message processing. *European Journal of Social Psychology*, *37*, 320–338.

Martin, P. Y., Laing, J., Martin, R. and Mitchell, M. (2005) Caffeine, cognition and persuasion: Evidence for caffeine increasing the systematic processing of persuasive messages. *Journal of Applied Social Psychology*, *35*, 160–182.

Martin, R. (1998) Majority and minority influence using the afterimage paradigm: A series of attempted replications. *Journal of Experimental Social Psychology*, *34*, 1–26.

Martin, R., Hewstone, M. and Martin, P. Y. (2007) Systematic and heuristic processing of majority- and minority-endorsed messages: The effects of varying outcome relevance and levels of orientation on attitude and message processing. *Personality and Social Psychology Bulletin*, *33*, 43–56.

Martin, R., Martin, P. Y., Smith, J. R. and Hewstone, M. (2007) Majority versus minority influence and prediction of behavioral intentions and behavior. *Journal of Experimental Social Psychology*, *43*, 763–771.

Martinie, M-A., Olive, T., and Milland, L. (2010) Cognitive dissonance induced by writing a counterattitudinal essay facilitates performance on a simple task but not on complex tasks that involve working memory. *Journal of Experimental Social Psychology*, *46*, 587–594.

Masicampo, E. J. and Baumeister, R. F. (2011) Consider it done! Plan making can eliminate the cognitive effects of unfulfilled goals. *Journal of Personality and Social Psychology*, *101*, 667–683.

Matz, D. C. and Wood, W. (2005) Cognitive dissonance in groups: The consequences of disagreement. *Journal of Personality and Social Psychology*, *88*, 22–37.

Mayer, N. D. and Tormala, Z. L. (2010) 'Think' versus 'feel' framing effects in persuasion. *Personality and Social Psychology Bulletin*, *36*, 443–454.

McClelland, D. C. (1985) *Human Motivation*. Glenview, IL: Scott, Foresman.

McConnell, A. R. and Brown, C. M. (2010) Dissonance averted: Self-concept organization moderates the effect of hypocrisy on attitude change. *Journal of Experimental Social Psychology*, *46*, 361–366.

McGregor, I., Newby-Clark, I. R. and Zanna, M. P. (1999) 'Remembering' dissonance: Simultaneous accessibility of inconsistent cognitive elements moderates epistemic discomfort. In E. Harmon-Jones and J. Mills (eds), *Cognitive Dissonance: Perspectives on a Pivotal Theory in Social Psychology* (pp. 325–353). Washington, DC: American Psychological Association.

McGregor, I., Zanna, M. P., Holmes, J. G. and Spencer, S. J. (2001) Compensatory conviction in the face of personal uncertainty: Going to extremes and being oneself. *Journal of Personality and Social Psychology*, *80*, 472–488.

McGuire, W. J. (1960a) Cognitive consistency and attitude change. *Journal of Abnormal and Social Psychology*, *60*, 354–358.

McGuire, W. J. (1960b) Direct and indirect effects of dissonance-producing messages. *Journal of Abnormal and Social Psychology*, *60*, 345–353.

McGuire, W. J. (1964) Inducing resistance to persuasion: Some contemporary approaches. In L. Berkowitz (ed.), *Advances in Experimental Social Psychology* (Vol. 1, pp. 191–229). San Diego, CA: Academic Press.

McGuire, W. J. (1968) Personality and attitude change: An information-processing theory. In A. G. Greenwald, T. C. Brock and T. A. Ostrom (eds), *Psychological Foundations of Attitudes* (pp. 171–196). San Diego, CA: Academic Press.

McGuire, W. J. (1983) A contextualist theory of knowledge: Its implications for innovation and reform in psychological research. In L. Berkowitz (ed.), *Advances in Experimental Social Psychology* (Vol. 16, pp. 1–47). San Diego, CA: Academic Press.

McGuire, W. J. (1985) Attitudes and attitude change. In G. Lindzey and E. Aronson (eds), *Handbook of Social Psychology* (3rd edn, Vol. 2, pp. 233–346). New York: Random House.

McGuire, W. J. (1986) The vicissitudes of attitudes and similar representational constructs in twentieth century psychology. *European Journal of Social Psychology*, *16*, 89–130.

McGuire, W. J. and Papageorgis, D. (1961) The relative efficacy of various types of prior belief defense in producing immunity against persuasion. *Journal of Abnormal and Social Psychology*, *62*, 327–337.

Meissner, F. and Rothermund, K. (2013) Estimating the contributions of associations and recoding in the Implicit Association Test: The ReAL model for the IAT. *Journal of Personality and Social Psychology*, *104*, 45–69.

Mellema, A. and Bassili, J. N. (1995) On the relationship between attitudes and values: Exploring the moderating effects of self-monitoring and self-monitoring schematicity. *Personality and Social Psychology Bulletin*, *21*, 885–892.

Millar, M. G. and Millar, K. U. (1990) Attitude change as a function of attitude type and argument type. *Journal of Personality and Social Psychology*, *59*, 217–228.

Millar, M. G. and Tesser, A. (1986) Thought-induced attitude change: The effects of schema-structure and commitment. *Journal of Personality and Social Psychology*, *51*, 259–269.

Miller, R. C. (1976) Mere exposure, psychological reactance and attitude change. *Public Opinion Quarterly*, *40*, 229–233.

Monahan, J. L., Murphy, S. T. and Zajonc, R. B. (2000) Subliminal mere exposure: Specific, general and diffuse effects. *Psychological Science*, *11*, 462–466.

Moons, W. G. and Mackie, D. M. (2007) Thinking straight while seeing red: The influence of anger on information processing. *Personality and Social Psychology Bulletin*, *33*, 706–720.

Moreland, R. L. and Beach, S. R. (1992) Exposure effects in the classroom: The development of affinity among students. *Journal of Experimental Social Psychology*, *28*, 255–276.

Moreland, R. L. and Topolinski, S. (2010) The mere exposure phenomenon: A lingering melody by Robert Zajonc. *Emotion Review*, *2*, 329–339.

Morwitz, V., Johnson, E. and Schmittlein, D. (1993) Does measuring intent change behavior? *Journal of Consumer Psychology*, *20*, 46–61.

Moscovici, S. (1980) Toward a theory of conversion behavior. In L. Berkowitz (ed.), *Advances in Experimental Social Psychology* (Vol. 13, pp. 209–239). San Diego, CA: Academic Press.

Moscovici, S., Lage, E. and Naffrechoux, M. (1969) Influence of a consistent minority on the responses of a majority in a color perception task. *Sociometry*, *32*, 365–379.

Moscowitz, G. B., Skurnik, I. and Galinsky, A. D. (1999) The history of dual-process notions and the future of preconscious control. In S. Chaiken and Y. Trope (eds), *Dual-process Theories in Social Psychology*. New York: Guilford Press.

Murphy, S. and Zajonc, R. B. (1993) Affect, cognition and awareness: Affective priming with optimal and suboptimal stimulus exposures. *Journal of Personality and Social Psychology*, *64*, 723–739.

Murphy, S. T., Monahan, J. L. and Zajonc, R. B. (1995) Additivity of nonconscious affect: Combined effects of priming and exposure. *Journal of Personality and Social Psychology*, *69*, 589–602.

Murray, H. A. (1938) *Explorations in Personality*. New York: Oxford University Press.

Murray, S. L., Haddock, G. and Zanna, M. P. (1996) On creating value-expressive attitudes: An experimental approach. In C. Seligman, J. M. Olson and M. P. Zanna (eds), *The Psychology of Values: The Ontario Symposium* (Vol. 8, pp. 107–133). Mahwah, NJ: Erlbaum.

Neal, D. T., Wood, W. and Drolet, A. (2013) How do people adhere to goals when willpower is low? The profits (and pitfalls) of strong habits. *Journal of Personality and Social Psychology*, *104*, 959–975.

Neumann, R., Hülsenbeck, K. and Seibt, B. (2004) Attitudes towards people with AIDS and avoidance behavior: Automatic and reflective bases of behavior. *Journal of Experimental Social Psychology*, *40*, 543–550.

Newby-Clark, I. R., McGregor, I. and Zanna, M. P. (2002) Thinking and caring about cognitive inconsistency: When and for whom does attitudinal ambivalence feel uncomfortable? *Journal of Personality and Social Psychology*, *82*, 157–166.

Newcomb, T. M. (1956). The prediction of interpersonal attraction. *American Psychologist*, *11*, 575–586.

Nickerson, D. W. and Rogers, T. (2010) Do you have a voting plan? Implementation intentions, voter turnout and organic plan making. *Psychological Science*, *21*, 194–199.

Nisbett, R. E. and Wilson, T. D. (1977) Telling more than we can know: Verbal report on mental processes. *Psychological Review*, *84*, 231–259.

Nordgren, L. F., van Harreveld, F. and van der Pligt, J. (2006) Ambivalence, discomfort and motivated information processing. *Journal of Experimental Social Psychology*, *42*, 252–258.

Norman, R. (1975) Attitude-cognitive consistency, attitudes, conformity and behavior. *Journal of Personality and Social Psychology, 32*, 83–91.

Norton, M. I., Monin, B., Cooper, J. and Hogg, M. A. (2003) Vicarious dissonance: Attitude change from the inconsistency of others. *Journal of Personality and Social Psychology, 85*, 47–62.

Nosek, B. A. (2007) Implicit–explicit relations. *Current Directions in Psychological Science, 16*, 65–69.

Ochsner, K. N. and Lieberman, M. D. (2001) The emergence of social cognitive neuroscience. *American Psychologist, 56*, 717–734.

Olson, J. M. (1990) Self-inference processes in emotion. In J. M. Olson and M. P. Zanna (eds), *Self-inference Processes: The Ontario Symposium* (Vol. 6, pp. 17–41). Mahwah, NJ: Erlbaum.

Olson, J. M. (1992) Self-perception of humor: Evidence for discounting and augmentation effects. *Journal of Personality and Social Psychology, 62*, 369–377.

Olson, J. M., Goffin, R. D. and Haynes, G. A. (2007) Relative versus absolute measures of explicit attitudes: Implications for predicting diverse attitude-relevant criteria. *Journal of Personality and Social Psychology, 93*, 907–926.

Olson, J. M., Vernon, P. A., Harris, J. A. and Jang, K. (2001) The heritability of attitudes: A study of twins. *Journal of Personality and Social Psychology, 80*, 845–860.

Olson, M. A. and Fazio, R. H. (2001) Implicit attitude formation through classical conditioning. *Psychological Science, 12*, 413–417.

Olson, M. A. and Fazio, R. H. (2002) Implicit acquisition and manifestation of classically conditioned attitudes. *Social Cognition, 20*, 89–104.

Olson, M. A. and Fazio, R. H. (2003) Relations between implicit measures of prejudice: What are we measuring? *Psychological Science, 14*, 36–39.

Olson, M. A. and Fazio, R. H. (2004a) Reducing the influence of extrapersonal associations on the Implicit Association Test: Personalizing the IAT. *Journal of Personality and Social Psychology, 86*, 653–667.

Olson, M. A. and Fazio, R. H. (2004b) Trait inferences as a function of automatically activated racial attitudes and motivation to control prejudiced reactions. *Basic and Applied Social Psychology, 26*, 1–11.

Olson, M. A. and Fazio, R. H. (2006) Reducing automatically activated prejudice through implicit evaluative conditioning. *Personality and Social Psychology Bulletin, 32*, 421–433.

Olson, M. A. and Fazio, R. H. (2009) Implicit and explicit measures of attitudes: The perspective of the MODE model. In Petty, R. E., Fazio, R. H. and Briñol, P. (eds), *Attitudes: Insights from the New Implicit Measures* (pp. 19–64). Mahwah, NJ: Erlbaum.

Oppenheimer, D. M. and Trail, T. E. (2010) Why leaning to the left makes you lean to the left: Effect of spatial orientation on political attitudes. *Social Cognition, 28*, 651–661.

Orbell, S., Hodgkins, S. and Sheeran, P. (1997) Implementation intentions and the theory of planned behavior. *Personality and Social Psychology Bulletin, 23*, 953–962.

Orne, M. T. (1962) On the social psychology of the psychological experiment: With particular reference to demand characteristics and their implications. *American Psychologist, 17*, 776–783.

Ortony, A., Clore, G. L. and Collins, A. (1988) *The Cognitive Structure of Emotions*. Cambridge: Cambridge University Press.

Osgood, C. E., Suci, G. J. and Tannenbaum, P. H. (1957) *The Measurement of Meaning*. Urbana, IL: University of Illinois Press.

Osterhouse, R. A. and Brock, T. C. (1970) Distraction increases yielding to propaganda by inhibiting counterarguing. *Journal of Personality and Social Psychology*, *15*, 344–358.

Oswald, F. L., Mitchell, G., Blanton, H., Jaccard, J. and Tetlock, P. E. (2013) Predicting ethnic and racial discrimination: A meta-analysis of IAT criterion studies. *Journal of Personality and Social Psychology*, *105*, 171–192.

Ottati, V., Fishbein, M. and Middlestadt, S. E. (1988) Determinants of voters' beliefs about the candidates' stands on issues: The role of evaluative bias heuristics and the candidates' expressed message. *Journal of Personality and Social Psychology*, *55*, 517–529.

Ottati, V., Terkildsen, N. and Hubbard, C. (1997) Happy faces elicit heuristic processing in a televised impression formation task: A cognitive tuning account. *Personality and Social Psychology Bulletin*, *23*, 1144–1156.

Ouellette, J. A. and Wood, W. (1998) Habit and intention in everyday life: The multiple processes by which past behavior predicts future behavior. *Psychological Bulletin*, *124*, 54–74.

Oyserman, D., Coon, H. M. and Kemmelmeier, M. (2002) Rethinking individualism and collectivism: Evaluation of theoretical assumptions and meta-analysis. *Psychological Bulletin*, *128*, 3–72.

Paulhus, D. (1982) Individual differences, self-presentation and cognitive dissonance: Their concurrent operation in forced compliance. *Journal of Personality and Social Psychology*, *43*, 838–852.

Paulhus, D. L. and John, O. P. (1998) Egoistic and moralistic biases in self-perception: The interplay of self-deceptive styles with basic traits and motives. *Journal of Personality*, *66*, 1025–1060.

Payne, B. K. (2001) Prejudice and perception: The role of automatic and controlled processes in misperceiving a weapon. *Journal of Personality and Social Psychology*, *81*, 181–192.

Payne, B. K. (2006) Weapon bias: Split second decisions and unintended stereotyping. *Current Directions in Psychological Science*, *15*, 287–291.

Payne, B. K., Burkley, M. A. and Stokes, M. B. (2008) Why do implicit and explicit attitude tests diverge? The role of structural fit. *Journal of Personality and Social Psychology*, *94*, 16–31.

Payne, B. K., Cheng, C. M., Govorun, O. and Stewart, B. D. (2005) An inkblot for attitudes: Affect misattribution as implicit measurement. *Journal of Personality and Social Psychology*, *89*, 277–293.

Payne, B. K., Lambert, A. J. and Jacoby, L. L. (2002) Best laid plans: Effects of goals on accessibility bias and cognitive control in race-based misperceptions of weapons. *Journal of Experimental Social Psychology*, *38*, 384–396.

Payne, B. K., Shimizu, Y. and Jacoby, L. L. (2005) Mental control and visual illusions: Toward explaining race-biased weapon identifications. *Journal of Experimental Social Psychology*, *41*, 36–47.

Pelham, B. W. and Neter, E. (1995) The effect of motivation on judgment depends on the difficulty of the judgment. *Journal of Personality and Social Psychology*, *68*, 581–594.

Perlman, D. and Oskamp, S. (1971) The effects of picture content and exposure frequency on evaluation of Negroes and Whites. *Journal of Experimental Social Psychology*, *7*, 503–514.

Perloff, R. M. (2003) *The Dynamics of Persuasion: Communication and Attitudes in the 21st Century* (2nd edn) Mahwah, NJ: Erlbaum.

Perugini, M. Richetin, J. and Zogmaister, C. (2010) Prediction of behavior. In B. Gawronski and K. Payne (eds), *Handbook of Implicit Social Cognition: Measurement, Theory and Applications* (pp. 255–277). New York: Guilford Press.

Peterson, A. A., Haynes, G. A. and Olson, J. M. (2008) Self-esteem differences in the effects of hypocrisy induction on behavioral intentions in the health domain. *Journal of Personality, 76,* 305–322.

Peterson, R. S. and Nemeth, C. J. (1996) Focus versus flexibility: Majority and minority influence can both improve performance. *Personality and Social Psychology Bulletin, 22,* 14–23.

Petrocelli, J. V., Clarkson, J. J., Tormala, Z. L. and Hendrix, K. S. (2010) Perceiving stability as a means to attitude certainty: The role of implicit theories of attitudes. *Journal of Experimental Social Psychology, 46,* 874–883.

Pettigrew, T. F. and Tropp, L. R. (2006) A meta-analytic test of intergroup contact theory. *Journal of Personality and Social Psychology, 90,* 751–783.

Petty, R. E. and Briñol, P. (2006) A meta-cognitive approach to 'implicit' and 'explicit' evaluations: Comment on Gawronski and Bodenhausen. *Psychological Bulletin, 132,* 740–744.

Petty, R. E. and Briñol, P. (2012) The Elaboration Likelihood Model. In P. A. M. Van Lange, A. Kruglanski and E. T. Higgins (eds), *Handbook of Theories of Social Psychology* (Vol. 1, pp. 224–245). London: SAGE.

Petty, R. E. and Cacioppo, J. T. (1981) *Attitudes and Persuasion: Classic and Contemporary Approaches.* Dubuque, IA: Brown.

Petty, R. E. and Cacioppo, J. T. (1983) The role of bodily responses in attitude measurement and change. In J. T. Cacioppo and R. E. Petty (eds), *Social Psychophysiology: A Sourcebook* (pp. 51–101). New York: Guilford Press.

Petty, R. E. and Cacioppo, J. T. (1984) The effects of involvement on responses to argument quantity and quality: Central and peripheral routes to persuasion. *Journal of Personality and Social Psychology, 46,* 69–81.

Petty, R. E. and Cacioppo, J. T. (1986) The Elaboration Likelihood Model of persuasion. In L. Berkowitz (ed.), *Advances in Experimental Social Psychology* (Vol. 19, pp. 123–205). New York: Academic Press.

Petty, R. E. and Cacioppo, J. T. (1990) Involvement and persuasion: Tradition versus integration. *Psychological Bulletin, 107,* 367–374.

Petty, R. E. and Krosnick, J. A. (eds) (1995) *Attitude Strength: Antecedents and Consequences.* Hillsdale, NJ: Erlbaum.

Petty, R. E. and Wegener, D. T. (1998a) Attitude change: Multiple roles for persuasion variables. In D. T. Gilbert, S. T. Fiske and G. Lindzey (eds), *The Handbook of Social Psychology* (4th edn, Vol. 1, pp. 323–390). Boston, MA: McGraw-Hill.

Petty, R. E. and Wegener, D. T. (1998b) Matching versus mismatching attitude functions: Implications for scrutiny of persuasive messages. *Personality and Social Psychology Bulletin, 24,* 227–240.

Petty, R. E. and Wegener, D. T. (1999) The Elaboration Likelihood Model: Current status and controversies. In S. Chaiken and Y. Trope (eds), *Dual Process Theories in Social Psychology* (pp. 41–72). New York: Guilford Press.

Petty, R. E., Briñol, P. and DeMarree, K. G. (2007) The Meta-Cognitive Model (MCM) of attitudes: Implications for attitude measurement, change and strength. *Social Cognition, 25,* 657–686.

Petty, R. E., Cacioppo, J. T. and Goldman, R. (1981) Personal involvement as a determinant of argument-based persuasion. *Journal of Personality and Social Psychology, 41,* 847–855.

Petty, R. E., Cacioppo, J. T. and Schumann, D. (1983) Central and peripheral routes to advertising effectiveness: The moderating role of involvement. *Journal of Consumer Research, 10,* 135–146.

Petty, R. E., Fabrigar, L. R. and Wegener, D. T. (2003) Emotional factors in attitudes and persuasion. In R. J. Davidson, K. R. Scherer and H. H. Goldsmith (eds), *Handbook of Affective Sciences* (pp. 752–772). Oxford: Oxford University Press.

Petty, R. E., Fazio, R. H. and Briñol, P. (eds) (2009) *Attitudes: Insights from the New Implicit Measures.* New York: Psychology Press.

Petty, R. E., Fleming, M. A. and White, P. H. (1999) Stigmatized sources and persuasion: Prejudice as a determinant of argument scrutiny. *Journal of Personality and Social Psychology, 76,* 19–34.

Petty, R. E., Gleicher, F. and Baker, S. M. (1991) Multiple roles for affect in persuasion. In J. P. Forgas (ed.), *Emotion and Social Judgments* (pp. 181–200). New York: Pergamon.

Petty, R. E., Haugtvedt, C. and Smith, S. M. (1995) Elaboration as a determinant of attitude strength: Creating attitudes that are persistent, resistant and predictive of behavior. In R. E. Petty and J. A. Krosnick (eds), *Attitude Strength: Antecedents and Consequences* (pp. 93–130). Mahwah, NJ: Erlbaum.

Petty, R. E., Schumann, D. W., Richman, S. A. and Strathman, A. J. (1993) Positive mood and persuasion: Different roles for affect under high- and low-elaboration conditions. *Journal of Personality and Social Psychology, 64,* 5–20.

Petty, R. E., Tormala, Z. L., Briñol, P. and Jarvis, W. B. G. (2006) Implicit ambivalence from attitude change: An exploration of the PAST Model. *Journal of Personality and Social Psychology, 90,* 21–41.

Petty, R. E., Wells, G. L. and Brock, T. C. (1976) Distraction can enhance or reduce yielding to propaganda: Thought disruption versus effort justification. *Journal of Personality and Social Psychology, 34,* 874–884.

Petty, R. E., Wells, G. L., Heesacker, M. H., Brock, T. C. and Cacioppo, J. T. (1983) The effects of recipient posture on persuasion: A cognitive response analysis. *Personality and Social Psychology Bulletin, 9,* 209–222.

Petty, R. E., Wheeler, S. C. and Bizer, G. Y. (1999) Is there one persuasion process or more? Lumping versus splitting in attitude change theories. *Psychological Inquiry, 10,* 156–163.

Petty, R. E., Wheeler, S. C. and Bizer, G. Y. (2000) Attitude functions and persuasion: An elaboration likelihood approach to matched versus mismatched messages. In G. R. Maio and J. M. Olson (eds), *Why We Evaluate: Functions of Attitudes* (pp. 133–162). Mahwah, NJ: Erlbaum.

Phelps, E. A. (2006) Emotion and cognition: Insights from studies of the human amygdala. *Annual Review of Psychology*, *24*, 27–53.

Phelps, E. A., O'Connor, K. J., Cunningham, W. A., Funayma, E. S., Gatenby, J. C., Gore, J. C. and Banaji, M. R. (2000) Performance on indirect measures of race evaluation predicts amygdala activity, *Journal of Cognitive Neuroscience*, *12*, 1–10.

Pierro, A., Mannetti, L., Kruglanski, A. W. and Sleeth-Keppler, D. (2004) Relevance override: On the reduced impact of 'cues' under high-motivation conditions of persuasion studies. *Journal of Personality and Social Psychology*, *86*, 251–264.

Pietri, E. S., Fazio, R. H. and Shook, N. J. (2013) Recalibrating positive and negative weighting tendencies in attitude generalization. *Journal of Experimental Social Psychology*, *49*, 1100–1113.

Pillaud, V., Cavazza, N. and Butera, F. (2013) The social value of being ambivalent: Self-presentational concerns in the expression of attitudinal ambivalence. *Personality and Social Psychology Bulletin*, *39*, 1139–1151.

Pomerantz, E. M., Chaiken, S. and Tordesillas, R. S. (1995) Attitude strength and resistance processes. *Journal of Personality and Social Psychology*, *69*, 408–419.

Powell, M. C. and Fazio, R. H. (1984) Attitude accessibility as a function of repeated attitude expression. *Personality and Social Psychology Bulletin*, *10*, 139–148.

Pratkanis, A. R., Greenwald, A. G., Leippe, M. R. and Baumgardner, M. H. (1988) In search of reliable persuasion effects: III. The sleeper effect is dead. Long live the sleeper effect. *Journal of Personality and Social Psychology*, *54*, 203–218.

Prentice, D. A. (1987) Psychological correspondence of possessions, attitudes and values. *Journal of Personality and Social Psychology*, *53*, 993–1003.

Prentice, D. A., Gerrig, R. J. and Bailis, D. S. (1997) What readers bring to the processing of fictional texts. *Psychonomic Bulletin and Review*, *4*, 416–420.

Pretty, G. H. and Seligman, C. (1984) Affect and the overjustification effect. *Journal of Personality and Social Psychology*, *46*, 1241–1253.

Priester, J. R. and Petty, R. E. (1995) Source attribution and persuasion: Perceived honesty as a determinant of message scrutiny. *Personality and Social Psychology Bulletin*, *21*, 637–654.

Priester, J. R. and Petty, R. E. (1996) The gradual threshold model of ambivalence: Relating the positive and negative bases of attitudes to subjective ambivalence. *Journal of Personality and Social Psychology*, *71*, 431–449.

Priester, J. R. and Petty, R. E. (2001) Extending the bases of subjective attitudinal ambivalence: Interpersonal and intrapersonal antecedents of evaluative tension. *Journal of Personality and Social Psychology*, *80*, 19–34.

Priester, J. R. and Petty, R. E. (2003) The influence of spokesperson trustworthiness on message elaboration, attitude strength and advertising effectiveness. *Journal of Consumer Psychology*, *13*, 408–421.

Priester, J. R., Cacioppo, J. T. and Petty, R. E. (1996) The influence of motor processes on attitudes toward novel versus familiar semantic stimuli. *Personality and Social Psychology Bulletin*, *22*, 442–447.

Priester, J. R., Wegener, D., Petty, R. E. and Fabrigar, L. (1999) Examining the psychological process underlying the sleeper effect: The elaboration likelihood model explanation. *Media Psychology, 1*, 27–48.

Prislin, R. and Christiensen, P. N. (2005) Social change in the aftermath of successful minority influence. *European Review of Social Psychology, 16*, 43–73.

Prislin, R. and Pool, G. J. (1996) Behavior, consequences and the self: Is all well that ends well? *Personality and Social Psychology Bulletin, 22*, 933–948.

Prislin, R. and Wood, W. (2005) Social influence in attitudes and attitude change. In D. Albarracín, B. T. Johnson and M. P. Zanna (eds), *The Handbook of Attitudes* (pp. 671–705). Mahwah, NJ: Erlbaum.

Raghunathan, R. and Trope, Y. (2002) Walking the tightrope between feeling good and being accurate: Mood as a resource in processing persuasive messages. *Journal of Personality and Social Psychology, 83*, 510–525.

Razran, G. H. S. (1940) Conditioned response changes in rating and appraising sociopolitical slogans. *Psychological Bulletin, 37*, 481.

Reber, R., Winkielman, P. and Schwarz, N. (1998) Effects of perceptual fluency on affective judgments. *Psychological Science, 29*, 45–48.

Regan, D. T. and Fazio, R. H. (1977) On the consistency between attitudes and behavior: Look to the method of attitude formation. *Journal of Experimental Social Psychology, 13*, 28–45.

Reich, T. and Tormala, Z. L. (2013) When contradictions foster persuasion: An attributional perspective. *Journal of Experimental Social Psychology, 49*, 426–439.

Rhodes, N. and Wood, W. (1992) Self-esteem and intelligence affect influenceability: The mediating role of message reception. *Psychological Bulletin, 111*, 156–171.

Richetin, J., Conner, M. and Perugini, M. (2011) Not doing is not the opposite of doing: Implications for attitudinal models of behavioral prediction. *Personality and Social Psychology Bulletin, 37*, 40–54.

Riketta, M. (2004) *Convergence of Direct and Indirect Measures of Attitudinal Ambivalence: A Meta-analysis.* Unpublished manuscript, University of Tübingen, Germany.

Rips, L. J., Brem, S. K. and Bailenson, J. N. (1999) Reasoning dialogues. *Current Directions in Psychological Science, 8*, 172–177.

Risen, J. L. and Critcher, C. R. (2011) Visceral fit: While in a visceral state, associated states of the world seem more likely. *Journal of Personality and Social Psychology, 100*, 777–793.

Robins, R. W., Hendin, H. W. and Trzesniewski, K. H. (2001) Measuring global self-esteem: Construct validation of a single-item measure and the Rosenberg self-esteem scale. *Personality and Social Psychology Bulletin, 27*, 151–161.

Rocklage, M. D. and Fazio, R. H. (2014) Individual differences in valence weighting: When, how and why they matter. *Journal of Experimental Social Psychology, 50*, 144–157.

Rogers, R. W. and Prentice-Dunn, S. (1997) Protection motivation theory. In D. Gochman (ed.), *Handbook of Health Behavior Research* (Vol. 1, pp. 113–132). New York: Plenum.

Rosenfeld, P., Giacalone, R. A. and Tedeschi, J. T. (1984) Cognitive dissonance and impression management explanations for effort justification. *Personality and Social Psychology Bulletin, 10*, 394–401.

Roskos-Ewoldsen, D. R. and Fazio, R. H. (1992) On the orienting value of attitudes: Attitude accessibility as a determinant of an object's attraction of visual attention. *Journal of Personality and Social Psychology*, *63*, 198–211.

Roskos-Ewoldsen, D. R., Bichsel, J. and Hoffman, K. (2002) The influence of accessibility of source likability on persuasion. *Journal of Experimental Social Psychology*, *38*, 137–143.

Ross, M., McFarland, C. and Fletcher, G. J. O. (1981) The effect of attitude on recall of past histories. *Journal of Personality and Social Psychology*, *40*, 627–634.

Rothermund, K., Teige-Mocigemba, S., Gast, A. and Wentura, D. (2009) Minimizing the influence of recoding in the Implicit Association Test: The Recoding-Free Implicit Association Test. *The Quarterly Journal of Experimental Psychology*, *62*, 84–98.

Rothman, A. J. and Salovey, P. (1997) Shaping perceptions to motivate healthy behavior: The role of message framing. *Psychological Bulletin*, *121*, 3–19.

Rothschild, M. L. (1979) Marketing communications in nonbusiness situations or why it's so hard to sell brotherhood like soap. *Journal of Marketing*, *43*, 11–20.

Rucker, D. D., Petty, R. E. and Briñol, P. (2008) What's in a frame anyway? A meta-cognitive analysis of the impact of one versus two sided message framing on attitude certainty. *Journal of Consumer Psychology*, *18*, 137–149.

Rule, N. O., Freeman, J. B., Moran, J. M., Gabrieli, J. D. E., Adams, R. B., Jr. and Ambady, N. (2010) Voting behavior is reflected in amygdala response across cultures. *Social Cognitive and Affective Neuroscience*, *5*, 349–355.

Russell, C. A. and Stern, B. B. (2006) Consumers, characters and products. *Journal of Advertising*, *35*, 7–21.

Rydell, R. J. and Gawronski, B. (2009) I like you, I like you not: Understanding the formation of context-dependent automatic attitudes. *Cognition & Emotion*, *23*, 1118–1152.

Rydell, R. J., McConnell, A. M. and Mackie, D. M. (2008) Consequences of discrepant explicit and implicit attitudes: Cognitive dissonance and increased information processing. *Journal of Experimental Social Psychology*, *44*, 1526–1532.

Sagarin, B. J., Cialdini, R. B., Rice, W. E. and Serna, S. B. (2002) Dispelling the illusion of invulnerability: The motivations and mechanisms of resistance to persuasion. *Journal of Personality and Social Psychology*, *83*, 526–541.

Sakai, H. (1999) A multiplicative power-function mode of cognitive dissonance: Toward an integrated theory of cognition, emotion and behavior after Leon Festinger. In E. Harmon-Jones and J. Mills (eds), *Cognitive Dissonance: Progress on a Pivotal Theory in Social Psychology* (pp. 267–294). Washington, DC: American Psychological Association.

Salancik, G. R. and Conway, M. (1975) Attitude inferences from salient and relevant cognitive content about behavior. *Journal of Personality and Social Psychology*, *32*, 829–840.

Sanbonmatsu, D. M. and Fazio, R. H. (1990) The role of attitudes in memory-based decision making. *Journal of Personality and Social Psychology*, *59*, 614–622.

Sargent, M. J., Kahan, T. A. and Mitchell, C. J. (2007) The mere acceptance effect: Can it influence responses on racial Implicit Association Tests? *Journal of Experimental Social Psychology*, *43*, 787–793.

Sawicki, V., Wegener, D. T., Clark, J. K., Fabrigar, L. R., Smith, S. M. and Bengal, S. T. (2011) Seeking confirmation in times of doubt: Selective exposure and the motivational strength of weak attitudes. *Social Psychological and Personality Science*, *2*, 540–546.

Sawicki, V., Wegener, D. T., Clark, J. K., Fabrigar, L. R., Smith, S. M. and Durso, G. R. O. (2013) Feeling conflicted and seeking information: When ambivalence enhances and diminishes selective exposure to attitude-consistent information. *Personality and Social Psychology Bulletin*, *39*, 735–747.

Scheier, M. F. and Carver, C. S. (1980) Private and public self-attention, resistance to change and dissonance reduction. *Journal of Personality and Social Psychology*, *39*, 390–415.

Scheier, M. F. and Carver, C. S. (1985) The self-consciousness scale: A revised version for use with general populations. *Journal of Applied Social Psychology*, *15*, 687–699.

Schneider, I. K., Eerland, A., van Harreveld, F., Rotteveel, M., van der Pligt, J., Van der Stoep, N. and Zwaan, R. A. (2013). One way and the other: The bidirectional relationship between ambivalence and body movement. *Psychological Science, 24*, 319–325.

Schuette, R. A. and Fazio, R. H. (1995) Attitude accessibility and motivation as determinants of biased processing: A test of the MODE model. *Personality and Social Psychology Bulletin*, *21*, 704–710.

Schwarz, N. (1999) Self-reports: How the questions shape the answers. *American Psychologist*, *54*, 93–105.

Schwarz, N. (2007) Attitude construction: Evaluation in context. *Social Cognition*, *25*, 638–656.

Schwarz, N. and Clore, G. L. (1983) Mood, misattribution and judgments of well-being: Informative and directive functions of affective states. *Journal of Personality and Social Psychology*, *45*, 513–523.

Schwarz, N. and Clore, G. L. (1997) Feelings and phenomenal experiences. In E. T. Higgins and A. W. Kruglanski (eds), *Social Psychology: Handbook of Basic Principles* (pp. 433–465). New York: Guilford Press.

Schwarz, N., Bless, H. and Bohner, G. (1991) Mood and persuasion: Affective states influence the processing of persuasive communications. In M. P. Zanna (ed.), *Advances in Experimental Social Psychology* (Vol. 24, pp. 161–199). San Diego, CA: Academic Press.

Schwarz, N., Strack, F. and Mai, H. P. (1991) Assimilation and contrast effects in part-whole question sequences: A conversational logic analysis. *Public Opinion Quarterly*, *55*, 3–23.

Sears, D. O. (1981) Life stage effects upon attitude change, especially among the elderly. In S. B. Kiesler, J. N. Morgan and V. K. Ooppenheimer (eds), *Aging and Social Change* (pp. 181–204). New York: Academic Press.

Sears, D. O. (1983) The persistence of early political predispositions: The roles of attitude object and life stages. *Review of Personality and Social Psychology*, *4*, 79–116.

Sears, D. O. (1986) College sophomores in the laboratory: Influences of a narrow data base on social psychology's view of human nature. *Journal of Personality and Social Psychology*, *51*, 515–530.

Sedek, G., Piber-Dabrowska, K., Maio, G. R. and von Hecker, U. (2011) Individual differences in prejudice and associative versus rule-based forms of transitive reasoning. *European Journal of Social Psychology*, *41*, 853–865.

Sedikides, C. and Strube, M. J. (1997) Self evaluation: To thine own self be good, to thine own self be sure, to thine own self be true and to thine own self be better. In M. P. Zanna (ed.), *Advances in Experimental Social Psychology* (Vol. 29, pp. 209–269). San Diego, CA: Academic Press.

See, Y. H. M., Petty, R. E. and Fabrigar, L. R. (2008) Affective and cognitive meta-bases of attitudes: Unique effects on information interest and persuasion. *Journal of Personality and Social Psychology*, *94*, 938–955.

See, Y. H. M., Petty, R. E. and Fabrigar, L. R. (2013) Affective-cognitive meta-bases versus structural bases of attitudes predict processing interest versus efficiency. *Personality and Social Psychology Bulletin*, *39*, 1111–1123.

See, Y. H. M., Valenti, G., Ho, Y. Y. A. and Tan, M. S. Q. (2103) When message tailoring backfires: The role of initial attitudes in affect-cognition matching. *European Journal of Social Psychology*, *43*, 570–584.

Seligman, C., Fazio, R. H. and Zanna, M. P. (1980) Effects of salience of extrinsic rewards on liking and loving. *Journal of Personality and Social Psychology*, *38*, 453–460.

Serenko, A. and Bontis, N. (2011) What's familiar is excellent: The impact of exposure effect on perceived journal quality. *Journal of Informetrics*, *5*, 219–223.

Settle, J., Dawes, C. and Fowler, J. H. (2009) The heritability of partisan attachment. *Political Research Quarterly*, *62*, 601–613.

Shavitt, S. (1990) The role of attitude objects in attitude functions. *Journal of Experimental Social Psychology*, *26*, 124–148.

Shavitt, S. and Nelson, M. R. (2000) The social identity function in persuasion: Communicated meanings of product preferences. In G. R. Maio and J. M. Olson (eds), *Why We Evaluate: Functions of Attitudes* (pp. 37–57). Mahwah, NJ: Erlbaum.

Sheeran, P. (2002) Intention–behavior relations: A conceptual and empirical review. In W. Stroebe and M. Hewstone (eds), *European Review of Social Psychology* (Vol. 12, pp. 1–36). Chichester: Wiley.

Sheeran, P., Milne, S., Webb, T. L. and Gollwitzer, P. M. (2005) Implementation intentions. In M. Conner and P. Norman (eds), *Predicting Health Behaviour: Research and Practice with Social Cognition Models* (2nd edn, pp. 276–323). Buckingham: Open University Press.

Sherif, C. W. (1980) Social values, attitudes and the involvement of the self. In H. E. J. Howe and M. M. Page (eds), *Nebraska Symposium on Motivation, 1979* (Vol. 27, pp. 1–64). Lincoln, NB: University of Nebraska Press.

Sherif, C. W. and Sherif, M. (eds) (1967) *Attitude, Ego-involvement and Change*. New York: Wiley.

Sherman, D. A. K., Nelson, L. D. and Steele, C. M. (2000) Do messages about health risks threaten the self? Increasing the acceptance of threatening health messages via self-affirmation. *Personality and Social Psychology Bulletin*, *26*, 1046–1058.

Shook, N. J. and Clay, R. (2012) Interracial roommate relationships: A mechanism for promoting sense of belonging at university and academic performance. *Journal of Experimental Social Psychology*, *48*, 1168–1172.

Shook, N. J. and Fazio, R. H. (2008) Interracial roommate relationships: An experimental test of the contact hypothesis. *Psychological Science*, *19*, 717–723.

Sia, T. L., Lord, C. G., Blessum, K. A., Ratcliff, C. D. and Lepper, M. R. (1997) Is a rose always a rose? The role of social category exemplar change in attitude stability and attitude–behavior consistency. *Journal of Personality and Social Psychology*, *72*, 501–514.

Simon, L., Greenberg, J. and Brehm, J. (1995) Trivialization: The forgotten mode of dissonance reduction. *Journal of Personality and Social Psychology*, *68*, 247–260.

Sinclair, R. C., Mark, M. M. and Clore, G. L. (1994) Mood-related persuasion depends on (mis) attributions. *Social Cognition*, *12*, 309–326.

Singelis, T. (1994) The measurement of independent and interdependent self-construals. *Personality and Social Psychology Bulletin*, *20*, 580–591.

Smallman, R., Becker, B. and Roese, N. J. (2014) Preferences for expressing preferences: People prefer final evaluative distinctions for liked than disliked objects. *Journal of Experimental Social Psychology*, *52*, 25–31.

Smit, H. J. and Rogers, P. J. (2000) Effects of low doses of caffeine on cognitive performance, mood and thirst in low and higher caffeine consumers. *Psychopharmacology*, *152*, 167–173.

Smith, A. P., Maben, A. and Brockman, P. (1994) The effects of evening meals and caffeine on performance, mood and cardiovascular functioning. *Appetite*, *22*, 39–55.

Smith, C. A. and Ellsworth, P. C. (1985) Patterns of cognitive appraisal in emotion. *Journal of Personality and Social Psychology*, *48*, 813–838.

Smith, C. T., De Houwer, J. and Nosek, B. A. (2013) Consider the source: Persuasion of implicit evaluations is moderated by source credibility. *Personality and Social Psychology Bulletin*, *39*, 193–205.

Smith, E. R. and DeCoster, J. (2000) Dual process models in social and cognitive psychology: Conceptual integration and links to underlying memory systems. *Personality and Social Psychology Review*, *4*, 108–131.

Smith, J. R., Hogg, M. A., Martin, R. and Terry, D. J. (2007) Uncertainty and the influence of group norms in the attitude–behaviour relationship. *British Journal of Social Psychology*, *46*, 769–792.

Smith, M. B., Bruner, J. S. and White, R. W. (1956) *Opinions and Personality*. New York: Wiley.

Smith, P. K. and Trope, Y. (2006) You focus on the forest when you're in charge of the trees: Power priming and abstract information processing. *Journal of Personality and Social Psychology*, *90*, 578–596.

Smith, P. K., Dijksterhuis, A. and Chaiken, S. (2008) Subliminal exposure to faces and racial attitudes: Exposure to Whites makes Whites like Blacks less. *Journal of Experimental Social Psychology*, *44*, 50–64.

Smith, S. M. and Shaffer, D. R. (1995) Speed of speech and persuasion: Evidence for multiple effects. *Personality and Social Psychology Bulletin*, *21*, 1051–1060.

Smith, S. M. and Shaffer, D. R. (2000) Vividness can undermine or enhance message processing: The moderating role of vividness congruency. *Personality and Social Psychology Bulletin*, *26*, 769–779.

Snyder, M. (1974) The self-monitoring of expressive behavior. *Journal of Personality and Social Psychology*, *30*, 526–537.

Snyder, M. (1986) *Public Appearances/Private Realities: The Psychology of Self-monitoring.* New York: Freeman.

Snyder, M. and DeBono, K. G. (1985) Appeals to image and claims about quality: Understanding the psychology of advertising. *Journal of Personality and Social Psychology, 49,* 586–597.

Snyder, M. and Kendzierski, D. (1982) Acting on one's attitudes: Procedures for linking attitudes and behavior. *Journal of Experimental Social Psychology, 18,* 165–183.

Soldat, A. S., Sinclair, R. C. and Mark, M. M. (1997) Color as an environmental processing cue: External affective cues can directly affect processing strategy without affecting mood. *Social Cognition, 16,* 55–71.

Son Hing, L. S., Li, W. and Zanna, M. P. (2002) Inducing hypocrisy to reduce prejudicial responses among aversive racists. *Journal of Experimental Social Psychology, 38,* 71–78.

Sparks, P. and Manstead, A. S. R. (2006) *Moral Judgements as Constitutive of Attitudes in the Evaluation of Actions.* Unpublished manuscript.

Sritharan, R. and Gawronski, B. (2010) Changing implicit and explicit prejudice: Insights from the Associative-Propositional Evaluation model. *Social Psychology, 41,* 113–123.

Srull, T. K. (1983) Affect and memory: The impact of affective reactions in advertising on the representation of product information in memory. *Advances in Consumer Research, 10,* 244–263.

Srull, T. K. (1984) The effects of subjective affective states on memory and judgment. *Advances in Consumer Research, 11,* 530–533.

Staats, A. W. and Staats, C. K. (1958) Attitudes established by classical conditioning. *Journal of Abnormal and Social Psychology, 57,* 37–40.

Stang, D. J. (1974a) Intuition as artifact in mere exposure studies. *Journal of Personality and Social Psychology, 30,* 647–653.

Stang, D. J. (1974b) Methodological factors in mere exposure research. *Psychological Bulletin, 81,* 1014–1025.

Staw, B. M. (1974) Attitudinal and behavioral consequences of changing a major organizational reward: A natural field experiment. *Journal of Personality and Social Psychology, 29,* 742–752.

Steele, C. M. (1988) The psychology of self-affirmation: Sustaining the integrity of the self. In M. P. Zanna (ed.), *Advances in Experimental Social Psychology* (Vol. 21, pp. 261–302). San Diego, CA: Academic Press.

Steele, C. M. and Josephs, R. A. (1990) Alcohol myopia: Its prized and dangerous effects. *American Psychologist, 45,* 363–375.

Steele, C. M. and Liu, T. J. (1983) Dissonance processes as self-affirmation. *Journal of Personality and Social Psychology, 45,* 5–19.

Steffens, M. C. (2004) Is the Implicit Association Test immune to faking? *Experimental Psychology, 51,* 165–179.

Stone, J. and Focella, E. (2011) Hypocrisy, dissonance and the self-regulation processes that improve health. *Self and Identity, 10,* 295–303.

Stone, J., Aronson, E., Crain, A. L., Winslow, M. P. and Fried, C. B. (1994) Inducing hypocrisy as a means of encouraging young adults to use condoms. *Personality and Social Psychology Bulletin, 20,* 116–128.

Strack, F. and Deutsch, R. (2004) Reflective and impulsive determinants of social behavior. *Personality and Social Psychology Review*, *8*, 220–247.

Strack, F., Martin, L. L. and Stepper, S. (1988) Inhibiting and facilitating conditions of the human smile: A nonobtrusive test of the facial feedback hypothesis. *Journal of Personality and Social Psychology*, *54*, 768–777.

Strack, F., Schwarz, N. and Gschneidinger, E. (1985) Happiness and reminiscing: The role of time perspective, mood and mode of thinking. *Journal of Personality and Social Psychology*, *49*, 1460–1469.

Strahan, E. J., Spencer, S. J. and Zanna, M. P. (2002) Subliminal priming and persuasion: Striking while the iron is hot. *Journal of Experimental Social Psychology*, *38*, 556–568.

Strick, M., Holland, R. W., Van Baaren, R. B. and Van Knippenberg, A. (2012) Those who laugh are defenceless: How humor breaks resistance to influence. *Journal of Experimental Psychology: Applied*, *18*, 213–223.

Stroebe, W. (2000) *Social Psychology and Health*. Buckingham: Open University Press.

Taylor, C. A., Lord, C. G. and Bond, C. F., Jr. (2009) Embodiment, agency and attitude change. *Journal of Personality and Social Psychology*, *97*, 946–962.

Taylor, S. E. and Brown, J. D. (1988) Illusion and well-being: A social psychological perspective on mental health. *Psychological Bulletin*, *103*, 193–210.

Taylor, S. E. and Brown, J. D. (1994) Positive illusions and well-being revisited: Separating fact from fiction. *Psychological Bulletin*, *116*, 21–27.

Tedeschi, J. T., Schlenker, B. R. and Bonoma, T. V. (1971) Cognitive dissonance: Private ratiocination or public spectacle? *American Psychologist*, *26*, 685–695.

Tesser, A. (1993) On the importance of heritability in psychological research: The case of attitudes. *Psychological Review*, *100*, 129–142.

Tesser, A. and Crelia, R. (1994) Attitude heritability and attitude reinforcement: A test of the niche building hypothesis. *Personality and Individual Differences*, *16*, 571–577.

Tetlock, P. E. and Boettger, R. (1989) Accountability: A social magnifier of the dilution effect. *Journal of Personality and Social Psychology*, *57*, 388–398.

Tetlock, P. E., Lerner, J. S. and Boettger, R. (1996) The dilution effect: Judgmental bias, conversational convention, or a bit of both? *European Journal of Social Psychology*, *26*, 915–934.

Thompson, E. P., Kruglanski, A. W. and Spiegel, S. (2000) Attitudes as knowledge structures and persuasion as a specific case of subjective knowledge acquisition. In G. R. Maio and J. M. Olson (eds), *Why We Evaluate: Functions of Attitudes* (pp. 59–95). Mahwah, NJ: Erlbaum.

Thompson, M. M. and Zanna, M. P. (1995) The conflicted individual: Personality-based and domain-specific antecedents of ambivalent social attitudes. *Journal of Personality*, *63*, 259–288.

Thompson, M. M., Zanna, M. P. and Griffin, D. W. (1995) Let's not be indifferent about attitudinal ambivalence. In R. E. Petty and A. J. Krosnick (eds), *Attitude Strength: Antecedents and Consequences*. Hillsdale, NJ: Erlbaum.

Thompson, R. and Haddock, G. (2012) Sometimes stories sell: When are narrative appeals most likely to work? *European Journal of Social Psychology*, *42*, 92–102.

Thurstone, L. L. (1928) Attitudes can be measured. *American Journal of Sociology, 33*, 529–554.

Thurstone, L. L. and Chave, E. J. (1929) *The Measurement of Attitude.* Chicago, IL: University of Chicago Press.

Tiedens, L. Z. and Linton, S. (2001) Judgment under emotional certainty and uncertainty: The effects of specific emotions on information processing. *Journal of Personality and Social Psychology, 81*, 973–988.

Tom, G., Pettersen, P., Lau, T., Burton, T. and Cook, J. (1991) The role of overt head movement in the formation of affect. *Basic and Applied Social Psychology, 12*, 281–289.

Tormala, Z. L. and Clarkson, J. J. (2007) Assimilation and contrast in persuasion: The effects of source credibility in multiple message situations. *Personality and Social Psychology Bulletin, 33*, 559–571.

Tormala, Z. L. and DeSensi, V. L. (2008) The perceived informational basis of attitudes: Implications for subjective ambivalence. *Personality and Social Psychology Bulletin, 34*, 275–287.

Tormala, Z. L. and Petty, R. E. (2002) What doesn't kill me makes me stronger: The effects of resisting persuasion on attitude certainty. *Journal of Personality and Social Psychology, 83*, 1298–1313.

Tormala, Z. L. and Petty, R. E. (2007) Contextual contrast and perceived knowledge: Exploring the implications for persuasion. *Journal of Experimental Social Psychology, 43*, 17–30.

Tormala, Z. L., Briñol, P. and Petty, R. E. (2006) When credibility attacks: The reverse impact of source credibility on persuasion. *Journal of Experimental Social Psychology, 42*, 684–691.

Tormala, Z. L., Clarkson, J. J. and Petty, R. E. (2006) Resisting persuasion by the skin of one's teeth: The hidden success of resisted persuasive messages. *Journal of Personality and Social Psychology, 91*, 423–435.

Tormala, Z. L., DeSensi, V. L. and Petty, R. E. (2007) Resisting persuasion by illegitimate means: A metacognitive perspective on minority influence. *Personality and Social Psychology Bulletin, 33*, 354–367.

Trafimow, D. and Finlay, K. A. (1996) The importance of subjective norms for a minority of people: Between-subjects and within-subjects analyses. *Personality and Social Psychology Bulletin, 22*, 820–828.

Trafimow, D. and Sheeran, P. (1998) Some tests of the distinction between cognitive and affective beliefs. *Journal of Experimental Social Psychology, 34*, 378–397.

Trafimow, D., Rice, S., Hunt, G., List, B., Nanez, B., Rector, N. and Brown, J. (2012) It is irrelevant, but it matters: Using confluence theory to predict the influence of beliefs on evaluations, attitudes and intentions. *European Journal of Social Psychology, 42*, 509–520.

Trafimow, D., Triandis, H. S. and Goto, S. G. (1991) Some tests of the distinction between the private self and the collective self. *Journal of Personality and Social Psychology, 60*, 649–655.

Triandis, H. C. (1989) The self and social behavior in differing cultural contexts. *Psychological Review, 96*, 506–520.

Tykocinski, O., Higgins, E. T. and Chaiken, S. (1994) Message framing, self-discrepancies and yielding to persuasive messages: The motivational significance of psychological situations. *Personality and Social Psychology Bulletin, 20*, 107–115.

Updegraff, J. A., Sherman, D. K., Luyster, F. S. and Mann, T. L. (2007) The effects of message quality and congruency on perceptions of tailored health communications. *Journal of Experimental Social Psychology*, *43*, 249–257.

Vallone, R. P., Ross, L. and Lepper, M. R. (1985) The hostile media phenomenon: Biased perception and perceptions of media bias in coverage of the Beirut massacre. *Journal of Personality and Social Psychology*, *49*, 577–585.

Van Boven, L., Judd, C. M. and Sherman, D. K. (2012) Political polarization projection: Social projection of partisan attitude extremity and attitudinal processes. *Journal of Personality and Social Psychology*, *103*, 84–100.

van der Pligt, J., Zeelenberg, M., van Dijk, W. W., de Vries, N. K. and Richard, R. (1998) Affect, attitudes and decisions: Let's be more specific. *European Review of Social Psychology*, *8*, 33–66.

van Harreveld, F., van der Pligt, J. and de Liver, Y. (2009) The agony of ambivalence and ways to resolve it: Introducing the MAID model. *Personality and Social Psychology Review*, *13*, 45–61.

Vargas, P. T., Von Hippel, W. and Petty, R. E. (2004) Using partially structured attitude measures to enhance the attitude–behavior relationship. *Personality and Social Psychology Bulletin*, *30*, 197–211.

Verhoeven, A. A. C., Adriaanse, M. A., de Ridder, D. T. D., de Vet, E. and Fennis, B. M. (2013) Less is more: The effect of multiple implementation intentions targeting unhealthy snacking habits. *European Journal of Social Psychology*, *43*, 344–354.

Verplanken, B. (2006) Beyond frequency: Habit as mental construct. *British Journal of Social Psychology*, *45*, 639–656.

Verplanken, B. and Aarts, H. (1999) Habit, attitude and planned behaviour: Is habit an empty construct or an interesting case of automaticity? *European Review of Social Psychology*, *10*, 101–134.

Verplanken, B. and Orbell, S. (2003) Reflection on past behavior: A self-report index of habit strength. *Journal of Applied Social Psychology*, *33*, 1313–1330.

Verplanken, B., Aarts, H., van Knippenberg, A. and Moonen, A. (1998) Habit versus planned behaviour: A field experiment. *British Journal of Social Psychology*, *37*, 111–128.

Verrier, D. B. (2012) Evidence for the influence of the mere-exposure effect on voting in the Eurovision Song Contest. *Judgment and Decision Making*, *7*, 639–643.

Verwijmeren, T., Karremans, J. C., Bernritter, S. F., Stroebe, W. and Wigboldus, D. H. J. (2013) Warning: You are being primed! The effect of a warning on the impact of subliminal ads. *Journal of Experimental Social Psychology*, *49*, 1124–1129.

Verwijmeren, T., Karremans, J. C. T. M., Stroebe, W. and Wigboldus, D. H. J. (2011) The workings and limits of subliminal advertising: The role of habits. *Journal of Consumer Psychology*, *21*, 206–213.

Visser, P. S. and Krosnick, J. A. (1998) Development of attitude strength over the life cycle: Surge and decline. *Journal of Personality and Social Psychology*, *75*, 1389–1410.

Visser, P. S., Bizer, G. and Krosnick, J. A. (2006) Exploring the latent structure of strength-related attitude attributes. In M. Zanna (ed.), *Advances in Experimental Social Psychology* (Vol. 38, pp. 1–67). San Diego, CA: Academic Press.

Vohs, K. D., Sengupta, J. and Dahl, D. W. (2014) The price had better be right: Women's reactions to sexual stimuli vary with market factors. *Psychological Science*, *25*, 278–283.

von Hecker, U. (1993) On memory effects of Heiderian balance: A code hypothesis and an inconsistency hypothesis. *Journal of Experimental Social Psychology*, *29*, 358–386.

Vonofakou, C., Hewstone, M. and Voci, A. (2007) Contact with out-group friends as a predictor of meta-attitudinal strength and accessibility of attitudes toward gay men. *Journal of Personality and Social Psychology*, *92*, 804–820.

Walther, E. (2002) Guilty by mere association: Evaluative conditioning and the spreading attitude effect. *Journal of Personality and Social Psychology*, *82*, 919–934.

Wang, C. L., Bristol, T., Mowen, J. C. and Chakraborty, G. (2000) Alternative modes of self-construal: Dimensions of connectedness-separateness and advertising appeals to the cultural and gender-specific self. *Journal of Consumer Psychology*, *9*, 107–115.

Wang, H., Masuda, T., Ito, K. and Rashid, M. (2012) How much information? East Asian and North American cultural products and information search performance. *Personality and Social Psychology Bulletin*, *38*, 1539–1551.

Watson, D., Wiese, D., Vaidya, J. and Tellegen, A. (1999) Two general activation systems of affect: Structural findings, evolutionary considerations and psychobiological evidence. *Journal of Personality and Social Psychology*, *76*, 820–838.

Webb, T. L., Sheeran, P. and Pepper, J. (2012) Gaining control over responses to implicit attitude tests: Implementation intentions engender fast responses on attitude-incongruent trials. *British Journal of Social Psychology*, *51*, 13–32.

Wegener, D. T. and Petty, R. E. (1995) Flexible correction processes in social judgment: The role of naive theories in corrections for perceived bias. *Journal of Personality and Social Psychology*, *68*, 36–51.

Wegener, D. T. and Petty, R. E. (1997) The flexible correction model: The role of naive theories of bias in bias correction. *Advances in Experimental Social Psychology*, *29*, 141–208.

Wegener, D. T. and Petty, R. E. (2001) Understanding effects of mood through the elaboration likelihood and flexible correction models. In L. L. Martin and G. L. Clore (eds), *Theories of Mood and Cognition: A User's Guidebook* (pp. 177–210). Mahwah, NJ: Erlbaum.

Wegener, D. T., Downing, J., Krosnick, J. A. and Petty, R. E. (1995) Measures and manipulations of strength related properties of attitudes: Current practice and future directions. In R. E. Petty and J. A. Krosnick (eds), *Attitude Strength: Antecedents and Consequences* (pp. 455–488). Mahwah, NJ: Erlbaum.

Wegener, D. T., Petty, R. E. and Smith, S. M. (1995) Positive mood can increase or decrease message scrutiny: The hedonic contingency view of mood and message processing. *Journal of Personality and Social Psychology*, *69*, 5–15.

Wegner, D. M., Fuller, V. A. and Sparrow, B. (2003) Clever hands: Uncontrolled intelligence in facilitated communication. *Journal of Personality and Social Psychology*, *85*, 5–19.

Wegner, D. M., Sparrow, B. and Winerman, L. (2004) Vicarious agency: Experiencing control over the movements of others. *Journal of Personality and Social Psychology*, *86*, 838–848.

Weisbuch, M., Mackie, D. M. and Garcia-Marques, T. (2003) Prior source exposure and persuasion: Further evidence for misattributional processes. *Personality and Social Psychology Bulletin*, *29*, 691–700.

Wells, G. L. and Petty, R. E. (1980) The effects of overt head movements on persuasion: Compatibility and incompatibility of responses. *Basic and Applied Social Psychology*, *1*, 219–230.

Wentura, D. and Rothermund, K. (2007) Paradigms we live by: A plea for more basic research on the IAT. In B. Wittenbrink and N. Schwarz (eds), *Implicit Measures of Attitudes* (pp. 195–215). New York: Guilford Press.

Werner, C. M., Stoll, R. B., Birch, P. and White, P. H. (2002) Clinical validation and cognitive elaboration: Signs that encourage sustained recycling. *Basic and Applied Social Psychology*, *24*, 185–203.

Wheeler, S. C., Briñol, P. and Hermann, A. D. (2007) Resistance to persuasion as self-regulation: Ego-depletion and its effects on attitude change processes. *Journal of Experimental Social Psychology*, *43*, 150–156.

Whittler, T. E. and Spira, J. S. (2002) Model's race: A peripheral cue in advertising messages? *Journal of Consumer Psychology*, *12*, 291–301.

Wicker, A. W. (1969) Attitude versus actions: The relationship of verbal and overt behavioral responses to attitude objects. *Journal of Social Issues*, *25*, 41–78.

Wiebe, G. D. (1951) Merchandising commodities and citizenship on television. *Public Opinion Quarterly*, *15*, 679–691.

Wiersema, D. V., van der Pligt, J. and van Harreveld, F. (2010) Motivated memory: Memory for attitude-relevant information as a function of self-esteem. *Social Cognition*, *28*, 219–239.

Wiersema, D. V., van Harreveld, F. and van der Pligt, J. (2012) Shut your eyes and think of something else: Self-esteem and avoidance when dealing with counter-attitudinal information. *Social Cognition*, *30*, 323–334.

Wilson, T. D. and Brekke, N. (1994) Mental contamination and mental correction: Unwanted influences on judgments and evaluations. *Psychological Bulletin*, *116*, 117–142.

Wilson, T. D., Dunn, D. S., Kraft, D. and Lisle, D. J. (1989) Introspection, attitude change and attitude–behavior consistency: The disruptive effects of explaining why we feel the way we do. In L. Berkowitz (ed.), *Advances in Experimental Social Psychology* (Vol. 22, pp. 287–343). Orlando, FL: Academic Press.

Wilson, T. D., Houston, C. E. and Meyers, J. M. (1998) Choose your poison: Effects of lay beliefs about mental processes on attitude change. *Social Cognition*, *16*, 114–132.

Wilson, T. D., Kraft, D. and Dunn, D. S. (1989) The disruptive effects of explaining attitudes: The moderating effect of knowledge about the attitude object. *Journal of Experimental Social Psychology*, *25*, 379–400.

Wilson, T. D., Lindsey, S. and Schooler, T. Y. (2000) A model of dual attitudes. *Psychological Review*, *107*, 101–126.

Wilson, T. D., Lisle, D. J., Schooler, J. W., Hodges, S. D., Klaaren, K. J. and LaFleur, S. J. (1993) Introspecting about reasons can reduce post-choice satisfaction. *Personality and Social Psychology Bulletin*, *19*, 331–339.

Winkielman, P. and Cacioppo, J. T. (2001) Mind at ease puts a smile on the face: Psychophysiological evidence that processing facilitation increases positive affect. *Journal of Personality and Social Psychology*, *81*, 989–1000.

Wittenbrink, B. and Schwarz, N. (eds) (2007) *Implicit Measures of Attitudes: Procedures and Controversies*. New York: Guilford Press.

Wittenbrink, B., Judd, C. M and Park, B. (2001) Spontaneous prejudice in context: Variability in automatically activated attitudes. *Journal of Personality and Social Psychology*, *81*, 815–827.

Wood, W., Kallgren, C. A. and Preisler, R. M. (1985) Access to attitude-relevant information in memory as a determinant of persuasion: The role of message attributes. *Journal of Experimental Social Psychology*, *21*, 73–85.

Wood, W., Lundgren, S., Ouellette, J. A., Busceme, S. and Blackstone, T. (1994) Minority influence: A meta-analytical review of social influence processes. *Psychological Bulletin*, *115*, 323–345.

Wood, W., Quinn, J. M. and Kashy, D. (2002) Habits in everyday life: Thought, emotion and action. *Journal of Personality and Social Psychology*, *83*, 1281–1297.

Woodall, W. G. and Burgoon, J. K. (1984) Talking fast and changing attitudes: A critique and clarification. *Journal of Nonverbal Behavior*, *8*, 126–142.

Wyer, R. S., Jr. and Goldberg, L. A. (1970) A probabilistic analysis of the relationships among attitudes and beliefs. *Psychological Review*, *77*, 100–120.

Ybarra, O. and Trafimow, D. (1998) How priming the private self or collective self affects the relative weights of attitudes and subjective norms. *Personality and Social Psychology Bulletin*, *24*, 362–270.

Yoshida, E., Peach, J. M., Zanna, M. P. and Spencer, S. J. (2012) Not all automatic associations are created equal: How implicit normative evaluations are distinct from implicit attitudes and uniquely predict meaningful behavior. *Journal of Experimental Social Psychology*, *48*, 694–706.

Young, A. I., Ratner, K. G. and Fazio, R. H. (2014) Political attitudes bias the mental representation of a presidential candidate's face. *Psychological Science*, *25*, 503–510.

Zajonc, R. B. (1968) Attitudinal effects of mere exposure. *Journal of Personality and Social Psychology Monograph Supplement*, *9*, 1–27.

Zajonc, R. B. (1980) Feeling and thinking: Preferences need no inferences. *American Psychologist*, *35*, 151–175.

Zajonc, R. B. (2001) Mere exposure: A gateway to the subliminal. *Current Directions in Psychological Science*, *10*, 224–228.

Zald, D. H. (2003) The human amygdala and the emotional evaluation of sensory stimuli. *Brain Research Reviews*, *41*, 88–123.

Zanna, M. P. and Cooper, J. (1974) Dissonance and the pill: An attribution approach to studying the arousal properties of dissonance. *Journal of Personality and Social Psychology*, *29*, 703–709.

Zanna, M. P. and Rempel, J. K. (1988) Attitudes: A new look at an old concept. In D. BarTal and A. W. Kruglanski (eds), *The Social Psychology of Knowledge* (pp. 315–334). Cambridge: Cambridge University Press.

Zanna, M. P. and Sande, G. N. (1987) The effect of collective actions on the attitudes of individual group members: A dissonance analysis. In M. P. Zanna, J. M. Olson and C. P. Herman (eds), *Social Influence: The Ontario Symposium* (Vol. 5, pp. 151–163). Mahwah, NJ: Erlbaum.

Zanna, M. P., Kiesler, C. A. and Pilkonis, P. A. (1970) Positive and negative attitudinal affect established by classical conditioning. *Journal of Personality and Social Psychology, 14*, 321–328.

Zhao, X. and Nan, X. (2010) Influence of self-affirmation on responses to gain- vs. loss-framed anti-smoking messages. *Human Communication Research, 36*, 493–511.

Ziegler, R. (2010) Mood, source characteristics and message processing: A mood-congruent expectancies approach. *Journal of Experimental Social Psychology, 46*, 743–752.

Ziegler, R. (2013) Mood and processing of proattitudinal and counterattitudinal messages. *Personality and Social Psychology Bulletin, 39*, 482–495.

Zimbardo, P. G., Weisenberg, M., Firestone, I. and Levy, B. (1965) Communicator effectiveness in producing public conformity and private attitude change. *Journal of Personality, 33*, 233–255.

# AUTHOR INDEX

# SUBJECT INDEX